Second Temple Studies

2. Temple Community in the Persian Period

Edited by
Tamara C. Eskenazi
and
Kent H. Richards

Journal for the Study of the Old Testament
Supplement Series 175

JOURNAL FOR THE STUDY OF THE OLD TESTAMENT SUPPLEMENT SERIES

175

JSOT Press
Sheffield

Published by JSOT Press
JSOT Press is an imprint of
Sheffield Academic Press Ltd
343 Fulwood Road
Sheffield S10 3BP
England

Typeset by Sheffield Academic Press
and
Printed on acid-free paper in Great Britain
by Bookcraft
Midsomer Norton, Somerset

British Library Cataloguing in Publication Data

A catalogue record for this book is available
from the British Library

ISBN 1-85075-472-1

Contents

PREFACE

The international dialogue represented in this volume has been conducted largely under the auspices of the Society of Biblical Literature (SBL). Most of the papers (Baltzer, Carroll, Clines, Davies, Garbini, Grabbe, Marinkovic and Van Rooy) form part of a symposium on 'The Temple in the Persian Period', held at the International Meeting of SBL in Rome (1991). Others were presented at subsequent Annual Meetings of SBL (Carter, Eskenazi/Judd, Washington and Willi). The book, thus, reflects both the diversity of voices in the field and an actual, international conversation among scholars who meet and jointly explore issues pertaining to the Second Temple Period. We thank SBL for its role in promoting such a conversation.

We dedicate this volume to Peter R. Ackroyd in appreciation for his contribution to the study of the Persian period and its literature. Although Ackroyd did not attend these particular sessions, his presence and work constitute the necessary and influential backdrop for any scholarly discussion of this formative era and has decisively shaped our own perceptions of its importance.

Tamara C. Eskenazi
Hebrew Union College–Jewish Institute of Religion
Los Angeles, CA
USA

Kent H. Richards
Iliff School of Theology
Denver, CO
USA

ABBREVIATIONS

AASOR	Annual of the American Schools of Oriental Research
AB	Anchor Bible
ABD	D.N. Freedman (ed.), *Anchor Bible Dictionary*
ANET	J.B. Pritchard (ed.), *Ancient Near Eastern Texts*
ATD	Das Alte Testament Deutsch
AUSS	*Andrews University Seminary Studies*
BA	*Biblical Archaeologist*
BAR	*Biblical Archaeology Review*
BASOR	*Bulletin of the American Schools of Oriental Research*
BETL	Bibliotheca ephemeridum theologicarum lovaniensium
BHS	*Biblia hebraica stuttgartensia*
BHT	Beiträge zur historischen Theologie
Bib	*Biblica*
BJS	Brown Judaic Studies
BKAT	Biblischer Kommentar: Altes Testament
BTB	*Biblical Theology Bulletin*
BWANT	Beiträge zur Wissenschaft vom Alten und Neuen Testament
BZ	*Biblische Zeitschrift*
BZAW	Beihefte zur *ZAW*
CBC	Cambridge Bible Commentary on the New English Bible
CBQ	*Catholic Biblical Quarterly*
CBQMS	*CBQ* Monograph Series
EncJud	*Encyclopaedia Judaica*
ETL	*Ephemerides theologicae louvanienses*
FOTL	The Forms of the Old Testament Literature
FRLANT	Forschungen zur Religion und Literatur des Alten und Neuen Testaments
HALAT	W. Baumgartner *et al.*, *Hebräisches und aramäisches Lexikon zum Alten Testament*
HAR	*Hebrew Annual Review*
HAT	Handbuch zum Alten Testament
HeyJ	*Heythrop Journal*
HTR	*Harvard Theological Review*
ICC	International Critical Commentary
IDBSup	*Interpreter's Dictionary of the Bible*, Supplementary Volume
IEJ	*Israel Exploration Journal*
JAOS	*Journal of the American Oriental Society*

JBL	*Journal of Biblical Literature*
JJS	*Journal of Jewish Studies*
JNES	*Journal of Near Eastern Studies*
JSOT	*Journal for the Study of the Old Testament*
JSOTSup	*JSOT* Supplement Series
JSS	*Journal of Semitic Studies*
KAT	Kommentar zum Alten Testament
KB	B.L. Koehler and W. Baumgartner, *Lexicon in Veteris Testamenti libros*
KS	Kleine Schriften
NCB	New Century Bible
NCBC	NCB Commentary
NICOT	New International Commentary on the Old Testament
NJB	New Jerusalem Bible
OBO	Orbis biblicus et orientalis
OTL	Old Testament Library
OTS	*Oudtestamentische Studiën*
PEQ	*Palestine Exploration Quarterly*
RB	*Revue biblique*
SBL	Society of Biblical Literature
SBLDS	SBL Dissertation Series
SBLMS	SBL Monograph Series
SBT	Studies in Biblical Theology
SPAW	*Sitzungsberichte der preusschen Akademie der Wissenschaften*
SSN	Studia semitica neerlandica
TDOT	G.J. Botterweck and H. Ringgren (eds.), *Theological Dictionary of the Old Testament*
ThWAT	G.J. Botterweck and H. Ringgren (eds.), *Theologisches Wörterbuch zum Alten Testament*
TOTC	Tyndale Old Testament Commentary
TT	*Teologisk Tidsskrift*
TTS	Trierer Theologische Studien
TynBul	*Tyndale Bulletin*
USQR	*Union Seminary Quarterly Review*
VF	*Verkündigung und Forschung*
VT	*Vetus Testamentum*
VTSup	*Vetus Testamentum*, Supplements
WBC	Word Biblical Commentary
WHJP	H. Tadmor and I. Eph'al (eds.), *World History of the Jewish People*
WMANT	Wissenschaftliche Monographien zum Alten und Neuen Testament
ZAW	*Zeitschrift für die alttestamentliche Wissenschaft*
ZDPV	*Zeitschrift des deutschen Palästina-Vereins*
ZTK	*Zeitschrift für Theologie und Kirche*

LIST OF CONTRIBUTORS

Klaus H. Baltzer
University of Munich, Munich, Germany

Robert P. Carroll
University of Glasgow, Glasgow, Scotland, Great Britain

Charles E. Carter
Seton Hall University, South Orange, NJ, USA

David J.A. Clines
Department of Biblical Studies, University of Sheffield, Sheffield, England

Philip R. Davies
University of Sheffield, Sheffield, England

Tamara C. Eskenazi
Hebrew Union College—Jewish Institute of Religion, Los Angeles, CA, USA

Giovanni Garbini
University of Rome, La Sapienza, Rome, Italy

Lester L. Grabbe
University of Hull, Hull, England

Sara Japhet
The Hebrew University, Jerusalem, Israel

Eleanore P. Judd
University of Denver, Denver, CO, USA

Peter Marinković
University of Munich, Munich, Germany

Kent H. Richards
Iliff School of Theology, Denver, CO, USA

Daniel Smith-Christopher
Loyola Marymount University, Los Angeles, CA, USA

Harry F. Van Rooy
Potchefstroom University for Christian Higher Education, Potchefstroom, South Africa

Harold C. Washington
Saint Paul School of Theology, Kansas City, MO, USA

Thomas Willi
University of Greifswald, Germany

INTRODUCTION: THE PERSIAN PERIOD: COMING OF AGE

Kent H. Richards

Persian Period discussions are ripe with new ideas, controversies and hypotheses important not only for the literature traditionally ascribed to this period but for the entire Hebrew Bible. This volume of Second Temple Studies, while focusing on the concepts of Temple and community, adds to the growing number of Persian Period studies that support the idea that the evaluation of the period is undergoing some radical changes. The period has gone from being described as the dark ages to being acclaimed as *the* most generative time for the formation of the library of books that we call the Hebrew Bible. This shift is remarkable. While the elevation in status is certainly not accepted as the standard scholarly view, its proponents are no small band of insulated, like-minded scholars. They come from more than a dozen countries, use diverse methods and represent no single 'school'. The articles and monographs that portray this shift have appeared during the last quarter of a century. However, the seeds were sown over a longer time in a fertile field of literary, historical and social-scientific methods.

In re-examining the period no issue or question is *verboten*. The meaning of the name Israel is questioned. Is Israel a political, geographical, ethnic, social or religious term, or some combination? Is the name itself more an obstacle to the interpretation of the Hebrew Bible than help? Questions about the geographical extent of Judah, not only in the Second Temple period, but earlier, where little corroborative evidence exists, have emerged. The extent to which a second temple existed and in what form also stands among the issues. Such an almost frenzied set of basic questions typically leads to turmoil and disagreement. However, a metaphor of warring parties is less appropriate and descriptive than one of a fertile field. Of course, when the field is rich, diverse ideas will grow.

This second volume of Second Temple Studies is illustrative of the diversity of methods and scholars working in the Persian Period. The essays vary from methodological issues to discussions of texts dealing with the temple, institutions, society and history. These essays, like those of the first volume, do not primarily settle the issues. Rather, they help shape the ongoing discussions and give the reader an opportunity to join the debate.

Davies proposes in his essay the necessity of writing a sociology of the literature of the Hebrew Bible. He points out the tension between the Israel depicted in the biblical writings and the historical Israel emerging from extrabiblical sources. He therefore challenges the scholarly constructed picture. As Davies has shown elsewhere, the scholarly constructed picture of Israel is more problem than datum. He highlights the significance of the Persian Period because he thinks that the most likely period for the type of literary Israel created in the Hebrew Bible is a Judah of the late sixth and early fifth century BCE. Not just the literature normally associated with this period, but also the patriarchal, monarchical Israel depicted in Genesis–2 Kings is an important creation of this age. Garbini's essay also elaborates on the intellectual and religious climate of the Persian Period, which might have produced more of the Hebrew literature than the critical orthodoxies have generally thought possible until the last 25 years.

Carroll, Clines, Baltzer, Marinković and Van Rooy focus on prophetic texts and traditions. They use diverse historical and literary methods with distinctive results. Carroll observes at the beginning of his essay the puzzling fact that there are no substantial accounts of building the second temple. This is all the more remarkable in light of the rather impressive accounts of earlier temple building in the Hebrew Bible. This fact, coupled with the obvious concern among Persian Period writers about the temple, leads him to propose that the Second Temple period may well be a time of disputed temples. The battle between a real temple and a textual temple depicts a society likely to have existed during the Persian Period.

Clines, after a survey of the various ideas about Haggai's temple, uses a deconstructive literary method à la Frederic Jameson to suggest that Haggai arose out of a social context of suppression. The Haggai book deconstructs the temple through noting that it is filled not with glory, but gold and silver. The people are encouraged to rebuild the temple, yet told that all the work of human hands is unclean. Finally, the odd shift at the end of Haggai from temple to the future world leader, Zerubbabel, completes the suppression. According to Clines, Haggai becomes a book that suppresses a social reality of deep conflict between people and leaders.

While Carroll and Clines develop understandings of two debates depicted during the Persian Period, Baltzer sees yet another *Auseinandersetzung* regarding the polemic against the gods. Through literary, comparative religions and historical analysis Baltzer ties together the polemic with the known tendency in antiquity to associate gods with cities and communities. He demonstrates how the depictions of Zion-Jerusalem give evidence of Israel's shaping their own understandings of city, land and people over against the tendencies of others sometimes to deify, among other entities, cities.

Marinković challenges the tendency to harmonize Haggai and Zechariah and underscores the ways in which they present contrasting emphases. While taking a different tack than Carroll and Clines, he attempts to understand the reasons the two prophetic figures, Haggai and Zechariah, are seen together, especially in the Ezra book. He contends that they compliment each other. Haggai stresses temple building and Zechariah 1–8 focuses on community building. The outward and visible sign of the temple reaches toward the real goal of what it means to 'build' when expressed in Zechariah's terms of a renewal of covenant and a relationship between the people and their God.

Marinković contends that 'house' in Zechariah is best understood as community, not temple. Haggai and Zechariah thus complement each other. Haggai stresses temple building and Zechariah 1–8 focuses on community building. For Zechariah, the real goal of what it means to 'build' a 'house' (i.e. the community) is a renewal of covenant and a relationship between the people and their God. Later traditions (editors who placed Haggai and Zechariah in that order and those responsible for Ezra–Nehemiah) influence the conjoining of this distinctive vision with that a temple. The building of the temple does not serve as a end in itself or represent the goal of the early post-exilic community. The goal, in Zechariah, is the renewal of the community itself.

In the final essay focusing on prophets, Van Rooy attempts to discover through anthropological and sociological methods the function of prophets in a changing society. He recognizes that all literary depictions are historically conditioned, and assumes certain historical realities as he compares the Deuteronomistic historians' portrayal of prophets with those of the Chronicler. In the final analysis, Chronicles portrays the diminishing role of prophets in the Persian Period, over against the increasingly important role of the contemporary Levites. Yet, the prophets in Chronicles serve as authoritative figures from the past over against the rise of apocalypticism's 'unclear figures of speech'. Chronicles, by way of a strange twist, is able to deflect the problem of the failure of prophecy in a changed world and to reclaim the importance of the temple.

Turning from the essays which focus on the prophets to the Carter essay, one is at the heart of the new directions in Persian Period studies. He brings together texts and archaeological evidence. While recognizing how little either text or archaeological evidence disclose regarding this period, he is able to construct from demographic data and site distribution just how small Judah was. The extrabiblical literary, historical and archaeological data regarding Judah has long been known to be inferior to what is available for Israel. Carter compensates for these limits by combining ethnography and archaeology to assess the demographic scope of the Persian period Judah. New studies such as Carter's provide the kind of 'hard' data many are calling for as re-evaluations of the Persian Period continue. If the idea of a small but increasingly important Judah and Jerusalem, with interconnections to other provinces such as Samaria and Ashdod, turns out to be the most accurate understanding, it will provide major assistance in evaluating the competing conceptualizations of society during the sixth through fourth centuries.

Willi's more literary study directly addresses the ways in which literature serves the goals of the Judaean society. He illustrates how certain geographical and genealogical details provide the hermeneutical key for understanding both the literature and the history. Some of his assumptions about the scope of Judah are in tension with those of Carter's reconstruction. Importantly, Willi is able to illustrate the Chronicler's interpretation of significant older traditions (often reaching different conclusions from Van Rooy's about the relationship of Chronicles to prophetic and apocalyptic traditions). With 1 Chron. 2.9 as a springboard, Willi shows how genealogy meets the Judaean communal need of citizen lists, but, in addition, the more theological need of understanding Judah as indeed linked to the Israel of the past as well as to a future hope. The genealogy of Judah is more than an ideology about the family of David but articulates the wider sense of the nature of Israel as a whole. Here one confronts discussions regarding the diverse images of Israel and Judah that were competing during the Persian period.

Japhet proposes a hermeneutical key for interpreting Ezra–Nehemiah. Japhet probes the problematic relation between 'story' and 'history' by focusing on Ezra–Nehemiah and analyzing its historiography, given the discrepancy within its narrative(s) and the conflict with other sources. Her essay advances the discussion by uncovering the book's compositional techniques as a prerequisite for interpreting its depictions of temple and community in the Persian period Judah. Japhet not only reviews previous attempts to resolve this thorny problem of the compositional nature of Ezra–Nehemiah, but offers a fresh theory concerning the ways chronology and ideology intersect in Ezra–Nehemiah to express distinctive meanings.

The three essays by Washington, Christopher-Smith and Eskenazi–Judd utilize various dimensions of social scientific method. These methods are applied to issues surrounding the role of women in Persian Period society. Washington explores the economic factors that gave rise to the necessity of speaking out against 'foreign' women in Proverbs 1–9. Women so designated were not only outsiders to the community; they in fact represented a genuine danger to land holdings of the community. Corporate survival was put at risk when these women took advantage of their increasing ability to hold land during the Persian Period. Washington assists our recognition of the prohibition of exogamous marriage not just as a religious matter or part of a patrilineal system but one that endangered the very existence of all communal claims in a land occupied at the pleasure of the Persians.

Smith-Christopher applies comparative sociological analysis to the intermarriage texts in Ezra–Nehemiah. He observes that religious issues were dominant in the Ezra book and political issues in the Nehemiah book. His separation of Ezra and Nehemiah represents yet another one of the ongoing debates about the literary character of these books. Smith-Christopher uses contemporary intermarriage studies to provide concepts of boundary maintenance and hypergamy theory (attempts on the part of one party to 'marry up', thus taking advantage of the higher status of the other party). While raising new questions about the historicity of the Ezra text, given the sociological analysis,

Smith-Christopher is persuaded that major questions remain about the extent to which the Persian Period community represented a clearly defined group. In any case, he is certain that, given current comparative studies, neither the communities in Ezra nor those in Nehemiah make much sense as a 'greatly privileged' group.

Judd and Eskenazi also use sociological concepts (system and power conflict) as well as a contemporary analogue to better understand the marriage to a stranger in Ezra 9–10. They confirm, as others have, that the women portrayed are not necessarily foreigners. Aided by the sociological methods, Judd and Eskenazi make several major advances in understanding the Ezra text and the community out of which it may have emerged. The sociological theory highlights certain dynamics. First, during times of extensive immigration it is necessary to provide rules regarding the definition of people in diverse groups. Secondly, over a period of time the definitions change because of factors internal to the immigrating groups and external to the larger society. Thirdly, persons from an earlier period of time who were defined as a part of a group may find themselves outside the definition at a later period of time. A kind of 'grandfather clause' needs to be created in order to deal with this factor.

The implications for understanding Ezra 9–10 are clear. Not only are the women not foreigners, they may well have fallen under the rubric of legitimate marriage partners at an earlier stage. However, because of changed conditions and evolving identities of groups, these same women became 'foreigners'.

The essays in this volume point toward the complex and diverse problems regarding the identity of the society and its major symbols in the Persian Period. Not to be excluded from the unknowns already discussed is the figure of Ezra. While Ezra's historical existence and the authenticity of his portrayal have been challenged before, the question has received new energy from Garbini's work (to mention just one writer in this volume). Grabbe's essay takes a synchronic look at Ezra's mission, especially as related to the Artaxerxes decree whose authenticity is debated. He concludes that the many proposals that designate Ezra as high priest, governor, commissioner, lawgiver or whatever, are based on slim and even conflictory textual references. Greater clarity is demanded in understanding the social dynamics of the time from which this Ezra mission is drawn. In some sense Grabbe's essay circles back into the realm of Davies's piece which calls for a sociology of the literature of the Hebrew Bible.

The essays in this volume, even as they resolve few issues, raise new questions and a surprising number of new proposals. They disclose the range of work being done on temple and society in the Persian Period. They invite response and participation in the debate, and illustrate the interdisciplinary nature of the tasks before us. No single individual is likely to write a definitive sociology of the period that gave rise to the Hebrew Bible, however one might delimit the period. The model of a solitary scholar sitting at a computer needs to be replaced by that of a team of individuals. Only the combined efforts of scholars adept at using different methods and theories will assist with this task. More insightful studies of the shifting roles in a volatile, emerging society depend on a careful use of evidence from both text and material remains. Of course, this is not a new demand, but it does gain a new level of urgency for a period not likely to be identified again as the dark ages.

Part I

TEMPLE

The Society of Biblical Israel

Philip R. Davies

I

The adoption of a sociological stance, and the application of sociological methods, within biblical scholarship is not a new development (for it goes back at least to Causse and Weber). Its success at least in Hebrew Bible/Old Testament studies has been patchy. The modesty of its success is partly due to the inevitable problems attending the analysis of a defunct society. There is a paucity of non-literary data. The quantity of such data will probably remain unsatisfactory, though it is certainly improving as the agendas and techniques of Palestinian archaeology conform to the requirements of social scientific analysis.

But the paucity of data is not the paramount issue. The real problem with a sociological approach to the problems of biblical scholarship lies in a change of disciplinary domain: the replacement of one set of critical assumptions with another. The writing of a critical history of Israel was at one time distinguished from the retelling of the biblical story with the result that rationalistic assumptions about individual and social motivation replaced theocentric and idealistic ones. Human causality began to supplant divine causality. This change in the realm of historical studies is now more or less universally applauded in biblical scholarship as a triumph of scholarship over dogma.

Palestinian archaeology has also had to fight for its autonomy, to distinguish itself from 'biblical archaeology', and to replace biblically-derived periodizations and constructs of history and culture with those deriving from its own data. This has been difficult because of the systematic interpretation of the data themselves with reference to biblical criteria. The process is yet to be exhausted, though the outcome seems increasingly promising. But in the case of neither history nor archaeology is the separation from a Bible-centred and to some degree dogmatic determination yet complete: the distinctions between a biblically-derived context and a non-biblically derived one have been conceptually and theoretically established, but the *practice* of biblical scholarship still adheres in many ways to a biblically-guided agenda, which includes its methodology and assumptions. Sometimes this adherence is unconscious, since the language of biblical scholarship itself has assimilated so much theological jargon ('covenant', 'preaching', 'God', 'faith', 'disciples'), but it can also be conscious, and indeed could be defended on the grounds that without the biblical record no account of either history or archaeology is possible. (On the same lines, one might argue that the origins of Rome cannot be studied without the aid of Virgil's *Aeneid*).

Any sociological approach is similarly confronted with the obstacle of the Bible itself, for the method needs to free itself from the premises supplied by the biblical description of a society called by it (and by scholars) 'Israel', and to set about establishing its *own* definition of the social systems of Palestinian populations. Most of the work pretending to be critical social-scientific analysis stumbles at this obstacle, since it takes for granted exactly what is required to be demonstrated and analyzed, namely a society known to scholarship by the name 'ancient Israel'.[1] N.K. Gottwald's *The Tribes of Yahweh*[2] illustrates both the possibilities of social-scientific analysis and its pitfalls. This investigation—which despite the criticisms to follow ought to be hailed as a very important breakthrough in many respects—attempts to gain access to a historical society by means of analysis of a literary corpus whose relationship to that society remains dubious apart from an uncritical adoption of the conclusions of Martin Noth's traditio-historical work. Gottwald has produced, in large measure, a sociology of a *biblical* society, a *literary* society, and not *necessarily* a historical one. The society *behind* the text and the society *within* the text are not, as they need to be, distinguished with clarity. The theological investment in the text[3] is transferred, along with

1. I have attempted to expound this phenomenon in my *In Search of Ancient Israel* (JSOTSup, 148; Sheffield: JSOT Press, 1992).

2. N.K. Gottwald, *The Tribes of Yahweh: A Sociology of the Religion of Liberated Israel* (Maryknoll, NY: Orbis Books, 1979).

3. By this I mean Gottwald's transfer, in the manner of the 'Biblical Theology' movement, of the theological value of the Hebrew Bible away from its literary manifestation and onto the historical phenomenon to which it attests. It is not clear to me (nor to most other critics) that Gottwald succeeded in driving divine causality out of

much else, to a hypothetical historical entity.

Gottwald's work grows out of—though it certainly departs from in many respects—a history of biblical scholarship whose assumptions are that (a) the society depicted in the Bible was a real historical one, whatever amendments might be needed here and there to the details, and therefore that (b) the literature must be a product of that society, so that the literature's *forms and ideas*, as well as its descriptions of society and history, offer direct evidence of that society's culture. The literature and its implied producers are wound together into a circle which a sociological analysis needs to penetrate. It is precisely the aim of such an analysis of the biblical literature to define the relationship between text as cultural artifact and the society whose artifact it is, rather than to inherit a set of answers provided by theological and literary-critical arguments.

'Biblical Israel' has always furnished the starting point of any investigation of ancient Palestine in the Late Bronze and Iron Ages. For instance, at any archaeological site in Palestine where Iron Age buildings or artifacts are being unearthed, one is likely to find a debate about whether these are 'Israelite'. However, such debates are seen increasingly as sterile, so long as there is no *archaeological* basis for making the decision, for applying the name 'Israel'. 'Israelite' is certainly a slippery category for an archaeologist to employ, because it is a literary category first and foremost, and a historical and political one only by inference. It is the biblical writings that tell us what criteria make a building, settlement or artifact 'Israelite', and not archaeological data. We know, of course, from non-biblical sources, that there was an ancient kingdom called 'Israel' (although this was not its only name). We know also that there was a kingdom called Judah, but only the biblical writings give us any cause to call Judah 'Israelite'. Equally, only the biblical writings give us cause to speak of the Jezreel or Galilee as 'Israelite' for most of the Iron Age. By 'Israelite' an archaeologist, or historian, ought to mean the kingdom called Israel which lasted for a couple of centuries in the northern Palestinian highlands. Such a criterion is much easier to apply and certainly less misleading. Where archaeology is following *literary* distinctions and trying to give them archaeological substance,

history. Certainly, he seems to have accorded a greater value to religious belief systems and their capacity to generate new social systems than most anthropologists would want to concede.

problems can be expected, and they are occurring with increasing frequency. The root problem lies with the nature of biblical Israel and its relationship to history. This relationship is one that any sociological analysis must seek to establish and then examine. It cannot be taken over from the existing discourse of biblical scholarship.

II

The first task of any biblical scholar who would also be a sociologist, or, conversely, any sociologist who would also be a biblical scholar, must be to focus upon the primary data. In the case of Iron Age Palestinian societies, these primary data are what the societies left behind, namely artifacts, buildings, inscriptions and debris of various kinds. In the case of the Bible itself, the data are texts that describe a society located in what we would now call Palestine and for the most part in what we call the Iron Age (1250–650 BCE). The two sets of data are not automatically commensurate. One set of data is the direct product of Iron Age people, the other is not. For there can be no serious claim that the biblical texts as we have them derive directly from the Iron Age. Nor can any such claim be pursued until and unless it can be shown that there is a positive correlation between the biblical and archaeological descriptions of Iron Age Palestine. Until that correlation is shown (and not simply assumed as a working hypothesis), *we must accept the archaeological data as primary* and regard biblical 'Israel' as what it is, a literary construct. The identity of the society that produced it remains an open question. This self-evidently critical approach has never been adopted as the norm in biblical studies. Instead, it has been assumed that the society that the biblical literature portrays is essentially a real, historical one, and that this real society is the original producer of the literature.

It follows that the theologically inspired discipline of biblical studies has bequeathed to sociology the modest task of explicating a society of dubious and untested historical reality. For the sociologist, the biblical literature must serve in the first instance as evidence for the society that produced it, not the one that is depicted in it regardless of its historicity. It is the culture of the producer society that the texts will reflect, a principle enunciated by Wellhausen regarding the patriarchal narratives, and obviously applicable to the remainder of the biblical material.

III

The first task, then, of a biblical sociology is a *sociology of the literature*, to address these texts as cultural artifacts, to discern from them the economic, political, social and intellectual structures that both enabled them to be produced, and then participated in producing them in the forms that they have. An agenda such as this seems quite similar to the traditional pursuits of biblical scholarship. But in both conception and execution, the sociological agenda is vastly different from the essentially theological one that biblical scholarship has hitherto pursued. The difference is that the society which the biblical writings describe is excluded as an object of direct investigation, because its historical reality cannot be taken for granted. 'Ancient Israel' is not at the outset a historical construct, but an ideological one. The question of historicity is not important. The sociologist can take for granted that recording events that really happened, or were even believed to have happened, is not necessarily the most obvious motivation behind the production of narratives in an ancient agrarian society.

IV

The difference between what I would call a sociological approach to biblical studies and the approach hitherto adopted as the norm can be neatly illustrated by importing a distinction that biblical critics have now become well aware of through their familiarity with literary criticism, particularly narrative criticism. The distinction is between the author and the narrator. The writing and the reading of narrative texts necessarily involves the creation, by writer and reader, of a world that is, of necessity, an imaginary one, however much it resembles a real one. By reading the narrative, the reader interacts with that projected world. This act of reading constitutes looking *through* a text that refers directly to a world outside of itself, imaging that world; indeed, by reading between the lines and filling in the gaps, the reader enlarges that world in scope and detail. The layperson is familiar with this through the phrase 'willing suspension of disbelief', referring to the mechanism by which the world of the text is allowed temporarily to replace the historical world of the reader. In temporarily suspending the real world, the readers forget not only themselves (they 'get lost' in a book) but they also, necessarily, obliterate the author. Part of the technique of suspending belief is to supplant the author with the narrator.

Thus, we enjoy narratives by looking *through* instead of *at* them, in accordance with the intentions of the author, and her/his created text. Few readers of books are interested in what a text tells them of the manner of its production, of its real author. Few authors and texts in any case wish to allude to these circumstances, since of course such allusions break the spell of the created world.[4]

However, it is possible to read a book as the work of an author, as a critic, to analyze the style and technique, to hear the voice of the author, to see the real, known author within his or her artifact. The critic is thus a special kind of reader, who does not suspend disbelief at all, but frequently reads the *author*. Both writer and reader have real, historical identities.[5] Critical reading, then, is a reading of non-suspension of disbelief; of addressing author, not narrator; of looking *at* a text. In reading ancient narratives such as the Bible, one may read as a reader, suspending disbelief, accepting the world of the text in place of the real one, and, most importantly, deliberately mistaking the narrator for the author. Or one may read as a historian or critic, in which case narrator and author will be clearly separated.

Biblical scholarship does not always exercise this distinction carefully. The world that the Bible creates is not very often sharply and critically distinguished by the critical reader from the world in which its authors lived. Indeed, the narrator and the author are often identical when scholars speak of 'Israel' in connection with the Bible. 'Israel' is frequently spoken of as both its author *and* its narrator. The society implied by the text (narrator), in other words, is taken to be the society generating the text (author).

4. Space does not permit the treatment of that special kind of narrative called autobiography. Even here the author and the narrator are not necessarily the same. At any rate, autobiography is not the major concern among the biblical narratives.

5. The same may be true when the author is personally known to the reader, for the anonymity (or pseudonymity) of the author aids the independence of the narrator. This is not denied by the fact that people have favourite authors and choose to read their books, for these authors are not 'known' except through what they write; their historical identities do not obstruct their narratorial ones.

V

There is also another dimension to this question of authorship and narration. Even once 'Israel' has been supplanted as the term (and concept) of the society from which historically the biblical literature arose, we may still speak only qualifiedly of 'the society' generating such writings. Historically 'Israel' is quite a different society from what is depicted in the biblical writings. It is certainly arguable that literature (whether all or some) bears the stamp of society as a whole. A greater influence may well be exerted by the character and interests of the class, group and individual. The distinction between these different levels is virtually axiomatic to students of ideology. It is, of course, a highly disputed matter to identify the economic and ideological factors at these various levels that assist in shaping literature. Unless the distinction is borne in mind no critical account of the relationship between writing and society (and thus history) can be entertained. A simple illustration: it is no more self-evident that the book of Ecclesiastes is more influenced by class or individual ideology than Proverbs, or that Jonah is less influenced by social perceptions of prophets than Isaiah or Amos. The fact that we cannot identify a single one of the biblical authors, and that we know very little about the economics and the ideologies within their society, may prevent us from ever reaching a satisfactory level of analysis; but awareness of the complexity of this issue should at least prevent us from the kinds of simple inferences from text to society that predominate the scholarly literature.

Certainly, one key to understanding the relationship is a focus on realia and indeed minutiae. The precise 'how, why and when' of authorship, indeed authorship itself as an economic and ideological activity, are fundamental topics. The authors of the Bible are in fact all too seldom depicted in biblical scholarship as individuals, sitting in a stone chamber, in a temple or palace somewhere, copying or composing for a patron, or for practice, or to fill in leisure time, and certainly in most cases catering to readers of their own class (if they imagine being read in every case). The anonymity of biblical authorship has encouraged a more general categorization: the theologoumenon 'Israel' very often becomes a historical entity whose beliefs and practices correspond to the writings of the few literati in their midst. Along with the impossibly vague 'Israel' go terms such as 'circles', 'tradition' and 'schools'. These categories are sometimes informed by valid historical sources, though all too often they are inferences from a sociologically ill-informed approach to the biblical literature and need to be replaced by an attempt to describe the social system under which the biblical literature was produced; and this is not to be done by merely trying to read between the lines of the text!

Social systems cannot easily be inferred from texts. If it is true that there can be no 'objective' description of any social system—either from within or from outside (again, a central and disputed problem in social anthropology)—then at least the critic needs to adopt as a standard of reference something outside of the literature itself. This will enable the critic to explain literature as a function of the system, and avoid the circularity by which the literature's own reflection (or invention) of a social system is assumed as an objective historical datum. How often is the social critique of Amos taken as an objective description? Would any other point of view be entertained? Is it because the book of Amos is scriptural that we are inclined to accept it as authoritative social analysis? Does theological commitment, perhaps, preclude such critical doubt? Or was its author, or were its authors, in any way biased towards or against certain other groups in society? This question can be applied again and again to biblical writings, whose modern students are encouraged by their textbooks to take as 'objective' the obviously subjective views of the unknown authors of this ancient literature.

Thus, a sociological approach to the biblical literature, having identified the society responsible for it, might ask who, within that society, could write, or read, and why anyone would write *this* sort of stuff that we find in the Bible. For example, one might ponder the feasibility of, say, the book of Jeremiah as a consciously crafted literary composition intended for a particular readership. Asking the question soberly is likely to generate perplexity as to why any individual or group would generate such an incoherent product and whether any person would consider reading it. The fact that biblical scholars and religious people are prone to read Jeremiah as scripture perhaps obscures the fact that this particular way of reading cannot have been valid for the time of its creation, since 'scripture' presupposes the creation of the literature and not vice-versa!

VI

The implication of a sociological approach to biblical literature is thus different from a theological, literary or historical one. In my own view, at least, each of these methods establishes and accords a certain kind of autonomy. The theological approach grants autonomy to theological propositions, and analyzes and accounts for the biblical literature in relation to them. It sometimes claims also to be dealing with the religion of Israel at the same time, but this delusion is a good deal less pervasive now than when I was a student. A literary approach accords autonomy to the text, its inherent structures and capacities for meaning. A historical approach accords autonomy to events and circumstances. A sociological approach gives autonomy to the social system. In each case, the biblical literature is constructed as a different sort of phenomenon, with implicitly different causes and effects.

None of these approaches is exclusive, and many readers will chide me for excessive, even crude oversimplification. Few biblical scholars would wish to have their work pigeonholed in this manner. But the simplification is quite deliberate. Unless some such distinction is borne in mind, even theoretically, the various approaches will encroach on one another to the point where they transgress on a domain not their own. Thus, conclusions about the literary unity of a text may lead (as could be exemplified endlessly) to historical conclusions about authorship; theological judgments may become historical evaluations or assumptions, and historical questions light disguises for confessional biases towards the 'authenticity' of the Bible. On the other hand, no sociological approach, which is interested in literature as a social cultural product, can operate in isolation from historical research, nor, I would argue, from literary analysis. These texts are artistic works, the products of some skill, and a certain skill is required to understand them; even more skill is required to psychoanalyze them and discern the motivations that the author does not wish to disclose. Thus, while a sociological approach is distinct from other approaches in its assumptions and its goals, it is neither divorced from, nor inimical to, all other approaches. On the other hand, while the voice of God is still claimed to be heard in biblical texts and the hand of God seen in history, the sociologists ought to resist seeking divine principles in the ordering of societies too. As ideally with the disciplines of history and literature, so too sociologically informed biblical scholarship ought to analyze its subject as part of a comprehensive search for human self-understanding, scrutinizing the Bible's genesis and transmission as part of human history, its art as part of human literature and its production as an achievement of human society, rather than subscribing to a precondition that the object of studying the Bible is to get to the root of its uniqueness, or find its God. For all human historical events, writings and societies are unique, and gods have no place in either the data or the domain assumptions of the social sciences except as projections. Whether any of them exists is a question not to be denied, but ignored.

VII

How do the methodological remarks made above belong in a volume about the Second Temple? I have tried elsewhere to offer a fuller explanation (see *Second Temple Studies* I). Here I shall summarize the thesis. It is that the society of Israel described in the biblical literature is a literary construct. Attempts to identify it with the social history of Palestine in the Late Bronze and Iron Age are becoming increasingly futile as the picture drawn of ancient Palestine from non-biblical sources diverges ever more from the biblical picture.

This divergence will perplex biblical scholars so long as they adhere to the belief that the biblical society (i.e. the one described in the biblical writings) is a real one, and to the belief that springs from this, that this society essentially began to create the biblical writings, and thus that analysis of the biblical Israel provides the historical and social context for the writings themselves. However, the divergence of biblical and non-biblical Israels leads towards the conclusion that the biblical writing is a product of a different society from the one that it creates in its narratives. What is that other society, and why did it create a literary 'Israel'? The earliest candidate, historically, for this role must be the society established in Judah (Yehud) towards the end of the sixth century and the beginning of the fifth century, which represented a Persian initiative of transportation of populations into the province, grafted onto the indigenous population, with the aim, probably, of reviving the provincial economy and perhaps securing a stable buffer against Egypt. The encouragement of local religious identities was part of the imperial strategy, and the biblical writings are one of the results of this initiative. The prominence of Judah, the invention of a fictitious monarchic past (including a mini-empire), the many stories reflecting immigration, the theory of ethnic identity, the invention of 'prophecy'—all these make more sense as the products of social neuroses (I intend the word technically, not pejoratively) than they do as less and less credible historical 'facts' to be asserted in the face of increasingly contradictory evidence.

If the above line of argument is valid—and whether or not accepted at the moment, I think something like it will soon appear inevitable—then the 'biblical period' moves forward from its traditional datings and settles in the Persian-Hellenistic period. It is to this period, and this population, that sociologists need to direct their attention in exploring the origin and character of the biblical literature as a cultural product. Rather than explaining the character of the book of Jeremiah in terms of the political and social profile of the period in which the prophet is placed, this highly curious literature needs to be analyzed in terms of the ideological influences—social, class, group and personal—of those who contributed to its authorship. As a social phenomenon, biblical prophecy is not to be construed as the behaviour of recognized types of intermediation, but as a literary exercise, created at a writing table and not in a marketplace. The question for the sociologist is not, then, why Ezekiel lay on the ground eating food cooked with human excrement, or ate a scroll, but why a writer created these particular fictions. Not whether the period of the Judges led inevitably to the formation of a monarchy, but the function of, and purpose behind, the creation of this non-existent historical period.

Thus, no sociological approach must set out with a notion of 'ancient Israel' as its object of study, unless it wishes stillbirth; this particular society has no historical existence, but is the result of an attempt by scholars to blend a literary construct with a historical society, or, more correctly, several societies. The biblical writing belongs to another society. The task of describing and understanding, largely without the use of any biblical material, the social system of the province of Judah under the Persians and their successors is not a minor speciality within the range of interests circumscribed by biblical scholarship. It is the central objective of any scholar who seriously wants to explain the biblical literature as a product of human social activity—which I take to be the aim of a sociological approach. The adoption of such a programme will be symptomatic of the extent to which biblical scholarship is finally able to liberate itself from the theological house of bondage in which it has been enslaved. Among the other approaches that should continue to be exercised legitimately, the sociological one is worthy of a central place in biblical studies. Especially, however, it deserves its own proper agenda and methods.

SO WHAT DO WE *KNOW* ABOUT THE TEMPLE? THE TEMPLE IN THE PROPHETS

Robert P. Carroll

> Thus the unfacts, did we possess them, are too
> imprecisely few to warrant our certitude
> —James Joyce[1]

> You consider that to be important? he asked.
> Exceedingly so.
> Is there any other point to which you would
> wish to draw my attention?
> To the curious incident of the dog in the night-time.
> The dog did nothing in the night-time.
> That was the curious incident, remarked Sherlock Holmes.
> —Arthur Conan Doyle[2]

What must strike any serious (i.e. competent) reader of the Hebrew Bible is the absence of any account of the building of the second temple. Excessive details are given of the dimensions and building of the Mosaic *miškān*, Solomon's temple and Ezekiel's temple, but the very temple that provided the background to the production of the Hebrew Bible is astonishingly lacking any account of its dimensions or its building. This is so strange and surprising a lack in a book over-determined by accounts of temple building, that Sherlock Holmes' 'curious incident of the dog' comes instantly to mind as a fruitful analogy for biblical studies. The relevance of the quotation from James Joyce's *Finnegans Wake* must also be obvious to everybody

1. *Finnegans Wake* (London: Faber & Faber, 3rd edn, 1964), p. 57.

2. 'The Adventure of Silver Blaze', in *The Memoirs of Sherlock Holmes* (*Sherlock Holmes: The Complete Illustrated Short Stories*, by Sir Arthur Conan Doyle [London: Chancellor Press, 1985]), p. 250. This is not the place to explore the intertextuality of this famous point from a Sherlock Holmes story and the legend of the original Passover night when it was said that as the children of Israel left the land of Egypt the Egyptian dogs *did not bark* at them.

involved in studying the Persian Period or engaged in second temple studies. We are faced with a curious absence of a very necessary account about the building of the second temple, replete with details about its actual dimensions, and what few 'facts' we do appear to have about the period are both too few and too imprecise to allow us to assert anything about the construction of the second temple with any certitude. In this essay I shall take up issues discussed elsewhere in relation to second temple studies[3] and seek to explore somewhat further the strange silence, or perhaps better still, the reticence of the text about the second temple in the period when the Hebrew Bible was being produced. That reticence, that refusal to describe adequately or to address the issue of the building of the second temple, is most curious and poses the important question, 'Why in a book made up of so many accounts of temple building projects should the second temple lack any sustained account of its building?'

A monographic treatment might do justice to this question, but within the severe limits of a paper I shall confine my explorations to the material contained in the prophetic books of the Bible. Before looking at the prophets the following *odd* fact about the second temple should be noted. The second temple is actually described in passing in Ezra 6.3-4 in the letter of Cyrus the king:

> Concerning the house of God at Jerusalem, let the house be rebuilt... its height shall be sixty cubits and its breadth sixty cubits, with three courses of great stones and one course of timber...

So there we have it! The second temple was a building sixty cubits by sixty cubits—roughly ninety feet high and ninety feet across—but of no length. No information whatsoever is given about the length of the building, so commentators on the text have to have recourse to conjectural emendation of or restoration to the text. In 1 Kgs 6.2 the house

3. See R.P. Carroll, 'Textual Strategies and Ideology in the Second Temple Period', in P.R. Davies (ed.), *Second Temple Studies*. I. *Persian Period* (JSOTSup, 117; Sheffield: JSOT Press, 1991), pp. 104-24 and Carroll, 'The Myth of the Empty Land', *Semeia* 59 (1992), pp. 79-93; *idem*, 'Israel, History of (post-monarchic Period)', *ABD*, III, pp. 567-76. To complete the record, acknowledgement should be made of my unpublished SBL International paper, '"Silence, Exile, and Cunning": Reflections on the "Bürger-Tempel-Gemeinde" Thesis Approach to the Early Second Temple Period', given in Vienna (7 August 1990), and my SBL Annual Meeting paper, '"No Peace for the Wicked": The Prophetic Word in the Second Temple Period', given in New Orleans, 19 November 1990.

of YHWH, the first temple, is represented as having the dimensions 'sixty cubits long, twenty cubits wide, and thirty cubits high' (with additional dimensions given for the vestibule). If the length of the first temple is assumed for the second temple and inserted into the text of Ezra 6, then the second temple becomes a cube of sixty cubits (a ninety foot cube).[4] Changing the text of Ezra 6 to fit the dimensions given in 1 Kings 6 necessitates some 'drastic textual surgery' and only further highlights the unsatisfactory state of the biblical text in Ezra.[5] What begins to look like a sixty cubit stone cube of a building is let down by textual inadequacies (cf. 1 Esdras 6.25) and only dubiously sustained by the conjectures of commentators or turned into an exact replica of the first temple (i.e. sixty cubits by twenty cubits by thirty cubits) without any textual warrants. That is a most unsatisfactory state of affairs which is too often overlooked by commentators and scholars eager to assume a level of information not provided by the actual biblical text.

We do not have adequate textual information for the dimensions of the second temple. Whatever the reasons for this inadequate and somewhat terse notation in Ezra 6.3-4—whether it is traceable to parablepsis caused by confusion of the various occurrences of *'āmmîn* 'cubits' or whatever the reason for such a defective text—the *fact* remains that the biblical text is remarkably quiescent on the subject of the physical representation of the second temple. How is that fact to be explained? Should that reticence (or simple absence of information) be taken as implicit evidence for the similarity of the second temple to the first temple? Is the defective text of Ezra to be made good from the text of 1 Kings? We would have to ignore the Chronicler's different dimensions of the overall structure of the temple (2 Chron. 3.4 makes the vestibule of the temple 120 cubits high and no height is given for the house of YHWH) and assume that 1 Kings 6 should be related intertextually to Ezra 6 to justify such a move. If we take 1 Kings 6, 2 Chronicles 3 and Ezra 6 together as an intertextual statement about the two temples, confusion cannot be avoided. Arbitrary decisions as to which text should supplement a defective text can easily

4. Cf. J. Blenkinsopp, *Ezra–Nehemiah: A Commentary* (OTL; London: SCM Press, 1988), pp. 123-25.

5. The phrase used is cited from Blenkinsopp, *Ezra–Nehemiah*; for such drastic surgery see H.G.M. Williamson, *Ezra–Nehemiah* (WBC, 16; Waco, TX; Word, 1985), pp. 68, 71.

conceal from the modern reader the most obvious and important fact of our ignorance of the actual dimensions of the second temple. Perhaps something has been lost over time from the Ezra text and should be conjecturally restored or perhaps, given the Chronicler's two dimensions in 2 Chronicles 3, the writer of Ezra 6 (if different from the Chronicler) was following suit in providing only two dimensions for the second temple.[6] At this point in my argument the posing of questions is more important than the attainment of answers. To explore further those questions in directions that might yield some clarification of the issues as they bear on the matter of the second temple I shall move on to consider the evidence afforded by the prophets on the subject of the temple in the hope that it may prove possible to say something further on the question constituting the title of this essay—'So What Do We *Know* about the Temple?'

The Temple in the Prophets

With the most obvious exception of the book of Ezekiel (especially chs. 40–48), the temple is not a particularly significant feature of the prophetic books. The paucity of detail and the generality of reference to the temple in the prophets do not permit the modern reader of the Hebrew Bible to determine whether first or second temple is being indicated (with the possible exception of Haggai–Zechariah where the rebuilt temple indicates that the second temple is the focus of the text). Working from the redactional information supplied by the colophons to the prophetic books, readers tend to apply anything said about the temple to the first temple without remarking on the lack of any real information about the temple that would allow the reader to determine *which* temple is meant in the text. As far as the prophetic books are concerned the temple is at best a textual one, lacking specificity of detail and reference, and therefore may be either the first or the second temple. The referentiality of the text may not even be that specific, so that the temple referred to is purely textual and fictional.

6. I do not propose to enter into the vexed discussion about whether the Chronicler also wrote Ezra–Nehemiah or there were different authors of Chronicles and Ezra–Nehemiah. The data available are too inadequate to determine the matter. The curious may be referred to the already cited commentaries of Blenkinsopp and Williamson (along with the invaluable work of D.J.A. Clines on Ezra–Nehemiah, esp. *Ezra, Nehemiah, Esther* [NCB; Grand Rapids: Eerdmans, 1984]).

For example, Jonah's psalmic reference to it 'How shall I again look upon your holy temple?' (2.4) and Habakkuk's general reference to 'YHWH is in his holy temple; let all the earth keep silence before him' (2.20) are fairly characteristic of the non-specificity of references to the temple in the prophets. Other more concrete references tend to fall foul of the standing caveat on all biblical rhetoric, especially the highly rhetorical language of the prophets, *caveat lector* 'let the reader beware'—such language *always requires interpretation*. The term 'temple' may refer to YHWH's heavenly or earthly temple, to the first temple or to the second temple, or to a specific temple in the text, present to the text or even to a future temple. But without further specification of defining information, how is the reader of the text to determine which it is? How is the reader to decide that a specific or actual temple is being referred to or that the temple in the text is not itself a textual construct? When is the temple in the text a real temple and when is it a textual temple?

These questions will remain throughout this paper and will have direct bearing on the construction of the notion of a 'textual' or 'midrashic' temple as an important element in the study of the Second Temple period. To give more shape to this approach, I must first review the material on the temple in the prophets. General references to YHWH's 'holy mountain' (e.g. Obad. 16; Zeph. 3.11; Joel 3.17) do not give any information whatsoever about the temple complex. Allusions to Jerusalem/Zion as the 'mountain of the house' (e.g. Mic. 3.12) are equally unhelpful in providing concrete information about the temple. In Isaiah and Jeremiah references to the temple are formal and narratological. In either case little or no specificity of detail is given in the text. Allusions to the temple in Isaiah 60–66 are distinctly unhelpful: general references to the rebuilding of cities and the use of cultic language (e.g. priests in 61.6) do not describe a temple-centred community with any degree of informed precision. Phrases such as 'the courts of my sanctuary' (62.9), 'our adversaries have trodden it [i.e. your sanctuary] down' (63.18), 'our holy and beautiful house, where our fathers praised you, has been burned by fire' (64.11), 'my holy mountain' (65.11, 25; cf. 11.9), 'a voice from the temple, the voice of YHWH' (66.6), 'what is the house which you would build for me?' (66.1) really convey very little information indeed. The holy mountain is as likely to be the city of Jerusalem (66.20) as it is to refer to the temple mound (cf. Exod. 15.17). As a city that once had a temple, that perhaps has a temple, and that may yet have a temple—the once and future temple—Jerusaleam is easily described as YHWH's holy mountain. But such rhetoric of holiness tells us absolutely nothing about the temple, be it first, second or third. From the sixth century BCE to the first century CE (and on down the centuries to this day) such rhetoric is at home (see the appropriated and transformed temple language in the New Testament, especially in the Fourth Gospel, some of the writings of Paul, and the Apocalypse) without specificity of focus or reference. The material in Isaiah 60–66 eludes precision of dating or exactitude of allusion.

The well known story of the vision in the temple of Isaiah 6 equally tells us remarkably little about the temple. The divine being surmounted by the *śᵉrāpîm*—an unknown species of anthropogriff, unattested elsewhere in the Bible—a smoke-filled building, burning coals on an altar, antiphonal singing and elements from the rhetoric of expiation/purification all point to the use of the language of the cult, but really afford very little hard information about the temple. In fact, Isaiah 6 reads more like a story constructed in symbols derived from temple furnishings and language associated with the temple than a story reflecting real events in an actual temple. In order to produce a story such as that in Isaiah 6 it would not be necessary ever to have been in the temple. The details are neither photographic nor structured in a way that provides specific information about the temple building. There are also, of course, too many questions of an interpretative nature to be asked of the story, the answers to which will take the reader further away from access to hard, reliable information concerning the temple. Most conventional readers of Isaiah 6 would understand the story to be an encounter between the speaker and the divine being in the first temple. Other readers who find Otto Kaiser's treatment of Isaiah 6–8 more persuasive than the traditional understanding of the text will be more inclined to think of the setting of ch. 6 as that of the second temple or what, in my opinion is even more likely, may be called a narratological construct of 'the temple'.[7] Where else would a visionary encounter the divine *as depicted* in Isaiah 6 but in the temple? The elements in the temple may appear real to readers and so mislead them into thinking that the story reflects 'real' events, but what kind of reality is depicted by *śᵉrāpîm* flying

7. Cf. O. Kaiser, *Isaiah 1–12: A Commentary* (OTL; London: SCM Press, new edn, 1983), pp. 114-33.

about the place, chanting to one another, manipulating tongs and touching people's lips with burning coals? If those are not imaginary elements in a fantasy (however skilfully manipulated in the text by a skilled writer) set in an imagined temple, then I do not know imaginative literature when I encounter it. The literary character of Isaiah 6 yields a literary or textual temple. Such a construct may also be described as a 'midrash'[8] and hence as 'a midrashic temple' because it is based on a highly symbolic use of textual material bearing on the temple. Readers may test for themselves the reality of the hypothesis being put forward here by writing a short story set in a temple. See if it is necessary to give more concrete details of a temple setting than appear in Isaiah 6.

In the book of Jeremiah the temple has a similar symbolic role to play in the narratological construction of the story of Jeremiah. As a priest from the priests of Anathoth it would be natural for Jeremiah to live and function in the temple. Hence we find many of the narratives place him in the temple. Hardly any of those narratives provide any serious details about the temple structures. Perhaps only the story of Jeremiah and the Rechabites in ch. 35, with its reference to 'the chambers' of the house of YHWH (v. 2), has a detail worth nothing. But even in that story the symbolic factor determining the force of the story is far more to the fore than any detail about the temple complex. In ch. 36 there are also chambers in the temple which provide space for Baruch to read the scroll to the people. Elsewhere in the book, Jeremiah stands at the gate or in the courtyard of the temple (7.2; 26.2; cf. 19.14) or is confined to the stocks in the upper Benjamin gate of the temple (20.2; cf. 29.26). All of these stories posit a temple setting for Jeremiah's activities, but the detail is never more than narratological. Perhaps that is what you would expect from such stories, but it does not help the historian reconstruct 'the historical temple' because it never provides the kind of detail that would allow the reader to differentiate a midrashic temple from a real temple. The temple remains textual throughout the prophetic books and its 'reality'

8. The term is Michael Owen Wise's and appears in his book *A Critical Study of the Temple Scroll from Qumran Cave 11* (Studies in Ancient Oriental Civilization, 49; Chicago: The Oriental Institute, 1990), p. 199, where he observes, 'I argue that the consensus position had not sufficiently reckoned with the literary character of the TS text. It is "midrash"; it does not 'describe' any historical event. This portion of the TS simply interprets the Bible.'

is never more than an open question for the historically minded reader.

The one group of prophetic texts that might be regarded as being indisputably the product of the second temple period is that of Haggai–Zechariah–Malachi. In Ezra 5.1-2 (1 Esdras 6.1-2) the prophets Haggai and Zechariah are associated with the rebuilding of the temple. In Haggai preparations for the project of the rebuilding are discussed in oracular forms and the beginnings of the rebuilding programme are depicted as a popular enterprise—'all the remnant of the people; and they came and worked on the house of YHWH' (1.14b). Implicit in the contrast between the rebuilt house and its former glory (2.3) is the notion that the rebuilt temple is a lesser building than the first temple. Nothing more is said about the physical details of the building, so Haggai as a book offers very little to the historian seeking information about the Second Temple. Hope for a great reversal is expressed in Hag. 2.6-9 whereby a divine shaking of the four elements of the heavens and the earth, the sea and the dry land will cause the wealth of nations to be brought to the new temple. This sudden influx of treasure into the temple will reverse the judgment that it was inferior to the first temple. Thus we may read Haggai as describing the new temple as a potential storehouse or treasury of the empire. It is hardly a holy place for worship or the celebration of cultic rituals, but it is to be a place for the generating of great wealth. With its building the economic welfare of the community will be transformed (2.15-19). In Haggai 2 the essence of the divine house is that of a *bourse* or centre of the generation of wealth. It looks more like an imperial taxation centre than a holy house. The book of Haggai—whatever its dating, milieu or production values may be—presents a disorganized and dispirited community which needs to build a centre in order to become a thriving economic concern. The lack of a divine temple is given as the explanation for the community's economic impoverishment and therefore the function of such a rebuilt temple must be seen in terms of its potential for generating wealth.

The book of Zechariah is much more complex because its narratological structure focuses on night visions which are *per definitionem* symbolic constructions which require complex interpretative strategies to be understood. The literary device of the night visions focuses on the rebuilding of the temple in various ways and is a highly reflective construction. The complexity of the visions suggests a considerable degree of reflective construction in their making and this factor in turn undermines the datings in the text. Unless the temple elements in the visions are purely literary or textual constructs (i.e. midrashic in the sense of being derived from texts about the temple rather than elicited from experiences in an actual temple), then they presuppose a setting in a temple built in the past rather than in the process of being rebuilt or proposed for rebuilding. The visions are too convoluted to be as stated in the text.

Elements of the rebuilding project are associated with Zerubbabel and features of the temple become the focus of some of the visions—for example, the golden *menōrâ* of 4.2. But again, as in Isaiah 6, the force of these visions is a symbolic one rather than a literal description of the temple furniture. A golden *menōrâ* flanked by two olive trees—cf. Isaiah 6's notion of YHWH superintended by *śᵉrāpîm*—represents the all-seeing power of YHWH's (divine) council.[9] Now whether the details of the *menōrâ* and the things associated with it in Zechariah 4 should be accepted as technical information about the physical contents of the second temple or whether we (i.e. modern readers of the text) should read the text as symbolic reflection on the temple literature is a matter for much debate. It might be reasonable to say that if Zechariah 4 is to be taken literally *at any point*, then the second temple probably contained a *menōrâ* ('lampstand') with seven lamps on or suspended from it. On the other hand, if, as C. Meyers and E. Meyers claim in their commentary, 'Zechariah's vision of the lampstand was influenced much more by the single lampstand tradition of the Pentateuch',[10] then the *menōrâ* is more likely to be a textual construct than a depiction of actual furniture in the Second Temple. The *miškān* of Moses then becomes the real source of the imagery in Zechariah and the text offers no concrete information about the temple (first or second). As a conflation of the traditions about the *miškān* and the first temple (so Meyers and Meyers), it would be a very reasonable hypothesis to say that the *menōrâ* of Zechariah had no real existence outside the text. In the text the *menōrâ* functions as a statement about YHWH's imperial control of the whole earth—like the

9. See the discussion of the text in C.L. Meyers and E.M. Meyers, *Haggai, Zechariah 1–8: A New Translation with Introduction and Commentary* (AB, 25B; Garden City, NY: Doubleday, 1987), pp. 228-59, and D.L. Petersen, *Haggai—Zechariah 1–8: A Commentary* (OTL; London: SCM Press, 1984), pp. 214-44.

10. *Haggai, Zechariah 1–8*, p. 232.

Persian empire (or its historical successors) with its structured control throughout its domains, so the divine being YHWH observes everything that goes on throughout the earth.[11] The *menōrâ* of the later post-Herodian temple should not necessarily be associated with Zechariah's vision.

Zech. 8.9-13 also represents the temple as an economic centre, and the burgeoning of the economy is associated directly with the building of the temple. Other facets of temple language and routine are used in Zechariah, for example, 'the mountain of YHWH of hosts, the holy mountain' (8.3) or the clothing of Joshua the high priest (3.1-5). None of it, however, adds to our knowledge of what the second temple may have looked like. If everything said or hinted at in Haggai–Zechariah were to be added together we would have remarkably little real information about the temple. Visions or oracles about the day of YHWH, when all the pots in the temple would be the same as the bowls before the altar and all the pots in Judah and Jerusalem would be sacred, hardly afford any concrete information about the temple (Zech. 14.20-21). The hope expressed in Zech. 14.21 that such a day would see the cessation of trade in the temple ('there shall no longer be a trader in the house of YHWH') is indicative of the role of the temple as a kind of 'merchant city', much given to commerce and business transactions. The language of the sacred used in 14.20-21 may suggest a hoped for transformation of the temple city from being a mercantile centre to becoming solely a cult centre. Thus Zechariah 14 repristinates the Haggai–Zechariah material in a direction away from Haggai's bourse and Zechariah's centre of commerce.

The material in Malachi refers to the temple a number of times. Various places deal with questions about altar pollution and the acceptability (or otherwise) of offerings of the altar (cf. 1.6-14; 2.13; 3.4). Criticisms are directed against the priests (2.1-9), but they will be purified by the 'messenger of the covenant' (3.1-4). YHWH is represented as coming 'suddenly to his temple' (3.1).[12] That reference to the divine *hêkāl* is not developed further and no details of the

11. Cf. A. Oppenheim, 'The Eyes of the Lord', *JAOS* 88 (1968), pp. 173-80; Oppenheim relates the 'eyes' to 'informers, accusers, internal spies, censors, secret agents and their like' (p. 180). Petersen (*Haggai—Zechariah 1–8*, p. 227) sees the 'eyes' as a 'symbol of divine beneficence' (cf. 2 Chron. 16.9; Ezra 5.5).

12. In citing Mal. 3.1 Mk 1.2 stops short of the coming of YHWH to his temple—evidence of the New Testament's tendency to decentre the temple.

temple appear anywhere in Malachi. In 3.10 the house of YHWH (i.e. the temple) is equated with a storehouse (*bêt hā'ôṣār*). The bringing of all the tithes into the storehouse or treasury will guarantee the prosperity of the land by providing 'food' (*ṭerep* 'prey') for the temple. The connection between the temple and fertility may reflect older connections of land and sacred enclave, but in Malachi it also seems to represent the same point made in Haggai–Zechariah about the temple as the economic centre of the community.

The one aspect of the prophetic books that I have not considered so far is that of the book of Ezekiel. Ezekiel is a minefield for the interpreter. Represented as living in Babylonia, the prophet Ezekiel nevertheless wanders all over Jerusalem behaving like a denizen of that city. In visions he sees the first temple on the eve of its destruction (chs. 8–11) and in subsequent 'visions of god' (40.2) he sees the reconstruction of the temple. Between the destruction of the first temple and the construction of a new temple the bulk of Ezekiel's work takes place. So the book is very much one dominated by temple considerations and appears (to the modern reader) to be a highly ideological document written in support of temple politics in the Persian (or Greek) period. Apart from chs. 40–48, which may be said to have an exactitude of detail bespeaking blueprints and plans for temple building, the material in chs. 1–39 on the first temple is symbolical rather than literal. Just as in the book of Zechariah physical details of founding, building and furnishing a temple are used to construct a symbolism of vision and oracle, so the book of Ezekiel represents physical details as giving way to symbolic interpretations. The textuality of Ezekiel may conceal from the conventional reader the lack of serious connection between the symbolism of the temple in the book and the physical features of real temples, but even biblical texts should not just be assumed to be operating with a simplistic scheme of referentiality to something imagined to be outside the text.[13]

Ezekiel 40–48 poses immense problems of interpretation and placement in the Second Temple period. Do the plans represent an enterprise submitted for consideration in the building and organization of the second temple? Is Ezekiel's temple the first or the second temple? What is the relationship between Ezekiel's vision and the second

13. On the textuality of Ezekiel see E.F. Davies, *Swallowing the Scroll: Textuality and the Dynamics of Discourse in Ezekiel's Prophecy* (JSOTSup, 78; Bible and Literature Series, 21; Sheffield: JSOT Press, 1989).

temple? Was the temple of Ezekiel 40–48 ever built? Was it ever meant to be built? In other words, the vision may be literary rather than aspirational, symbolic rather than blueprints for an actual building programme. Like the Temple Scroll from Qumran, Ezekiel's temple may never have been other than a textual temple.[14] Scholars have provided many different answers to these questions (where they have been asked in the first place) and it would take a very different paper from this one to explore all those interpretative constructions based on Ezekiel 40–48. But like Sherlock Holmes's curious incident of 'the dog in the night-time' what I find most curious about Ezekiel 40–48 and the second temple is the complete lack of an account in the Hebrew Bible represented as the account of the building of the second temple to parallel those accounts of the *miškān* of Moses or the temple of Solomon. It is conceivable that such an omission was not deliberate and that there was no need for such an account because the second temple was perceived by the ideologues who produced the Hebrew Bible to be the replacement of the first temple. Built in exactly the same place and to exactly the same specifications, there was no need to give an account of its construction because Kings (and Chronicles to some extent) contained that account. Equally conceivable is the viewpoint that Ezekiel 40–48 provides the details of the rebuilding of Jerusalem and its temple. There are insuperable problems with either conception and so it is necessary to offer some alternative reflections on the origins and nature of the Second Temple.

Observations on the Second Temple

It is possible to devote much further space to exploring the role of the temple in the prophetic writings, but very little of it would have direct bearing on the problem of describing the temple in terms of what we could be said to know about the Second Temple. There is also much coming and going about the building of the temple in the Ezra–Nehemiah literature, but again there is very little substantive detail given. I find the text of Nehemiah to be so egocentric that I am not at all sure how I should read that text, especially in terms of being a historically reliable document about the rebuilding of either city or temple.[15] The textuality of Ezra–Nehemiah also militates against

14. See Wise, *A Critical Study of the Temple Scroll.*

15. On Nehemiah's unreliable memoirs, see D.J.A. Clines, 'The Nehemiah Memoir: The Perils of Autobiography', in *What Does Eve Do to Help? And Other*

taking what is said in the text literally or even as a reliable account of events imagined to be taking place outside the text.[16] I very much suspect the text of Ezra–Nehemiah to be a highly fictionalized account with little historical worth. While that may be a debatable point, it is a point worth making about all the biblical literature bearing on the Second Temple period. It cannot be demonstrated to the satisfaction of all parties that the material in Ezra–Nehemiah and Haggai–Zechariah–Malachi is to be taken at face value *qua* history. Furthermore, all these texts constitute sites of struggle and contested readings. I think what we need here to assist us in our readings of biblical texts is something like the category of 'the biblical fact'. This category is analogous to what Hugh Kenner calls 'the Irish fact'. For Kenner an 'Irish Fact' is 'definable as anything they will tell you in Ireland'.[17] He provides many examples of such 'facts' and also warns the receiver of such facts that they 'had best assume a demeanour of wary appreciation'. My version of Kenner's phrase would be 'the Biblical Fact'. What you read in the Bible are 'Biblical Facts'. Not facts in the external world but textual facts or 'history in inverted commas'.[18] Such 'Biblical Facts' as relate to the Second Temple need to be treated in some such manner so as not to fool the modern reader into thinking that they are reading something that approximates to what *we* call history. 'Biblical Facts' require serious interpretation and evaluation as to their weight in any reconstruction of what it is we imagine we do know about the second temple—whether its origins, its structure, its nature or its datings.

A very different approach to the subject might be attempted along the following lines. Seeing that we know so very little about the physical structure of the second temple and that we have no account of its construction comparable with the other three great textual *miškān*/

Readerly Questions to the Old Testament (JSOTSup, 94; Sheffield: JSOT Press, 1990), pp. 124-64.

16. On the textuality of Ezra–Nehemiah see T.C. Eskenazi, *In An Age of Prose: A Literary Approach to Ezra–Nehemiah* (SBLMS, 36; Atlanta: Scholars Press, 1988). For a more conventional overview of the second temple, see S. Japhet, 'The Temple in the Restoration Period: Reality and Ideology', *USQR* 44 (1991), pp. 195-251.

17. *A Colder Eye: The Modern Irish Writers* (London: Allen Lane, 1983), pp. 3-10 (3).

18. On the Bible and history see R.L. Fox, *The Unauthorized Version: Truth and Fiction in the Bible* (London: Viking, 1991).

temples of the Bible, what about a different tack? Let us imagine for a moment that there never was a *significant* Second Temple before Herod (re)constructed his famous temple. Let us also support that imaginative possibility by asking 'what actual, concrete evidence do we have of a pre-Herodian temple?' What archaeological or material remains have been found for such a building? This is to start from first principles. Let us then suppose—just for the sake of argument—that there was some physical structure of a temple that was elaborately developed by Herod but which, in some sense, preexisted Herod's building. That modest building (bourse, treasury, commercial centre) we will assign to what Joel Weinberg calls the *Bürger–Tempel–Gemeinde* (or civic temple community). Such a modest building could be detected in the Haggai–Zechariah material (whatever the dates assigned to such literature). If Weinberg's notion of a guild or community associated with a temple building is correct, such a building need not be grandiose. Its role as a district bourse with a ritualized cult and funded by families wishing to belong to such a guild would fit all the textual information available in the Bible. What would differentiate it from the major texts on *miškān*, temple and Ezekiel's vision would be its actuality.

The actuality of this modest building is not important for the biblical writers. What the great texts of constructing the *miškān* and the temples of Solomon and Ezekiel are about is not the literal building of actual sanctuaries but representations of complex metaphoric and metonymic structures which bear on how the community is to live in the world.[19] I do not think that any of the descriptions of temple building in the Bible is of such a nature that we could reproduce (i.e. build now from scratch) the building in a tridimensional architectonic fashion today.[20] Such narratological accounts in the Bible are doing something other than giving architectural information. Those texts describe buildings that never were: grandiose, ideological constructions with no real existence outside of the text. The actual temple

19. On this see the wise observations of G. Josipovici, *The Book of God: A Response to the Bible* (New Haven: Yale University Press, 1988), pp. 90-107.

20. All the various architectural models which I have seen for the *miškān* and the temple have to assume information that is *not* in the text and have to make arbitrary judgments to overcome the lack of adequate data in the Bible. These lacunae ought to persuade the reader that the biblical stories belong to the symbolic discourse world of the Bible rather than to the architect's drawing-board.

around which the guild families lived in the Persian period (or more likely in the Graeco-Roman periods) had little interest for the biblical writers. Hence the great difficulty in finding adequate information on it in the Bible. Even the Chronicler who (presumably) lived during the period of the second temple ignored it in order to rewrite the account of Solomon's temple (i.e. to rewrite the past rather than encounter the present).

The temple in Ezra–Nehemiah appears peripherally in the focus on the legitimation disputes about building projects in Jerusalem. Just look at the text of Ezra, where the building of the temple is constantly interrupted in order to send to distant lands to check and read the authorization for the temple's construction. The text is profoundly textual in its obsession with *documentary authorization* and is much more concerned with such documentation than it is with the actual building of the temple. The authorization of the temple is more important than the building project. That all reads more like problems of legitimation than problems of building. The text wishes to impress on its readers (hearers) that the project of building was legitimate and so keeps forgetting *or* refusing to give the details of its actual building. When the building of the temple is completed its authorization is emphasized in terms of being legitimated by 'command of the God of Israel *and* by decree of Cyrus *and* Darius *and* Artaxerxes king of Persia' (Ezra 6.14). Who could question or oppose such fourfold legitimation!

Now why would legitimation be such a problem? The text responds to charges of illicit building and reflects a setting of extreme hostility to the temple project. If the *Bürger–Tempel–Gemeinde* were indeed a minority or clique group in that period, then opposition to or rejection of the temple project would be natural and understandable. If the temple had been simply a replacement of the older temple built on the same spot, why should there have been any problems whatsoever? On the other hand, opposition to the temple would have been guaranteed if the temple had been designed to be the exclusive property of a specific ideological group or of interlopers from Babylon. Whereas all the blueprints of temples contained in the Bible are national or universal entities, the temple represented in Ezra–Nehemiah is the ideological property and private concern of a pressure group determined to be as exclusive as possible. That is a fundamental difference between all the largescale representations of temples in the Bible and the barely discernible building project in the texts discussed in this paper. No wonder detail of physical construction is so hard to come by and no wonder symbolic representations play such a large part in these texts. The building of the so-called second temple may have been a 'hole-in-the-wall' affair (if you will excuse the idiom). It was at best a sectarian activity reflecting a minority point of view, even though it was to become a major generative force in the later development of Judaism. But the absence of direct information about its construction allows the reader of the Bible to assume profound family resemblances between it and the Kings–Chronicles accounts of Solomon's temple.

This approach to the matter can be taken further. We know from the Qumran literature of a temple scroll giving details of the (potential) construction of a significantly large temple. This scroll fits into the typology of the temple accounts in the Bible: the *miškān* of Moses, the temple of Solomon and the temple of Ezekiel. What is significant in that list is the absence of any similar typological account of the second temple. That absence could be explained (in the sense of rationalized) in terms of the second temple having been seen as the equivalent (i.e. replacement) of the first temple—note how the Chronicler ends the work in anticipation of building the temple by having Cyrus the king of Persia say 'YHWH...has charged me to build him a house at Jerusalem' (2 Chron. 36.23) while focusing on the first temple in the body of the work. A different explanation is favoured in this paper. If Ezekiel's temple and the Qumran temple scroll were produced and could exist in the Second Temple period, then we must accept the inevitable conclusion that the second temple was not widely accepted as the legitimate temple. In other words, we must think of the 'second temple period' as a period of *contested* temple projects. In fact, we should be questioning the use of the phrase 'second temple' to cover the Persian-Graeco-Roman period. Its continued usage entails accepting the ideology of the Second Temple group and adopting their point of view. That is to side with one faction in a period of many factions contesting important issues. We must stand outside that struggle rather than siding with one particular faction.

At some point in the Persian–Greek period a temple was built in Jerusalem—space does not permit an exploration of when and by whom—but it was the exclusive property of a specific ideological party and was not recognized by other groups. The scrolls associated with Qumran indicate some of the opposition to and rejection of the Jerusalem temple community. The general indifference of the prophetic books to the temple—with the obvious exception of the Haggai–Zechariah–Malachi additions to the prophetic collection—may indicate indifference or opposition. The Ezra–Nehemiah material reflects strong opposition but belittles it and marginalizes it in various ideological ways. Opposition to the temple may be read from Isa. 66.1-6, but like any prophetic text it is open to considerable interpretation. The little temple group in Jerusalem may have carried on with their ritualized way of life, but the producers of some of the prophetic traditions were rather hostile to that kind of ideology. Running through most of the prophetic books (epitomized by the opening and closing chapters of Isaiah) is the most trenchant critique of the temple cult.

Outside the canon of the Hebrew Bible are numerous books that do not recognize any cessation of the so-called 'exile' (i.e. for them there was no 'return' with Ezra or rebuilding of the legitimate temple).[21] For the producers of these books Zerubbabel, Cyrus, Ezra and Nehemiah do not figure as major architects of the Jerusalem community. The auspicious legitimation of the rebuilding of city and temple finds no echo in their work. All *that* (i.e. restoration, rebuilding, etc.) lies in the future when YHWH will cause a temple to be built. Such a point of view could either ignore the Jerusalem temple or denounce it as having fallen into the hands of wicked priests. What the Ezra–Nehemiah material does is to offer authentication of the rebuilt temple by associating its rebuilding with the great Persian emperors of the remote past (Cyrus, Darius, Artaxerxes). That legitimation puts the temple's foundation in the distant past rather than in the future (as in Qumran and elsewhere) and makes the biblical documents party to a major ideological conflict in the Graeco-Roman period.

In conclusion I can only appeal, in defence of my speculative enquiry, to the problems of finding adequate factual information to back up any viewpoint in this vexed area of biblical studies. And there

21. On this see M.A. Knibb, 'The Exile in the Literature of the Intertestamental Period', *HeyJ* 17 (1976), pp. 253-72, and my *Anchor Bible Dictionary* article referred to above in n. 3. Echoes of these ideological struggles sound throughout the New Testament, especially in relation to the temple in the Gospels and the Apocalypse.

is so very little information because there was very little to know about that temple in the so-called Second Temple period. As Joyce's great work puts it, 'thus the unfacts, did we possess them, are too imprecisely few to warrant our certitude...'

THE POLEMIC AGAINST THE GODS AND ITS RELEVANCE FOR SECOND ISAIAH'S CONCEPTION OF THE NEW JERUSALEM

Klaus R. Baltzer

Second Isaiah is a document concerned with the reconstitution of Judah-Israel and Zion-Jerusalem:

> 'Comfort, comfort my people', says your God,
> 'Speak tenderly to Jerusalem!' (40.1-2)

At the same time it is a document in the middle of the debate. This debate—this *Auseinandersetzung*—is most evident in the polemic against the gods. A standard treatment of this subject can be found in H.D. Preuss, *Verspottung fremder Religionen im Alten Testament.*[1] As he has shown, the polemic forms an integral part of Second Isaiah's message, with wide-reaching consequences.[2]

It is therefore striking that, while we know the details of the polemic, we do not know which gods are being referred to. Second Isaiah only mentions Bel and Nebo (46.1-3).[3] A proper assessment of these Babylonian gods was important for the exiles,[4] but the question of their veneration was not restricted to Babylon, as the Elephantine texts[5] make clear. It is possible that Second Isaiah knew of many gods. But in this essay I want to focus on just one clear example.

In antiquity the gods were known by their names, as well as by their titles and their general characteristics. They could also be distinguished by their relationship to cities, countries or specific groups of

1. (BWANT, 5; Stuttgart: Kohlhammer, 1971).

2. *Verspottung*, p. 192-247 (§6).

3. *Verspottung*, pp. 217-18, n. 139: 'Bel is another name for Marduk', according to Skinner and Muilenburg.

4. Cf. Cyrus Cylinder, *ANET*, pp. 315-16.

5. Cf. B. Porten, *Archives from Elephantine* (Berkeley: University of California Press, 1968), pp. 164-79; *ANET*, p. 491: Ostracon,'Greeting from a Pagan to a Jew'.

people. In pictorial representation they were identified by their emblems. Only a few details were necessary to make clear which god was meant. This very fact creates problems for us (though it keeps the authors of museum guidebooks in business!).

Idol manufacturing is first mentioned in Second Isaiah in the prologue (40.18-20) which serves to introduce all the book's major themes. It is a sub-theme of the larger topic: Israel's god compared to the other gods (דמה, v. 18).[6]

In v. 19 and v. 20 two idols are referred to, along with the descriptions of their production.[7] Let us start with the first idol (פסל) in v. 19. It consists of a poured metal core, overlaid with gold. Abundant examples of this sort of idol have been collected by archeologists. The technique itself indicates a costly item, but it says nothing about the actual god in question. In addition, specific mention is made of 'silver chains' (רתקות כסף) which the smith produces and then applies to the idol. The commentaries do not know what to do with this reference to רתקות.[8] The root itself (רתק) is mentioned in Nah. 3.10 together with זק ('chains').[9] רתקות is therefore something that one ties or binds up. It is only attested in the plural. The combination 'silver' and 'smith' has led to the translation 'chains'. This corresponds to the translation of the Targum. K. Elliger[10] notes: 'Most commentators adopt "chains" but then differ over the use to which they are put'.[11] Normally they are explained as some type of jewelry chain. Yet why do we not hear of 'covering...of every precious stone', as in Ezek. 28.13?

Could it be that the chains are in fact emblematic and at one time helped to identify the deity? 'Chained gods' are attested in antiquity.

6. Cf. Preuss, *Verspottung*, pp. 193-201.

7. Cf. Preuss, *Verspottung*, pp. 195-96; Paul Trudinger, 'To Whom Then Will You Liken God?', *VT* 17 (1967), pp. 220-25.

8. See *KBL*^{3} *s.v.*; K. Elliger, *Deuterojesaja* (BKAT, 11, 1; Neukirchen–Vluyn: Neukirchener Verlag, 1978), p. 76.

9. See Isa. 45.14: 'they shall follow you, they shall come over in chains' (בזקים). The chains of the prisoners of war are real! Note also Ps. 148.8; Job 36.8; also רתיקות in 1 Kgs 6.21.

10. Cf. *Deuterojesaja*.

11. Cf. now H.E. Spykerboer, *The Structure and Composition of Deutero-Isaiah* (Meppel: Krips Repro, 1976), p. 44. Contrast T.N.D. Mettinger, 'The Elimination of a Crux? A Syntactic and Semantic Study of Isaiah XL 18–20', *Studies on Prophecy* (VTSup, 26; Leiden: Brill, 1974), p. 80, who translates 'plates'.

Karl Meuli[12] has collected considerable data. Most of the examples are Greek and Roman, though undoubtedly older cultic forms and traditions are represented. His examples need to be critically handled and better differentiated, but his basic observation stands: the chained gods were originally, in most instances, goddesses associated with trees, represented in columns or pillars. Their veneration took place in the context of sacred processions, in which masks were frequently worn. As an example, Meuli mentions in particular the various ways in which Artemis is venerated.

In both cult legend and pictorial representation, Hera appears as a chained figure. In addition, Meuli mentions Kronos, Dionysos and Hermes. We learn from Plato's reference to Socrates that even sculptures required chains from time to time.[13] The point of the chains or similar sorts of binding[14] is, in any event, to make sure that the god is securely fixed in one place.[15]

12. 'Die gefesselten Götter', *Gesammelte Schriften*, II (ed. T. Gelzer; Basel: Schwabe, 1975) pp. 1035-81; cf. R. Merkelbach, 'Gefesselte Götter', *Antaios*, XII (ed. M. Eliade and E. Jünger; Stuttgart: Klett, 1971), pp. 549-65.

13. Plato, Meno 97c-e (trans. W.R.M. Lamb, LCL edn):

> Socrates: Then right opinion (δόξα) is just as useful as knowledge (ἐπιστήμη)... It is because you have not observed with attention the images of Daedalus. But perhaps there are none in your country.
> Meno: What is the point of your remark?
> Soc.: That if they are not fastened up they play truant and run away; but, if fastened, they stay where they are.
> Men.: Well, what of that?
> Soc.: To possess one of his works which is let loose does not count for much in value; it will not stay with you any more than a runaway slave: but when fastened up it is worth a great deal, for his productions are very fine things. And to what am I referring in all this? To true opinions.

See also Plato, Euthyphro 11a-e; Aristotle, Politikon 1253b.33–1254d.1; Diodor 4.76.

14. Note in this respect Meuli's observation: 'What at first had been chains later often has been given a new interpretation as bands (στέμματα) and tassels (θύσανα)' ('Die gefesselten Götter', p. 1064; cf. p. 1054); see further p. 1077 n. 1: 'The chains especially of female deities always could be given a new interpretation as a sort of jewelry'.

15. The 'local stability' of an idol is parodied also in Isa. 46.5-8: 'he will remain standing, he will not move from his place' (v. 7). I presume that here another deity is in view, namely—spoken in Greek terminology—Hermes, the god of the merchants (cf. 46.6: 'who shake gold out of the bag'). He will not run, as he is

When one turns, against this backdrop, to the depiction of Zion-Jerusalem in the second half of Second Isaiah (49.14–55.13), one can ask: are there iconographic elements used here that correspond to the depiction of the goddess as the Tyche of the city?[16]

In 52.1-3 the renewal of Zion-Jerusalem's enthronement is described. It begins in v. 1 with her investiture:

> Put on your strength, O Zion
> put on your beautiful garments,
> O Jerusalem, the holy city [or: city of the sanctuary?]!

One can imagine this more concretely by comparing the representations of Athena.[17] Over her chiton she is clothed with the *aegis*, a piece of armor that she either wears or carries as a shield to terrify her enemies. Usually it contains the figure of gorgon's head. Over this comes her mantle.

According to v. 2 Jerusalem stands up and then takes her seat (note שבי). That is, Zion-Jerusalem appears as one enthroned.[18] What follows in the course of events is peculiar, for Zion-Jerusalem is spoken of as one in bonds. The Qere and Kethib differ here. Kethib reads indicative: 'the bonds of your neck are loosened', while Qere has the imperative: 'loose the bonds from your neck!' (התפתחי מוסרי צוארך).[19] The Kethib emphasizes the wondrous character of the event: YHWH is the one who has loosened Jerusalem's bonds. In the Qere, Zion-Jerusalem is herself involved in the sequence of events: she is commanded to stand up, take her seat, and loosen her bonds. The bonds are interpreted in this context as signs of captivity. They are *real and symbolic* at the same time.[20] With a play on words, the enthroned one (שבי) is no longer the captive one (שביה). The bonds do not hold her in

supposed to do as a messenger of the gods, but 'remain standing'!

16. See L. Ruhl, 'Tyche', *Ausführliches Lexikon der griechischen und römischen Mythologie* (ed. Roscher; Hildesheim: Olms, 1916–24; repr. 1965), pp. 1309-80; O. Waser, 'Tyche in bildlicher Darstellung', *ibid.*, pp. 1357-80; G. Herzog-Hauser, 'Tyche 1', *Pauly-Wissowa*, VII A 2 (1948), pp. 1643-89; M.P. Nilsson, *Geschichte der griechischen Religion*, II (Munich: Beck, 3rd edn, 1974), pp. 200-18.

17. See, e.g., D. Ohly, Glyptothek München; *Griechische und römische Skulpturen* (Munich: Beck, 4th edn, 1977), pp. 28-29.

18. See Targum: 'on the throne of your magnificence'.

19. For מוסר 'fetter' see also the derivates.

20. See also 51.14: 'hastily the fettered shall be freed' (צעה להפתח). Probably here it refers to real imprisonment of debt slaves, which will be ended.

place. Zion-Jerusalem is the opposite of the chained city-goddess.

The most telling mark of identification for the city goddess, especially in her form as Tyche, is the walled-crown. In their roles as the protective goddesses of the city, Kybele and Astarte wore walled-crowns. The thing that makes a city a city is a wall. Of course a wall has to do with defense, but also with legal considerations. The walled-crown is quite realistically portrayed, complete with gates and battlements. The techniques of building and defense from this time can be readily identified. A classic example is the Tyche of Antiochia on the Orontes.[21] There can be no question that she is modeled on earlier tradition. The walled-crown later becomes an actual piece of jewelry worn by women.[22]

When one reads Isa. 54.11-14 with this picture in mind, it appears as though the coronation of Jerusalem is being portrayed. YHWH is himself the smith (צרף) who fashions the precious crown (see 40.19; 41.7; 46.6; 48.10). What may as well be hinted at is the actual construction of a new wall for Jerusalem, splendid and richly ornamented. The crown is thus a model[23]—a *tabnit*—for the walls of the city. The fact that YHWH presents a crown to Zion-Jerusalem indicates that he sanctions the building of walls for Jerusalem. And as such, the city again has full legal status. This imagery has been taken from the representations of the Tyche. As the personification of a city, Zion-Jerusalem is no less magnificently outfitted.

It can be assumed that Second Isaiah has made use in other places of the iconography of the Tyche because further elements appear. One typical emblem of the Tyche is the cornucopia. Originally this horn of plenty was a goat's horn belonging to Amaltheia, a nymph from Crete, who, according to legend, nourished the child Zeus on goat's milk. In order to thank her, Zeus filled the horn with plenty: richness and bounty are portrayed by the produce of the land which now spills

21. See B. Fehr, 'Lectio Graeca—Lectio Orientalis; Überlegungen zur Tyche von Antiocheia', *Visible Religion: Annual for Religious Iconography*. VII. *Genres in Visual Representations* (ed. H.G. Kippenberg; Leiden: Brill, 1990); T. Dohm, *Die Tyche von Antiocheia* (Berlin, 1960) with pictures; for predecessors see esp. p. 41.

22. W. Deonna, 'Histoire d'une emblème; La couronne murale des villes et pays personifiés', *Bulletin du Musée d'Art et d'Histoire de Geneve* 18 (1940); S.M. Paul, 'Jerusalem—A City of Gold', *IEJ* 17 (1967), pp. 259-63.

23. See the 'model' (תבנית) of the Tabernacle in Exod. 25.9, 40.

out of the horn, most especially corn, oil and wine.[24]

Here we may stumble onto the curious reference to the 'bowl of staggering' in Isa. 51.17. Jerusalem receives the bowl from YHWH and 'drinks it to the dregs'—even to drunkenness. Second Isaiah interprets an otherwise positive image, the cornucopia, negatively: the drunkenness is not from wine, but on account of the wrath of YHWH (51.20-21). Bowl of staggering instead of horn of plenty—for Second Isaiah this means: it is not the Tyche who provides the fruit of the land, not a city goddess, but YHWH, as Hosea had insisted:

> She did not know that it was I who gave her
> the grain, the wine and the oil (Hos. 2.10).

There may also be an element of parody in the Second Isaiah scene, in that we hear of the children of Jerusalem who have failed to lead their drunken mother:

> There is none to guide her
> among all the sons she has borne.
> There is none to take her by the hand
> among all the sons she has brought up (51.18).

The Tyche is likewise frequently depicted with the child Pluto, symbol of bounty, on her arm.

We began with a question about the curious reference to chains in Isa. 40.19, and then moved to the various depictions of Zion-Jerusalem in the second half of Second Isaiah (49.14-21; 51.17; 52.1-3; 54.11-12). Could it not be that these various elements belong to a larger presentation in which Zion-Jerusalem is set over against the city-Tyche of antiquity? This could suggest that Second Isaiah's polemic against the gods—far from being a secondary development concerned with idol manufacturing—is in fact closely linked to the personification of Zion-Jerusalem. The close connection between these two groups of texts—polemics against the gods and depictions of Zion-Jerusalem—can be understood within the context of Second Isaiah's larger conception and within the historical circumstances of the Persian period.

Second Isaiah is a document that is concerned with the reconstruction of Jerusalem as a city. As such, the question of Zion-

24. See K. Wernicke, 'Amaltheia 1', *Pauly-Wissowa*, I.2 (1894), pp. 1720-23; H. Hunger, *Lexikon der griechischen und römischen Mythologie* (Vienna: Hollinek, 8th edn, 1988), p. 32.

Jerusalem's identity is raised again. The way the identity of the new community is made explicit is not by deifying the city. By no means is Zion-Jerusalem to be regarded as deified in Second Isaiah's conception, even though personification is both possible and well attested.[25] Nevertheless, YHWH alone is God. He provides blessing and bounty. He guarantees the balance between what is now breaking in—'Behold, I do a new thing' (43.19)—and what is everlasting, because, as Second Isaiah repeatedly insists, YHWH is a God of creation. The city and its destiny, the well-being of the land and its people, and the sense of final world order—these three realms cannot be separated in Second Isaiah's theological understanding.

In this same period one can observe the 'twilight of the gods'. The cities must now rely on their good luck—and even then only for those who have their wits about them. At the same time what is experienced is a sense of insecurity before a world in change. This accounts for the emergence of official veneration of the Tyche in the cities and their subsequent rise in importance. In Third Isaiah one hears mention of Gad and Meni, gods of fortune (65.11), which the Septuagint renders Δαίμων and Τύχη.

Historically speaking, one would like to know more about the development of cities in the Persian period, before Alexander as well as later in the Hellenistic period. We do have some sense of the part Nehemiah played in the reconstruction of Jerusalem, particularly with respect to the building of the walls. It would be nice to be able to clarify the exact relationship between Nehemiah's activity and the larger working conception of Second Isaiah.[26] The *Auseinandersetzung* with the gods of the time is particularly acute in Second Isaiah with respect to the Tyche, as our examples have shown. The significance of Zion-Jerusalem is explored by means of a contrast with the emblematic depictions of the city-Tyche. The iconographic

25. Cf. the studies (with lit.!) of G. Stählin, 'Das Bild der Witwe; Ein Beitrag zur Bildersprache der Bibel und zum Phänomen der Personifikation in der Antike', *Jahrbuch für Antike und Christentum* 17 (1974), pp. 5-20; O.H. Steck, 'Zion als Gelände und Gestalt; Überlegungen zur Wahrnehmung Jerusalems als Stadt und Frau im Alten Testament', *ZTK* 86 (1989), pp. 261-81.

26. See my 'Liberation from Debt Slavery after the Exile in Second Isaiah and Nehemiah', *Ancient Israelite Religion: Essays in Honor of Frank M. Cross* (ed. P.D. Hanson, P.D. Miller and S. Dean McBride; Philadelphia, Fortress Press, 1987), pp. 477-84.

tradition of Zion-Jerusalem as found in Second Isaiah forms the basis for the later depiction of the heavenly Jerusalem in the book of Revelation (see Rev. 21.21). Even Constantine knows of the close connection between fetters, chains, the Tyche and the city when he founds his new capital Constantinople in the fourth century CE.

According to Meuli,[27]

> When Constantine built his new capital, he had a Tyche of the city constructed. It was a statue with a chain connected to it (κατήνιον κλειδωμένον). The statue was consecrated by invoking the star gods (ἐστοιχειωμένον). It was fastened to a cross, which was in turn placed in the midst of statues of the emperor and his mother and oriented toward the east. The entire group was set up in the Milion. The chains were securely locked and the key buried beneath the base on which the statues stood. Thus it was assured that the city would always enjoy much bounty and be victorious over all.[28]

27. See 'Die gefesselten Götter', p. 1081. Text: Ps.-Kodinos, *Patria Konstantinupoleos*; edn: T. Preger, *Scriptore Originum Constantinopolitanarum*, II (Leipzig: Teubner, 1907), p. 166.

28. Christopher Seitz helped in translating this article for the SBL Congress at Rome. In a revised form it is a translation from 'Stadt-Tyche oder Zion-Jerusalem', in J. Hausmann and H.-J. Zobel (eds.), *Alttestamentlicher Glaube und Biblische Theologie: Festschrift für Horst Dietrich Preuss zum 65. Geburtstag* (Stuttgart: Kohlhammer, 1992), pp. 114-19.

HAGGAI'S TEMPLE, CONSTRUCTED, DECONSTRUCTED AND RECONSTRUCTED*

David J.A. Clines

1. *The Temple Constructed*

The Second Temple was not just an edifice built by Judaeans; it was also a mental artifact constructed by Haggai. It was Haggai's intention, according to the book, to get the temple constructed; but we have to ask ourselves, What kind of a temple was it he had in mind? How did he himself construct the temple? What construction, we might say, did he put on the term 'temple'?

Here are eleven building materials the text of the book provides us with. Let us see whether by taking an inventory of them we can reconstruct Haggai's construction of the temple.

1. The temple is to be 'the house of Yhwh' (1.2). This apparently means a building that will be owned by Yhwh; he obviously does not need it for living in, or for being in Jerusalem himself in person; for even before the temple is rebuilt he already is 'with' the people of Judah (1.13).

2. The temple stands in need of 'rebuilding' (1.2)—which means

* The impetus for this paper arose from a conversation with Ms Sue Campbell, a Sheffield graduate student working under my supervision on Haggai and my teaching assistant in 1991–92. I gladly acknowledge the stimulus her creative researches have given me, but I do not of course hold her responsible for the contents of this paper. The paper was read in different versions to the International Meeting of the Society of Biblical Literature in Rome, July 1991, to the Old Testament Seminar at the University of Cambridge in March 1992, and at the symposium on The Old Testament and Literature held in celebration of the fiftieth anniversary of the Faculty of Theology at the University of Aarhus in May 1992. It has been published also in *SJOT* 7 (1993), pp. 51-77, together with other papers from the Aarhus symposium.

(a) that it is to be the same building as the one that once stood in this place (you cannot rebuild a new building, only an old one), and (b) that it is at present unbuilt or derelict (as also in 1.4, where it 'lies in ruins').

3. The people, whom I will take to mean the Jews of the province,[1] say that the time has not yet come for the house to be rebuilt (1.2). This saying of theirs presumes that they think there *is* a time, in the future, when the house *should* be rebuilt.[2] Now perhaps we are meant to believe that they will *always* be saying this, as a way of forever avoiding building the temple; but we had better not jump to that conclusion.[3] Certainly we can assume that what Haggai thinks, as against the people, is that the right time is *now*. And now *we* must ask, Why would *one* person think the time is right when everyone else does not? Must we not answer, It looks as if he knows something that the rest of the people do not know.

4. Zerubbabel and Joshua do not apparently know what the people are saying about the time for rebuilding the temple (or perhaps they are only 'thinking' it, since *'āmar* can mean that too). For the report of what they are saying or thinking is not something Zerubbabel and Joshua know for themselves; it is information delivered to them as a 'word of Yhwh' via Haggai the prophet (1.2).[4]

1. The identity of Haggai's audience has at times been a contentious issue, but scholarly opinion seems to have settled down in favour of this, the simplest, view. See e.g. D.L. Petersen, *Haggai and Zecharaiah 1–8* (OTL; London: SCM Press, 1985), pp. 80-82 (with particular reference to 2.14).

2. Some older commentators (e.g. Jerome, Rashi, Kimchi) thought that the people may have been awaiting the fulfilment of the 70 years prophecy of Jeremiah (Jer. 25.11-14). But most moderns would agree with T.T. Perowne that 'It is clear from the sharp rebuke here administered, and from the severe judgments with which their procrastination had been visited (v. 6, 9-11), that the excuse was idle and the delay worldly and culpable' (*Haggai and Zechariah* [Cambridge Bible; Cambridge: Cambridge University Press, 1893], p. 27). This seems to me, however, to be something of a shallow moralizing interpretation that does not reckon with Haggai's notion of the eschatological 'time'.

3. Nor had we better invent pseudo-economic and pseudo-psychological explanations such as that of J. Bright: 'The people, preoccupied with the struggle for existence, had neither resources nor energy left over to continue the project' (*A History of Israel* [London: SCM Press, 2nd edn, 1972], p. 366). This does not take account of the question of the right 'time'.

4. Commentators do not seem to be troubled by the fact that the divine speech to Zerubbabel and Joshua consists, not of a divine oracle of judgment or promise, but

5. What is needed if the temple is to be built is timber, to be fetched from the hills (1.8). Now if we can permit ourselves a little excursion *hors du texte* in the company of the Meyers, we will find that the only trees growing on the Judaean hills are the sycamore; and their timber is unsuitable for large buildings. So the timber Haggai demands for the temple cannot be for the construction of the temple itself. It must be for the scaffolding and ladders the builders will need.[5]

6. When the temple is rebuilt, Yhwh will 'take pleasure in it' and 'be honoured' (1.8). This means that he is at the moment displeased and dishonoured by having a ruined temple.[6]

7. The temple had been, before its destruction, 'glorious'. 'Who is there among you who survives who saw this house in its original glory (כָּבוֹד)?', asks Yhwh in 2.3,[7] certifying that 'glory' is something quintessential to the nature of the temple. Merely beginning the

only of a piece of information such as we would rely on Gallup polls to give us these days. For Petersen, the verse 'points to a demonstrable unwillingness...to participate in the reconstruction of the temple' (p. 48); but I would have thought that if the unwillingness were 'demonstrable' there would have been no need for a divine message to Zerubbabel and Joshua to inform them.

5. C.L. Meyers and E.M. Meyers give this explanation (*Haggai, Zechariah 1–8* [AB, 25b; Garden City, NY: Doubleday, 1987], pp. 27-28), as had Koole earlier. For a lengthy list of other explanations offered, see P.A. Verhoef, *The Books of Haggai and Malachi* (NICOT; Grand Rapids: Eerdmans, 1987), pp. 65-66. There are others who think that the timber could be firs, oaks, poplars, cypresses, palms or olives—and indeed *some* of these could be used, could they be found, for the building proper; see further, H.W. Wolff, *Haggai: A Commentary* (trans. M. Kohl; Minneapolis: Augsburg, 1988), p. 45.

6. The RSV tells us that the purpose of building the temple is so that 'I [Yhwh] may appear in my glory', which sounds like a 'theophany'; but וְאֶכָּבְדָ can hardly mean that. Wolff also thinks that the verb is best rendered by 'I will show myself in my glory' (cf. W. Baumgartner *et al.*, *Hebräisches und aramäisches Lexikon zum Alten Testament*, II [3rd edn; Leiden: Brill, 1974], p. 434a), which means 'the manifestation of that acceptance [as God's house] through God's presence, power, and compassion' (p. 46). P.R. Ackroyd also, in my opinion, overinterprets the word by translating, 'I will let myself be honoured', which means, he says, 'I will accept the worship which tends to my honour' (*Exile and Restoration: A Study of Hebrew Thought of the Sixth Century BC* [London: SCM Press, 1968], p. 160). There is simply nothing about *worship* here.

7. According to Meyers and Meyers, *kābôd* 'here designates splendor and perhaps also [is] a term which can be related to God's presence as bestowing glory' (p. 50). 'Splendor' is what I always thought 'glory' was, so the second part of the definition does not convey a very precise sense.

rebuilding of the temple does not make it glorious, we observe, for even a month after the work of rebuilding has been renewed,[8] it still remains without glory; for YHWH attributes to the people the opinion that the temple must still be 'as nothing in your eyes by comparison with it [the former temple]' (2.3).[9]

8. Yet, in a 'little while' (עוֹד אַחַת מְעַט הִיא, 2.6), the temple will become full of 'glory' (כָּבוֹד). Perhaps it will by that time have been rebuilt, perhaps it will not; we do not know.[10] But what we do know is that it is not the builders of the temple who will fill it with 'glory'. It is YHWH himself who will do that ('and I will fill this house with glory', וּמִלֵּאתִי אֶת־הַבַּיִת הַזֶּה כָּבוֹד, 2.6).

9. How the temple will be filled with glory is that Yhwh will 'shake' all the nations so that the 'riches'[11] of all nations will come into the temple (2.7).[12] *Riches* are what make the temple glorious.[13] These

8. The date is 21.vii.2 compared with 24.vi.2 as the date of recommencement of building (cf. 2.1 with 1.15).

9. The text does not mean exactly 'To you does it not seem as if it were not there?' (REB) or 'Does it not seem as though there is nothing there?' (NJB), for the issue is not whether there is anything there, but whether what is there has any glory or not.

10. Some scholars seem to know this; O. Eissfeldt, for example, thinks of Haggai and Zechariah 'depicting the grace of Yahweh and the coming of the age of salvation as being primarily dependent upon the building of the Temple' (*The Old Testament: An Introduction* [trans. P.R. Ackroyd; Oxford: Basil Blackwell, 1966], p. 433). Similarly G. von Rad: '[F]or these two prophets the rebuilding of the Temple is actually the necessary precondition of Jahweh's advent and of his kingdom' (*Old Testament Theology*, II [trans. D.M.G. Stalker; Edinburgh: Oliver & Boyd, 1965], p. 281). Similarly G. Fohrer, *Introduction to the Old Testament* (trans. D. Green; London: SPCK, 1970), p. 460: 'Haggai...expects, upon completion of the building, a convulsion that will shake all nature and all nations'.

11. It perhaps does not make a great difference whether we read the MT חֶמְדַּת 'desire of, i.e. desirable things of' (as Verhoef) or emend to חֲמֻדֹת (as K. Elliger in *BHS*, p. 1062, Meyers and Meyers, *et al.*).

12. I think we are right in assuming that the text speaks of an event that *will* happen, but I am nevertheless attracted by the possibility that it is all hypothetical, as A.P. Stanley put it: '[E]ven if the present tranquillity of the world must needs be broken up, even if some violent convulsion should once again shake all nations, yet abundant treasures would flow into the Temple' (*Lectures on the History of the Jewish Church*, III [new edn; London: John Murray, 1883], pp. 91-92).

13. So also Verhoef, *Haggai and Malachi*, p. 104: 'This is not God's glory but the abundance and preciousness of the desired things which will become available to the temple'; and Petersen, p. 68: 'The possessions, rather than God, will provide

riches take the form of silver and gold,[14] and YHWH lays claim to them already, even while they are still in the possession of the nations: 'mine is the silver and mine is the gold, says YHWH of armies' (2.8)—with a certain determination if not actually aggressively.[15] Presumably '*the* silver' (הַכֶּסֶף) and '*the* gold' (הַזָּהָב) mean 'silver and gold in general', 'all the silver and gold there is'.[16]

10. What this 'shaking' of the earth will amount to is unclear. The language itself suggests a *physical* cosmic upheaval, with a shaking of the heavens and the earth, of the sea and the dry land (2.6); but it is

kābôd'; and cf. E. Jacob, *Theology of the Old Testament* (trans. A.W. Heathcote and P.J. Allcock; London: Hodder & Stoughton, 1958), p. 79: '*Kabod* designates whatever had weight—it is used of riches: Gen. 31.1... Hag. 2.7'. What we cannot say is: '[W]hat need has he of earthly splendor, when all silver and gold are his?' (E. Achtemeier, *Nahum–Malachi* [Interpretation; Atlanta: John Knox Press, 1986], p. 100).

14. What kind of interpretation is it to say: '[T]he nations' treasures consist of more than material resources, even though the text mentions only silver and gold. In Israel's history the nations contributed such cultural achievements as architectural styles, musical instruments, and melodies for singing (1 Kgs. 4–5), titles for addressing Yahweh, and consequently insights into the mysteries of faith (Ps. 29; 48.1-8; 89.5-13)' (C. Stuhlmueller, *Rebuilding with Hope: A Commentary on the Books of Haggai and Zechariah* [International Theological Commentary; Grand Rapids: Eerdmans, 1988], p. 30). Given interpreters like this, what does a prophet have to do to be believed if he actually means 'silver and gold'?

15. Cf. G. von Rad, 'The City on the Hill', in *The Problem of the Hexateuch and Other Essays* (trans. E.W. Trueman Dicken; Edinburgh: Oliver & Boyd, 1966), pp. 232-42 (240): 'A starkly challenging sentence proclaims Yahweh's exclusive right to possess them. It is as if they have been hitherto on temporary loan, and are still held back from their true purpose as the property of Yahweh. In the eschaton, however, they will return from this misappropriation into the exclusive control of Yahweh, their rightful owner.'

16. Similarly Petersen, *Haggai and Zechariah 1–8*, p. 69: 'Yahweh might be claiming that all silver and gold are ultimately his in order to justify taking them away from the nations'. It can hardly be a matter of the precious vessels stolen from the first temple, for they could hardly be called the 'riches of the nations' (contrast p. 68: 'Haggai does not expect ingots of gold but, rather, precious vessels and other metallic accoutrements for the temple cultus... [P]recious objects belonging to the temple had been lost to the nations. And their return was a necessary part of a proper restoration'). Can it be the spoils from his victories in holy war (Verhoef, *Haggai and Malachi*, p. 105)? Perhaps (cf. Nah. 2.10 [EVV 9]; Mic. 4.13; Ps. 60.8-10 [EVV 6-8]; Josh. 6.19), but there is a marked absence of hostile intent in Haggai's depiction.

hard to see how a universal *earthquake* could bring the wealth of the nations into the temple.[17] Presumably the language of *physical* upheaval is symbolic of a *political* upheaval that will issue in Judah's dominance over all other nations. Whether the upheaval will be by military means[18] or some more pacific rearrangement we cannot tell. And how the wealth will 'come' to Jerusalem, whether as booty or as taxes,[19] is equally inexplicit.[20]

11. There is so much silver and gold out there waiting to be shaken into the temple that, when it is all in, 'great shall be the glory of this house, the latter more than the former' (2.9).

The data are not complete and at times not entirely clear. But the resultant picture is unambiguous. Haggai constructs the temple as nothing but a *treasure-house*. It is a place where precious objects can be stored and displayed. When it is in ruins it obviously cannot serve as a storehouse and display-case. Its owner, the god Yhwh, is inevitably dishonoured by having a 'house' that is in disrepair, and worse, a house that by being in disrepair cannot display the *kābôd* that comes from owning many precious objects. It is therefore essential, for the deity's self-respect, that the house should be rebuilt. All the silver and gold in the world may belong to him by rights and in principle; but they bring him no honour unless they are gathered together in a 'house'.

There is another dimension to Haggai's construction of the temple. It is that there is an *urgency* about rebuilding the house. For it is only

17. According to J.G. Baldwin (*Haggai, Zechariah, Malachi: An Introduction and Commentary* [Tyndale OT Commentaries; London: Tyndale Press, 1972], p. 48), Haggai sees 'the whole universe in such a series of convulsions that every nation will gladly part with its treasures' (why would convulsions make them do that, I wonder?), but, as Verhoef observes (*Haggai and Malachi*, p. 102), this explanation would require us to attach a literal meaning to רעש in v. 6 and a figurative meaning in v. 7.

18. Verhoef sees here the language of holy war, the wealth being spoils dedicated to the victor (*Haggai and Malachi*, p. 103).

19. Meyers and Meyers, *Haggai and Zechariah 1–8*, p. 53, envisage the nations 'send[ing] tribute through their ambassadors and emissaries'.

20. We might even consider, with Dean Stanley, whether freewill offerings from gentiles might not be in mind: 'If its own children should neglect it, the heathen whom they despised would come to the rescue' (*Lectures on the History of the Jewish Church*, III, p. 91). Cf. Achtemeier, *Nahum–Malachi*, p. 101: '[A]ll peoples will finally come with their offerings to the Lord of Hosts'.

a short time, 'yet a little while', before the cosmic upheaval is going to occur that will bring the wealth of all the nations flooding into Jerusalem.[21] Preparations must be made for the arrival of all that silver and gold. The *people* do not realize that the 'time' is pressing, for they do not have Haggai's conviction about the imminent overthrow of all the kingdoms. Haggai, on the other hand, knows that Yhwh is about to 'shake' the heavens and the earth—perhaps he has already started[22]—so it is high time that the temple be readied to receive the treasures that will fall out of the pockets of the nations when Yhwh will imminently turn them upside down (הפך) and give them a good shaking.

Everything in the book of Haggai becomes coherent when we recognize how Haggai constructs the temple. How rebuilding the temple connects with 'glory', how 'glory' connects with silver and gold, how silver and gold connect with world upheaval, and, especially, how world upheaval connects with the 'right time' for rebuilding the temple—all make sense when Haggai's temple is understood as a *treasury*.

Of course, there are many other ways of constructing the second (or, rebuilt) temple, some of which a Haggai would no doubt have consented to. It would be hard to deny, for example, that the author of the book of Haggai, whether or not that person was the historical Haggai, would have thought of the temple, or the temple to be, as a place of sacrifice. Where this essay stands, however, is on the observation that the author of the book chose not to speak of the temple in that way, ever.

It proves very difficult for modern scholars, however, to believe that an author could have such a restricted vision of the temple. We all know, and our dictionaries and encyclopaedias confirm it, that the Jewish temple had many significances, and our tendency is to recall those significances whenever we read the word 'temple', as if all

21. I can hardly agree that with the phrase 'yet a little while' Haggai 'refers not so much to the shortness of the interval as to the vastness of the powers involved' (Achtemeier, *Nahum–Malachi*, p. 102).

22. We note that the present participle in 2.21, 'I am shaking', is not preceded by 'yet a little while' (as in 2.6); does this perhaps not mean that the shaking has already begun? The commentators do not observe this difference from 2.6, and generally translate the participle as a future, even if a *futurum instans* (Verhoef, *Haggai and Malachi*, p. 143).

of them were present in the minds of speakers and hearers of the language at every moment. James Barr has invented the *mot juste* for this habit of ours: it is 'illegitimate totality transfer' when we insist on reading all the possible meanings of a word into each of its occurrences.[23]

Here are some of the ideas that occur to commentators when they read 'temple' in Haggai.

1. It is the 'place of the presence of God'. So, for example, Verhoef (a Calvinist who nevertheless lapses into Latin in the face of the almost palpable holiness of the temple) writes:

> The second major theme of Haggai's message concerns the rebuilding of the temple... To appreciate the importance of this message, we will have to consider the theological significance of the temple. In the history of Israel the tabernacle and subsequently the temple were the places of the *praesentia Dei realis* among his people.[24]

Another way of putting it is this:

> God's presence is reestablished through the powerful symbolic means of his dwelling made habitable.[25]

Or,

> God's presence is made manifest in his 'glory'. In fact, God's 'glory', as distinct from his 'name', appears to represent an extraordinary and dramatic manifestation of God's presence and power.[26]

2. It is a symbol of the glory of Yhwh. So Petersen writes that YHWH will have

> greater prestige now that this house is finished.[27]

23. J. Barr, *The Semantics of Biblical Language* (London: Oxford University Press, 1961), p. 222 (it is 'illegitimate *identity* transfer' on pp. 218, 235).

24. Verhoef, *Haggai and Malachi*, p. 34.

25. Meyers and Meyers, *Haggai and Zechariah 1–8*, p. 28.

26. Meyers and Meyers, *Haggai and Zechariah 1–8*, p. 28, referring to J.G. McConville, 'God's "Name" and God's "Glory"', *TynBul* 30 (1979), pp. 149-63. Does this mean that there are *unextraordinary* manifestations of this divine 'presence' in the temple? What would a 'manifestation' of a divine presence look like? Am I alone in thinking that not a lot has been explained when I read that God's presence is made manifest 'in' something that is a manifestation of his presence?

27. Petersen, *Haggai and Zechariah 1–8*, p. 51.

And Mason:

> [F]or [Haggai], the significance of the Temple is *eschatological*. It will be the place where God appears again in His glory.[28]

And, more simplistically, Smith:

> [Haggai] believed that the temple must be rebuilt so the glory of the Lord might return and dwell with his people. Any person who longs for the presence of the Lord is a good man.[29] [And, we might add, any female person who would like to become a man now knows how to achieve that.]

3. It is a place of God's self-revelation. So Ackroyd:

> The divine presence... expresses itself in the Temple as the chosen place of divine revelation... The God who is lord of heaven and earth, who cannot be contained in a building, nevertheless condescends to reveal himself and to localize his presence in order that blessing may flow out.[30]

4. It is a place of worship, of human encounter with the divine. So Achtemeier:

> [T]he prophet concentrates almost singlemindedly on the necessity for the Judeans to restore their place of worship... When Haggai... calls for temple rebuilding, it is... an announcement that the Lord of Hosts yearns to give himself again... to enter into covenant fellowship with the Chosen People once more. Their years of abandonment under God's judgment are over. They should prepare themselves for the Lord's return... The temple will be sign and seal of their renewed hearts' devotion—the evidence that they have finally come to terms with reality.[31]

And Ackroyd:

> [T]he failure to rebuild is much more than a matter of reconstruction of a building. It is the reordering of a Temple so that it is a fit place for worship... Without a properly built temple, that is a ritually correct place for the worship of God, such worship is impossible.[32]

28. R. Mason, 'The Prophets of the Restoration', in R.J. Coggins *et al.* (eds.), *Israel's Prophetic Traditions: Essays in Honour of Peter R. Ackroyd* (Cambridge: Cambridge University Press, 1982), pp. 137-54 (143).

29. R.L. Smith, *Micah–Malachi* (WBC, 32; Waco, TX: Word Books, 1984), p. 149.

30. Ackroyd, *Exile and Restoration*, pp. 154, 160.

31. Achtemeier, *Nahum–Malachi*, pp. 94-95, 97-98.

32. Ackroyd, *Exile and Restoration*, pp. 156-57, 160.

5. It is a sacral centre, necessary both for Israel's survival and as the focus of a universal religion. Thus von Rad:

> The Temple was, after all, the place where Jahweh spoke to Israel, where he forgave her her sins, and where he was present for her. The attitude taken towards it therefore determined the attitude for or against Jahweh... [T]he eschatological Israel was to have a sacral centre, and... this alone would guarantee her existence... It was for this time, when Jahwism would throw off its national limitations and become a universal religion—the time of the Messiah—that the temple had to be rebuilt.[33]

And J. Bright:

> The community desperately needed a focal point about which its faith could rally.[34]

Similarly S.R. Driver had described Haggai's temple as

> the religious centre of the world (Isa. ii. 2-4), nations coming in pilgrimage to it, delighting to honour it with their gifts, and so making it more glorious even than the temple of Solomon.[35]

6. It is the channel of salvation. Thus Wolff writes:

> Haggai does not press for the temple to be rebuilt in order that the priestly cult may function. The purpose is 'so that Yahweh may enter into it, and may appear for the salvation of the people' (K.M. Beyse, 'Serubbabel und die Königserwartungen der Propheten Haggai und Zacharja', *Arbeiten zur Theologie* I/48 [1972] 75).[36]

7. It is also a symbol of, or, rather, a vehicle for, the community itself and its identity. Thus Meyers and Meyers:

> The restoration of the sacred temple in Jerusalem is the key to the establishment of the new, largely ecclesiastical system of community autonomy under Persian rule.[37]

8. It is the economic and administrative centre of the post-exilic Yahwistic community. So Petersen,[38] following the hypothesis of Joel Weinberg that the community is best understood as a 'Bürger–

33. Von Rad, *Old Testament Theology*, II, pp. 281-82.

34. Bright, *History of Israel* (2nd edn), pp. 368-69.

35. S.R. Driver, *The Minor Prophets: Nahum, Habakkuk, Zephaniah, Haggai, Zechariah, Malachi* (Century Bible; Edinburgh: T.C. & E.C. Jack, 1906), p. 152.

36. Wolff, *Haggai*, p. 46.

37. Meyers and Meyers, *Haggai and Zechariah 1–8*, p. xlii.

38. Petersen, *Haggai and Zechariah 1–8*, pp. 30-31.

Tempel-Gemeinde',[39] a collectivity that provided its members with an identity and a rudimentary administration based on the 'father's house' as the primary unit of social administration.

Each of these views can be argued on its own merits, and they may well be correct accounts of ideas that were abroad in Haggai's time.[40] But whatever their validity in reference to the historical actuality of the sixth century BCE, if we have them in our mind when we read the book of Haggai we inevitably misunderstand the book, for *it* thinks of the temple as a treasure-house, no more, no less.

2. *The Temple Deconstructed*

If I have now rightly reconstructed Haggai's construction of the temple, it remains a question whether this construction is open to *deconstruction*. Now to deconstruct a discourse, according to Jonathan Culler, is 'to show how it undermines the philosophy it asserts, or the hierarchical oppositions on which it relies'.[41] And there are in this text, to my mind, three points at which a deconstruction of such a nature imposes itself.

1. *Honour*

The book's initial set of oppositions is between the unbuilt temple and the built temple. (a) The unbuilt temple is a site of shame, lack of glory; the built temple will be a place of honour. (b) The unbuilt temple is a signal of human disregard of the divine, or disobedience (cf. 'obey', 1.12): they live in ceiled houses, while the deity's dwelling is in ruins. The built temple will be a testimony to human enthusiasm for the divine. (c) The unbuilt temple causes divine displeasure; the built temple will be an object YHWH will take pleasure in (1.7). (d) The unbuilt temple brings economic disaster to the populace; the

39. J. Weinberg, 'Das *beit 'abôt* im 6.–4. Jh. v.u. Z.', *VT* 23 (1973), pp. 400-14; *idem* (J. Vejnberg), 'Probleme der sozialökonomische Struktur Judäas vom 6. Jahrhundert v.u. Z. Zu einigen wirtschaftshistorischen Untersuchungen von Heinz Kreissig', *Jahrbuch für Wirtschaftsgeschichte* (1973), pp. 237-51.

40. See, for a survey of the kinds of ideas that may have been held about the temple in the Persian period, D.L. Petersen, 'The Temple in Persian Period Prophetic Texts', *BTB* 21 (1991), pp. 88-96 (also appears in *Second Temple Studies*. I. *Persian Period*, pp. 125-43).

41. J. Culler, *On Deconstruction: Theory and Criticism after Structuralism* (London: Routledge & Kegan Paul, 1983), p. 86.

built temple will spell blessing upon the grain, the new wine, the oil and what the ground brings forth (cf. 1.11).

Now it comes as something of a surprise, amounting (I think) to a deconstruction, that it turns out that the rebuilding of the temple, though demanded so strongly, will *not* in fact achieve the aim of bringing 'honour' (*kābôd*) to the deity and his house. For in 2.7 we learn that it will be when the treasures of silver and gold from the other nations come into the temple that it will be filled with *kābôd*. If filling the temple with precious objects is what produces *kābôd*, then it cannot be finishing the building itself that does so. And vice versa. We may call this a deconstruction because the text itself shows no hint of awareness of the conflict between the two statements; the conflict is hidden, and so we may say that the text *undermines* itself.

It is a further element in the deconstruction that whereas the book initially made out that the producing of *kābôd* for the temple is entirely in the hands of the people who build or who fail to build, 2.7 affirms that it is Yhwh's own personal filling of the temple with treasure that will bring *kābôd*, as if the people's activity was nugatory. Perhaps, of course, we should harmonize the text, avoiding the deconstructive possibility, and say that if the people do not finish rebuilding the temple, there will be no temple for Yhwh to fill with his treasures; so in that sense the people's activity may be a *precondition* of the divine activity that will ensure the deity's honour.[42] But the simple fact is that the text itself does not confront the tension between the people's contribution to the *kābôd* and the deity's, so each of the poles of the tension tends to undermine or deconstruct the other.

2. *Uncleanness*

A more deep-seated deconstruction arises from the obligation laid on the people to rebuild the temple, on the one hand, and the affirmation that 'every work of their hands' is unclean (2.14), on the other.[43]

42. Similarly R.P. Carroll, *When Prophecy Failed: Reactions and Responses to Failure in the Old Testament Prophetic Traditions* (London: SCM Press, 1979), p. 161: '[U]ntil the temple was rebuilt the wealth of nations could not flow into it. So the rebuilding of the temple had become a prerequisite for the expected event of salvation.'

43. I am ignoring the argument that the 'people' in question are not the Judaeans but the Samarians (as e.g. J.W. Rothstein, *Juden und Samaritaner: Die grundlegende Scheidung von Judentum und Heidentum* (BWANT, 3; Leipzig: Hinrichs, 1908); D. Winton Thomas, 'Haggai', *IB*, VI, p. 1047; von Rad, *Old Testament*

To put the matter more fully: on the one hand, the people of Judah are reproached for neglecting the rebuilding of the temple, and urged to 'build the house' (1.8) and 'work' (2.4). There is indeed no means of rebuilding the house apart from the labour of the Judaeans. Yet, on the other hand, Haggai seems to go out of his way to insist that everything the Judaeans do is somehow 'unclean' or 'defiled' (2.10-14). If this is so, then the temple building itself, as the work of Judaean hands, is going to be 'defiled', with evident consequences for the programme of acquiring *kābôd.* This is not an outcome the book envisages explicitly, but nevertheless, deconstructively, it sets out the impossibility of the people's achieving what it demands. The result will be that the more the Judaeans build the temple, the more they will defile it and dishonour it. And conversely, the less they build the temple, the less defiled it will be *but* the more dishonoured. So it is impossible to 'please' (1.8) this deity and impossible to honour him. It is perhaps not surprising that all the honour he expects to get will be by his own efforts ('I will fill this house with glory', 2.7).

To appreciate most fully the deconstructive possibilities in the text over this issue we have to examine more closely the dialogue of Haggai with the priests over the question of the transmissibility of holiness and defilement (2.10-19). There is a great deal that is uncertain about the exegesis of this pericope, and not surprisingly so, from a deconstructionist point of view, since the text has suddenly found itself in deep and disturbing waters. Most crucial for the present purpose is the phrase 'all the work of their hands' (כָּל־מַעֲשֵׂה יְדֵיהֶם, 2.14), which seems to designate what it is that Haggai says is defiled. Now this term seems at first sight as comprehensive as it is possible to be. Nevertheless there is some evidence that it might refer only to agricultural produce.[44] For in Deut. 14.29, 16.15, 24.19, 28.12 and

Theology, II, p. 283; Bright, *History of Israel* (2nd edn), pp. 368, 371; W. Rudolph, *Haggai—Sacharja 1–8—Sacharja 9–14—Maleachi* (KAT, 13/4; Gütersloh: Mohn, 1976), pp. 49-50; Wolff, *Haggai*, p. 94. The most recent scholarship has generally professed itself convinced by the argument of K. Koch to the contrary ('Haggais unreines Volk', *ZAW* 79 [1967], pp. 52-66; similarly H.G. May, '"This People" and "This Nation" in Haggai', *VT* 18 [1968], pp. 190-97); so e.g. R. Rendtorff, *The Old Testament: An Introduction* (trans. J. Bowden; London: SCM Press, 1985), p. 237.

44. It seems a mistake to restrict the 'work of their hands' to their offerings, as is done for example by Ackroyd, *Exile and Restoration*, p. 168: 'The emphasis in

30.9 we have the phrase 'all the work of your hand(s)'[45] in reference unmistakably to the produce of the fields; and, more importantly, within the book of Haggai itself the phrase can be shown to have this meaning. For in 2.18 we find, 'I smote you—all the work of your hands—with blight and mildew and hail'.[46] If 'agricultural produce' is all the phrase means, were we then right to think of the building of the temple when we read in 2.14 that 'all the work of their hands' was unclean?

Yes, I believe so. I would argue that it is not at all surprising that in the context of agricultural labour, such as we encounter in those passages in Deuteronomy, 'the work of your hands' should refer to field produce and not to pots, silverware or linen, or any other of the hundred and one things that could reasonably be called 'the work of the hands'. In other contexts, 'the work of the hands' can mean quite different things. For example, in 2 Kgs 19.18 images are called 'the work of the hands of a human'; in Jer. 32.30 the Israelites have been angering Yhwh 'by the work of their hands', presumably transgressions in general; and in Song 7.2 (EVV 7.1) jewels are 'the work of the hands of a craftsman'. Even in Deuteronomy itself the phrase quite commonly refers to human activity in general (e.g. 2.7, 'Yhwh your God has blessed you in all the work of your hands' while travelling through the wilderness; 31.29, 'provoking Yhwh to anger through the work of your hands', not specifically making idols, as in 4.28). Only the immediate context can give the phrase a more specific meaning than 'activity'.

The question can be answered yet another way also. Let us suppose that 'all the work of their hands' (2.14) means specifically their produce from the fields (as, admittedly, it does in 2.17). May we not go on to ask: if the people are unclean and are consequently defiling their agricultural produce, will they not equally be defiling everything they touch?[47]

Haggai's own message to the people concentrates on the uncleanness of the people's offerings in the shrine'. On the contrary, the emphasis is on *all* the works of their hands, of which their offerings are only one example.

45. Deut. 16.15 and 24.19 have כל מַעֲשֵׂה יָדֶיךָ; 28.12 and 30.9 have כָּל־מַעֲשֵׂה יָדֶךָ; and 14.29 has כָּל־מַעֲשֵׂה יָדְךָ אֲשֶׁר תַּעֲשֶׂה.

46. 'The people ("you") are defined in terms of the work of their hands... agricultural commodities' (Petersen, *Haggai and Zechariah 1–8*, p. 93).

47. How the people come to be unclean, in Haggai's view, is not a question we

Strangely enough, the text of Haggai remains very innocent over this question of defilement, not realizing its significance for the building of the temple. And so do the commentators, who only very rarely recognize how problematic is a building of a temple by workers in a state of ritual impurity.[48] Uncleanness is very contagious, so Haggai avers, and he has not needed any consultation with priests to know that; it was a commonplace for any Jew of whatever period. The idea of building a temple, by definition a holy place, using the labour of unclean builders is almost ludicrous. But Haggai represses the implicit conflict between the uncleanness of the builders and the cleanness of the building. Why? He is not stupid; he must know at some level that there is a conflict. But he cannot cope with it. Either he has to give up his dream of seeing the temple rebuilt, or he has to allow that the people are not after all in a state of ritual impurity. He cannot do either, and the result is a text that deconstructs itself.

What is truly intriguing about this deconstruction is how it comes to be inscribed in the text in the first place. Why does the whole issue of the transmissibility of holiness and uncleanness get raised at all?[49] The

need to go into here. I cannot accept Petersen's elaborate argument that it is not the people but the temple that is unclean ('the impurity can only derive from the place to which the sacrifices are being brought', *Haggai and Zechariah 1–8*, p. 84). Cf. also Baldwin: 'The ruined skeleton of the Temple was like a dead body decaying in Jerusalem and making everything contaminated' (*Haggai, Zechariah, Malachi*, p. 33). It would be a strange way to go about demanding a ceremony of ritual purification for the temple to blame the people for letting themselves be contaminated by the temple whenever they bring offerings to it. The text implies, in my opinion, that the sacrifices are unclean before they arrive at the temple.

48. R. Mason, 'The Prophets of the Restoration', in *Israel's Prophetic Tradition: Essays in Honour of Peter R. Ackroyd* (ed. R.J. Coggins *et al.*; Cambridge: Cambridge University Press, 1982), pp. 137-54 (144), believes indeed that we should see the phrase 'the work of their hands' as referring to their building activity; but he does not draw the conclusion that the temple must therefore be ritually unclean. Rather, he merely ethicizes the 'uncleanness' into an '[in]capacity for self-regeneration', observing that it is not the work of the people but the eschatological 'Coming' of God that will fill the temple with glory. He overlooks the fact that uncleanness transmits itself to temples but incapacity for self-regeneration is quite harmless to *sancta*.

49. It can hardly be, as Achtemeier would have it, that the temple-builders are in danger of becoming self-righteous and believing that 'association with the things of God automatically communicates moral purity... Haggai addresses this temptation with a parable and its explanation... The question is,... Having dealt with God's

elaborate question and answer process between Haggai and the priests seems designed, not to elicit authoritative answers to currently debated or unclear issues, but principally to lead up to an explanation of why the Judaean harvests have been so poor. The logic seems to be as follows (though there are no causal connectives in the text): everything the people do is unclean; their offerings at the altar are unclean; God punishes them for this infringement of cultic purity by sending blight, mildew and hail to decrease the productivity of their fields.

This is in itself a quite unexceptional line of reasoning, but its appearance at this point is startling. In the first place, it runs counter to the explanation that has hitherto been the burden of the text. From the beginning of the book, the logic has been: 'You have sown much, and harvested little... Why? Because of my house that lies in ruins' (1.6, 9). The *reason* why they do not build the temple is because they think the time has not yet come; and the *result* of not building the temple is that the deity withholds prosperity from them. The *next step* that they can take if they want to change things is to start to build the temple. Given the presuppositions, everything in this line of argument makes good (and familiar) sense. But how is this explanation to be squared with the other, that their lack of prosperity is a punishment for their *uncleanness*? Are they being punished for their *neglect* of the temple or for their *impurity*? If it is for both offences, if they are *both* negligent and unclean, why is not a word about their uncleanness breathed until three months after they have resumed work on the temple (cf. 1.15 with 2.10)?

In the second place, where is the logic in the second explanation? Where is the *reason* or *cause* for their uncleanness? They have been contracting the uncleanness from somewhere, but do they know where? Since they do not, what are they to do about it as a *next step*? Assuming they do not want to remain in a state of impurity, what move can they make? Even if it is not literal impurity that we are reading about here, but some sort of moral incapacity, what are they expected to do about it? It can hardly be, can it, that the 'uncleanness' is a metaphor for their unreadiness for the work?[50] If that were so,

holy place, have they themselves become holy?' (*Nahum–Malachi*, pp. 102-103). Cf. also Ackroyd, *Exile and Restoration*, p. 169: 'There is no automatic efficacy in the temple, no guarantee that by virtue of its existence it ensures salvation'.

50. So e.g. Perowne, *Haggai and Zechariah*, p. 24: 'Their one sin in neglecting the Temple spreads its moral pollution over "every work of their hands"'; May,

they would surely have been 'purified' from such a uncleanness by their commencement of the work on the twenty-fourth of the sixth month, a good three months ago. And furthermore, how is the promised blessing of 2.19 connected with the uncleanness? It's all very well to be blessed, but what does that do to the impurity? Is that to be removed? And if so, how? How can the category of impurity drop out of sight, and be replaced by the category of blessing? Impurity is got rid of only by rituals of purification; impurity is impervious to 'blessing'. All the 'blessing' in the world will not turn an unclean thing into a clean, will it?

There is at bottom something gratuitous (must we not conclude?) in this excursion into matters of the holy and the clean. All that arises from it are complications that deflect the force of the original thrust of the book.

So must we conclude that the text exhibits a kind of 'bad faith', according to which the people can never be praised for doing what they are encouraged to, and are required only to do what it is impossible for them to do? If they don't build the temple they will be punished for their negligence, and if they do build the temple they will defile it.

3. *Zerubbabel*

We have just now observed a case where the text suddenly takes off in an unexpected direction, implicitly undermining what has preceded. Now we find, in the final four verses of the book (2.20-23), an even more striking divergence from the previous course of the book, and an equally disturbing deconstructive situation. It is fascinating that both these deconstructive texts (2.10-19; 2.20-23) are signed with the same dateline: the twenty-fourth day of the ninth month of the second year of Darius. According to this text, therefore, Haggai the prophet deconstructs the whole of his prophetic ministry on its last day![51]

'"This People" and "This Nation" in Haggai', p. 196: 'Through their failure to honor Yahweh with proper attention to his house, they had become, as it were, unclean'.

51. In the older scholarship this day has sometimes been very differently esteemed, as the 'birthday of Judaism', the day when the temple was founded and the prophet definitively 'rejected willing but cultically suspect helpers, thereby inaugurating the sequestration that was to be typical of later Judaism' (Fohrer, *Introduction to the Old Testament*, p. 460).

The final oracle, addressed to Zerubbabel, is a quite remarkable one, designating him as nothing less than the universal and eschatological ruler. This significance of the oracle is, surprisingly, not generally recognized by commentators.[52] But the eschatological framework is quite clearly signalled by the language of cosmic upheaval we already met with at 2.6. The heavens and the earth are to undergo a 'shaking', symbolical no doubt of the political shaking that the writer envisages. More explicitly than in 2.6, where it was simply a matter of 'shaking' the nations, here we learn that YHWH will also 'overthrow the throne of kingdoms', 'destroy the strength of the kingdoms of the nations' and 'overthrow the chariot and its riders', the horses and their riders 'going down', each by the sword of his fellow (2.22). This prediction signifies a new political order corresponding to the picture of the dominance of Jerusalem reflected in 2.7.[53] Into that new eschatological political order there is to be inserted Zerubbabel as its chief ruler.

52. Meyers and Meyers, for example, think that the day in question is 'the day in which the Yehudites will once again achieve political independence and self-rule under the Davidide Zerubbabel' (*Haggai and Zechariah 1–8*, p. 67)—which hardly seems to match the cosmic language of 2.21-22. But elsewhere they speak of Zerubbabel's appointment as an eschatological event (e.g. pp. 70, 82). And Wolff sees the announcement to Zerubbabel that Yhwh would 'overthrow (הפך) all nations' as Haggai's 'offer[ing] to the worried Zerubbabel the immediate and lasting reminder that Yahweh is the God who controls all the political conditions and affairs of the great powers' (p. 102). In Zerubbabel's shoes I would not need this reminder, nor would I glean it from Haggai's words; I would be more likely to start drafting my policy as world ruler. Wolff thinks that 2.23 'designates [Zerubbabel] as the personal bearer of hope' (*Haggai*, p. 108); this is an amazingly other-worldly reading of what is transparently a political statement. Smith (*Micah–Malachi*, p. 163) also fails to grasp the immediacy of this revolution in world order when he writes: 'Zerubbabel of the line of David was only a Persian governor of a tiny community. But it would not always be that way. Yahweh was going to shake the nations.'

53. The text is being domesticated by Achtemeier when she writes: 'He speaks not of the overthrow of Persia but of the subjection of all nations to God' (*Nahum–Malachi*, p. 105)—as if Haggai dealt in ethical platitudes and had no agenda you could call political. Ackroyd's reading is more sophisticated, but still fails to satisfy: 'The events are not necessarily to be thought of in military terms, but rather in terms of the subordination to the divine will of those powers which set themselves up as authorities in their own right' (*Exile and Restoration*, p. 163). For how does he (or the prophet) imagine such a subordination as coming about, then, if not by military means (including, no doubt, supernatural military means)?

The language about Zerubbabel in 2.23 is unmistakable. Zerubbabel's appointment will take place 'on that day', which (even if we did not recognize the phrase already as the technical term for the eschaton) must be the eschatological time, for the 'day' when he will be appointed is plainly the time of cosmic 'shaking'. Having 'chosen' (בחר) Zerubbabel, Yhwh will 'take' (לקח) him, as various persons have previously been 'taken' for high office.[54] Further, Zerubbabel is termed 'my servant' (עבדי),[55] whom Yhwh will 'set as a signet-ring' (חותם), presumably upon his own finger as a symbol of Zerubbabel's appointment as ruler (cf. the language used of Jehoiachin, 'Coniah, king of Judah', in Jer. 22.23-25 as 'the signet-ring on my right hand').

So the book of Haggai ends with the announcement that Zerubbabel is to be appointed world ruler.[56] No matter how brief the oracle, the claim it makes is astounding. When we recollect how the envisaged eschatological ruler is portrayed elsewhere in the prophetic literature (e.g. Isa. 9.6-7; 11.1-3; 16.5; 55.4; Jer. 23.5; 30.9; Ezek. 34.23-24; 37.24-25; Mic. 5.1-4 [EVV 4.14–5.3]; Zech. 3.8; 6.12-13), we are drawn up sharp by the realization that here for the first time in Old

54. The term signifies 'interventions that are going to bring about a change of place, calling, and function' (Wolff, *Haggai*, p. 105).

55. According to Wolff, 'Zerubbabel is... addressed in the same way as David... According to Haggai's line of thinking, this relationship will have been related to Zerubbabel's efforts for the building of the temple' (p. 105). I doubt this, for why would Joshua, equally responsible for the temple building, not be in view here also? And in any case, was David responsible for the first temple? I doubt, in other words, that the promise to Zerubbabel is connected with temple building at all. And that 'Zerubbabel, as Yahweh's seal, would then be the guarantor of the temple's completion' (Wolff, *Haggai*, p. 106).

56. Wolff is remarkably reticent in allowing only that 'it is not entirely improbable that... Zerubbabel will in the future be declared the new David. But it must be stressed that this promise is couched in extremely muted terms.' His argument is that important messianic terms like משח and מלך are missing and there is nothing said of the struggle, victory and peace of the messianic age (*Haggai*, p. 106). I myself find what Haggai says much more persuasive than what he does not say. In contrast with Wolff, von Rad, *Old Testament Theology*, II, p. 284, says: 'He clearly and unequivocally designated as the coming anointed one David's descendant Zerubbabel'; cf. Rendtorff, *The Old Testament: An Introduction*, p. 236: 'a clear messianic expectation'; J.A. Soggin, *Introduction to the Old Testament* (trans. J. Bowden; London: SCM Press, 1976), p. 325: 'The messianic kingdom was about to be inaugurated, its sovereign was to be the last scion of the house of David, Zerubbabel'.

Testament prophetic books a prophet actually knows the name of this hoped-for figure, and moreover that it turns out to be the name of a contemporary of the prophet,[57] a man who is at this moment walking about the streets of Jerusalem. The historical Zerubbabel was, so far as we know, only a governor (פחה) of the Persian province of Yehud and a member of the Judaean royal house, nothing more startling; so the astonishing boldness of the identification can hardly be exaggerated. He must be the first real person to have been identified with the eschatological son of David.[58]

Now where a deconstruction begins to open up is over the question, So what is the important thing for this prophetic text? What is the *point* of the book of Haggai?

Until we have read to within four verses of the end of this book we are in little uncertainty about its overall point. No one doubts that it concerns the rebuilding of the temple, the consequences of ignoring it and an encouragement to begin it.[59] But, suddenly, in the last four verses we encounter an entirely new theme, the appointment and naming of the world ruler. And the former issue of temple building suddenly becomes invisible—just as, for its part, the universal significance of Zerubbabel had been in all that preceded.

Any book, of course, may have more than one topic, more than one aim. A book does not deconstruct itself merely by taking up a new topic, even in its last four verses. Where the deconstructive aspect lies, I think, is in the fact that the two topics, each of such moment, and

57. According to the chronology of the book of Zechariah, Zechariah will be saying something very similar in two months' time (cf. 1.7) about 'the Branch'; but although the identity of the Branch is an open secret, Zechariah does not go so far as Haggai in giving his name as Zerubbabel.

58. Von Rad says that 'It is common to point out that Haggai here differs radically from the pre-exilic prophets by naming a living member of the house of David as the coming anointed one' (*Old Testament Theology*, II, p. 284); but I have not found any other traces of this 'common' observation.

59. So too Wolff, *Haggai*, p. 22: 'Haggai is impelled by a single question: how can the devastated temple in Jerusalem be rebuilt?' Wolff relates the address to Zerubbabel to this theme by the assumption that Zerubbabel is 'appointed authorized guarantor of the temple's completion' (*ibid.*); but of course there is nothing in the Zerubbabel oracle about the temple. A focus on the temple has not, however, been universally recognized; cf. e.g. Perowne, *Haggai and Zechariah*, p. 22: '[I]t was the stern call, "Repent ye", with which he was principally charged'. Here the pragmatic demands of the text have been moralized, as so often happens.

each not self-evidently subordinate to the other, are nevertheless not brought into relation with one another, so that the reader experiences an aporia over what should be designated the overall theme of the work.[60] It is not that the two purposes flatly contradict one another, as if, for example, part one had said that Joshua was to become the world ruler and part two had said Zerubbabel. It is that in the first and major part of the book the one thing worthy of attention is the glory of YHWH evidenced by the influx of treasures to the temple and in the second part of the work the one object of attention is the glory of Zerubbabel as world ruler designate. Zerubbabel is not, it is true, in *competition* with Yhwh for glory, for it is Yhwh who is appointing Zerubbabel to his glorious office. But it is hard to see how the two themes are related.

It is not that Zerubbabel himself is going to bring about the achievement of the glory of Yhwh which the first part desiderates; for it is not Zerubbabel as distinct from Joshua who leads the work of rebuilding (1.1, 12, 14; 2.2, 4); and in any case it is not the rebuilding that is going to acquire glory but the filling of the temple with wealth by Yhwh himself (2.7). Nor, on the other hand, does the completion of the temple bring about in any way the success of Zerubbabel, for his appointment is not linked to the completion of the temple (in fact, the *completion* of the temple hardly seems to be the issue; it is the *working on* the temple that seems to matter).

As a result, every attempt we make to state the aim or theme of the book seems doomed. In this major respect too the book deconstructs itself, professing to be about one thing and then, without telling us that it has changed its mind, turning out to be about something different (without ceasing to be about the first thing at the same time).

60. Attempts to relate the two parts of the book are extraordinarily unsuccessful; thus Petersen, *Haggai and Zechariah 1–8*, p. 105: 'Through [Haggai's] efforts... the temple was well on the way to reconstruction. Now it was time to focus on other issues, including the civil polity of Israel.' Is that what 2.20-23 is about, 'the civil polity of Israel'? And is a phrase like 'now it was time to focus on other issues' not an elaborate way of saying that we cannot see the connection between the first issue and the second? See also Stuhlmueller, *Haggai and Zechariah*, p. 16: 'Haggai's focus was exceptionally clear. All of his energies were directed toward two goals: the rebuilding of the temple and the restoration of the Davidic rule'. But he does not even hint at what the relation of the two goals might be.

The Temple Reconstructed

I always worry about what to do with a text after it has been deconstructed. In this paper I want to propose a *reconstructive* process. I will focus first upon reconstructing the realities surrounding the text's composition, and secondly upon reconstructing the eventualities surrounding the text's reception.

1. *The Composition of the Text*

Why was this text written? I will not try to answer that question by speculating about the author's intention or the psychology of the prophet, of course, and especially not by double-guessing Persian political strategy or extrapolating from archaeological artifacts. Taking a leaf out of Frederic Jameson's book,[61] I will assume that this text, like others, is written in order to suppress or repress (using the Freudian metaphor) a social conflict. Texts are written on paper, and paper is used for pasting over cracks, especially cracks in the social fabric. The question, Why was this text written?, can then be answered by reconstituting the social reality it implies. Now this is not quite the same as reconstructing the actual social reality in Jerusalem in 520 BCE, to which of course we have no access, since all we have are texts, texts that purport to give us access to those times, indeed, but that are, being texts, constitutionally incapable of doing so. No matter; we cannot access the actual first *readers* of Haggai's book either, but we *can* reconstitute its implied readers. We cannot ever grasp the social reality of Haggai's time, but we *can* profile the social reality implied in the book.

If texts are written to suppress conflicts, and we want to bring those conflicts to the surface, deconstruction seems to me a good way of doing it. In a deconstruction, a chasm in the text opens up; and we have the choice of timidly averting our gaze from the giddy depths or of boldly peering down into them to what lies hidden (or partly hidden) at the unconscious level.

a. The first deconstruction I identified concerned the issue of honour. It appeared that the people are dishonouring the deity by not rebuilding the temple, and yet for all their rebuilding they will not

61. *The Political Unconscious: Narrative as a Socially Symbolic Act* (London: Methuen, 1983).

achieve the honour the deity requires. There is a conflict here between the people and what they can do, on the one hand, and the leadership (the prophet and his accomplices, the high priest and the governor) and what they want on the other. There is, in other words, a social conflict lurking beneath the text and coming to expression in its deconstructability.

In this case, of course, the conflict is not entirely latent. For the text itself portrays the very same conflict, though it does not tell us the whole truth about it. It represents the conflict as being between the enthusiasts for rebuilding the temple and the 'people'. On the one side are Haggai the 'prophet', Zerubbabel the governor and Joshua the high priest. These leaders will have their support groups, presumably of prophets, administrators and priests. On the other side are the 'people', everyone else. They are farmers and householders. The conflict comes about when the people with power think that the people without power should stop farming and putting ceilings in their houses and should spend their days in unpaid labour on building the temple. The people without power do not think this is a good idea.

In whose interest is this rebuilding? Not the people's. Even if they are not economists, they can see that temple building is not contributing to the gross national product, and even if they are not atheists they can see that the worship of the deity is not being impeded in any way by the incompleteness of the temple. Sacrifices are being offered, prayers are being said, priests and levites are being fed by tithes. The temple is a prestige project promoted by the elite, and its construction serves *their* sense of fitness, their vanity. The people at large are understandably not so enthusiastic, for they have little to gain and plenty to lose by the project.

So there is a social conflict beneath the text, implied by the text. The text by no means obscures it completely, but it does try to suppress it. And the way it does so is to tell the story of how the conflict was overcome, i.e. resolved. We recall that Jameson regards texts as attempts to suppress *unresolved* social conflicts. If a conflict has been resolved, it will not generate a text; if everything in the garden is lovely, there is nothing to write about. Now the way this text tries to suppress the conflict that generated it is to claim that the people were won over to the opinion of the leadership, and so set about rebuilding the temple, thereby removing the tension. What the text suppresses (almost) is that the conflict was *not* resolved, for not all the people *did* co-operate in the building of the temple. Only a *remnant* worked on the temple—which implies that the majority did not. We can tell that this is the case, for while 'the people' as a whole are claimed to say that the 'time is not yet come' (1.2), and it is the people as a whole who are unclean and defiling the temple (2.14), it is only the 'remnant of the people' who obey the prophet's demand, have their spirit stirred and are addressed as its builders (1.12, 14; 2.2).[62] A remnant is a good thing to be; it is the nearest the proletariat can get to being an elite. If you are a remnant, you are still there; you are still in the reckoning. If you don't belong to the remnant, you have been written off. Now the text of course says not a word about the non-remnant, those who did *not* obey the prophetic word; it tries to write them out of existence. But the word 'remnant' gives the game away; for any semiotic square with 'remnant' at one corner is bound to have 'non-remnant' at another. In short: after Haggai had finished all his prophesying, the conflict between those who wanted the temple built and those who did not remained—so a text was called into being. *That* is the implication of the text.[63]

b. The second deconstruction, concerning the issue of uncleanness, points up more sharply the same implied social conflict, between the leadership and the populace. Where it differs from the first is that it expresses not just the fact of the conflict but the feelings of the elite about the conflict. The prophet, and therewith his class, cannot cope with the fact that they despise the people they are dependent on, and they express their anxiety about the tension by creating a deconstructable text. That is to say, they recognize that without the labour of the 'people' there will be no temple building; indeed, without the free and voluntary labour of the lower orders the prestige project of the elite will not be accomplished. Haggai (the character in the book of Haggai) expresses his distaste for the 'people' by pronouncing them

62. Another way of suppressing the conflict is to translate שאר as 'the rest' of the people (as REB at 1.12, 14; 2.2); everyone knows, on the contrary, that '[i]n Hg and Zc "the remnant of the people" means the faithful grouped around Jerusalem' (so NJB footnote)—or rather, the supporters of the leaders in Jerusalem. It is, incidentally, not a problem for the distinction between 'the people' and 'the remnant of the people' that in 1.12 it is 'the people' who fear before Yhwh and that in 1.13 it is to 'the people' that Yhwh says, 'I am with you'; for the 'people' in question here have just now been defined by 'the remnant of the people' at the beginning of 1.12.

63. Whether it was the historical reality is more than we can say, of course.

'unclean', and he attempts to gain a secure vantage point for himself over against the people by setting up an artificial dialogue with the priests as his power base. But his categorization of the people as 'unclean' backfires on him when it leads him to declare 'all the work of their hands' unclean. Implicitly that must include the temple building, but he and the class he represents cannot allow that; the text is generated by the unresolved conflict.

c. The third deconstruction, concerning Zerubbabel, evinces a different social or political conflict implied by the text, namely over the status of the governor. At its most simple, the point is that Haggai does not need to pronounce this oracle about Zerubbabel if everyone already agrees with it, and he does not need to write it down if everyone has accepted his prophecy about Zerubbabel at the time when he delivered it. The very existence of the Zerubbabel oracle in the text is prima facie evidence of resistance to it in the historical reality the text implies. Commentators indeed often recognize that the oracle addresses a situation of conflict, but, since they tend to think in psychological, personalistic and theological categories, they don't see that it is a *political* conflict. They think it is a conflict within Zerubbabel's own psyche, that he needs 'encouragement'. Maybe anyone in Zerubbabel's position *does* need encouragement, but more than that he needs a public announcement of support from his various power bases. Haggai provides that here on behalf of the prophetic cadre.[64]

There is bound to be conflict in a society when one group begins promoting one of its number as a world dictator and promising a shaking of all fixed points of reference. Shopkeepers and farmers are not going to welcome a cosmic upheaval; they need weather they can rely on and steady trade. A shaking of the heavens and the earth that will result in one ruler being substituted for another is more attractive to potential rulers and their hangers-on than to folk who have to earn a living by the 'work of their hands', to coin a phrase. And even if the wealth of all the nations is going to come pouring into Jerusalem, no one expects it to end up in the pocket of Joe Citizen; turning the local shrine into Fort Knox is not everyone's idea of eschatological bliss. Everyone under their own vine and fig tree...now that is a different matter. Haggai's elite do not know this; they think everyone should be

64. Cf. the notation of Ezra 5.2 that, at the rebuilding of the temple by Zerubbabel and Jeshua, 'with them were the prophets of God, helping them'. How? We may presume that the prophets did not carry stones.

impressed by the idea of Zerubbabel's being the signet ring on the deity's finger. The text actually represents this elite as so out of touch with reality as needing to be informed by a divine oracle what their people are thinking: the time is not yet come, say the people, says the Lord, by the hand of Haggai. Do rulers so ignorant deserve to be rulers?, we ask ourselves. The gulf between the governors and the governed is intolerably wide; even the surface of the text witnesses to that fact, and the deconstruction confirms it.

2. *The Reception of the Text*

Haggai's book was plainly not a 'popular' work; it is not the product of the 'people'. Rather, it portrays, from the point of view of the leadership, a conflict between them and that section of the people that does not belong to the 'remnant'. But equally plainly, it found its way into the biblical canon, and was accepted by the 'people'. How did they cope with its inconcinnities? Why did they not notice its self-deconstructability? Why did no one see through its papering over of the social conflicts it so revealingly attests?

Being professedly the words of a prophet has a lot to do with it. Being a *book* attributed to a prophet is even more important. It is writing that creates truth, for the truth about the past is what is remembered about the past. Writing a book of prophecy is therefore what makes a prophet a true prophet—even if that prophet tells palpable falsehoods like 'yet a little while and I will shake the heavens'.

That is to say, if you regard the words of Haggai as essentially the words of the deity written down 'by the hand of' Haggai, which means to say, if you believe 1.1, all tensions in the text have to be explained away, for everyone knows that the deity does not contradict himself. In fact, you don't need to explain away tensions, for if you believe that these are the words of the deity you will not be expecting to find tensions, and you will not believe the evidence of your eyes when you encounter one. It will also not occur to you to side with anyone in the text except Haggai, for he is the prophet of the god; the people therefore *are* unclean, and the temple most certainly *should* be built, the moment Haggai says it should. In short, through most of the history of the reception of the book, its deconstructability and its suppression of social conflict has simply been ignored because of the authentication of the prophet by the religious community.

What has happened, however, in the days since the interpretation of the Hebrew Bible was wrested from the control of ecclesiastical authorities? Sad to say, not a lot. The prophet's book remains canonical scripture, and most interpreters feel some constraint to offer readings in accord with the parameters of doctrinal purity.

Two quotations from latterday readers of the book of Haggai should be enough to testify to the reception the book enjoys in our own time. In response to the depiction of the wealth of the nations flowing into Jerusalem, in which many a reader might well see a touch of the grandiose and of wishful thinking, Hans Walter Wolff writes,

> What is being expressed here is not greed on Israel's part, or some kind of Jewish egoism; it is the sovereign claim of Yahweh, who turns to his impoverished people in their necessity.[65]

Compare with this the words of Wolff's Heidelberg predecessor, Gerhard von Rad:

> There is no question here of greed for gain, but a proclamation by Yahweh which the prophet sets down with uncompromising boldness, and any exegesis which casts doubt upon this mighty purposefulness of Yahweh in the present world-order stands self-condemned in its own supposed spirituality.[66]

The text, that is to say, cannot possibly represent any kind of unlovely motivation on the part of the prophet or his supporters. In fact, say Wolff and von Rad, what we find here are not really words of the prophet himself, but 'the sovereign claim of Yahweh', 'a proclamation by Yahweh' that is consequently as unassailable as the moral character of Yhwh himself. These are not the words of some post-exilic Jew, poverty-stricken and marginalized in some far-flung outpost of the empire, giving voice to a fantasy about world dominion and economic supremacy for his kinsmen; no, these are the very words of the 'mighty purposefulness' of the universal god, 'turning to his impoverished people in their necessity'. Let no reader of these esteemed Hebrew Bible scholars reflect for a moment on the social divisiveness of Haggai's book, or remark that it is a funny way of turning to your impoverished people to promise them all the silver and gold lining the

65. Wolff, *Haggai*, p. 82.

66. G. von Rad, 'The City on the Hill', in *The Problem of the Hexateuch and Other Essays* (trans. E.W. Trueman Dicken; Edinburgh: Oliver & Boyd, 1966), pp. 232-42 (240-41).

pockets of the Gentiles and then do nothing about it. Such exegeses stand self-condemned, von Rad assures us, so we know in advance where we stand with the guild if we try to write a paper like the present one. The text owed its origin to its suppression of a social conflict in ancient Israel; and it owes its continuing existence (does it not?) to its facility to suppress conflict among its readers. And in the same way, and in the same 'prophetic' succession, the works of Wolff and von Rad also owe *their* continued existence to *their* power to suppress divergent readings, outlawing in advance 'any exegesis that casts doubt'.

This is the depth of the corruption in our academic discipline that surrounds us, even in this year of grace 1994, for all the splendours of the Enlightenment and the glories of scientific biblical criticism. It would be ironic if Haggai's book should come to serve for the unmasking of the abomination of religious authority standing where it should not and for the breaking loose of conflicts within the scholarly community that have been too long hushed up in the name of collegiality and tolerance.

WHAT DOES ZECHARIAH 1–8 TELL US ABOUT THE SECOND TEMPLE?*

Peter Marinkovic

Zechariah as Promoter of the Building of the Temple: A Thesis and its Problems

The prophet Zechariah is still regarded as having promoted the building of the second temple, and is, more or less closely, associated with the prophet Haggai and the latter's message. Noteworthy in this respect is—as one example among many—the statement by Herbert Donner in his study *Geschichte des Volkes Israel und seiner Nachbarn* with regard to the effectiveness and proclamation of the two prophets: 'Kurze Zeit danach (520) traten in Jerusalem zwei Propheten auf und riefen zum Tempelbau: Haggai und Sacharja'.[1] It is interesting that Donner can here point to an instance in the Bible in which mention has been made of the two prophets, for already in the book of Ezra there are notes that state that Haggai and Zechariah appeared together. We read the following in Ezra 4.24–5.2:[2]

> Then the work on the house of God which is in Jerusalem stopped; and it ceased until *the second year of the reign of Darius, king of Persia*.
>
> Now Haggai, the prophet, and Zechariah, the son of Iddo,[3] the prophets, prophesied to the Jews who were in Judah and Jerusalem, in the name of the God of Israel (who was watching) over them.

* I would like to thank Dr Ingrid L. Semaan for her help in translating this paper.

1. H. Donner, *Geschichte des Volkes Israel und seiner Nachbarn in Grundzügen*, II (ATD/E, 4/2; Göttingen: Vandenhoeck & Ruprecht, 1986), p. 412.
2. For my translation of Ezra, I have consulted A.H.J. Gunneweg, *Esra: Mit einer Zeittafel von Alfred Jepsen* (KAT, XIX/1; Gütersloh: Mohn, 1985).
3. See also Neh. 12.16 for Zechariah's genealogical relationship with the family of Iddo (cf. Zech. 1.1, 7).

> At that time, Zerubbabel, the son of Shealtiel, and Joshua, the son of Jozadak, arose and began to build [Aram. בנא] the house [Aram. בַּיִת] of God which is in Jerusalem; and with them were the prophets of God, supporting them.

Ezra 6.14[4] states this point in the same explicit manner:

> And the elders of the Jews built and prospered through the prophesying of Haggai, the prophet, and Zechariah, the son of Iddo. They finished the constructing[5] by command of the God of Israel and by decree of Cyrus and Darius (and Artaxerxes, the king of Persia).[6]

It is striking to note that these passages, reminiscent of summaries, do not indicate that either Haggai or Zechariah called explicitly for building a temple. Similarly, there is no mention made that both prophets ever proclaimed the same message or, at least, emphasized the same points in their individual messages. The text merely stresses their simultaneous appearance (5.1)[7]—implied in the text—and their support of the building of the 'temple' (5.2); in other words, the progress of this undertaking on account of the proclamation of their messages (6.14). Nevertheless, it is quite possible that both of these passages (Ezra 5.1-2 and 6.14) have contributed substantially to the fact, that in traditional Zechariah scholarship not only the chronological appearance of the two prophets is observed (which, historically speaking, is more than likely the case), but furthermore, the heart of their messages has finally been regarded as parallel, if not identical.

4. Gunneweg, *Esra*, pp. 95-96, 112, discusses in detail the Chronistic revision of this verse, which, most likely, led to the inclusion of Haggai and Zechariah in the so-called Aramaic basic account (Ezra 4.6–6.14*). Ezra 5.1-2, in Gunneweg's opinion, is nothing but a Chronistic creation (pp. 95-96). This interpretation shows great similarity to the idea proposed by Beuken and others that the present form of Haggai and Zechariah 1–8 is the result of the same Chronistic revision (cf. n. 34 below). Both texts, to mention just one example, present introductory dating formulas (see n. 34 below) in the same striking manner (these dates correspond to those given in Ezra 5.1-2; 6.14).

5. Aram. בנא. Literally: 'built and completed'.

6. Most commentators regard the passage given in parentheses to be supplementary material; see Gunneweg, *Esra*, p. 112.

7. The texts do not mention the places of their appearance. But those details that are given about the persons who are addressed make it possible to come to the following rough division: Judah and Jerusalem (Ezra 5.1; indirectly Ezra 6.14 as well). It is, however, not possible to determine on the basis of Ezra 5.1 alone whether or not Gola was another location where they proclaimed their message.

The assumption is *that the proclamations of the two prophets have been shaped* by the call to build the 'temple',[8] or, to phrase it more literally, *by the call to build the house of God in Jerusalem.*[9]

I have based *the point of departure of my study* on an *obvious discrepancy*: If we examine Zechariah 1–8—having in mind the question 'What do the texts really say about the building of the second temple?'—we can see an obvious discrepancy with Ezra 5.1-2; 6.14 and the subsequent scholarly interpretation of Ezra and Haggai and Zechariah 1–8 as well. First of all, the texts of Zechariah 1–8 contain hardly any statements about the temple. There are very few verses that deal with this matter, and those few that we have are basically marginal, or are part and parcel of pronouncements that express other concerns. Secondly, the greater part of the text of Zechariah 1–8 deals with other thematic matters. For example, not one of the eight visions is thematically connected with the temple as such or with its reconstruction.[10]

Compared to Ezra 5.1-2 and 6.14, there are, relatively speaking, far fewer statements in Zechariah 1–8 that deal with the temple (and its construction) than in Haggai.[11] In order to gain a clearer understanding of the basic themes of Zechariah 1–8 (and thus of the main concerns of Zechariah's message), I would like, first of all, to present a survey of the content of the basic message contained in Zechariah 1–8. Then, as my second step, I will discuss all those verses in Proto-Zechariah that contain significant terms that are related to 'house' and 'temple', that is to say, to בית and היכל. This means that I will pay special attention to the passages in which these words are used in

8. See Donner, *Geschichte*, p. 412. The passage to which I have already referred (cf. n. 1) expresses an *opinio communis*.

9. And this means that Zechariah's message usually has been interpreted through the perspective of the prophecy of Haggai. This becomes obvious upon a thematic examination of the contents of the book of Haggai, as will be shown later.

10. Compare also with Ezek. 40–48. Several of these chapters deal directly and some passages deal indirectly with the new temple and its construction, or with its management and its organization (priests, Levites, regulations pertaining to offerings). For the possibility of interpreting the lampstand and the Joshua visions (Zech. 3–4) as possible components of a Judaic equivalent of the (Akk.) Babylonian *kalū* ritual for the reconstruction of the temple, see below.

11. Haggai will be discussed in detail later. Here, however, I will merely point to the fact that the terms עיר, ירושלם, ציון do not occur at all in Haggai, while the terms בית and היכל are frequently used.

connection with expressions that denote 'building' and 'founding'/ 'completing' (בנה and בצע/יסד *pi.*). Finally, applying the results of this study, I will answer the following question: 'What could have possibly contributed to the fact that Zechariah, along with Haggai, is regarded in Ezra 5.1-2 and 6.14 as promoter of the building of the house of God in Jerusalem?'

Survey of Concerns Expressed in Zechariah 1–8

Let us now turn to the basic concerns expressed in Zechariah 1–8. In Zechariah 1–8, we find three thematic concerns. First, *YHWH's return to Jerusalem and his abode is regarded as the turning point for his people's return to Jerusalem.* Statements about the return of YHWH to Jerusalem and his renewed abode are found in the first and third vision (Zech. 1.8-17; 2.5-9), in the immediately following collection of oracles (2.10-17), and in the promise made in the so-called 'Fastenrede' (8.1-8). These pronouncements thus constitute a type of frame, or better yet, a foundation for the remaining themes of Zechariah 1–8.

The first vision (1.8-17) deals most obviously with the question pertaining to the end of the exile as a time of divine judgment: 'How long wilt thou have no mercy on Jerusalem and the cities of Judah, against which thou hast had indignation these seventy years?' (1.12). And YHWH answers: 'I have returned[12] to Jerusalem with compassion' (1.16). Consequently, YHWH's return to Jerusalem has already taken place, at least in intention. This perspective is established at the beginning of the cycle of visions, and this fact determines the meaning of all subsequent pronouncements of Proto-Zechariah.

In the third vision (2.5-9), the intention to measure the breadth and length of Jerusalem (probably in preparation for a future building activity)[13] is brought to an end. The following explanation is given:

12. For the translation of *qatal*, bearing in mind its characteristic that indicates the completion of an action (and therefore translating it as perfect tense: 'I have returned'), see R. Bartelmus, *HYH: Bedeutung und Funktion eines hebräischen 'Allerweltswortes', zugleich ein Beitrag zur Frage des hebräischen Tempussystems* (ATS, 17; St Ottilien: EOS–Verlag, 1982), pp. 51-54; as well as R. Hanhart, *Sacharja* (BK, XIV/7.1; Neukirchen–Vluyn: Neukirchener Verlag, 1990): 'Die Rückkehr ist als Entschluss Vergangenheit, geschehen...' (p. 57).

13. The text does not indicate explicitly whether or not anything is to be built, and if something is to be built, it does not name what it is. The YHWH-oracle (2.8b-9: the

'Jerusalem shall be inhabited as a town without walls with regard to the multitude of men and cattle in its midst' (2.8b). God announces: 'And I will be to her, says YHWH, a wall of fire round about, and I will be the glory within her' (2.9). This complementary description expresses in vivid images the all embracing nature of YHWH's beneficial presence in Jerusalem: on the one hand, God encircles the city as a protective burning wall; on the other hand, he is (simultaneously!) in her midst as 'the glory' (and thus becomes her splendour, her glory, her fame, her honour). This promise of YHWH, seen in its context, stands in immediate relationship with the promise that the future life of both human and animal in Jerusalem will be bountiful. This pledge is interpreted as an implicit reference to the return of the exiles to Jerusalem.

This supposition is confirmed by the oracle sequence that follows (2.10-17). There the exiles are commanded from the very outset to flee from the land of the north and find refuge from Babylon (2.10-11). In the second part of these oracles, YHWH exorts the Daughter of Zion to rejoice and to be glad: '"For lo, I am coming to dwell in the midst of you", says YHWH' (2.14).[14] God's renewed taking up of his abode in the midst of the Daughter of Zion as YHWH'S community is about to occur. Zech. 2.15 mentions the accessibility of the YHWH community to many peoples some time in the future, their ability to become YHWH'S people, and repeats that YHWH will dwell in their midst. Zech. 2.17, finally, announces that God is departing for his new dwelling.

According to the oracle of Zech. 8.3a, YHWH says: 'I have returned to Zion and have taken up my abode in the midst of Jerusalem'.[15] The return of YHWH to Jerusalem has taken place. Zech. 8.4-5 then presents the picture of the populated city, and 8.7-8 announces that the

openness of Jerusalem, YHWH as protective wall of fire), which in the context of the vision should be taken to mean YHWH's response to human endeavour, seems to indicate that we are dealing with the construction of a city wall.

14. The *futurum instans* (הנני + *qotel*) is continued by a *w*^{e}*-qatal* so that this tense indicating a process that is about to happen or that is almost already happening should therefore be applied to the second predicate as well. See Bartelmus, *HYH*, pp. 73-79.

15. Statements containing *qatal* with emphasis on the completed action (see n. 12 above).

return of the people to Jerusalem under God's guidance is about to take place.[16]

Let me summarize. In the first place, it is striking that in all these instances, with the exception of Zech. 1.16,[17] when referring to YHWH's renewed taking up of his abode in Jerusalem, *absolutely no mention is made of the temple.* It is always the whole city of Jerusalem that is regarded as the place where God is about to or has already taken up his abode—or it is in the midst of the Daughter of Zion (and the many peoples) as a community of YHWH, in the midst of whom God will be present. Never is the temple itself mentioned as a unique place in which God is present.

In the second place, it is striking (when compared to Haggai) that in the passages under discussion no mention is made of any condition that would have to be fulfilled by humans (God's people) *before* the return of YHWH (and God's people) to Jerusalem. Therefore, this is a *return of God without any condition*, a return that is free of any precondition and thus is also free of the prerequisite of the building of the temple. In Haggai, the story is completely different. Haggai traces the bad harvest experienced by the people, in other words, the absence of the blessings of the land, directly back to the absence, or the not-yet-presence, of the wholesome presence of YHWH. This latter event, in turn, has not yet taken place because the temple, the place and visible sign of the presence of YHWH, has not yet been rebuilt. Instead, Haggai deplores the fact that the people are only concerned with the building of their own houses (Hag. 1.2, 3-11).

In the third place, Jerusalem, as YHWH'S dwelling in Zechariah 1–8, is in most instances connected with the future residence of his people after their return (see the reiteration of the covenant formula, in Zech. 2.15; 8.8, and the mention of the great number of people living in Jerusalem in 2.8; 8.4-5). Zechariah 1–8 is basically concerned with the return of YHWH *and* his people to Jerusalem and their living together there. The return of YHWH constitutes the turning point, and thus the beginning, of the process. The other two basic assertions of Zechariah 1–8 support this as a main point: the 'Neuordnung des Gottesvolkes', as Heinz-Günther Schöttler has formulated it in the subtitle to his study of Zechariah 1–6, *Gott inmitten seines Volkes.*[18]

16. *Futurum instans* with following w^{e}-*qatal* sequence, cf. n. 14 above.

17. For further information about 1.16, see below.

18. H.-G. Schöttler, *Gott inmitten seines Volkes: Die Neuordnung des*

The second major theme in Zechariah 1–8 concerns the *leadership of the community of YHWH in Jerusalem.* Visions four and five (Zech. 3.1–4.14) deal mainly with the new leadership of the YHWH community in Jerusalem/Judah. A point in the future is therefore examined, a time in which the events that have been announced in the first three visions have already taken place, that is, the return of the exiles has already been accomplished, or the process is already well under way. Two 'sons of oil', mostly interpreted as two anointed men, one with royal and the other with priestly background (Zech. 4),[19] have been placed in charge of the new YHWH community. Furthermore, before assuming office, the priest will have to undergo a cleansing ritual (3.1-5).

The visions dealing with Joshua and the seven-branched lampstand are interpreted not so much as an Israelite version of the (Akkadian) Babylonian *kalū* ritual; rather, they offer statements about the future positions of leadership within the community of YHWH in Jerusalem.

Gottesvolkes nach Sacharja 1–6 (TThSt, 43; Trier: Paulinus Verlag, 1987). In late exilic/early post-exilic times, the question of the nature and organization of the people of God is of great importance. The following studies deal with this point: J. Hausmann, *Israels Rest: Studien zum Selbstverständnis der nachexilischen Gemeinde* (BWANT, 124; Stuttgart: Kohlhammer, 1987), or H. Utzschneider, *Das Heiligtum und das Gesetz: Studien zur Bedeutung der sinaitischen Heiligtumstexte (Ex. 25–40; Lev. 8–9)* (OBO, 77; Göttingen: Vandenhoeck & Ruprecht, 1988).

19. This, however, is the usual critical interpretation (frequently used with reference to Joshua and Zerubbabel); for instance, cf. W. Nowack, *Die kleinen Propheten* (HK, III/4; Göttingen: Vandenhoeck & Ruprecht, 3rd edn, 1922), p. 358; E. Sellin, *Das Zwölfprophetenbuch* (KAT, XII; Leipzig: Scholl, 2nd/3rd edn, 1930), p. 506; F. Horst (T. Robinson–F. Horst), *Die zwölf kleinen Propheten* (HAT, I/14; Tübingen: Mohr, 3rd edn, 1964), p. 231; J.G. Baldwin, *Haggai, Zechariah, Malachi* (TOTC; Downers Grove, IL: Inter-Varsity, 1972), p. 124; W. Rudolph, *Haggai—Sacharja 1–8—Sacharja 9–14—Maleachi* (KAT, XIII/4; Gütersloh: Mohn, 1976), p. 108; R.A. Mason, *The Books of Haggai, Zechariah and Malachi* (CBC; Cambridge: Cambridge University Press, 1977), p. 48; K. Elliger, *Das Buch der zwölf kleinen Propheten*, II (ATD, 25; Göttingen: Vandenhoeck & Ruprecht, 8th edn, 1982), pp. 110-11; A. Deissler, *Zwölf Propheten*, III (Die Neue Echter Bibel; Würzburg: Echter Verlag, 1988), p. 281. In contrast to this view, see the following scholars who accept only the authorization of a dyarchical basis structure for post-exilic Judah: D.L. Petersen, *Haggai and Zechariah 1–8: A Commentary* (OTL; Philadelphia: Westminster Press, 1984), p. 234; C.L. Meyers and E.M. Meyers, *Haggai, Zechariah 1–8: A Translation with Introduction and Commentary* (AB, 25B; Garden City, NY: Doubleday, 1987), pp. 258-59.

Therefore, in these two visions we will find hardly any pronouncements about the temple (if at all, it will be a presupposition, except in 3.7 and 4.9). We are dealing here with delineations of public figures and their future functions in the life of a community.[20]

The third major theme of Zechariah 1–8 consists of the *main features of the rules of conduct that order daily life in the YHWH community in Jerusalem.* Visions six and seven (Zech. 5.1-11) deal, among other topics, with the internal nature of the re-established YHWH community in Jerusalem. Vision six emphasizes the fact that perjurers and thieves will be removed from this community. It is especially the nature of perjury and theft that burdens the relationships within the community and can thus jeopardize the harmonious coexistence of the members of the group. Vision seven even goes one step further when it describes how the land, is purged of sin, personified as a woman in an ephah which is expelled to the land of Shinar (5.5-11).[21]

The so-called 'Fastenrede' (Zech. 7–8) provides more concrete instructions on how to lead an ethical life and how to deal with each other within the YHWH community of Jerusalem. The oracles given in Zech. 7.9-10 and 8.16-17 demand fair judgment, mutual love, mercy and truth from the members of the community. Oppression of widows, orphans, strangers and the poor, the devising of evil plots against each other and perjury are forbidden. The instructions on how to lead an ethical life are very much in the prophetic (legal) tradition (for instance: Amos 5.24; Hos. 12.7; Isa. 1.17, 23; Jer. 7.5-6; 21.12; 22.3; cf. Exod. 22.21, 24 as well).

20. The thematic concern of Zech. 3 is the purification of the high priest Joshua; it is not the purification of the site of the old temple before the rebuilding of the temple. This latter would be in keeping with the (Akk.) Babylonian *kalū* ritual connected with the restoration of the temple. For the controversial authenticity of Zech. 3, see the following commentaries: Horst, *Die zwölf kleinen Propheten*, p. 210; Elliger, *Das Buch der zwölf kleinen Propheten*, p. 120; Deissler, *Zwölf Propheten*, p. 267, who argue that Zech. 3 was a later addition to the cycle of visions, while others, for instance Rudolph, *Haggai–Sacharja*, p. 94; Petersen, *Haggai and Zechariah 1–8*, p. 112; Meyers, *Haggai, Zechariah 1–8*, pp. lvi-lviii, 215, maintain that the vision belongs to the original Zechariah material. The Meyers, especially, emphasize the special position of Zech. 3 within the framework of the other visions ('7 + 1', p. lvii).

21. It is interesting that a בית will be built there for the ephah (Zech. 5.11). The ephah, into which all wickedness has been banned, will be set up in it.

The conclusions drawn from the examination of the passages in Zechariah are the following:

In his proclamations, Zechariah basically advocated a concept for the living community in Jerusalem, that is, a concept for a renewed YHWH community in Jerusalem. According to Zechariah 1–8, the return of YHWH to Jerusalem and the return of his people—including all those who wish to join YHWH (and his people)—belong together so that it will be possible to build up the YHWH community in Jerusalem. This community will function according to the ethical rules of conduct that have been instituted by YHWH. In short, the basic issue of Zechariah 1–8 concerns the renewed establishing of the relationship between YHWH and his people in Jerusalem.[22] In my opinion, Zechariah did not see the goal of this so-called restoration primarily in the reconstruction of the temple; for him, its purpose lay in the restoring, or the designing and organizing of a YHWH community in Jerusalem.

Consequently, the proclamation of Proto-Zechariah has a very different message at its center from that of his presumed contemporary Haggai who emphasized the need for the reconstruction of the temple (Hag. 1.2-11, 14; 2.1-9, 15-19). In contrast, Zechariah is much more concerned with 'concepts for a community'.[23] For him, as has already been pointed out, the building of the temple is not so much a basic issue (house as *building*: size of structure, cf. Haggai), but the 'building of the community' (house as *family*, *community*: sociomorpheme = socio-religious size). The few statements that deal with his understanding of the temple (Joshua vision, Zech. 3.1-10, and other passages as well) show a much greater concern for questions

22. The key-word 'covenant' is not used in Zech. 1–8, but through the two instances where the complementing parts of the covenant formula are used, precisely in those crucial passages in Zech. 1–8 that deal with YHWH's dwelling in Jerusalem (2.15; 8.8), it becomes evident that this is meant; see K. Baltzer, *Das Bundesformular* (WMANT, 4; Neukirchen: Neukirchener Verlag, 2nd edn, 1964 [1960]), pp. 69-70.

23. The use of the uniform term 'community', when seen in the context of the rather patchy social structure that came into being in Jerusalem at the beginning of the Persian period, is somewhat problematic and needs to be discussed and explained in an independent study. For these reasons, I have replaced the term in most cases with the compound noun 'YHWH community'. In this manner I have dealt with the fact that the expression YHWH community is the smallest common denominator all these various groups share.

pertaining to the leadership of a group, than with the problems related to the progress of the building of the temple.[24]

The Establishment of a YHWH Community in Jerusalem
ביתי יבנה בה

So far we have seen that, unlike Ezra 5.1-2 and 6.14 and Haggai, the main point of Zechariah 1–8 is not the—building of the—temple. The latter text is more or less concerned with the city of Jerusalem as such and with the dwelling of YHWH and his community there (forms of living together, leadership of the community, and related matters).

Nevertheless, there are (when compared with Haggai[25]) only a few texts in Zechariah 1–8 that contain the significant terms for 'house' and 'temple' (בית and היכל) in connection with the terms used for 'building' (בנה) and 'founding'/'completing' (בצע/יסד *pi.*). Before I discuss these passages in greater detail, I would like to offer a brief survey of the various possible meanings of the two most important terms: בית and בנה, especially since both words can also be found in Ezra 5.1-2 and 6.14 (Aram.).

בית is often used to refer to a building; in such cases it should be translated as 'house'. If this term is used in connection with the name of a god, it would be more appropriate to translate it as 'temple' or 'temple building'. On the other hand, the word בית can also be used as sociomorpheme; then it denotes 'community'/'group', 'family', 'household', 'kinship' or 'dynasty'. The house of Joseph, the house of Judah, the house of Israel, or the house of Ahab and the house of David[26] are all examples of this usage. These construct chains that are joined with a name in which the second meaning of בית is important are very interesting in still another respect: grammatically speaking, when בית is used in conjunction with the name of a god, we are dealing with the same linguistic phenomenon. In the case of 'the house

24. Visions 2 and 8 (2.1-4; 6.1-8) that have not been discussed so far in this paper deal with the effects that the end of the exile and the return of YHWH and his people to Jerusalem have on what is happening in the world (outside of Jerusalem and Judah). Neither vision mentions the temple and its construction at all.

25. I point here again to the fact that in Haggai the terms עיר, ירושלם, ציון are not used at all, whereas the words בית and היכל occur frequently.

26. See H.A. Hoffner, 'בית', *ThWAT*, I, pp. 629-38 (ET *TDOT*, I). Hoffner provides a great number of examples for this point.

David' we will hardly ever think of a palace that belonged to David—not to mention the fact that so far we have hardly concerned ourselves about which buildings could possibly be meant when we talk about the 'house of Judah' or 'the house of Israel'. Therefore, I would like to set myself the following task: when we translate and interpret the term בית יהוה we should not think automatically of a temple structure, but think as well of the (temple) community that it represents.[27] This means that the term בית יהוה should not in every context be interpreted immediately and exclusively to mean 'temple'. Instead, we should first of all examine whether or not the second meaning—the meaning denoting family, people or community of YHWH—is more appropriate. Especially with regard to the conclusions we have reached about the message contained in Zechariah 1–8, such a task could be useful, though we should also be aware that such a reading could be pushed too far. Tamara C. Eskenazi in her study of Ezra/Nehemiah, *In an Age of Prose: A Literary Approach to Ezra–Nehemiah*, has shown that the concept of the 'house of God' can be understood to be broader than the mere temple. It can include the whole city of Jerusalem as well.[28]

The word בנה in its original meaning signifies 'building', 'constructing', 'reconstructing' (of walls, buildings and similar structures). בנה is also often used in a figurative sense and signifies in such instances, among other things, the organization of a community, family, tribe or dynasty; especially when it is used in conjunction with the word בית. We find such a usage, for example, in Ruth 4.11 (in which instance it is said that Rachel and Leah have built the house of Israel) and in Deut. 25.9 (Levirate marriage).[29]

The use of these two terms is very striking in the prophecy of Nathan (2 Sam. 7, parallel in 1 Chron. 17). In these instances, the writers of the texts are on several occasions playing with the ambiguous meaning

27. Cf. the ambiguity and unclarity in our own usage of the word 'church': building, community, worship.

28. T.C. Eskenazi, *In an Age of Prose: A Literary Approach to Ezra–Nehemiah* (SBLMS, 36; Atlanta: Scholars Press, 1988), pp. 53ff. In my interpretation of Ezra 5.1-2; 6.14, I differ from the understanding proposed by Eskenazi who regards the construction of the whole city as an appropriate rendering of the 'building of the house of God'. See also D.L. Petersen, 'The Temple in Persian Period Prophetic Texts', *BTB* 21 (1991), pp. 90-91.

29. See S. Wagner, 'בנה', *ThWAT*, I, pp. 689-706. He lists a great number of references.

of the words. For instance, when David decides to build a house for God's abode, YHWH does not accept this offer and rebukes the king, saying that he himself, namely YHWH, will build a house for David, meaning a family, a dynasty (2 Sam. 7.11, 27, parallel in 1 Chron. 17.10, 25). It should be noted, however, that the term עשה is used in 2 Sam. 7.11, while in 1 Chron. 17.10 the word has been changed to בנה in approximation of the second text. In 2 Sam. 7.27, as well as in 1 Chron. 17.25, the word בנה is used throughout.[30] It is obvious that the meaning of the original narration shows that it is not the building of an actual temple that is preferred by YHWH; rather, it is the building of a community, that is, the building of a family or dynasty.

I will now examine more closely those passages in Zechariah 1–8 that contain these terms, or a corresponding linguistic combination, keeping in mind the basic issues of Zechariah 1–8 pertaining to the building of the YHWH community in Jerusalem, and keeping in mind all the ambiguities contained in the expression בנה בית. Then I will try to examine whether or not the second and figurative meaning does not offer a more appropriate interpretation.

1. 'Therefore, thus says YHWH, "I have returned to Jerusalem with compassion; my house shall be built in it", says YHWH Sabaoth' (Zech. 1.16a).

'House' in this context could be interpreted to mean 'temple' as well as 'community'. At this moment, neither meaning can be preferred over the other.

2. 'Thus says YHWH Sabaoth: "If you will walk in my ways and keep my charge, then you shall judge over my house and have charge over my courts, and I will give you the right of access among these who are standing here"' (Zech. 3.7).

Both meanings of ביתי work equally well, but it is difficult to use the verb דין (to judge) in connection with the temple as building. Most of the interpreters of this passage, in order to avoid this problem, have therefore added the preposition ב (reading thus בביתי) to make a judgment *in* the temple.[31] The translation, 'You will judge my community', however, grammatically speaking, fits into this passage much better than 'You will judge the temple', or, 'in the temple'; and it

30. This could indicate that language usage had undergone changes from exilic to post-exilic times; this point, however, has to be examined in the case of a number of significant passages.

31. See the discussion of Meyers and Meyers, *Haggai, Zechariah 1–8*, p. 195.

provides a meaningful reading as well, especially since the so-called Joshua vision (3.1-7) does not deal at all with the building of the temple as such, but with putting a person in a position of leadership. The courts, חצרים, a term often translated as outer courts of the temple—a debatable interpretation—could be taken to mean (as, for example, in Neh. 12.29) the open and unfortified settlements that surrounded Jerusalem, belonged to its sphere of influence and were consequently governed by the city. I propose, therefore, to translate the passage in Zechariah in the following manner: 'You will judge my community and be in charge of my farmsteads'. Furthermore, ביתי appears also in Num. 12.7 as part of a YHWH oracle. In that instance, the word should not be understood to indicate 'temple'. It is used as a synonym for terms that indicate social importance, as, for instance, עמי ('my people'). I propose to interpret the term ביתי in this passage, and perhaps in 1.16, as 'my community' ('my people').

3. 'The hands of Zerubbabel have laid the foundation of this *house*; his hands shall also complete it' (Zech. 4.9a).

4. 'Thus says YHWH Sabaoth: "Let your hands be strong when in these days you shall be hearing these words from the mouths of the prophets, on the day on which the *house* of YHWH Sabaoth was founded, that the *temple* might be built"' (Zech. 8.9).

Both passages deal with the founding of the house. The context of 4.6b-10a makes it more plausible to think of יסד as indicating the laying of the foundation-stone, rather than to see in the activity a ceremonious inauguration of the YHWH community in Jerusalem (corresponding, for instance, to the events in Nehemiah 8 or 9–10). The second passage, however, could be interpreted in the second manner, especially since mention is made in the immediate context 8.7-8 of the return of the people to Jerusalem, and since only there in the whole of Zechariah 1–8 are the words of the covenant formula fully quoted. But the use of the appositive היכל, which in no other place in Zechariah 1–8 is used together with בית, seems to make it more logical to translate the word here to indicate the laying of the foundation-stone. All this seems reasonable, provided the term היכל was originally used in this passage, for the subordinate clause does not really fit into the sentence. This lack of grammatical coherence has made the editors of the BHS speculate that this is a later gloss.[32]

32. Many commentators (among them Rudolph, *Haggai–Sacharja*, pp. 148-49) regard Zech. 8.9-13 to be an editorial addition because in the whole of Zech. 1–8 this

5. 'Thus says YHWH Sabaoth, "Behold, the man whose name is Branch: for wherever he stands, things will bud in this place, and he will build the *temple* of YHWH. It is he who will build the *temple* of YHWH... And the crown will be in the *temple* of YHWH as a reminder... And those who are far off will come and build at the *temple* of YHWH"' (Zech. 6.12, 13a, 14, 15a).

This passage in the present context referring to the high priest Joshua, speaks about היכל, a term that, in my opinion, is used in no other place in the Bible as sociomorpheme. The symbolic action that concludes the cycle of visions almost certainly points to the building of the temple. A close examination of the passage seems to indicate that 6.9-15 has been subjected to editorial revision; the original text probably contained instructions for the coronation of Zerubbabel. On the occasion of this future ceremonial and symbolic action, YHWH will promise that he will be the future ruler and the future builder of the temple (according to the royal duties that were traditional in the ancient Near East).

Zerubbabel did lay the foundation-stone and was promised that at some time in the future he would complete the building of the temple (Zech. 4.9; 6.12-13). Others (returning exiles?) would participate in the construction. Zechariah 1–8 does not add any further tangible information. Also, there is no mention made of an explicit demand that the people participate actively in the building of the temple.[33] Consequently, in Zechariah 1–8, the temple is of minor importance when compared with the main concern of the texts: the building of the community of YHWH and his people in Jerusalem.

Concerning the Understanding of Haggai and Zechariah in Ezra 5.1-2 and 6.14 as Complementary Concepts

The building of the outer and inner 'house' of YHWH was the task of the early post-exilic period. According to my thesis, it is possible to interpret the message contained in the books of Haggai and Zechariah

is the passage that is closest to Haggai (esp. 1.6, 9-11; 2.15-19).

33. Two points are especially striking in these texts: first, the contradictory statements of Zech. 4.9 and 6.12-13 pertaining to the person of the founder of the house, or, rather, the temple (Zerubbabel or Joshua); second, the different usage of these terms when mention is made of the house or the temple. Whereas Zech. 1.16; 3.7; 4.9 use the word בית (house, temple), Zech. 6.12-13, 15 uses היכל (palace, temple). Only Zech. 8.9 employs both terms together.

1–8 as complementing as well as completing each other. This can perhaps be best expressed through an image: their relationship to each other *can* be seen in the same way as that of the two sides of a coin. Haggai stressed the building of the temple, while Zechariah 1–8 is concerned with the building of the YHWH community in Jerusalem. The message of these prophets *was not necessarily* conceived as complementary. However, the traditional interpretation in Ezra has assigned them this relationship and, perhaps, has led to the understanding that both prophets were regarded as promoting the building of the house of God in Jerusalem.

In my opinion, the structure of the book of Ezra provides a good example for this solution to the problem. After the initial introductory remarks about the return of the exiles (Ezra 1–2), Ezra 3.1–6.22 proceeds to describe the building of the temple as well as related matters. This is followed in Ezra 7.1–10.44 (see also, Neh. 8.9-10) by a report about the important steps in the construction of the temple community (including the announcement of rules, some of which pertain to the life within the community: the so-called law of Ezra). This arrangement of events corresponds to the ordering of the book of Haggai (with its emphasis on the building of the temple as the outer house of YHWH) to precede Zechariah 1–8 (with its concern for the need to establish the YHWH community, the 'later' temple community, that is, the inner 'house' of YHWH), an editorial ordering that probably emerged later.[34] These two aspects of the building of the house of YHWH, according to Ezra (or the editors of the book of Ezra)[35] therefore belong together.

34. P.R. Ackroyd has pointed this out on several occasions—for example, 'The Books of Haggai and Zechariah I–VIII', *JJS* 3 (1952), pp. 151-56; *Exile and Restoration: A Study of Hebrew Thought of the Sixth Century BC* (OTL; London: SCM Press, 1968), pp. 154-55; 'Historical Problems of the Early Achaemenian Period', *Or* 20 (1984), pp. 12-14—repr. in: P.R. Ackroyd, *The Chronicler in his Age* (JSOTSup, 101; Sheffield: JSOT Press, 1991), pp. 152-54. For further discussion of the very obvious parallelism of the introductory dating formulas in Haggai and Zech. 1–8 (Hag. 1.1, 15; 2.1, 10, 20; Zech. 1.1, 7; 7.1), see also the careful discussion of W.A.M. Beuken, in which he traces the more or less Deuteronomistic and Chronistic revisions of Haggai and Zech. 1–8: *Haggai–Sacharja 1–8: Studien zur Überlieferungsgeschichte der frühnachexilischen Prophetie* (SSN, 10; Assen: Van Gorcum, 1967), pp. 10-20, 331-36.

35. For the tradition of textual revision, understood by Beuken to be Chronistic, that both Haggai and Zech. 1–8 have in common, see also n. 34 above.

The building of the temple does not serve as an end in itself, and consequently does not represent the goal of the efforts of the early post-exilic period in Jerusalem. Rather, it is a symbol and visible sign of the relatedness of God and God's people and their living together as a community in Jerusalem. Thus the temple will become the visible sign of the renewal of the Covenant, the relationship between YHWH and his people, but the actual ultimate goal is the renewed community itself, the community that exists between God and God's people and not the mere building of a temple. Therefore, the main goal is emphasized by Zechariah (the internal reason for the building of the temple), while the construction of the external and visible sign is demanded by Haggai to support this goal.

Passages like 2 Samuel 7 and the parallel passage in 1 Chronicles 17 serve to remind us of the ambiguity conveyed through the expression בנה בית 'to build a building' or a 'community', especially when used in texts dating from the post-exilic period.

Part II

COMMUNITY

THE PROVINCE OF YEHUD IN THE POST-EXILIC PERIOD: SOUNDINGS IN SITE DISTRIBUTION AND DEMOGRAPHY*

Charles E. Carter

The Persian period has been one of the most neglected eras in Syro-Palestinian archaeology. Biblical scholars and archaeologists alike—though perhaps for different reasons—devoted most of their energies to uncovering the textual and artifactual secrets of either the 'golden ages' of the monarchy and Israelite prophecy on the one hand and setting the stage for the emergence of nascent Judaism and Christianity on the other. Sandwiched in between these two 'more interesting' periods, the 'dark age' of the post-exilic period seemed of little consequence.

In the last decade or two, however, scholars have begun to pay more attention to the period, spawning a number of significant studies (see introduction). But if interest in the Persian period has increased, so has an awareness of the difficulties inherent in reconstructing it, for both text and tell stubbornly yield their secrets. Numerous questions continue to be discussed. What were the boundaries of the post-exilic province of Judah (Yehud in the epigraphic witness)? When was Yehud granted autonomy? What socio-economic conditions prevailed

* Versions of this paper have been read at the W.F. Albright Institute for Archaeological Research in Jerusalem, and the Sociology of the Second Temple at the annual AAR/SBL/ASOR meetings in New Orleans (1990) and Kansas City (1991). A full treatment of the issues raised here may be found in my dissertation, 'A Social and Demographic Study of Post-Exilic Judah' (PhD dissertation, Duke University, 1991). I am particularly indebted to A. Ofer ('The Judean Mountains during the Biblical Period', forthcoming) and I. Finkelstein, N. Feig, A. Feldstein and Y. Kameisky (see I. Magen and I. Finkelstein [eds.], *Archaeological Survey in the Hill Country of Benjamin*, forthcoming) for granting me permission to use data from their latest surveys of Judah and Benjamin respectively, without which I would not have been able to project the site distribution and population of the province of Yehud. I would also like to thank my wife, Elyse M. Carter for creating figures 1, 2 and 4; figure 3 was generated by Byron Bumpass of Technology and Training Services, Durham, NC. Finally, Kenneth Hoglund and Avi Ofer read previous drafts of this article and offered several helpful comments, for which I am grateful.

in the province? In Syria-Palestine? How important was the province to the empire? How many sites were settled during the period, and how many people lived in Yehud?

This article addresses a number of these questions—in particular, those concerning the size of the province; the number, size and distribution of the sites within it; its population; and its significance—from the perspective of 'contextual' or 'social' archaeology. These approaches represent the shift in focus that has emerged as a result of the new archaeology, and seek to combine a close, critical reading of biblical traditions with a socio-economic analysis of the archaeological record.[1] Although I am indebted to those scholars and studies that preceded my own work, I frequently arrive at different conclusions because of advances in methodology or new sources of data. So, for example, based on the discipline of historical geography and a sensitivity to the natural features of Palestine, I suggest that the core of the province of Yehud was located in the central hills; thus, my proposal excludes the Shephelah and coastal plain.[2] How many people lived in Yehud? Previous population estimates have ranged from Albright's 20,000 for the late sixth century[3] to the 200,000 of Weinberg.[4] Although Albright's figures were influenced by his intimate knowledge

1. On contextual archaeology, see W.G. Dever, 'Biblical Archaeology: Death or Rebirth?', paper presented at the Second International Congress on Biblical Archaeology, Jerusalem, July 1990; on social archaeology, see C.L. Meyers and E.M. Meyers, 'Expanding the Frontiers of Biblical Archaeology', *Eretz Israel* 20 (1989), pp. 140*-47.* For a discussion of the 'new archaeology', see W.G. Dever, 'The Impact of the "New Archaeology" on Syro-Palestinian Archaeology', *BASOR* 242 (1981), pp. 15-29.

2. Although W.F. Albright (*The Biblical Period from Abraham to Ezra* [New York: Harper & Row], p. 87) suggested that the province extended along the 'watershed road' from Jerusalem to Beth Zur, it is not clear what the exact boundaries of the province were in his view. Avi-Yonah (*The Holy Land* [Grand Rapids, MI: Baker Books], pp. 20ff.) also excludes the coastal plain and Shephelah, but on a textual basis alone.

3. *The Biblical Period*, p. 87.

4. See, 'Demographische Notizen zur Geschichte der nachexilischen Gemeinde in Juda', *Klio* 54 (1972), pp. 45-59, as cited by J. Blenkinsopp, 'Temple and Society in Achaemenid Judah', in P.R. Davies (ed.), *Second Temple Studies*. I. *Persian Period* (Sheffield: JSOT Press, 1991), pp. 40-44. In discussing the range of population figures, Blenkinsopp considers that the population of the province was between Albright's and Weinberg's extremes, and 'closer to Albright than to Weinberg'. See 'Temple and Society', p. 43 n. 3.

of the archaeological setting of Palestine in the sixth and fifth centuries, they still treat the biblical data relatively uncritically;[5] Weinberg's are extrapolated from the Deuteronomic History and lists in Ezra–Nehemiah; and Weinberg's figures are, in essence, more intuitive than scientific.

My own population projections benefit from advances in methodology for population estimates as well as the most up-to-date surveys of both Benjamin and the Judaean Hills.[6] Based on these sources of data, I suggest that the population of Yehud ranged from a low of 11,000 in the late-sixth/early-fifth centuries BCE to a high of 17,000 in the late-fifth/early-fourth centuries BCE. Thus, according to my estimates, the province of Yehud was both relatively small and relatively poor for much of the Persian period. This accords with the general picture one gains from the biblical texts that date directly to the Persian period (in particular, Haggai and Nehemiah),[7] but raises some important questions concerning social setting of Yehud, the significance of such a small province to the Persian empire, and the ability of a small, poor province to sustain the literary activity traditionally attributed to it. I address these questions regarding the implications of my research briefly at the end of this article.

Biblical and Archaeological Problems

Before we can speak about site distribution and the population of the province of Yehud we must determine its borders. Recent events in Eastern Europe and the former Soviet Union remind us that national and provincial boundaries can change rapidly and dramatically as

5. For example, Albright viewed the figures in Ezra 2 and Neh. 7 as reflecting the population of Yehud in the mid-fifth century. According to his views, between 10 and 15 thousand people lived in and around Jerusalem at that time. See *The Biblical Period*, p. 93.

6. As noted in n. 1 above. One should remember that Albright's estimates were published before Kochavi's survey of 1967 (*Judea, Samaria, and the Golan: Archaeological Survey 1967–1968* [Jerusalem: The Archaeological Survey of Israel, 1972]) was undertaken.

7. These estimates also seem quite reasonable in light of the most recent projections for the population of Palestine in the Iron II period. According to Broshi and Finkelstein, the population of Judaea excluding the Shephelah and coastal plain was approximately 60,000 (7500 in Jerusalem; 22,500 from Jerusalem to Ramallah; 30,000 in the Judaean Hills). See M. Broshi and I. Finkelstein, 'The Population of Palestine in Iron Age II', *BASOR* 287 (1992), pp. 51-52.

imperial power ebbs and flows. So it was in Syria-Palestine in the eighth through sixth centuries BCE; those years witnessed the waxing and waning of Assyrian hegemony, the destruction of the Southern Kingdom at the hands of the Babylonians, and the rapid rise of the Persian empire. What had once been an autonomous kingdom, Judah, was reduced to a small piece of a world-class empire; many of its leading citizens were led away to Babylon while others fled to Egypt. But, after the Persian conquest of Babylon, and thanks to the largesse of the Persian king, exiles from many national or ethnic backgrounds were allowed to return to their respective homelands. So it was that Judah, now known as Yehud, was re-established, though only as a province, subject to an imperial governor. Still, certain problems face any attempt to reconstruct life in Yehud from a textual or archaeological perspective. For the texts had particular, often tendentious, agendas of their own (which may differ from those of the modern interpreter), and the archaeological artifacts are subject to competing interpretations.

The Biblical Agenda—Ezra and Nehemiah as Propaganda

Biblical scholars and archaeologists have traditionally turned to five lists from Ezra and Nehemiah in their attempts to determine the boundaries of the province: the lists of returnees in Ezra 2 and Nehemiah 7; the list of 'districts' and 'sub-districts' of the province that sent delegations to work on the walls of Jerusalem (Neh. 3); the list of cultic officials who settled in Jerusalem (Neh. 11); and the list of singers (Neh. 12).

Ezra 2.1-67 and Nehemiah 7.4-69

Ezra 2 and Nehemiah 7 contain slightly different versions of a list of returnees from the exile, of the towns and villages to which they are related, of temple functionaries, slaves and animals.[8] Even though lively debate has surrounded the function, date and provenance of the lists,[9] they, perhaps more than the other lists, have been the basis of

8. For a discussion of the theories concerning the relationship of the lists from Ezra 2 and Neh. 7 see H.G.M. Williamson, *Ezra, Nehemiah* (WBC, 16; Waco, TX: Word, 1988) and J. Blenkinsopp, *Ezra–Nehemiah* (OTL; Philadelphia: Fortress Press, 1988).

9. See G. Hölscher, 'Die Bücher Esra und Nehemia', in E. Kautzch (ed.), *Die Heilige Schrift des Alten Testaments*, II (Tübingen: Mohr, 4th edn, 1923); K. Galling, 'The "Gola-List" according to Ezra 2//Nehemiah 7', *JBL* (1951),

scholarly discussion of the borders of the province. The differences between the two lists are relatively minor, generally reflecting differences in spelling, order of villages, or population. Many of these sites are located close to Jerusalem, and more are within the boundaries of the tribal territory of Benjamin than within those of Judah.[10] Many familiar biblical sites are listed, each with the number of returnees that populate it; and Persian period remains have been discovered at a number of these sites through excavations or surface surveys. The total population of these villages is 7273 according to Ezra, and 7430 according to Nehemiah.

Nehemiah 3

This text from Nehemiah lists the villages that supplied the workers for rebuilding the walls of Jerusalem and includes some settlements not found in the roster of Ezra 2//Nehemiah 7 (Neh. 3.1-32). It is often used to delineate the districts and/or sub-districts of Yehud, with their rulers: Mizpah, Jerusalem, Beth-Haccerem, Beth-Zur and Keilah. Avi-Yonah suggests that when two cites are mentioned in connection with a district in Nehemiah 3, the second city 'represents the administrative center of the other half'.[11] According to this reading at least three of these districts were further divided into two 'sub-districts' (Jerusalem, vv. 9 and 12; Beth-Zur, v. 16; Keilah, v. 17) Jericho and the lands surrounding it, though not mentioned in Nehemiah 3, are typically added as a separate district.[12]

pp. 149-58; A. Alt, 'Die Rolle Samarias bei der Entstehung des Judentums', in *Festschrift Otto Procksch zum 60. Geburtstag* (Leipzig: J.C. Hinrichs, 1934); C. Shultz, 'The Political Tensions Reflected in Ezra–Nehemiah', in W.W. Hallo *et al.* (eds.), *Scripture in Context: Essays on the Comparative Method* (Pittsburg: Pickwick Press, 1980), pp. 221-44; and J.W. Betlyon, 'The Provincial Government of Persian Period Judea and the Yehud Coins', *JBL* 105 (1986), pp. 633-42.

10. See the discussion in Blenkinsopp's *Ezra–Nehemiah*, pp. 86-87.

11. *The Holy Land*, p. 20.

12. See E. Stern, *Material Culture of the Land of the Bible in the Persian Period* (Warminster, England: Aris & Philips, 1982), pp. 247-49. Aharoni, *The Land of the Bible* (London: Burns & Oates, 2nd rev. edn, 1979), pp. 411-19, agrees with the common position that the Persian officials did not alter the administrative structure of Palestine that they took over from the Babylonians and Assyrians; he divides Yehud into five districts with nine sub-districts. See also Kallai, *The Northern Boundaries of Judah*, pp. 82-94 (as cited by Stern, *Material Culture*, p. 249).

The Idealized Portrait of Yehud—Nehemiah 11.25-36

The list of cities in Neh. 11.25-36 includes many locales that were almost certainly outside the jurisdiction of the province, such as Beersheba, Lachish and Kiryat-Arba. It, more than those discussed above, represents an idealized portrait of Yehud, one that conforms more to Judaea during the late monarchy than to the reconstituted community of the post-exilic period.[13] Villages or geographic areas that are first mentioned in this list are from the Judaean Shephelah, the coastal plain, and the Negev.

If these biblical lists are used to draw a composite portrait of Yehud's borders, they would indicate a rather large province, extending from Kadesh-Barnea in the south to (Baal-)Hazor in the northeast and Lod, Hadid and Ono in the northwest coastal plain. Most scholars place the eastern border at the Dead Sea and Jordan River. The province would have extended westward into the Shephelah, thus including sites such as Gezer and Lachish. But should these lists be taken uncritically? Were they intended as boundary lists, or even as inventories of cities within the newly established province? In answering this question, it is important to note the character of each of the books containing these lists. Ezra is concerned largely with his attempts to re-institute the Mosaic Torah as the law of the land—a mission underwritten by the Persian empire—and his fight against intermarriage. Nehemiah gives an often self-serving account of his governorship, the fortification of Jerusalem, and the redressing of social oppression. Thus, the intent of the biblical writers, in so far as it can be recovered, was not to delineate the boundaries of the province of Yehud; this stands in direct contrast with the lists of tribal territories and their cities from the books of Joshua and Judges.[14] Rather, the lists in Ezra and Nehemiah function either as indicators of the sites to which Jews had returned in the years after Cyrus' decree

13. See Stern, 'The Province of Yehud in Vision and Reality', in L. Levine (ed.), *The Jerusalem Cathedra: Studies in the History, Archaeology, Geography, and Ethnography of the Land of Israel*, I (Jerusalem: Yad Izhak Ben-Zvi Institute, 1981), pp. 9-21; and J. Blenkinsopp, 'Temple and Society in Achaemenid Judah', in P.R. Davies (ed.), *Second Temple Studies*. I. *Persian Period* (Sheffield: JSOT Press, 1991), p. 44.

14. See the discussion on this point in Blenkinsopp, 'Temple and Society', pp. 44ff.

or sites in which returning exiles had ancestral connections, whether or not they were within the borders of the province.[15]

The Archaeological Data

Analysing the borders of Yehud from an archaeological perspective is no less difficult, for there is no consensus as to what types of data are appropriate. Three types of remains have often been used (usually coupled with the biblical lists) as the basis for reconstructing the province's borders: seal impressions, coins and fortresses. Stern has suggested that any site at which seals or coins have been discovered that bear the impression *yhd*, *yhwd*, *yhd*-plus-symbol or *yršlm* should be considered Judaean.[16] In addition, he interprets a series of fortresses dating to the Persian period as boundary fortifications. In his reconstruction, a line of fortresses extending from Beth-Zur[17] to Kh. ez-Zawiyye and Kh. el-Qaṭṭ marks the southern border of the province and a similar line of fortresses in the Shephelah (including Yarmuth, Azekah and Adullam) delimits its southwestern boundary. Apparently supporting Stern's line of reasoning is the fact that coins or seal impressions that Stern dates to the Persian period have been discovered at two of these sites: a Yehud coin was excavated at Beth-Zur and a *yršlm* seal impression was unearthed at Azekah.

This combination of fortresses and coins and/or seal impressions has its problems. The first problem concerns the location of fortresses. Recently, a line of fortresses dating to the mid-fifth century was excavated in the Negev Highlands, south of Arad and Beersheva. Their excavator, R. Cohen—following the logic of Stern's work—suggested that they may have been 'strongholds along the southern border of the province of Judah'.[18] But these sites are well beyond the limits of even

15. See A. Rainey, 'The Biblical Shephelah of Judah', *BASOR* 251 (1983), p. 18.

16. *Material Culture*, pp. 245-49, and 'The Persian Empire and the Political and Social History of Palestine in the Persian Period', in W.D. Davies and L. Finkelstein (eds.), *The Cambridge History of Judaism*. I. *Introduction*: *The Persian Period* (Cambridge: Cambridge University Press, 1984), pp. 82-86.

17. Here, Stern follows Albright's questionable identification of a fortress at this site as Persian; the architectural remains from this site more likely date to the Ptolemaic period. See the discussion of R.W. Funk, 'The History of Beth-Zur with Reference to its Defenses', in *The 1957 Excavation at Beth-Zur*, pp. 4-17.

18. See R. Cohen, 'Solomon's Negev Defense Line Contained Three Fewer

the most maximalist reconstructions of the province,[19] and show that the existence of a fortress in a strategic area does not necessarily imply that it was intended to defend provincial boundaries. Kenneth Hoglund has recently drawn attention to other weaknesses in Stern's position, at least for the fortresses in the southern central hill country, noting that

> The fortress (Kh. ez-Zawiyye) is located on the northern side of the ridge it sits on, and faces to the north toward Yehud. Any Edomite force that might come upon the fortress would command the higher elevation to the south and could easily overwhelm what forces may have been deployed in the fortress.[20]

Hoglund suggests that, rather than indicating borders, the fortresses represent an imperial concern to protect trade routes and communication lines necessary to maintain control of the empire.

Can the interpretation that coins and seal impressions may be used as markers of the boundaries of the province be more easily defended? Two types of issues must be addressed in answering this question: (1) the appropriate dating and, (2) the location of the impressions. On both counts, Stern's analysis is lacking. As noted, Stern assigns a Persian period date to any site at which *yhd*, *yhwd*, *yhd*-plus-symbol, or *yršlm* impressions or coins were found. But only *yhd* and *yhwd* seals are in fact clearly Persian; the latter two are better dated to the first part of the Hellenistic period, as Paul Lapp had suggested in 1963 and as the excavations at the City of David have confirmed.[21] Further, Cohen's excavations in the Negev demonstrate the problems involved in using seal impressions to determine boundaries. During his excavations, a *yhd* seal was discovered at Kadesh-Barnea; rather than extend Yehud's borders to include that site, Cohen suggests that the impression indicates that 'large numbers of Jews lived south of Judah', outside the province of Yehud.

Fortresses', *BAR* 12 (1986), pp. 40-45.

19. Cohen also suggests that the fortresses were under Arabian, rather than Jewish control ('Solomon's Negev Defense Line').

20. *Achaemenid Imperial Administration*, pp. 202-203.

21. See P. Lapp, 'Ptolemaic Stamped Handles from Judah', *BASOR* 172 (1963), pp. 22-35. On the impressions from the City of David excavations, see the discussion of Jerusalem below.

Historical Geography and Yehud

Since neither textual data nor the type of archaeological data (seal impressions, coins and fortresses) that have been used in previous attempts provide any conclusive reconstruction, I suggest a solution to the problem of the boundaries of the province based on historical and geographic considerations.[22] A number of studies, from the classic treatments of G.A. Smith to the recent works of D. Hopkins, C. Meyers and I. Finkelstein,[23] indicate that the natural geographical divisions of Palestine often formed the basis of distinct geopolitical entities. The limits on political influence were often determined in part by the power of a central government to overcome these natural boundaries. That this control is often fragile is seen in the ease with which the Israelite monarchy divided after the death of Solomon.

With this in mind, from a geographic standpoint alone, I would question any reconstruction of the province of Yehud that includes sites in the Shephelah (Gezer, Azekah, Ain Shems), or the Coastal Plain (Lod, Hadid, Ono). Why exclude the Shephelah? The Shephelah forms a natural buffer between the coastal plain and the central hill country of Judah. Its fertility led to protracted conflicts over its control and it was incorporated into Israel only during the reign of David. Though controlled by the united monarchy, and subsequently by Judah, it remained a self-contained geographic entity, as Rainey has demonstrated.[24]

One result of the Babylonian conquest in 587 may have been a return to more natural geographic borders, borders that had been expanded as the monarchy's geopolitical influence had grown. Such contraction of borders in times of military crisis is well attested, as is the difficulty of controlling territories located at a significant distance

22. This approach was suggested to me by K. Hoglund; the reconstruction that follows is my own.

23. See G.A. Smith, *The Historical Geography of the Holy Land* (London: Hodder & Stoughton, 25th edn, 1931); C.L. Meyers, 'Of Seasons and Soldiers: A Topological Appraisal of the Pre-Monarchic Tribes of Galilee', *BASOR* 252 (1983), pp. 47-59; D. Hopkins, *The Highlands of Canaan: Agricultural Life in the Early Iron Age* (Decatur, GA: Almond Press, 1985); and I. Finkelstein, *The Archaeology of the Israelite Settlement* (Jerusalem: Israel Exploration Society, 1988).

24. See A. Rainey, 'The Biblical Shephelah of Judah', p. 6.

from the ruling entity's heartland.[25] Given this difficulty, empires have generally tended to divide their provinces into geographically self-contained units.[26] On this basis, I would argue that the Shephelah, contiguous to but geographically distinct from the central hill country, would have formed a separate district from Yehud.

Two lines of independent witnesses, one textual and the other an interpretative model from anthropology, support this conclusion. I have suggested that the biblical texts from Ezra and Nehemiah that pertain to the returning exiles are concerned primarily with the extent of Jewish settlement in Palestine rather than the extent of the province itself. This interpretation is borne out in the account of the invitation extended to Nehemiah to meet the delegation from Samaria in the Vale of Ono. According to M. Avi-Yonah, in order for Ono to have been a plausible meeting place for these two parties it must have been neutral territory, outside the jurisdiction of the provinces of both Yehud and Samaria.[27] Further, the plots of Sanballat, Tobiah, and their co-conspirators to interrupt the work of fortifying the walls of Jerusalem, were made known by 'some of the Jews who lived near them', indicating that Jews whose loyalties lay with the province of Yehud and its leaders lived outside the province itself (cf. Neh. 4.7-15).

Another textual support for this conclusion comes from the funerary inscription of the Sidonian king, Eshmun'ezer II.[28] Eshmun'ezer, who reigned in the mid-fifth century BCE, claims to have received from the Persian overlords

25. See R. Collins, 'Some Principles of Long-Term Social Change: The Territorial Power of States', in L. Kriesberg (ed.), *Research in Social Movements, Conflicts, and Change*, I (Greenwich, CT: JAI Press, 1978); and 'Does Modern Technology Change the Rules of Geopolitics?', *Journal of Political and Military Sociology* 9 (1981), pp. 163-77.

26. See K. Hoglund, *Achaemenid Imperial Administration,* in particular, 'The Archaeology of the Imperial Response', pp. 165ff.

27. *The Holy Land*, pp. 13ff.

28. Inscription 3, *Corpus Inscriptionum Semiticarum, Pars Prima: Inscriptiones Phoenicias Continens*, I (Paris: Academia Inscriptionum et Litterarum Humaniorum, 1881), pp. 9-20. I am grateful to Professor Anson Rainey for referring me to this inscription.

> Dor and Joppa, the mighty lands of Dagon, which are in the Plain of Sharon, in accordance with the important deeds which I did. And we added them to the borders of the country, so that they would belong to Sidon forever.[29]

Anson Rainey[30] argued that the mention of these lands shows that the entire northern coastal plain (the plain of Sharon) was under Sidonian control and was therefore outside of the control of the province of Yehud. This, too, would exclude sites like Lod, Hadid and Ono from the province; and it would suggest that the Persians saw coastal plain and hill country as separate entities.[31]

The central place theory, used by anthropologists in discussions of hierarchies in site distribution, also supports this reconstruction.[32] It holds that relationships between and among sites may be represented by a series of hexagons, with influence from large, central sites radiating outward, incorporating intermediate and smaller-sized sites. This model, applied first to Germany, was revised as it was applied to ancient Mesopotamia. There, it was discovered that a rhomboid pattern depicted these interrelationships more accurately than the hexagon. Hoglund has recently applied the model to Palestine, noting that due to the different geological and environmental setting of Palestine, circles and ellipses may be better suited to depict these relationships.[33] Drawing circles with a radius of approximately twenty kilometers from Jerusalem, Lachish, and Gezer, all of which show evidence of functioning as regional centers ('central places') in the

29. Translation of F. Rozenthal in *ANET*, p. 662.

30. Personal communication. See also his discussion in 'Tel Gerisah and the Inheritance of the Danite Tribe', *Annual of the Eretz Israel Museum,* 23-24 (1987–89), pp. 59-72.

31. One may suggest that a funerary inscription is not a legitimate historical source, given the tendencies of ancient Near Eastern rulers for exaggeration and political propaganda. But the sources of Ezra and Nehemiah are no less tendentious. See, for example, the frequent petition from Nehemiah that YHWH 'look upon me for good' on account of his deeds (Neh. 5.19; 13.14, 6, 31).

32. See C. Redman, *The Rise of Civilization from Early Farmers to Urban Society in the Ancient Near East* (San Francisco: W.H. Freeman, 1978), pp. 240ff.; and Carter, 'A Social and Demographic Study', pp. 68-71.

33. See 'The Establishment of a Rural Economy in the Judean Hill Country During the Late Sixth Century', presented at the Southeastern Regional Meeting of AAR/SBL/ASOR, March 1989. Figures 1A and B are adapted from Hoglund's presentation.

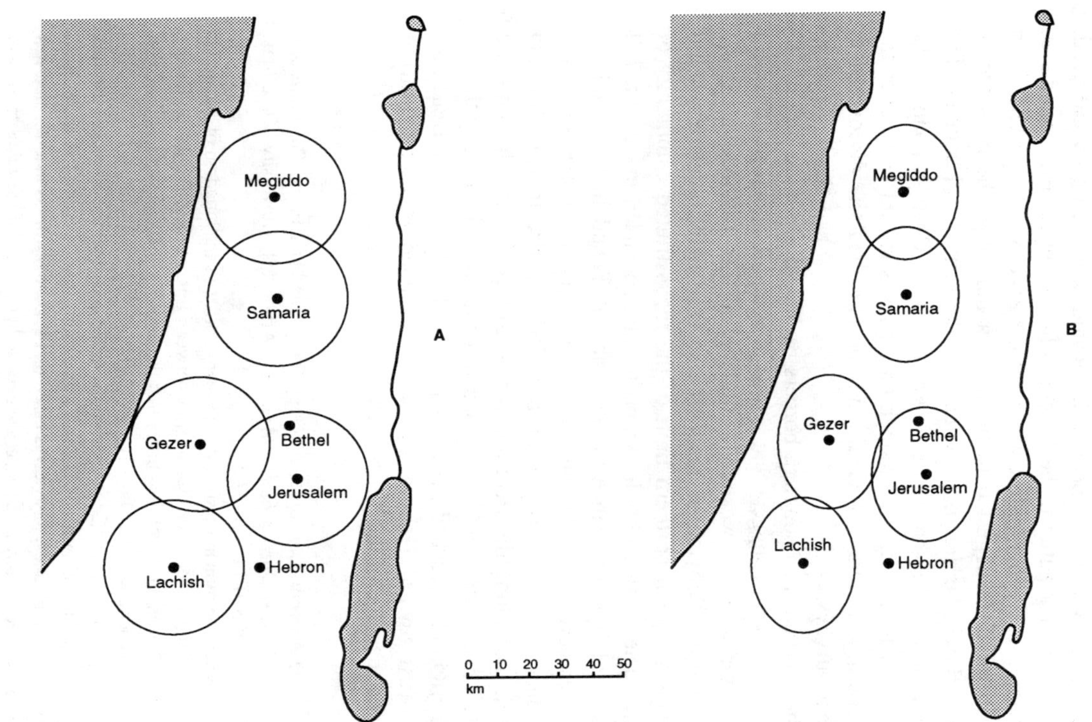

Figure 1. *The Central Place Theory Applied to Palestine. A. The Idealized Model B. The Model Adjusted for Palestine's Topography*

Persian period, the spheres of influence of these cities intersect at about the border of Shephelah and Hill Country (Figure 1A). This division is even more clearly delineated when ellipses are used. Plotting such a pattern, the border follows the natural boundaries between these geographic entities almost exactly (Figure 1B). With this in mind, I suggest that the western border of the province of Yehud should be drawn at the edge of the central hill country. The eastern border may have extended as far as the Dead Sea and, to the North, the Jordan River, although only three sites existed east of the hill country: Jericho, En Gedi, and one unnamed site discovered in surface surveys.

The northern and southern borders of Yehud are more difficult to establish. I would suggest that just as geographic considerations help one determine the western boundary of the province after the Assyrian and Babylonian conquests, so the tribal boundaries would provide a logical northern limit of the reconstituted community of Yehud. The northern border seems to have extended toward the hill country of Ephraim, since the province of Yehud incorporated the tribal territories of Judah and Benjamin. Benjamin's northern tribal boundary evidently ran just north of Jericho, Michmas, et-Tell and Bethel, then along the Beth-horon pass toward Gezer[34] though these borders had shifted during the divided monarchy.[35] It is likely that the southern border reached from En-Gedi, on the shore of the Dead Sea, northwest toward Hebron and then continued westward until it reached the edge of the hill country.[36]

34. See Aharoni, *Land of the Bible*, pp. 251-56 and D. Dorsey, *The Roads and Highways of Israel During the Iron Age* (Ann Arbor, MI: University Microfilms, 1981), pp. 269; 310-11; 336-37.

35. When the monarchy split, the northern border of the kingdom of Judah fell just south of the ancient tribal boundaries between Ephraim and Benjamin. During the reign of Josiah, however, it is likely that the territory of Judah went well beyond Bethel and Upper and Lower Beth Horon.

36. Here I am consciously departing from the conventional view that the area south of Beth-Zur and north of Hebron was under Edomite control in the Persian period. As Hoglund notes, this view is based on the textual witness that this area was under Edomite hegemony in the Maccabean period (1 Macc. 4–5) and thus must have been controlled by them in the earlier period. No archaeological or textual evidence places the Edomites here in the Persian period. Rather, the closest attested Edomite presence to Hebron in the Persian period is from Horvat Qitmit, which is located in the eastern Negev. The excavator, Itzhaq Beit-Arieh, dates the site, which he

Accordingly, the boundaries of Yehud in the late fifth–early fourth centuries BCE extended from approximately coordinates 1920/1422 at Jericho in the northeast, northwest to 1483/1733 at Bethel, then to coordinates 1580/1450 at Beit Ur et-Tahta. The southern border extended from 1872/0963 at Tell Goren, northwest toward Hebron (although the site was not occupied during the Persian period)[37] and continued westward to the border between the hill country and the Shephelah. The area of the province was approximately 1700 square kilometers (620 square miles), slightly smaller than one-half the area of the state of Rhode Island.

The location of the province in the central hill country of Palestine reveals something about the ecological setting of the province and its essential subsistence strategies. But since the central hills are not themselves homogeneous, I have divided Yehud into sub-areas, which I designate as environmental niches on the basis of a wide variety of criteria including climate, rainfall patterns, soil types and elevation.[38] In this reconstruction, the province contained four major environmental niches, three of which may in turn be sub-divided. At

identifies as cultic in nature, to the late seventh or early sixth centuries BCE, continuing into the Neo-Babylonian and Persian periods; see 'New Light on the Edomites', *BAR* 14 (1988), pp. 28-41. The archaeological data do not demand an Edomite presence in the hill country in the early Persian period, nor do the geographic data. The geographical division between the central hill country and the Negev falls approximately 8–10 km south of Hebron, at which point the average rainfall drops below 300 mm annually, the amount necessary to support traditional agrarian subsistence strategies. See Hoglund, 'Rural Economy', pp. 7-8.

37. See A. Ofer, 'The Judean Hill Country. From Nomadism to National Monarchy', in I. Finkelstein (ed.), *From Nomadism to Monarchy: Archaeological and Historical Aspects of Early Israel* (Jerusalem: Yad Izhak Ben-Zvi and The Israel Exploration Society, 1990), pp. 203-204. Ofer, who has conducted excavations at Hebron, considers it 'doubtful' that it was occupied in the Persian period.

38. This strategy follows the lead of Israel Finkelstein and Avi Ofer in their respective surveys of Ephraim, Benjamin and Judah. In the survey of Benjamin five distinct topographical areas were identified: foothills (outside the borders of Yehud), slopes, central hills, desert fringe and desert. The survey of Judah was divided into ten areas: the southern shephelah, the Negev hills, the southwestern Judaean desert, the 'southern springs', the mountain heights, the southern desert fringe, the Arkub triangle, the northern central hills, the northern desert fringe, and the Jerusalem hills. See I. Magen and I. Finkelstein, *Archaeological Survey of the Land of Benjamin* (forthcoming), and A. Ofer, *The Judean Mountains during the Biblical Period* (forthcoming), for a complete discussion of the nature of their zones.

the western edge of Yehud are the slopes that mark the transition from the central spur of Palestine towards the Shephelah and coastal plain. Next is the central spur or Judaean hills, followed by the desert fringe, which then leads toward the Judaean desert. All but the Judaean desert may be subdivided as follows: EN1. Northwestern Hills; EN2. North Central Hills; EN3. Northern Desert Fringe; EN4. Southwestern Hills; EN5. Central Hills; EN6. Southern Desert Fringe; EN7. Southern Central Hills; and EN8. Judaean Desert (Figure 2).[39]

Site Distribution and Population Estimates

The biblical lists of returnees in Ezra 2//Nehemiah 7, though composites and almost certainly telescoped, provide us with a rather high number of returnees, approximately 50,000. Archaeological data from excavations and surface surveys suggest a very different reconstruction. But before discussing population and site distribution, we must address a more basic question: How should the period from 586–332 be designated, and how, if at all, should it be divided? On the basis of historical, material cultural and textual evidence, I divide these years into three periods: 587/86 to 539/38 (Neo-Babylonian or Iron IIC); 539/38 to c. 450 (Persian I); and 450 to 332 (Persian II).[40]

From a historical standpoint, it is clear that Babylonian control of Judah had ceased by 539 with the rise of the Persian empire; Persian control ended in 332 with the conquest of Alexander the Great. Thus the beginning and ending of the Persian period is easily established. The material cultural evidence points to a period of transition in the sixth century, when many typical Iron II forms continued in use but showed a clear decline in quality. Thus, although the destruction in Judah at the hands of the Babylonians from 598–587/6 was extensive, it did not lead to an immediate change in material culture, a fact

39. These environmental niches are not to be associated with the districts and sub-districts of the province as outlined by Stern, Avi-Yonah and others. I have adopted the suggestion of A. Demsky that the Hebrew word פלך, traditionally translated 'district' is actually derived from Akkadian *pilku*, 'work detail'. See Demsky, '*Pelekh* in Nehemiah 3', *IEJ* 33 (1983), pp. 242-44. For a more complete discussion of Demsky's article, including some of the problems this interpretation raises, see my dissertation, 'A Social and Demographic Study', pp. 75-76.

40. For a detailed discussion of these problems see Carter, 'A Social and Demographic Study', pp. 93-96.

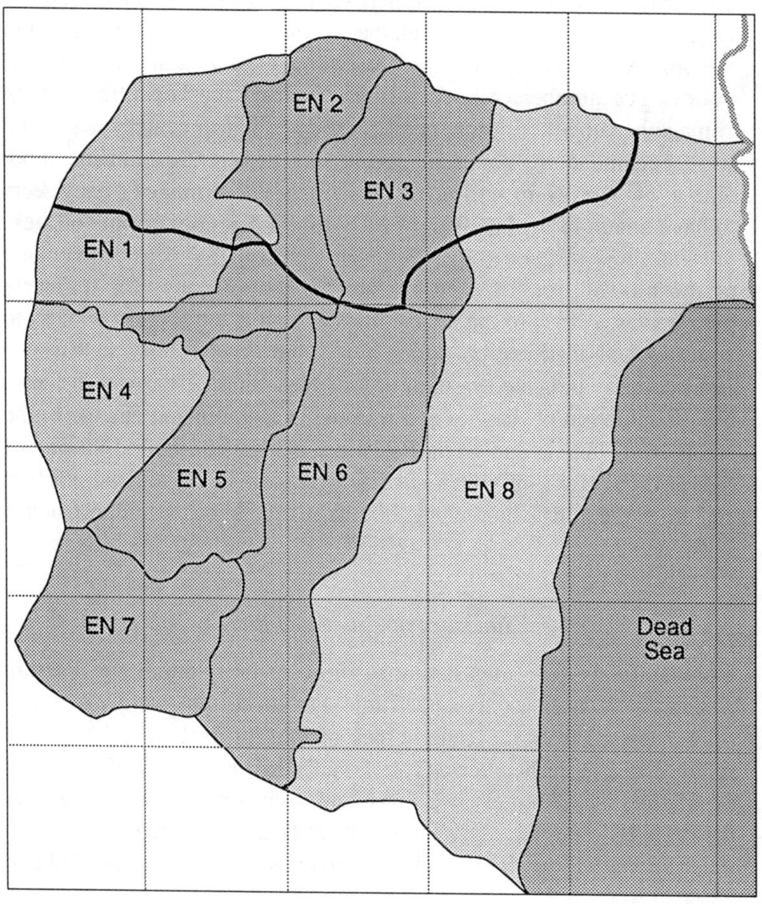

Figure 2. *The Eight Individual Environmental Niches of the Province of Yehud*

which may suggest that this period should be identified as Iron Age rather than Neo-Babylonian.[41]

The transitional forms that began in the mid-sixth century gradually gave way to more distinct Persian period pottery. This pottery has typically been identified as 'early' or 'late', with no real indications of the criteria for these designations. But there is ample evidence for significant changes in the nature and status of Yehud during the fifth and fourth centuries—evidence that supports a break in the period. As Hoglund has pointed out,[42] a number of fortresses were constructed in the mid-fifth century BCE, representing a new phase in imperial policy. The number of seals increased during the late fifth century, coinage became more prominent in the early fourth century, and Attic ware became more common during this period. In addition, more than a few sites were settled later than even the fortresses (many seem to have begun in the late fifth or early fourth centuries); some of these present a mix of Persian and Hellenistic pottery that is as problematic as the mix of Iron IIC and Persian period pottery is for the early period sites. Added to the archaeological data is the literary witness to a strategy of fortification during this same time period, at least for Jerusalem, as indicated in the book of Nehemiah. This in turn led to the repopulation of the city and resulted in a significant change in the status of Yehud within Syria-Palestine, if not the empire. No one of these shifts alone provides sufficient reason to divide the Persian period in the mid-fifth century, but taken together they support such a division.

Summary of Excavated Sites

Comparatively few sites dating to the Neo-Babylonian and Persian periods have been excavated (Table 1). Those that were excavated often suffered from the general lack of interest in the Persian period relative to the earlier periods of Israel's history and/or the lack of sophistication of pottery typology and architectural chronology for the period. Some, like the excavations at Bethany (el-'Ezariyeh), provide the student of the period with little useful information. Others,

41. See G. Barkay, 'The Redefining of Archaeological Periods: Does the Date 588/586 BCE Indeed Mark the End of the Iron Age Culture?' (forthcoming in the proceedings of the Second International Congress of Biblical Archaeology).

42. See his *Achaemenid Imperial Administration*, pp. 202-205.

like those at El-Jîb, while potentially valuable, suffered from minimal controls and a gross misunderstanding of pottery typology. Those at Bethel, Beth-Zur, Tell en-Naṣbeh and Jericho were more methodologically sound, but suffered from a general lack of knowledge of the period.

Neo-Babylonian (587/86–538)
Bethel I[43]
El-Jîb
Tell el-Fûl
Tell en-Naṣbeh[44]

Persian I (538–450)
Jerusalem
Tell Goren
Ramat Rahel
Beth-Zur

Persian II (450–332)
Bethel II
Ras el-Kharrubeh
Bethany (el 'Ezariyeh)
Jericho
Ketef Yeriḥo
Kh. Abu et-Twein
'Ain 'Arrub

Table 1. *Excavated Sites from the Neo-Babylonian and Persian Periods*

Determining, on the basis of the excavation reports, precisely when in the period sites were first occupied, reached their largest size, and were abandoned, is often difficult, if not impossible. These factors make any attempt to discuss the relative size of those sites and their population particularly problematic. Of all the sites excavated, only Jerusalem (in its most recent excavations of Kenyon and Shiloh) has

43. A chronology is given in the final report of the Bethel excavations (p. xiv), but note that a normal stratigraphic analysis is not provided. What I call Bethel I is called a 'sixth-century phase' and given the dates 587 to the late sixth century. Bethel II refers to the period that the excavators identified as 'Late Persian and Early Hellenistic'.

44. This site, as we shall see below, was not completely destroyed during the Babylonian conquest and continued to be inhabited through the Neo-Babylonian and Persian periods.

been characterized by sound excavations and relatively complete publication, and therefore provides the type of data that truly advances our understanding of the material culture of the period.

If this pessimistic view of the data is correct, what can the excavated sites tell us about the years 586–332? Four sites located within the province of Yehud were occupied in the exilic period: Tell el-Fûl, El-Jîb, Tell en-Naṣbeh and Bethel.[45] Of these only Tell en-Naṣbeh (biblical Mizpah), the seat of Babylonian rule in exilic Judah, continued to be occupied in the fifth and fourth centuries. The exact date of the abandonment of Bethel, El-Jîb and Tell el-Fûl is still open to question, but virtually all scholars agree that none of the sites survived into the fifth century.[46] Bethel was resettled late in the Persian period.

Several sites appear to be settled near the beginning of the Persian I period. **Ramat Rahel**, the site of an imperial citadel in the Iron II period and destroyed by the Babylonians in 587/86, was re-established early in the fifth century. Since the majority of the remains from the site are epigraphic rather than architectural, it is impossible to reconstruct its history with certainty. Aharoni suggested that it served a political/military function in the Persian period, but this is based almost solely on its function during the Iron Age.[47] **Tel Goren** (En-Gedi) appears to have been abandoned in the early sixth century, to be re-established sometime in the fifth century. It is one of the rare sites that reached its zenith during the Persian period, probably in the late

45. Even though many excavations have been conducted in Jerusalem in the last one hundred years, it is still unclear how soon after its fall in 587/86 Jerusalem began to be inhabited again. In the period directly after the Babylonian conquest, Mizpah (Tell en-Naṣbeh) was the regional capital; but it has recently been suggested that sacrifices began to be offered in Jerusalem soon after its fall (See M. Kochman, 'Status and Extent of Judah' [PhD dissertation, The Hebrew University of Jerusalem, 1980], pp. xiiff.). If this is the case, one would expect some small level of settlement to have begun before the first return to Yehud in 538. However, the most we can say on the basis of the archaeological evidence is that Jerusalem was resettled sometime in the sixth century. For this reason, I have identified Jerusalem as a Persian I and II site.

46. See the discussion in Carter, 'A Social and Demographic Study', pp. 97-109.

47. Aharoni admitted that the dating and size of the 'citadel' was 'extremely problematical' since no floors were found dating to the Persian or Hellenistic period. Some Persian period walls were uncovered but are insufficient to account for a substantial building phase. Given the paucity of hard architectural data, the citadel remains a hypothetical construct.

fifth century. Associated with the site, along with the full range of Persian period pottery, are several *yehud* seal impressions, a significant amount of Attic pottery, and a large building with industrial remains. The site evidently shrank in size in the early and middle fourth centuries. Also dating generally to the Persian I period was **Beth-Zur.** While the stratigraphy of the site is confused at best, it does contain some significant numismatic remains. These include an Attic tetradrachm, a Yehud coin inscribed with the name YḤZQYH,[48] and six other late-fifth/early-fourth-century coins.[49] Ceramic and architectural remains from the site are inconclusive and suggest a relatively small settlement at the site.[50]

Seven excavated sites date to the Persian II period, with five of those representing settlements.[51] **Bethel** was resettled sometime toward the end of the Persian period. Evidently the site was quite

48. This was dated to the Ptolemaic period by Albright and Sellers (see 'Echoes of the 1931 Campaign', in *The 1957 Excavation at Beth-Zur*, p. 2); it is more correctly dated to the latter part of Persian II. See L. Mildenberg, 'Yehud: A Preliminary Study of the Provincial Coinage of Judea', in O. Markholm and N.M. Waggoner (eds.), *Greek Numismatics and Archaeology* (Belgium: Wettern, 1979), pp. 183ff.; and Y. Meshorer, *Ancient Jewish Coinage*. I. *Persian Period through Hasmonaeans* (Dix Hills, NY: Amphora Books), pp. 13-34.

49. These include an inscribed imitation Attic drachm, one Palestinian obol, two Philisto-Arabian obols; one Tyrian hemiobol; and one Sidonian trihemiobol. Of these coins, all but the Attic drachm would date to the fourth century BCE.

50. The citadel that was excavated in 1931 has been interpreted variously as Persian and Hellenistic. Albright regarded the structure as Persian, and is followed by Stern in this interpretation (*Material Culture*, pp. 36-38). Sellers suggested it was Ptolemaic (See 'Echoes of the 1931 Campaign', pp. 1-3). The ceramic record indicates a break in settlement from 587–200 BCE in Field II, with some pottery dating to the mid-fifth century discovered in Fields I and III. The most significant cache of Persian period pottery was discovered in a cistern southeast of the citadel and is not sufficient to suggest widespread settlement at the site. The most interesting suggestion concerning the site comes from R. Reich, who has recently argued that the citadel was occupied in the Persian period and has parallels to the Assyrian-style governor's 'residences' discovered at Gezer and Lachish dating to the mid-fifth century. See 'The Beth-Zur Citadel II—A Persian Residency?', *Tel Aviv* 19 (1992), pp. 113-23.

51. The discussion that follows concentrates on the settled sites. Excavations at **Ketef Yeriḥo** and **'Ain 'Arrub** yielded important ceramic and economic remains dating to the latter third of the fourth century and the late fifth centuries respectively. See my 'A Social and Demographic Study', pp. 136-37 and pp. 141-42 for a complete discussion of the finds and their significance for the period.

small, as the architectural remains were meager and poorly built. The building phase that does date to the period was concentrated around a spring south of the main tell. **Ras el-Kharrubeh** was evidently a moderately-sized village during much of the Persian period. Excavations and survey data both revealed architectural and pottery remains.[52] Biran's first excavations suggested that the settlement reached its peak in the eighth through (early) sixth centuries and that it was a 'respectable village in the Perso-Hellenistic period'; this conclusion was essentially confirmed in the 1983 excavations in which architectural finds dating to both Persian and Hellenistic periods were discovered. **Jericho** was excavated in 1908–1909 by Sellin and Watzinger and by Kenyon from 1952 to 1958. Minimal architectural remains were discovered in the earlier excavations; the most significant artifacts are epigraphic. These include 10 *yh* and 3 *yhd* seals; and one each of the following impressions: *yhwd 'uryw*, *lyhw'zr*, and *mṣh*. All have parallels from other important sites and all date generally to the fifth or fourth centuries. Epigraphic remains were also most prominent at **El-'Ezariyeh (Bethany)**. There four seals, all dating to the Ptolemaic period but dated to the Persian period by the excavator were discovered in unclear stratigraphic contexts.[53] Subsequent surveys uncovered a small amount of Persian period pottery, indicating that whatever settlement may have been associated with the site was minimal. **Khirbet Abu et-Twein** was excavated by A. Mazar in 1974–75. Although Mazar identified it as Iron II, Hoglund has dated the fortress to the mid-fifth century according to his architectural typology.[54] If Hoglund is correct, the structure would represent the only fully excavated mid-fifth century fortress from the province

52. The site was excavated by Biran in 1936 and again in 1983. See 'Soundings at the Supposed Site of Old Testament Anathoth', *BASOR* 62 (1936), pp. 22-25; and 'On the Problem of the Identification of Anathoth', *Eretz Israel* 18 (1985), pp. 209-10. The site was surveyed by U. Dinur and N. Feig in 1988 as part of the new survey of the tribal territory of Benjamin. See Map 17-13 in *Archaeological Survey in the Hill Country of Benjamin* (Forthcoming, Israel Exploration Society).

53. One *yršlm* and three *yhd-ṭeṭ* seals were found. See S.J. Saller, *The Excavations at Bethany (1949–1953)*, pp. 192-96. Approximately 78 vessels or fragments dated either to the Persian or Persian–Hellenistic periods were identified by Saller; however, his knowledge of the pottery of the period was limited, as evidenced by his dating of the seals.

54. See 'Iron Age Fortresses in the Judaean Hills', *PEQ* 114 (1982), pp. 86-109; and Hoglund, *Achaemenid Imperial Administration*, pp. 193-97.

of Yehud. Near the fortress was a small settlement of ten buildings that were not excavated. Similar arrangements—with small settlements near Persian period fortresses—exist at Kh. el-Qaṭṭ, Kh. Umm el-Qala and Kh. ez-Zawiyye.[55]

Jerusalem as the Provincial Capital of Yehud

The destruction of Jerusalem at the hands of the Babylonians in 587/86 was evidently widespread, if not complete; and it is unclear to what extent, if any, settlement continued at the site after the defeat and exile. According to 2 Kings 25, the seat of Babylonian control of vanquished Judah transferred to Mizpah, where Gedaliah—installed by the new ruling empire as governor—was eventually assassinated. Jerusalem itself then faded into darkness throughout the exilic period, only to rise from oblivion (at least from a textual standpoint) with the missions of Haggai and Proto-Zechariah, Third Isaiah and Ezra–Nehemiah.

While it is probable that some settlement in Jerusalem continued into the exilic age, both text and artifact agree that it is only with the return from exile that it gradually regained its prominence. The debate concerning when Jerusalem was again designated the capital of an autonomous province must be left for others to settle. But the archaeological remains of the city allow us to draw some general conclusions about its size and patterns of growth in the Persian period.

The most important excavations of Jerusalem relating to the Persian period were conducted by Kenyon (1961–67) and Shiloh (1978–85) on the southeastern spur of the biblical city.[56] Kenyon's excavations established the line of the post-exilic walls of Jerusalem.[57] The eastern wall was discovered well within the lines of the Iron II walls; inside, but adjacent to the post-exilic wall, were remains dating from the fifth through third centuries. Excavations in three areas discovered sections

55. See Carter, 'A Social and Demographic Study', p. 141. These settlements near the fortresses may have been barracks for the conscripts assigned to the fortresses or villages that supported them economically.

56. For a more complete discussion of the excavations of Jerusalem in the exilic and post-exilic periods see Carter, 'A Social and Demographic Study', pp. 109-20.

57. Remarkably, Kenyon's finds had been anticipated by M. Avi-Yonah in his prescient article, 'The Walls of Nehemiah—A Minimalist View', *IEJ* 4 (1954), pp. 239-48.

of the southwest and western sides of the walls.[58] In the final year of her excavations, Kenyon discovered a joint between the Herodian temple platform and an earlier platform that she identified with Zerubbabel's temple.[59]

Shiloh's excavations showed evidence of Persian period settlement (Stratum 9 of 20 strata) in four areas within and outside the lines of the post-exilic walls. In three of those areas limited architectural and ceramic remains were mixed with fill associated with the quarrying undertaken in the effort to rebuild the city. Curiously, some of the best preserved buildings, forming 'a stratigraphically well-defined layer',[60] were discovered in Area G, outside the city walls. The pottery discovered was described as a 'rich repertory...typical of the Persian period'. Associated with the pottery were several inscribed and anepigraphic seals that 'fix the stratigraphical and chronological ascription of Stratum 9 in the Persian period'.[61]

Although other excavations have yielded Persian period remains outside the walls of Persian period Jerusalem,[62] it is unlikely that the

58. K.M. Kenyon, 'Excavations in Jerusalem, 1965', *PEQ* 98 (1966), pp. 83-84; 'Excavations in Jerusalem, 1966', *PEQ* 99 (1967), p. 69.

59. 'Excavations in Jerusalem, 1967', *PEQ* 100 (1968), pp. 104-105.

60. Shiloh, *Excavations at the City of David I, 1978–82, Interim Report of the First Five Seasons* (Monographs of the Institute of Archaeology), *Qedem* 19 (1984), p. 20.

61. Shiloh, *Excavations*. The seal impressions are extremely important for our understanding of the chronology of seals within the Persian period. For a full discussion of the data, see Carter, 'A Social and Demographic Study', pp. 115-17, and the forthcoming article by D.T. Ariel and Y. Shoham, 'Locally Stamped Handles and Associated Body Fragments of the Persian and Hellenistic Periods'. The article is to be published in a third volume of *Qedem* dedicated to the City of David excavations.

62. These include the excavations in the Armenian Garden (See A.D. Tushingham, *Excavations in Jerusalem 1961–1967*, I [Toronto: Royal Ontario Museum, 1985] and M. Broshi, 'Excavations on Mount Zion 1971–1972', *IEJ* 26 [1976], pp. 82-83); those at Ketef Hinnom on the grounds of the Scottish Presbyterian Church (see R. Barkay, 'An Archaic Greek Coin from the "Shoulder of Hinnom" Excavations in Jerusalem', *Israel Numismatic Journal* 8 [1984–85], pp. 1-5, and the report on the Persian period remains from Ketef Hinnom included in my dissertation, 'A Social and Demographic Study', pp. 117-18); and a salvage excavation on Mamilla Street near Jaffa Gate (see 'Tombs in the Mamilla Street Area, Jerusalem', in *Highlights of Recent Excavations* [Jerusalem: The Israel Antiquities Authority, 1990], pp. 16-17).

city extended onto the western hill during this period; rather, settlement was primarily confined to the southeastern spur and the Temple Mount. The western wall of the Persian period settlement was evidently identical with that of the Iron II city, and the eastern wall was located within the lines of the Iron II eastern wall but joining that wall near the Temple Mount.

How large was the city? Shiloh estimates that during the tenth through eighth centuries BCE the size of Jerusalem was approximately 160 dunams, with 100 dunams associated with the Temple Mount, forty-nine dunams with the southeastern spur, and eleven dunams on the eastern slope, evidently beyond the line of the Iron II city walls.[63] Because the data from Kenyon's excavations show that the eastern wall of the city was above the Iron I and II wall, I would estimate that the maximal size of Jerusalem in the Persian period was between 130 and 140 dunams, with eighty dunams dedicated to the Temple Mount and between fifty and sixty dunams settled, including intra- and extramural occupation.[64] This would represent the size of the city after the mission of Nehemiah and the effort, imperially sanctioned if not imposed, to repopulate and fortify Jerusalem. Before that time (i.e. between the first return under Sheshbazzar and the mission of Nehemiah) it is impossible to arrive at a conclusive estimate of Jerusalem's size; but given the textual traditions of Haggai and Nehemiah, both of which suggest an impoverished Jerusalem, I would doubt that Jerusalem was more than half of its Persian II size.

Surface Surveys and Site Distribution in Yehud

To fill out the picture of the number of sites and their distribution within the province one must turn to the surveys that have been carried out in the last 25 years.[65] But because of the intrinsic problems

63. Shiloh, *City of David*, p. 3.

64. This assessment is in general agreement with the suggestions of Avi-Yonah ('The Walls of Nehemiah'), Broshi ('Excavations on Mount Zion', pp. 82-83; 'Estimating the Population of Ancient Jerusalem', *BAR* 4 [1974], pp. 12-13) and D. Bahat (*The Illustrated Atlas of Jerusalem* [New York: Simon & Schuster, 1990], pp. 34-36), as well as those of Kenyon and Shiloh discussed above.

65. These include surveys conducted or edited by M. Kochavi (*Judea, Samaria, and the Golan*), I. Magen and I. Finkelstein (*Archaeological Survey of the Land of Benjamin*) and A. Ofer ('The Judean Mountains during the Biblical Period'), as discussed above.

associated with surveys they must be used with care.[66] Quadrants in a given survey may be canvassed unevenly, and few are surveyed entirely. Thus, areas in which more time is spent could conceivably yield higher numbers of sites with attendant percentages of pottery than those which are surveyed less extensively. Even the character of the same site may be interpreted quite differently if different surveyors canvass a site independently.[67] Another serious problem with surveys is the tendency to treat periods in a homogeneous fashion, without regard for the changes in settlement patterns and site distribution that invariably occur over an extended period of time.[68] This in turn leads to what archaeologists call 'inflated' settlement maps.[69]

Despite these problems, any attempt to reconstruct the site distribution and/or population of the province must use surface surveys; the limited information from excavations informs us only slightly of the broad patterns of settlement during the period. Taken together, excavations and surveys show a total of 113 sites in the province of Yehud that may date to the Persian period, of which 111 were occupied.[70] Of these sites, 45 (41 per cent) were located in the tribal territory of Benjamin, and 66 (59 per cent) in the territory of Judah (Chart 1). Examining site distribution by environmental niche shows the following patterns (Chart 2; Figure 3): EN1, the northwestern slopes—19 sites (17 per cent of all sites); EN2, the north central hills—15 sites (13 per cent); EN3, the northern desert fringe—11 sites (10 per cent);

66. For a discussion of the history of surveys and both their value and methodological problems associated with them, see A.J. Ammerman, 'Surveys and Archaeological Research', *Annual Review of Anthropology* 10 (1981), pp. 63-88.

67. See the examples I cite on pp. 143-44 and pp. 345-48 of my dissertation ('A Social and Demographic Study'). As I note in the former discussion, even though two people may discover slightly different settlement histories for a particular site in independent surveys, they will typically agree concerning the period or periods in which that site reached its peak(s) of occupation.

68. See Ammerman, 'Surveys', pp. 77-78. I have attempted to take this into account by separating the period into Persian I and II, with the dividing line being the middle of the fifth century BCE. However, it is much more difficult to distinguish between Persian I and II sites based on survey data, and any such distinction must be considered extremely tentative. And while I do distinguish between population trends in Persian I and II, the map I have drawn does show all the sites found in Yehud throughout the Neo-Babylonian and Persian periods.

69. Ammerman, 'Surveys', pp. 77-78.

70. The cave at Ketef Yeriḥo may not have been occupied, and if it was it would represent a minimal occupation; the site of 'Ain 'Arrub is a tomb-cave.

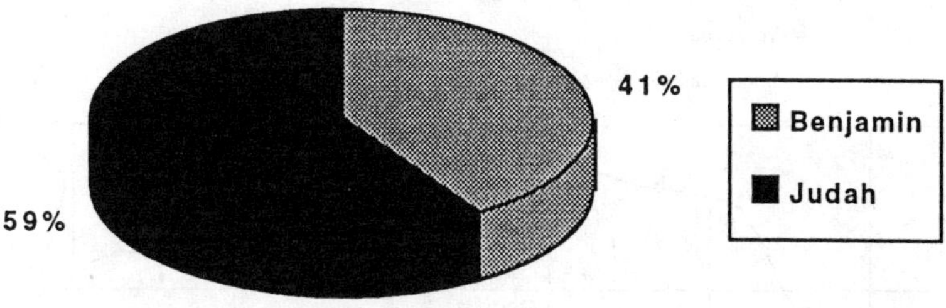

Chart 1. *Site Distribution by Biblical Territories, Persian Period Yehud*

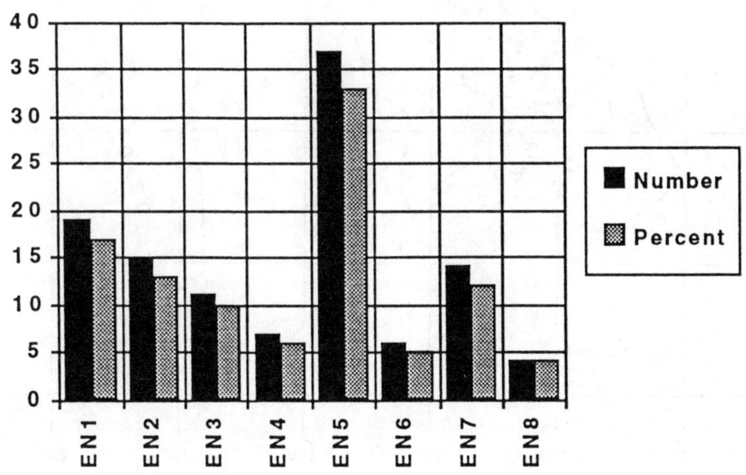

Chart 2. *Site Distribution by Environmental Niches, Persian Period Yehud*

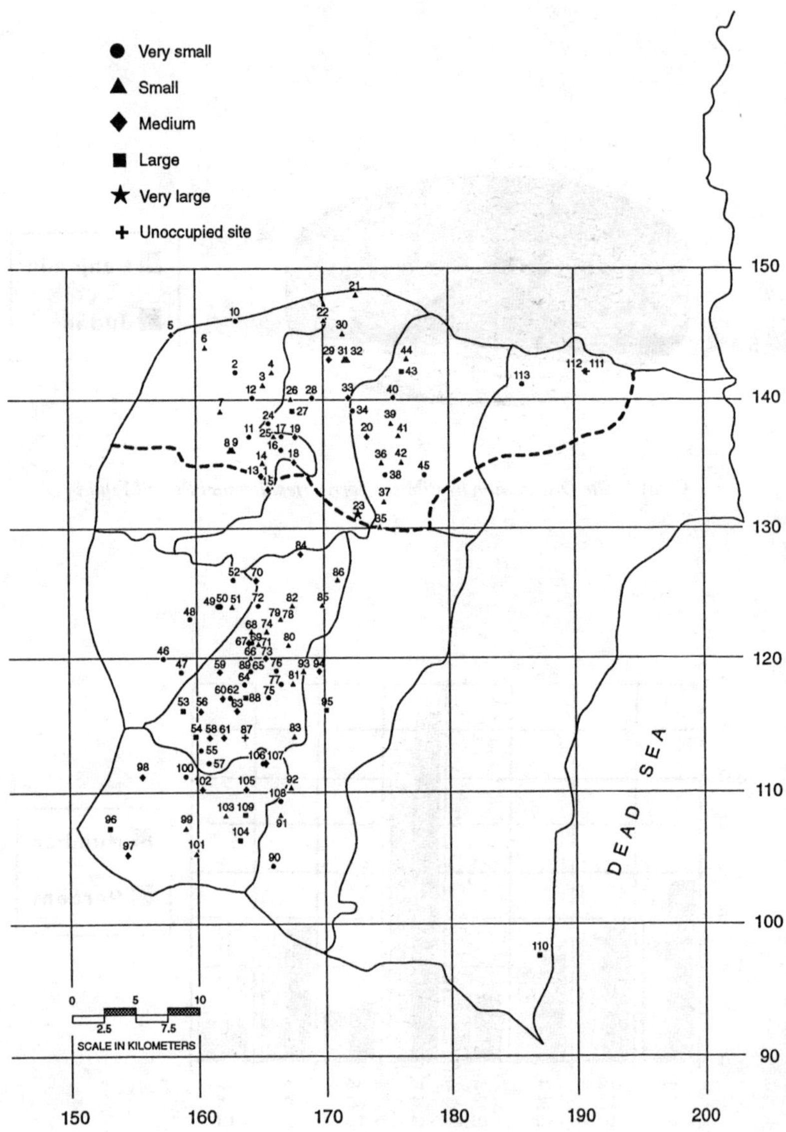

Figure 3. *Site Distribution in the Persian Period Province of Yehud*

EN4, the southwestern slopes—7 sites (6 per cent); EN5, central hills—37 sites, of which 36 were occupied (33 per cent of all sites); EN6, southern desert fringe—6 sites (5 per cent); EN7, south central hills—14 sites (12 per cent); and EN8, the Judaean Desert, contained 4 sites, of which 3 represent settlements (4 per cent).

The relative size of the sites is as important as site distribution for an understanding of the period. Based on earlier studies of population and site distribution of other archaeological periods, I divided the settlements in Yehud into five distinct categories: Very Small (VS), 1–2.0 dunams (median 1.5); Small (S), 2.1–5.0 dunams (median 3.5); Medium (M), 5.1–12.0 dunams (median 8.5); Large (L), 12.1–25.0 dunams (median 18.5); Very Large (VL), more than 25 dunams.[71] The vast majority of sites were very small (31 per cent) or small (36 per cent); this means that two-thirds of the sites of the Persian period had an area of five dunams or less and a population of less than 125. Slightly less than one-fourth (23 per cent) were medium, with a population range of 125–300. Approximately 11 per cent of the sites were large (10 per cent) or very large (less than one per cent), with a population of more than 300 (of these, only four were more than 20 dunams, and only Jerusalem exceeded 25 dunams).

The Population of the Province of Yehud

Population may be estimated in a variety of ways, including spatial analysis,[72] paleodemography, food remains analysis,[73] carrying

71. The site list included here is patterned after those of M. Broshi and R. Gophna in their studies of the population of the Early and Middle Bronze Ages, and the Roman-Byzantine period. See, M. Broshi, 'The Population of Western Palestine in the Roman-Byzantine Period', *BASOR* 236 (1980), pp. 1-10; M. Broshi and R. Gophna, 'The Settlements and Population of Palestine during the Early Bronze Age II–III', *BASOR* 253 (1984), pp. 41-53; 'Middle Bronze Age II Palestine: Its Settlements and Population', *BASOR* 261 (1986), pp. 73-90. The five categories of site sizes that I use here seem more appropriate than the schematization that Broshi and Gophna use for the Early or Middle Bronze Age in that the Persian period sites are markedly smaller than those of the periods that they analysed.

72. R. Narroll, 'Floor Area and Settlement Population', *American Antiquity* 27 (1962), pp. 587-89; and S.E. Casselberry, 'Further Refinement of Formulae for Determining Population from Floor Area', *World Archaeology* 6 (1974), pp. 117-22.

73. For a discussion of these two methods of population estimates, and a general discussion of the problems of such estimates, see R.M. Schacht, 'Estimating Past

capacity,[74] water supply[75] and areal analysis. All of these approaches are based in part on applying ethnographic data to the archaeological record. Areal analysis, which most easily lends itself to the particular problems of reconstructing Yehud's population, involves applying a population-to-land area coefficient to the total settled area.[76] Archaeologists first estimate the size of excavated and surveyed sites in either acres, hectares or metric dunams. To account for sites not discovered in areal surveys, they typically add a factor of 20 per cent to the total area. This total figure is then multiplied by the appropriate population coefficient to arrive at a population estimate.

I have adjusted this procedure slightly to account for the nature of the data concerning Yehud and arrived at the following estimates.[77] The total settled area of Yehud in the Persian I period approached 440 dunams (50+ dunams from excavated sites, 130 dunams from surveys of Benjamin, and 255 from the survey of Judah); its population would be approximately 11,000. In the Persian II period, the total settled area would have grown to approximately 678 metric dunams,[78] and the population increased to about 17,000. By the end of the fifth century, it is likely that Jerusalem would have grown to its full size of 50

Population Trends', *Annual Review of Anthropology* 10 (1981), pp. 119-40. Also helpful is F.A. Hassan, 'Demography and Archaeology', *Annual Review of Anthropology* 8 (1979), pp. 137-60.

74. See M. Broshi, 'Methodology of Population Estimates: The Roman Period as a Case Study', paper presented at the Second International Congress on Biblical Archaeology, Jerusalem, 1990.

75. J. Wilkinson, 'Ancient Jerusalem. Its Water Supply and Population', *PEQ* 106 (1974), pp. 33-51.

76. Recent ethnoarchaeological research on population density suggests a maximum coefficient of 250 people per hectare (= 25 people per metric dunam). I build consciously on the work of several prominent scholars for my population estimates. See Y. Shiloh, 'The Population of Iron Age Palestine in the Light of a Sample Analysis of Urban Plans, Areas and Population Density', *BASOR* 239 (1980), pp. 25-35; the works of Broshi and Gophna cited in n. 71; and I. Finkelstein, *The Archaeology of the Israelite Settlement*, and 'The Value of Demographic Data from Recent Generations for Environmental Archaeology and Historical Research', paper presented at the Society of Biblical Literature International Meeting, Sheffield, England, 1988.

77. For a complete discussion of the nature of those adjustments and the relevant data, see Carter, 'A Social and Demographic Study', pp. 155-62.

78. For a breakdown of the data and changes, see Carter, 'A Social and Demographic Study', pp. 155-62, n. 233.

to 60 occupied dunams and a population of approximately 1500.[79] The distribution of the population among the major and individual environmental niches also provides important data about the nature of the province. As one would expect, most of the population resided in the central hills. This area, accounting for only 20 per cent of the area of Yehud, contained approximately 69 per cent of its population. The western slopes comprised 17 per cent of the province and held 18 per cent of the total population. Approximately 12 per cent of the population was in the desert fringe, which accounted for 20 per cent of the area of Yehud. And the Judaean desert, which represented 41 per cent of the province's area, accounted for only 3 per cent of its population (see Table 3 for a niche-by-niche analysis).

	Persian I	*Persian II*
Excavated Area (in dunams)	51	88
Surveyed Area	348	536
Correction Factor	35	54
Total:	434	678
Population Coefficient	×25	×25
Approximate Population	10,850	17,000[80]

Table 2. *Settled Area in Yehud, Persian I & II*

79. Seventy to eighty dunams of the total area would have been dedicated to the temple and administrative complex; this, however, is considered public space rather than settled area and should not be included in the population estimates. Contrast this figure with Broshi's estimate of approximately 4500 persons in the post-exilic period ('Estimating the Population of Ancient Jerusalem', p. 12). Broshi and I have arrived at a similar area for the city; the discrepancy between our population estimates comes from two factors. Broshi used the entire area of the capital (30 acres = 120 dunams) for his estimate, not accounting for public space—a factor that he has addressed in his later writing on population estimates. He also used a higher population to land ratio than I do—his being 150 people per acre (= 37.5 per dunam).

80. These population figures should be considered provisional, at best. The reader should keep in mind that I have presented them with the conviction that some attempt to estimate the population of Yehud, however tentative, is worthwhile. The reader should also note that if I followed the more traditional procedure for estimating population noted above, the figures would increase by about 10 per cent, with the population during the Persian I period at about 12,000 and that during the Persian II period approximately 18,500.

	EN1	EN2	EN3	EN4	
Size	197	155	150	125	
Area %	10	8	8	6	
Population	2500	2700	1200	500	
Population %	14	16	7	3	
Density	13	17	8	4	
Settlements	19	15	11	7	
Site %	17	14	10	6	
	EN5	**EN6**	**EN7**	**EN8**	**Totals**
Size	141	246	139	790	1943
Area %	7	13	7	41	100
Population	5700	900	3300	500	17,300
Population %	33	5	19	3	100
Density	40	4	24	.63	9[81]
Settlements	36	6	14	3	111
Site %	32	5	13	3	100

Table 3. *Area, Site Distribution, Population, and Density in the Province of Yehud*[82]

The Implications of a Small Yehud

The size and population of Yehud projected here is far lower than any previous estimate, and considerably lower also than the biblical traditions of Ezra 2/Nehemiah 7, both of which record approximately 42,000 exiles leaving Babylon for Yehud. Weinberg, for example, has suggested that the population of the province was about 200,000 before the return that began in 539, a figure that is more than 10 times greater than my own projections.[83] And even if one agrees that the lists in Ezra and Nehemiah are composites, reflecting nearly 100 years of immigration to the province of Yehud, those who returned from exile joined a community of people who had remained in the land after the Babylonian conquest. Surely, one could argue, the population must have been greater than 17,000. If Yehud was this small

81. This figure represents the average population density for the entire province of Yehud.

82. In the table, Size refers to square kilometers in the niche; Area %, the percentage of the niche in the province; Population, its total population; Pop. %, the percentage of the population of Yehud that the niche contains; Density, the number of persons per square kilometer; Settlements, the total number of inhabited sites in the niche; and Site %, the percentage sites in Yehud contained in the niche.

83. See 'Demographische Notizen zur Geschichte der nachexilischen Gemeinde in Juda', *Klio* 54 (1972), pp. 45-59.

and this poor, how could the literary activity attributed to the exilic and post-exilic periods have been sustained? How could the temple have been built? What was the nature of the community that supported it? How could such a small province survive, let alone be considered significant to the security of the Persian empire? Although each of these questions is significant, each with far-reaching implications, only a few programmatic comments are possible.

Literary Genius in the Post-Exilic Period

Though scholars are divided as to what corpora of literature were produced in the post-exilic period, there is general agreement that the period was marked by a significant amount of literary activity. Recent suggestions have included placing the Deuteronomic School in Jerusalem in the Persian period[84] and the Priestly editing of the official history of Israel.[85] These may be added to the more traditional evidences of profound literary output: the activity of an Isaian community (Third Isaiah); the composition of Haggai and First and Second Zechariah; the books of Joel, Jonah and Malachi; the composition of Chronicles and editing of much of the Writings.

But could a small Jerusalem support this level of literary production? This question is really one of the size and nature of urban elites. In agrarian societies urban communities accounted for a relatively small proportion of the total population, usually less than 10 per cent,[86] but were responsible for a wide variety of social, political and religious functions. In such urban communities craft specialization is

84. See R.F. Person, *Second Zechariah and the Deuteronomic School* (JSOTSup, 167; Sheffield: JSOT Press, 1993). For the suggestion that many of the exilic works, including the Deuteronomic History, Ezekiel, Lamentations and Second Isaiah were not composed in Babylon but in Jerusalem, see H.M. Barstad, 'On the History and Archaeology of Judah during the Exilic Period. A Reminder', *Orientalia Louvaniensia Periodica* 19 (1988), pp. 25-36.

85. Van Seters suggests that the Yahwist dates not to the tenth/ninth centuries BCE, but composed Genesis–Numbers as an introduction to the Deuteronomic history sometime during the exile. This was followed by the Priestly version of the entire history in the fifth/fourth centuries BCE.

86. See G. Lenski, *Power and Privilege: A Theory of Social Stratification* (New York: McGraw–Hill, 1966), pp. 200-204; and G. Lenski, J. Lenski and P. Nolan, *Introduction to Human Societies: A Macro-Sociological Approach* (New York: McGraw–Hill, 1991), pp. 163-66.

ubiquitous; that is to say that elites with different functions concentrated in these communities, supported in large measure by extracting surplus from agrarian peasants in the surrounding villages. And, as G. Lenski points out, it is often the function of the religious elites to devise an ideology that will support the cultus and, perhaps, the state; such an ideology is generally necessary to convince the peasantry to part with surplus.[87] What type of elites were active in Jerusalem? Certainly, professional members of the cult were represented, including Aaronide and Levitical priests (Neh. 7.1, 39, 43; 8.1-9); singers (Neh. 7.1, 23, 45); temple servants (Neh. 3.26, 31; 7.46; 11.19); gatekeepers (Neh. 7.1, 23, 45); and a scribal class (Ezra 8.1, 9). The provincial governor would have had a staff (perhaps 'Solomon's servants' of Neh. 11.57-60); and, with the fortification of the city under Nehemiah, conscripts would have been garrisoned there (the 'men of the guard', Neh. 4.23; 7.3). Other specialists represented include goldsmiths (Neh. 3.8, 21-22); perfumers (Neh. 3.8); and both masons and carpenters (Ezra 3.7).[88] The population of Jerusalem in the Persian II period was between 1250 and 1500, or between 7.4 and 8.8 per cent of the population of Yehud; these figures are well within the 5 to 10 per cent average of urban centers in the pre-industrial age.[89] Thus, the level of literary creativity traditionally attributed to

87. '*Technological advance created the possibility of a surplus, but to transform that possibility into a reality required an ideology that motivated farmers to produce more than they needed to stay alive and productive, and persuaded them to turn that surplus over to someone else*. Although this has sometimes been accomplished by means of secular and political ideologies, a system of beliefs that defined people's obligations with reference to the supernatural worked best in most societies of the past' (*Human Societies*, p. 162; italics in original text). Evidently, by the mid-fifth century, that ideology was no longer entirely successful in Yehud; Neh. 13.10 records that many Levitical priests and singers had 'fled to their fields' since they had not received their payment from the tithe. It is possible that the tithes and 'portions' intended to support the Levitical priests had been collected, but not distributed to them because of official corruption. Nehemiah claims to have dealt with this problem, guaranteeing them payment, and restoring them to their rightful position. Note also that in Neh. 10.37 one function of the Levitical priests is collection of taxes.

88. This diversification is generally in keeping with urban elites and probably represents only a small portion of the elites of Jerusalem. See *Power and Privilege*, pp. 200-201.

89. If anything, the population of Jerusalem was higher than normal. Lenski notes that in seventeenth- and eighteenth-century Russia, urban population accounted for no more than 3 per cent of the total population, and by the mid-nineteenth century

the Persian period need not be questioned on the grounds either of a small province or a small Jerusalem.

Economic Security and a Small Yehud

One could argue that a small Yehud is equivalent to an insignificant Yehud. Further, one may wonder, given the relatively modest area of the province—restricted primarily to the central hills—and its even more modest population, how Yehud could have survived economically and supported the operation of the temple complex. A look at the relevant texts suggests that there were indeed problems with both. The prophet Haggai relates famine, blight, drought and general futility to the preoccupation of the people with their own affairs and the failure to rebuild the temple (Hag. 1.3-11; 2.15-19; see also Zech. 8.9-13). And though the ministry of Haggai and Zechariah stirred the people to lay the foundations of the temple and subsequently rebuild it, Nehemiah returned some 70 years later to find the walls of Jerusalem still in disrepair (Neh. 1–2) and the Levitical priesthood dispersed throughout the province because their base of economic support was severely eroded (Neh. 13.10-13). The people are also characterized as suffering from the effects of heavy taxation and administrative abuses (5.1ff.). The long-term effects of the latter was the institution of debt-slavery, the breakdown of the family structure, and general economic malaise. These kinds of problems, even if exaggerated for rhetorical or other purposes, reflect the kind of conditions one might expect in a relatively small province.

If these texts do support, in general terms, my reconstructions from archaeology, how could this struggling community have survived? It is here that the wider social, geographic and economic contexts must be brought into focus. For if one focuses solely on one component part of the empire, that is, the province of Yehud, one's conclusions concerning the nature of that part may become skewed. But Yehud did not exist in a vacuum; other important social, political and religious developments took place outside of the province in Syria-Palestine. Yehud was part of a larger administrative district, Eber-Nari, which was in turn part of the Persian empire. The temple-building program

was only 8 per cent of the total. Likewise, in fourteenth-century England, less than 5.5 per cent of the population lived in towns of more than 3200 people (*Power and Privilege*, pp. 199-200).

was part of a larger Persian policy of restoring cults and temples of peoples and religions that had been subjugated by the Neo-Babylonians.[90] As such, the project was financed at least in part by the empire; the total weight of fiscal responsibility did not fall on the *gōlâ* community. In this regard, the textual witness to returnees settling outside the border of the province becomes even more important. For as both Rainey and Ackroyd have pointed out, *Jewry is larger than Yehud*.[91] The loyalty of these returnees was not only financial,[92] but is also evident in their providing work details for the rebuilding of the walls of Jerusalem (Neh. 3).

One of the chief criticisms that could be leveled against a small Yehud is that it would not have been economically viable without the surplus that the Shephelah and coastal plain would have provided. And if these two geographic entities were not part of Yehud, to what province should they be attached? The situation on the coastal plain is relatively clear. According to L. Stager, it was under Phoenician control, with specific authority over the major cities of the plain alternating between Tyre and Sidon.[93] Dor was very likely the capital city of the province named after itself,[94] as was Ashdod.[95] Lachish

90. See the extended discussion of J. Blenkinsopp in 'Temple and Society in Achaemenid Judah', pp. 34ff.

91. P.R. Ackroyd, 'Archaeology, Politics and Religion: The Persian Period', *Iliff Review* 39 (1982), pp. 5ff.; Rainey, 'The Shephelah of Judah', pp. 18ff.

92. In this regard, see Blenkinsopp and his discussion of the wider temple economy (the so-called Bürger-Tempel-Gemeinde, or 'civic-temple-community') of Yehud. He maintains that 'Babylonian Jewry, therefore, shared with the imperial government the expenses of construction and maintenance. By means of this financial underwriting, and by reserving to themselves responsibility for the actual rebuilding to the exclusion of the native population (Ezra 4.1-5), the golah-community in effect claimed control of the Jerusalem cult under the supervision and protection of the imperial authorities'. See 'Temple and Society in Achaemenid Judah', pp. 39-40.

93. 'Why were Hundreds of Dogs Buried at Ashkelon?', *BAR* 17 (1991), p. 28. This arrangement evidently was in force as far south as Ashkelon, which was itself under Tyrian control. This view is supported by the Eshmun'ezer inscription which claims control the Sharon Plain.

94. See E. Stern, 'The Dor Province in the Persian Period in the Light of the Recent Excavations at Tel Dor', *Transeuphratène* 2 (1990), pp. 147-55.

95. See W.J. Bennett, Jr, and J.A. Blakely (eds.), *Tell el-Hesi: The Persian Period (Stratum V)* (Winona Lake, IN: Eisenbrauns, 1989), p. 337.

was probably the seat of another province, perhaps Idumea.[96] Gaza remained an independent city-state, but may have been linked to the provinces of Arabia.[97] Control of the Shephelah itself evidently alternated between Egypt and Persia; when controlled by the Persians, it is unclear to which province it was attached, although it would have fallen most naturally under the jurisdiction of Lachish.

How did Yehud relate to other provinces (Figure 4)? With loyal Judaeans living outside the borders of Yehud a network of economic exchange must have been developed, perhaps along the lines attested during the later Second Temple Period when Jews from the diaspora contributed to the upkeep of the temple.[98] Thus, former exiles who had returned to their homeland would have continued to offer sacrifices in Jerusalem and to celebrate the major pilgrim festivals there. The sacrifices themselves were a form of taxation designed to underwrite the priesthood and other temple officials; the income generated by the periodic influx of pilgrims would also have had wider effects on the economy of Jerusalem. And, according to Neh. 10.33-34, a one-third shekel temple-tax was imposed as a part of Nehemiah's mission, a tax that would have further supported temple operations.[99]

Just as economic support for the temple and its operations flowed into Yehud from beyond its borders, it is likely that other, non-cultic exchanges occurred as well. These may have been similar to those in effect in the late Iron II period. So, for example, by the late seventh century BCE, Tel Miqne/Ekron may have been producing up to 80 per cent of the olive oil of all of Palestine. Although Tel Miqne/Ekron

96. Bennett and Blakely (eds.), *Tell el-Hesi*. At the site a monumental building, called 'The Residency', dating to the Persian period, was excavated; Bennett and Blakely suggest that it may have been the governor's residence.

97. Bennett and Blakely (eds.), *Tell el-Hesi*. See also Stager, 'Hundreds of Dogs', p. 28.

98. See, for example, M. Broshi, 'The Role of the Temple in the Herodian Economy', *JJS* 38 (1987), pp. 31-37.

99. It is unclear how extensively this tax was collected; it is certainly possible that Jews from the diaspora paid it, as they did during the Herodian period. Broshi suggests that about 500,000 Jews lived in Palestine and paid the tax during that later period, and that as many as 2,000,000 diaspora Jews contributed to the temple in this manner. We also know that during the Persian period the *gôlâ* community had offers from other communities to assist in rebuilding the temple; although their offers were rebuffed, it is likely that Jewish communities existed in Galilee and perhaps the Transjordan during this time.

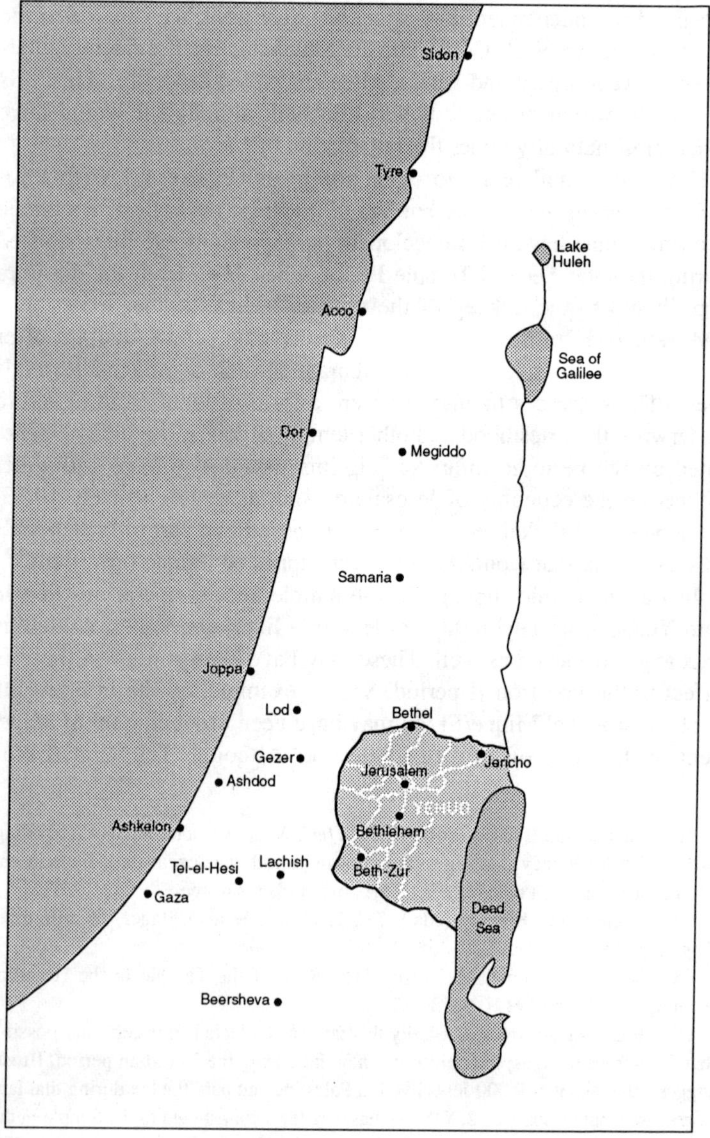

Figure 4. *The Province of Yehud in Palestine*

was destroyed by the Babylonians (perhaps as early as 603 BCE), the principle of regional production centers was probably maintained by the Neo-Babylonian and Persian empires.[100] These kinds of interrelationships with other provinces in Palestine would have been vital to the security of Yehud, and may explain the large granaries at Tell el-Hesi and, perhaps, El-Jîb (used in the earlier Neo-Babylonian period).

At issue, then, is not only the survival of a small province in the central hill country in Palestine in the sixth through fourth centuries BCE. Larger imperial policy dictated, to a certain degree, events in and around Yehud.[101] Thus, as Hoglund has pointed out, the refortification of Jerusalem was not merely an act of largesse on the part of the Persian emperor, designed to gain the loyalty of a small but important ethnic group in western Palestine. Rather, it was evidently intended to secure western Palestine, Yehud, Samaria and the southern coastal plain for the empire in the face of growing threats from Greece and Egypt, threats in which the city of Dor may have been involved. In this regard, the economic stability of Yehud was in the best interests of the empire;[102] even a small Yehud would have been guaranteed adequate resources from other provinces, including the Shephelah (when in Persian hands) and coastal plain sites. This does not mean that the interrelationships among the provinces would have been free from the petty rivalries that traditionally existed among city-states in earlier periods of Palestine's history. Instead, the apparent shift in imperial policy signified by the increased status of Jerusalem in the mid-fifth century led to just such rivalries between Yehud and

100. On the importance of and evidence for regional interrelationships in the seventh century BCE, see S. Gitin, 'Tel Miqne-Ekron: A Type Site for the Inner Coastal Plain in the Iron Age II Period', in S. Gitin and W.G. Dever (eds.), *Recent Excavations in Israel: Studies in Iron Age Archeology* (AASOR, 49; Winona Lake, IN: Eisenbrauns, 1989), pp. 48-51.

101. Yet, Ackroyd's point that too much can be made of the concept of 'imperial policy' is well taken. He points out that such policy 'is not necessarily always consistent. Pragmatic decisions may be at different levels, responding to different needs as they are perceived. Politicians, as we all know, can make mistakes of judgment, and they can show themselves inept. We must not look for a greater coherence and intelligibility in political action in the past than we should expect to find in our own time.' See 'Archaeology, Politics, and Religion', p. 17.

102. *Achaemenid Imperial Administration*, pp. 207ff.

representatives from Samaria, Ashdod and the Arab provinces.[103]

These brief paragraphs suggest that a distinction should be drawn between a small Yehud and an unstable Yehud. Yes, Yehud was probably smaller and poorer than many earlier reconstructions of the province have allowed. This would in turn explain the relatively minimal messianic expectations of the early Persian period and would suggest that little, if any, hope for independence existed at that time.[104] But small and relatively poor does not mean insignificant or isolated. The archaeological and textual data agree that as the Persian period progressed so did the size and status of the province.[105] Many significant questions remain to be answered, particularly concerning the social and economic setting(s) and structure(s) operative within the

103. On both the political and religious implications of the tensions between Samaria and Yehud, see Ackroyd, 'Archaeology, Politics, and Religion', pp. 13-15. He suggests a linkage in rule of the two areas, at least early in the Persian period, which is traceable in part to the correspondence from Elephantine addressed to both cities.

104. *Contra* P. Hanson, *The Dawn of Apocalyptic* (Philadelphia: Fortress Press, 1975), pp. 240-63, who sees a heated conflict within the post-exilic community between the so-called hierocratic party, represented by the dyarchy of Zerubbabel ben Shealtiel and Yehoshua ben Yehozadak, and the visionary party, represented in the prophecies of Third Isaiah. Among those who view the apocalyptic and messianic language of Haggai referring to Zerubbabel within the context of Judaean submission to the Persian throne are E.M. Meyers, 'The Persian Period and the Judean Restoration: From Zerubbabel to Nehemiah', in P. Hanson, D. McBride and P. Miller (eds.), *Ancient Israelite Religion: Essays in Honor of Frank Moore Cross, Jr.* (Philadelphia: Fortress Press, 1988), pp. 509-21; and J. Kessler, 'The Second Year of Darius and the Prophet Haggai', forthcoming in *Transeuphratène*. As E. Meyers points out, 'A concomitant of a strong high priest was the diminution, at least by First Zechariah, of the role of the Davidic scion, who is relegated to an eschatological status (Zech. 3.3; 4.6b-10a; 6.12). The attitude of the prophet is that the Davidic line will be re-established at a future time of God's choosing, but for the meantime a Davidic governor—possibly groomed for the job in the court of Darius I—was thought to be sufficient evidence of Persian goodwill and Yehudite aspirations.' ('The Persian Period and the Judean Restoration', p. 512).

105. Archaeologically, for example, it is apparent that, as the period progressed, seal impressions were more frequently stamped with governors' names and the authority to mint coins was granted to the province (Stern suggests a relative chronology of anepigraphic seals with Persian motifs coming early in the Persian period and epigraphic seals with the names of governors coming later in the period and representing increased socio-political and socio-economic autonomy. See his discussion in *Material Culture*, pp. 209-13).

province of Yehud and the degree to which Weinberg's Bürger–Tempel-Gemeinde model is a useful construct for viewing the period.[106] Future studies of the period will perhaps be able to use the present work as a starting point to answer these types of questions.

106. For a positive assessment of the contribution of Weinberg to the study of post-exilic community of Judah, see P. Dion, 'The Civic-and-Temple Community of Persian Period Judaea: Neglected Insights from Eastern Europe', *JNES* 50 (1991), pp. 281-87. Other discussions of Weinberg's general approach are found in J. Blenkinsopp, 'Temple and Society in Achaemenid Judah', and R. Horsley, "Empire, Temple and Community—But no Bourgeoisie! A Response to Blenkinsopp and Petersen', in Davies (ed.), *Second Temple Studies* I, pp. 163-74.

LATE PERSIAN JUDAISM AND ITS CONCEPTION OF AN INTEGRAL ISRAEL ACCORDING TO CHRONICLES: SOME OBSERVATIONS ON FORM AND FUNCTION OF THE GENEALOGY OF JUDAH IN 1 CHRONICLES 2.3–4.23*

Thomas Willi

The Historical Situation and Chronicles' Position in the History of Ideas

Quite a number of archeological, historico-cultural and ideological observations and evaluations have shown that Judaism in the early post-exilic time, that is, at the beginning of the Persian period, stood in practically unbroken *continuity* with the situation shortly before and during the exile.[1] This continuity had primarily been maintained by the cultural life in the villages and cities of the Judaean countryside. In the early Persian epoch the main question was that of preserving and maintaining former characteristics under the new circumstances of the Achaemenid empire. Only gradually did attempts arise in Judah to *redefine its own identity*. This happened together with the process of separation from the more powerful Samaria. Since the Neo-Babylonian period the territory of the former kingdom of Judah was

* This essay is a somewhat extended and reworked version of a paper presented at the AAR/SBL annual meeting at Kansas City, MO, November 24, 1991, at the invitation of SBL's Chronicles, Ezra, Nehemiah Group, under the title 'The Chronicler as Exegete'.

1. 'The dominant factor was the close bond between the province in the Persian period and the former kingdom of Judah in pre-Exilic times. It reflects a striving to establish continuity...' (E. Stern, 'The Province of Yehud: The Vision and the Reality', *The Jerusalem Cathedra* 1 [1981], p. 15). Further evidence in a forthcoming study by T. Willi, *Juda—Jehud—Israel: Studien zum Selbstverständnis des Judentums in persischer Zeit* (manuscript 1991), pp. 10, 14-19, to be published in Forschungen zum Alten Testament (FAT, 10).

politically subordinate to the province of Samaria.[2] Jerusalem and its surroundings succeeded only later, in the middle of the Persian period, in establishing its independence. Nehemiah's internal and external initiatives finally lead to the establishment of an independent province called Yehud in Aramaic (יְהוּד מְדִינְתָּא, Ezra 5.8). Nehemiah—and Ezra as well—represented for their contemporaries significant achievements, but more than that and above all they mark a deep break in the life and development of post-exilic Israel. The book of Ezra–Nehemiah was written in order to document the stages leading to this change in the fifth century BCE and preparing the establishment of an independent province Yehud.[3]

This transformation concerns equally the political and the cultural sector, as much as it has its impact on the ideological sphere. *Politically* we now find Yehud (יהוד מדינתא Ezra 5.8) firmly established as an independent province of the Achaemenid empire, covering some 600 square miles. *Material life* now differs markedly from the culture of the first half of the Persian period. So only now, right in the middle of the Persian time, do clear *signs of transition* appear in the political and cultural area. But what about spiritual life and history of ideas, the 'Geistesgeschichte'?

We possess a unique testimony to help us define the new state of mind. It shows how late Persian Judaism became aware of its specific role and task in relation to the entire Jewish people, in the diaspora as well as in Yehud. I am referring to Chronicles with its well-rounded,

2. A. Alt, in his 'Die Rolle Samarias bei der Entstehung des Judentums', *KS*, II (3rd edn, 1964), pp. 316-37 (originally published in the Festschrift O. Procksch [1934], pp. 5-28), notes 'einen sehr bedeutsamen Unterschied in den Schicksalen Samarias und Jerusalems...: Samaria ist schon durch die Assyrer, hingegen Jerusalem erst durch die Babylonier in die rechtliche Lage gebracht worden, deren Auswirkungen wir unter den Persern beobachten' (p. 318). He then regrets that we have 'kein klares Bild... von den Einrichtungen [in the territories of the former kingdom of Judah]... unter der Herrschaft der Babylonier... So wissen wir nicht einmal genau, ob das zuletzt von Zedekia verwaltete Gebiet als administrative Einheit bestehen blieb. Die Wahrscheinlichkeit spricht für das Gegenteil. Dann war aber die Frage, ob die Babylonier aus einem so kleinen Gebiet überhaupt eine Provinz für sich unter einem eigenen Statthalter zu machen für nötig hielten. Ich zweifle nicht, dass *Procksch* das Richtige getroffen hat, als er neuerdings diese Frage rundweg verneinte und die Vermutung aussprach, das Restgebiet um Jerusalem werde vielmehr dem Statthalter von Samaria zur Verwaltung überwiesen worden sein...'

3. Willi, *Juda–Jehud–Israel*, pp. 28-90.

coherent image of Israel—not just Judah!—and Israel's history. Through the concept of an integral Israel, the Chronicler holds up a mirror for his contemporaries, whether they live in the province Yehud or in the widespread גולה. It is an extensive, critical mirror, but equally one that also reminds and comforts.

Interpreter, Canon and Interpretation

With Chronicles we have already passed the decisive threshold and left behind the break that was supposed to have occurred in the middle of the Persian period. In Chronicles there is something new. It is no longer a continuation ('Fortschreibung') of former tradition. Even continuity of transmission includes a certain degree of explanation and interpretation. But from this interpretation to the exegetical methods of Chronicles there is not only a quantitative, but also a qualitative leap. If interpretation was formerly a mere concomitant of transmitting the old tradition, it is now a deliberately applied method of literary and historiographic work. Chronicles does not use interpretation in order to preserve and to transmit the former traditions. For the older tradition had already been firmly grounded. Interpretation now is practised in order to elucidate, to check and to establish one's own identity by means of Scripture.[4] Here, by the way, is where a kind of 'prospective historiography' belongs, what has been called the Chronicler's '*a priori* thinking', as Sara Japhet describes it: 'Israel's institutions were not produced by the historical reality, but the reverse. They anticipate history—history is the realization of their already-existing blueprint'.[5]

The Chronicler starts out from the assumption that *the premises and conditions of his own present are hidden in the wording of Scripture* and that they can be derived from it. When taking up the older traditions, scrutinizing, digesting them and presenting them afresh, he retells the past while at the same time he is speaking about the present.

4. T. Willi, *Die Chronik als Auslegung: Untersuchungen zur literarischen Gestaltung der historischen Überlieferung Israels* (FRLANT, 106; Göttingen: Vandenhoeck & Ruprecht, 1972), pp. 176-84, 205-207, 229-41.

5. S. Japhet, אמונות ודעות בספר דברי הימים ומקומן בעולם המחשבה המקראית. *The Ideology of the Book of Chronicles and its Place in Biblical Thought* (Heb.; Jerusalem: Bialik Institute, 1977), p. 199 (ET BEATAJ, 9; Berne: Lang, 1989), p. 230.

This inquiry into metahistorical relations is especially evident in the opening of his work, in the genealogies, which I propose to call 'citizenship-lists' of twelve-tribe Israel.[6]

The Chronicler's Israel is the people of its land. The patriarchs Abraham, Isaac and Israel certainly have their prominent position in the beginning of Chronicles—but only among humankind, the οἰκουμένη of 1 Chronicles 1, and not in connection with Israel's stock as described in 1 Chronicles 2–8 (–10)![7] The promises given to them are not dealt with, just as little is said of Moses and his mediation of the Torah—both go without saying and are presupposed.[8] Chronicles does not speak about all this, but it does speak about Israel, and actually it puts the emphasis on Israel in its entirety, on כל־ישׂראל, 'All-Israel'[9] with its connection to the land.[10] It is for this purpose that it begins with Judah and the regions where Judah grew to its complete form.

At the intersection of genealogy with geography the citizenship-lists have to be seen in close relation to the late prophetic utterances on 'the Land', utterances that have to be placed chronologically in the late Persian period.[11] This is how we can understand 1 Chronicles 2–10, and not as analogies to older, pre-exilic tribal stories, family trees or border systems. Certainly, the genealogies are based upon these older elements and expose them to the reader in a concise, fresh manner. In doing so they provide their formative influence on the self-consciousness of the target group's identity. The citizenship, the civil rights of such an 'All-Israel' are in a certain sense idealized. Nevertheless the wholistic, metahistoric concept of Israel is closely related to historical reality. It is this organic 'All-Israel' that is presented in 1 Chronicles 2–10 as *dramatis persona* of the retelling of its history.[12] So the

6. Willi, *Chronik* (BKAT, 24.1; Neukirchen–Vluyn: Neukirchener Verlag, 1991), p. 55.

7. 1 Chron. 29.18 is to be seen under this aspect, too.

8. S. Japhet, 'Conquest and Settlement in Chronicles', *JBL* 98 (1979), pp. 205-206.

9. H.G.M. Williamson, *Israel in the Book of Chronicles* (Cambridge: Cambridge University Press, 1977), see esp. pp. 98-99, 108-110, 120, 125-31.

10. Cf. S. Japhet, אמונות ודעות, pp. 309-333, see esp. p. 333 (= *Ideology*, pp. 363-93, esp. p. 393).

11. Cf. Jer. 24.10; Ezek. 33.23-29; Zech. 2.16; Isa. 11.11-16; 24.4-13; 62.4.

12. The same conclusion, but by different ways, is reached by W. Osborne, 'The Genealogies of 1 Chronicles 1–9' (PhD dissertation, The Dropsie University,

Chronicler is defining the place and the function of late Persian Judaism by referring to the much wider and broader Israel of the original twelve tribes.[13] Its Israelite legacy and tradition now constitute essential elements of Jewish identity in Yehud and abroad. They describe the role of Judaism in the framework of the multinational Persian empire. In this regard, the succession of the kingdom of Judah is no longer of primary relevance, rather Judah's function for this 'All Israel'. The Chronicler is now going to define Judah and its offspring, the 'chosen' kingship of David and his house. This is the theme of the historical narrative 1 Chronicles 11—2 Chronicles 36, which builds upon this 'All Israel' picture of the genealogies. And its base is to be found in 1 Chron. 2.3–4.23.

Exegetical Methods in the Composition of the Genealogy of Judah

We begin with a brief survey of the contents. The *chronistic frame,* sometimes a part of the picture itself and partially composed by elements of biblical tradition, is 1 Chron. 2.3-17, 25aα, 42aα, 50aα; 4.21-23. Add to this the *genealogical notice* 2.18-24, leading to the *genealogy of Jerahmeel* (2.25aβ-41) and to the *genealogy of Caleb* (2.42aβ-55). When looking at ch. 3 from the aspect of Israel's first settlement, we see that this passage makes good sense in a citizenship-list. It combines genealogical with geographical viewpoints. The same is the case in the concluding ch. 4, which deals with Judah's principal clans according to their main areas of settlement. In ch. 4 we have therefore an overall picture of Israelite population in the territory of Judah, from North to South, that is, as seen from Jerusalem.[14]

We find very different components pieced together to create a new unity of a higher order. Behind this we recognize an unceasing

1979). As a result of his investigations he too states that 1 Chron. 1–9 was deliberately composed as a part of the entire work.

13. Willi, *Die Chronik als Auslegung*, p. 162 n. 206, underlines what he calls 'den Gedanken des umfassenden Gottesvolkes'; and K. Strübind, *Tradition als Interpretation in der Chronik* (BZAW, 201; Berlin: de Gruyter, 1991), p. 60, speaks of the 'eschatologischer *Panisraelitismus*' of the Chronicler.

14. Further investigations concerning the composition of the Judah-genealogy may be found in H.G.M. Williamson, 'Sources and Redaction in the Chronicler's Genealogy of Judah', *JBL* 98 (1979), pp. 351-59; G. Galil, 'The Genealogies of the Tribe of Judah' (PhD dissertation, Hebrew University, Jerusalem, 1983) (Hebrew); Willi, *Chronik*, pp. 71-79.

endeavour to understand, to interpret and to expose preformed tradition. This is realized on three levels: the Chronicler deals with *scriptural tradition,* he uses *oral tradition*, and he gives this material the *systematical shape* of his presentation.[15]

Interrelation of Oral and Literal Tradition

Here we must include a brief statement about oral tradition. As we can see with the תורה שבעל פה, the 'oral teaching' of later rabbinical tradition, 'oral tradition' does not exclude a secondary stabilization by writing. In the late Persian period major parts of Israel's tradition, especially the Pentateuch and prophetic writings, had already been given normative, canonical status. At the same time this canonized tradition was read attentively. In this reading the past became the shape for the present, and even for the future. Discrepancies between past and present produced sorrow and repentance, but at the same time they inspired hope for a new fulfilment of the old word.[16] 'Canonical' in this ongoing process of Israel's tradition does not mean fossilization and loss of creativity. The תורה of Moses, the teachings of the prophets as the message of God's word remained valid and became validated again and again. Thus it became necessary to integrate the situation of the current generation. According to the fully developed rabbinic conception, such interpretation and application of Scripture took part in the authority and dignity of the original תורה שבכתב, the revelation preserved in Scripture, although it would appear on scene and be recognized much later. 'Orality' therefore is a formal description, not a judgment of value. It relates the sphere qualified in Israel's tradition as 'oral' to 'Scripture', notwithstanding that it might contain non-literary as well as literary documents. Chronicles is one of the most important witnesses to the canonical Scripture in the late Persian period. It contains non-literary elements of interpretation, which of course are to be related to 'what is written'. The interrelation of these components, or the different levels of transmission respectively, are an essential factor of the Chronicler's exegetic work.

15. Cf. Willi, *Chronik*, p. 72.
16. Cf. Willi, *Chronik*, pp. 58-59.

Selection

In order to connect different components to create a whole they must first be selected. In Chronicles, too, interpretation begins with a careful selection. To define the criteria the Chronicler followed for his selection we should proceed from the known to the unknown. 'Known' in this sense is the biblical material of the older traditions, that is, Scripture.

The Chronicler does not base his genealogy of Judah primarily on Numbers 26 or Genesis 46 as he does for most of the twelve tribes. The *starting point* of his conception of Judah is *Genesis 38*. In this respect the construction is not opaque. There is no 'Undurchsichtigkeit des Aufbaus', as W. Rudolph[17] claims. The Tamar story provides a reasonable framework for the exposition of all descendants of Judah in 1 Chronicles 2–4. Not only the content of the chapter, but its position in the flow of the book of Genesis as well was of prime importance for this choice.[18]

Positioning

Ordering and arranging the chosen material is another element of interpretation. The citizenship-lists describe Israel's structure according to aspects of geography as well as genealogy and family law. Within this structure Judah comes first. Judah's precedence does not correspond to the standard of Old Testament tradition about the twelve tribes; it is an exception.[19] Aside from the book of Numbers, which arranges the tribes around the tabernacle and later refers to the distribution of the land (Num. 2.3-31; 10.14-28; 7.12-83; 34.16-29), only 1 Chron. 2.3–9.1 and 12.25-38 place Judah at the head of the twelve tribes. In 1 Chronicles 2 this is done by transition from the twelve sons of the patriarch Israel (vv. 1-2) to the twelve tribes of all Israel (v. 3ff.), and it is done without any explanation. Nevertheless

17. *Chronikbücher* (HAT, 1/21; Tübingen: Mohr [Paul Siebeck], 1955), p. 10.

18. For the interpretation and historical evaluation of Gen. 38 itself, cf. the studies by J.A. Emerton, 'Some Problems in Genesis XXXVIII', *VT* 25 (1975), pp. 338-61; 'An Examination of a Recent Structuralist Interpretation of Genesis XXXVIII', *VT* 26 (1976), pp. 79-98 and 'Judah and Tamar', *VT* 29 (1979), pp. 403-15.

19. See Willi, *Chronik*, p. 60.

the Chronicler has reasons to do so, but he will not expound them until 1 Chron. 5.1-2, where he discusses first-born Reuben. Judah's precedence is not derived from the historical predominance of the tribe. It is not explained by the longer lasting existence of the Southern kingdom. It has not been conceived as an ideological sublimation of the Persian province Yehud. Rather it is the actualization of what has long ago been prefigured in the Tamar story of Genesis 38. The content and position[20] of this old tribal saga[21] are now filled with a new meaning and realized in Judah's development. Since 1 Chron. 1.35-54 had already taken up Genesis 36 as a list of the 'sons of Esau', after Gen. 35.23-26 (= 1 Chron. 2.1-2), there remained only the Joseph story, the blessing of Jacob—and precisely Genesis 38.

Genesis 38 as a closed narrative, as 'in sich abgeschlossene Einzelerzählung',[22] has always confronted its interpreters with a riddle. The old midrash[23] solved it biographically, tracing Judah's departure from his brothers (Gen. 38.1) to his advice to sell Joseph (Gen. 37.26-27). Rabbinic tradition[24] as well as modern exegesis refer to the 'Gesamtzusammenhang'[25] of Genesis. Without naming David this coherence leads directly to Jacob's blessing with its promise, 'Judah, it is you!' (Gen. 49.8-12).

This is the starting point for 1 Chron 5.1-2:

20. Later rabbinical interpretation knows the rule of דרישת סמוכים; see W. Bacher, *Die exegetische Terminologie der jüdischen Traditionsliteratur*, I (Leipzig: 1899 = Darmstadt: Wissenschaftliche Buchgesellschaft, 1965), p. 133; II (Leipzig: 1905 = Darmstadt: Wissenschaftliche Buchgesellschaft, 1965), p. 159. See further I.L. Seeligmann, 'Voraussetzungen der Midraschexegese', in J.A. Emerton and G.W. Anderson (eds.), *Congress Volume, Copenhagen 1953* (VTSup, 1; Leiden: Brill, 1953), p. 159.

21. When C. Westermann (*Genesis* [BKAT, 1/3; Neukirchen–Vluyn: Neukirchener Verlag, 1982]) states that Gen. 38 is a 'Familienerzählung... und nicht im Kern Stammesgeschichte', he nevertheless shortly after that declares, 'Familien—und Stammesgeschichte... sind... hier nahe beieinander'.

22. Westermann, *Genesis*, p. 42.

23. Quoted also by Rashi, see *Miqra'ot Gedolot* (Jerusalem: 1976), I, fol. 132b; ET R. Rosenbaum and A.M. Silbermann, *Pentateuch with Targum Onkelos, Haphtaroth and Rashi's Commentary*, I (Jerusalem: Feldheim, 1973), pp. 185-86.

24. *b. Soṭ.* 10b.

25. Westermann, *Genesis*, p. 52.

1 ובני ראובן בכור־ישראל כי הוא הבכור
ובחללו יצועי אביו נתנה בכרתו לבני יוסף בן־ישראל ולא להתיחש לבכרה:
2 כי יהודה גבר באחיו ולנגיד ממנו והבכרה ליוסף:

> [1]And the sons of Reuben the first-born of Israel—for he is the first-born, and because he defiled his father's bed, his birthright[26] was given to the sons of Joseph the son of Israel, but not to be enrolled in the genealogy [according to civil rights] to the birthright, [2]so that Judah prevailed over his brothers and from him came the leader; yet the birthright is Joseph's.

This is without doubt the Chronicler's own explanation. It accounts for his putting Judah at the beginning. He does not do so because of Judaean particularism, motivated by 'love of Judah and hatred of Israel', *Vorliebe für Juda und Hass gegen Israel.*[27] On the contrary, his view results from an All-Israelite, twelve-tribe perspective. Otherwise 1 Chron. 5.1-2 would not make sense. The verses refer to the dominant view about birthright. The Old Testament makes a distinction between the so-called, artificially construed, male *first-born of the mother* and the 'true' *first-born of the father*. The first case is related to cult and descent; the second one has a social impact, especially in matters of inheritance. The matriprimogeniture (Heb. פטר רחם),[28] is important in cases where human and animal first-borns are seen together and where there is a relation to cultic affairs. In certain cases the first-born can be redeemed. On the whole patriprimogeniture (Heb. ראשית און)[29] is prevalent in Israel, as it determines the law of family and inheritance. In historical times the first-born does not inherit the whole property of his father, but only a double portion of it (Deut. 21.17; 2 Kgs 2.9). This is the background of the notice about the בני יוסף בן־ישראל in 1 Chron. 5.1.[30] The wording refers to

26. G εὐλογίαν αὐτοῦ does not lead to a conjectural בִּרְכָתוֹ (contra *BHS* App.; Rudolph, *Chronikbücher*, pp. 42-43).

27. As W.M.L. de Wette (*Beiträge zur Einleitung in das Alte Testament*. I. *Kritischer Versuch über die Glaubwürdigkeit der Bücher der Chronik mit Hinsicht auf die Geschichte der Mosaischen Bücher und Gesetzgebung* [Halle: Schimmelpfennig, 1807 = Hildesheim: Olms, 1971], p. 126) entitles the corresponding ch. II/7.

28. Exod. 13.2, 12, 15; 34.19; Num. 3.12; 18.15; Ezek. 20.26. Cf. also Num. 8.16.

29. Gen. 39.2; Deut. 21.17; Pss. 78.51; 105.36.

30. Against *G* [-L] τῷ υἱῷ αὐτοῦ 'Ιωσηφ υἱῷ 'Ισραηλ, respectively against *S* (*A*) *lywsp' ḥwhy br ysryl*, 'to his son (*S* brother), the son of Israel', read MT.

Gen. 48.5-6 where a double portion—indicating first birthright—is divided in half between Ephraim and Manasseh and therefore neutralized. Now all future tribes of Israel would receive the same share. In other cases Chronicles, too, tends to neutralize patriprimogeniture, and thus to open up new possibilities, to ensure equality of opportunity and to make possible a charismatic development of history. That is why it 'uses a couple of terms to express the preferential position of a non-firstborn son, in deliberate opposition to √בכר: so גבר (1 Chron. 5.[1-]2 in relation to Gen. 27.37); נגיד (same verse); ראש (1 Chron. 26.20)'.[31]

1 Chronicles 5.1-2 therefore first explains the balancing of the double share by the distribution to the two sons of Joseph. But at the same time it emphasizes that this double share did not automatically indicate the *patria potestas* which after the father's death would normally have passed to the *patriprimogenitus* and would have made him *primus inter pares* of his brothers and family.[32] Such precedence quite naturally had to stay in the hands of a single person, which Judah now became by divine guidance and charismatic election.[33]

In the Chronicler's eyes these are the factors, as he deduces them from Scripture and tradition, which make David the first king over the ממלכת יהוה ביד בני דויד (2 Chron. 13.8). David's kingship only expresses and realizes Judah's predominance. From the very beginning this predominance has been related to 'All Israel', to the people of the twelve tribes in its entirety. According to Chronicles the kingship of David is the result of, rather than the reason for, Judah's special role. It is exactly this role that was now being put to the test in and by the province of Yehud—and with it the welfare of 'All Israel'. The manner in which the chronistic citizenship-lists present Judah as predominant, according to Scripture and tradition, κατὰ τὰς γραφάς, underlines this fact.

31. M. Tsevat, 'בכר', in *ThWAT*, I, cols. 643-50, the quotation on col. 647.

32. M.D. Johnson, *The Purpose of the Biblical Genealogies with Special References to the Setting of the Genealogies of Jesus* (SNTSMS, 8; Cambridge: Cambridge University Press, 1969), p. 64, formulates, relating to the 'militaristic... interests' in Chronicles: 'Reuben gives way to Joseph and especially Judah, who became strong among his brothers'. But this 'and' is nothing more than simplification and leveling.

33. Is it only by chance that here, in the beginning of the Chronicler's genealogy of Judah, 1 Chron. 2.3, that the name of יהוה occurs for the first time in the whole work?

Reworking Older Tradition

Every synopsis[34] shows the reader at first glance that interpretation is a substantial element in Chronicles. One can ascertain without difficulty the *direct quotations* from Scripture. In the genealogy of Judah they are Gen. 38.(6-)7; Gen. 46.12bβ (cf. Num. 26.21); 1 Kgs 5.11aβ; Josh. 7.1bα,17b, 25aαβ, 1aβ; Num. 2, 3 = 7.12 (Ruth 4.18-22 looks more like a parallel than like a *Vorlage*); 1 Sam. 16.6-9 (cf. 1 Samuel 17, 13bβ); Exod. 31.2b = 38.22a; 2 Sam. 3.2-5; 5.5, 14-16. Literal quotations which we would put in quotation marks are Gen. 38.7; 46.12bβ; Josh. 7.1aβ; Exod. 31.2b = 38.22a; 2 Sam. 3.2-5; 5.5, 14-16.

The very enumeration of these references shows that the different books of the older tradition are considered equally and dealt with in the same manner: we see no different valuation. As Genesis 38 provides the framework for the Chronicler's Judah-genealogy, so 2 Samuel 3 and 5, quoted literally, furnish the *Leitwort*, the leading expression, the √ילד, 51 times in the 100 verses of our passage.[35] Its counterpart is the expression X ªbi- *Place Name*, (PN), 'X, father of such and such place', that operates as a *Leitwort* as well.[36] The Chronicler did not invent this expression on his own. He found it in the older tradition[37] and made it the central theme of his exposition. The √ילד is embedded not only in Gen. 38.27-28, but also in 2 Sam. 3.2, 5 and, in different form, in 5.14 (with passive meaning). The Chronicler standardized them to נולד לו and used this form not only in

34. P. Vannutelli, *Libri synoptici Veteris Testamenti*, I (Rome: Pontificium Institutum Biblicum, 1931); A. Bendavid, *Parallels in the Bible: Genesis, Joshua/Samuel/Psalms/Chronicles* (Jerusalem: Carta, 1969); J. Kegler and M. Augustin, *Synopse zum Chronistischen Geschichtswerk* (BEATAJ, 1; Bern: Lang, 1984).

35. 1 Chron. 2.3, 4, 9, 10 (2×), 11 (2×), 12, 13, 17, 18, 19, 20 (2×), 21, 22, 24, 29, 35, 36 (2×), 37 (2×), 38 (2×), 39, 40 (2×), 41 (2×), 44 (2×), 46 (2×), 48, 49; 3.1, 4, 5; 4.2 (2×), 6, 8, 9, 11, 12, 14 (2×), 18.

36. 28 times in all: 1 Chron. 2.21, 23, 24, 42 (2×), 44, 45, 49, 50, 51 (2×), 52, 55 (13 occurrences) ; 1 Chron. 4.3, 4 (3×), 5, 11, 12, 14, 17,18 (3×),19, 21 (2×) (15 occurrences).

37. Cf. Gen. 4.20, 21; 33.19; 34.6; Josh. 24.32; Judg. 9.28. See also 1 Chron. 7.14, 31; 8.29 = 9.35. *Contra* M. Noth, 'Eine siedlungsgeographische Liste in 1. Chr. 2 und 4', *ZDPV* 55 (1932), pp. 97-124, who takes the filiation as proof of a very old document (to be dated 'in die Zeit nicht lange nach dem Tode Salomos', p. 119), combining 1 Chron. 2 and 4.

3.1, 4, 5 (pl.), but already in 2.3a, at the beginning of the genealogy, and shortly after in the key verse 2.9a.[38]

Chapter 2 is, by means of this נולד לו, continued by ch. 3, being based on the quotations of 2 Sam. 3.2-5 and 2 Sam. 5.5.14-16. Both passages make specific reference to David's sons having been 'born in Hebron' (3.2) and 'born to him in Jerusalem' (5.14) respectively. The latter case is connected to the beginning of Israelite settlement in Jerusalem. David's children therefore figure as representative members of the first generation born in Jerusalem, and their descendants in 3.10-24 are a sign of continuing Jewish settlement of the town, in spite of all interruptions as for instance by exile (vv. 16-19). 1 Chronicles 3 then concludes the first, genealogical part (√ילד!) of the genealogy of Judah, thematized by 2.9.

Chapter 4 in its turn does not emphasize genealogy as much as geography. By means of the filiation X *ᵃbi–* PN it shows us Judah's land, not only in general, but especially by listing the individual villages, starting points for new settlements and connections from mother- to daughter-cities, centers and areas of settlement in the sense of human geography.[39] The Chronicler's 'Israel' is essentially defined by the land of its emergence. That is why he reminds Judaism of his province and of the wide diaspora of those everlasting connections and relations to the origins. For they are part of the identity of Israel as the Chronicler sees it.

38. This may be held as a subsidiary argument favouring the view that 1 Chron. 3 forms an integral part of the Chronicler's Judah genealogy. At the same time it indicates chronistic authorship for such a central verse as 1 Chron. 2.10.

39. We might see in our list a biblical parallel to notices of contemporary Greek authors referring to founders of cities and colonies, οἰκισταί—by the very term evoking the idea of a 'father-*house*'. See e.g. Thucydides (before 455–c. 400), *Hist.* 1.24, 1-2, or, very similar, the reports about the foundation of Heracleia, *Hist.* 3.92, 1.4-5, or Notium, *Hist.* 3.34, 4, another case is Sicilian Katane (today Catania), *Hist.* 6.33 (cf. Strabo 6.272). See further Plato (428/27–349/48), *Republic* 379a, and Herodotus (484?–after 430), *Hist.* 4.155; cf. 159; 4; 6.34-38. 'No city sent out... colonists without appointing a founder, who had complete power over the colony', states J.E. Fontenrose in his article 'City-Founders', *The Oxford Classical Dictionary* (Oxford: Clarendon Press, 1964 [1949]), p. 195. Herodotus in his *History* (7.51 and 8.22), as Plutarch (*Them.* 9), even uses the term πατέρες as does our list in Chronicles.

The Integration of Caleb

In Chronicles' genealogy of Judah the non-Israelite relationships are conspicuous. Attention to non-Israelites begins with 2.3: '[three], born to him by the daughter of Shua, the Canaanite'. The descendants of the third son from Judah's Canaanite marriage, Shelah, frame the whole genealogy, closing it in 4.21-23, which thus reverts to the beginning in 2.3. Obviously, they are regarded as genuine members of the tribe of Judah. Just as Canaanite ancestors contributed to the development of Judah—see the Tamar story![40]—, so did 'the Ismaelite Jether' (2.17), 'an Egyptian servant named Jarha' (2.34), and 'Bithia the daughter of Pharaoh' (4.18; NASB 4.17), whereas 4.22 indicates a connection with Moab. For an adequate impression of the Chronicler and his conception of Israel it is important to keep in mind how openly he exposes the non-Israelite components in Judah's heritage—right against the background of 1 Chronicles 1!

In the genealogical ch. 2 the Chronicler deals substantially with Caleb. Here we see an author and interpreter applying older tradition to the present circumstances. Central to this is 2.18-24. In contrast to J. Wellhausen[41] I cannot take these verses as a competing doublet to 2.42-50aα, because the two passages do not really represent two different Caleb-genealogies. 2.18-24 is not as much a genealogy as it is a genealogical notice by which the Chronicler explains the duplication he himself found in the genealogical tree 2.42-55: on the one hand Caleb in the South, and on the other Caleb in the North. Verses 18-24 thus account for the fact that at a given time there were not any genuine Hezronites populating the Bethlehem area, as one would have presumed, but, in their place, descendants of Caleb.[42] Instead of settling in Judaean territory, the progenitor Hezron preferred to undertake his activities in east-Jordanian Gilead. Caleb filled the resulting settlement-vacuum. By his behaviour favouring Judah, Caleb obtained citizenship in Judah.

The identity and composition of Judah are therefore the central

40. This remains valid even if Shua should not be the name of a Canaanite clan, as C. Steuernagel (*Die Einwanderung der israelitischen Stämme in Kanaan* [1901], p. 79) assumes.

41. J. Wellhausen, *De gentibus et familiis Judaeis quae 1. Chr. 2.4 enumerantur* (Diss. theol.; Göttingen: Dieterich, 1870), p. 16.

42. By maternal law, as is indicated by the role of Ephrath and the Hur lineages.

theme of our list. We have to start from the fact that originally neither Jerahmeel nor Caleb belong to Judah's family tree. *But that is exactly what the key verse 2.9 frankly declares*! Nowhere else in the Old Testament are Jerahmeel and Caleb presented as sons of Hezron or even as brothers.[43] Of course there were indications in tradition relating Caleb to Judah (see for example Num. 13),[44] but by descent and genealogy he was not Judaean. The difference between Caleb and the genuine Judaean clans had, it seems, to last at least until the exile.[45] Things changed only after that, when Calebites, retreating from Edomite pressure in the South,[46] settled in and around Jerusalem, in the North of Judah. By cultivating and developing the land they maintained continuity of settlement and life in this region. They contributed to overcoming the exile and its effects, devastation and depopulation. This Calebite contribution to a continued settlement of Judah, Jerusalem and the surrounding area seems to be reflected in the Chronicler's citizenship-list of Judah. As soon as the civil rights of Israel, and of its forerunner Judah, respectively, had to be recorded, one was faced with the question of *interpretation and adaptation of the tradition*. This was the situation that allowed, nay, demanded, the Chronicler's inclusive view of Judah. Within his synchronic perspective he came to the obvious conclusions and, at the same time, provided the reasons for the fact that 'the new community politically [was] by no means and [could] not be exclusive', 'das neue Gemeinwesen politisch durchaus nicht exclusiv [war] und nicht sein [konnte]', as E. Meyer[47] has already formulated it. Unfortunately Meyer's point is not widely known. We thus would propose to recognize the Chronicler's own contribution[48] in his integrating Jerahmeel

43. H.G.M. Williamson, 'Sources and Redaction in the Chronicler's Genealogy of Judah', *JBL* 98 (1979), p. 352.

44. The Chronicler thus completes a line already indicated by priestly and other OT traditions: Caleb stays faithful and obedient to God's promises and commandments in contrast to a majority of Israel.

45. T. Willi, *Chronik*, pp. 26-27.

46. The Edomites in their turn were forced out by the Nabataeans; see J.R. Bartlett, 'From Edomites to Nabataeans: A Study in Continuity', *PEQ* 111 (1979), pp. 53-66.

47. *Die Entstehung des Judentums: Eine historische Untersuchung* (Halle: Niemeyer, 1896 = Hildesheim: Georg Olms, 1965), p. 119.

48. This in addition to the position taken by H.G.M. Williamson, 'Sources and Redaction in the Chronicler's Genealogy of Judah', p. 352, who holds that the

and Caleb into the framework of the Judah-genealogy, provided by Genesis 38. Verse 2.9 serves as hermeneutic key to the very different and heterogeneous materials and information which he collected.[49] He constantly bases his picture of Judah on tradition; but he courageously applies and adapts this tradition to his own time. Certainly the spirit of interpretation differs from the spirit of prophecy—but it has the same source. And it develops by authority as well. As for the field of historiography, Chronicles, through its interpretation and exegetical method, turns out to be a predecessor and a premise for later apocalyptic.[50]

Judah as Part and Representative of Israel

Judaism as it portrays itself in our Judah-list and in Chronicles' genealogies is as Israelite-minded as it is Judah-orientated, that is, Jewish. It is not confined to the reality of the province Yehud. On the contrary it sets this humble political entity in a much wider frame, by means of history, genealogy and geography. By doing so, Chronicles shows the Judaism of its time the importance of its heritage and its task as if in a mirror. *The Chronicler's Judah understands itself as member and part of Israel.* However, within this larger frame of twelve-tribe All-Israel, Judah occupied a special position.

The Judah-list is thus more than a simple reflection about the family and background of David. True, we find information about Davidic descent integrated, but it is derived, according to the Chronicler's view, from a broader genealogical perspective of the entire tribe of Judah. The data about David and his family—this is what matters to the Chronicler—finally follow from the overall picture of Judah. In short: *It is not David who makes Judah, but it is Judah that makes David David*! This is indicated by the position the Chronicler assigns to Judah in the genealogies of Israel. Here, too, it can be said that it is *not Judah* (or Judaism inside or outside the province Yehud) *that is*

Chronicler found the integration of Jerahmeel and Caleb already in some source before him.

49. This is the main difference between the analysis proposed here and the view of J. Wellhausen (*De gentibus …*): Wellhausen, too, takes 1 Chron. 2.9 as a central point of the composition (on p. 13 he writes: 'proficiscar a versu nono qui totius capitis proponit quasi summam'), but in combining this verse with the (old) genealogy of a Caleb in the South, 2.42-50aα ('cum Kelubaeo v. 9 conferri debet Kaleb v. 42 sqq.') he automatically declares it as belonging to an old source.

50. See Willi, *Chronik*, pp. 27 and 53.

defining Israel, but the preformed, so to say preexisting, Israel of the twelve tribes that determines the way Chronicles understands Judaism, its task and its promise. To this end the Chronicler goes on to track down the lines of the one Israel as it is manifested in the history of the Northern kingdom as well as in that of the Southern.

It is the organic entity of Israel that stands behind the kingship of David and his successors. Kingship, the rule by a David, a Solomon and their sons thus was not incidental. It had been preformed by Judah's development and history. But Judah itself is only one member in the organism of twelve-tribe Israel. Representing a function necessary for the whole, it always remains related to 'All Israel'. In relation to this whole kingship, even the kingship of David and his sons remains secondary. As Edom's example already indicated in 1 Chron. 1.35-54, it has only provisional, essentially catalytic and revealing character.[51] It shows God's 'ruling' (משל 1 Chron. 29.12; 2 Chron. 20.6) over Israel. In a time to come it will be carried out, under quite different circumstances, in a different way, but authorized by the same God, by the מְלֹךְ, the 'reigning' of the מלכות פרס, 'the reign of Persia' (2 Chron. 36.20).[52]

The Judaism of his time, as the Chronicler sees it, has its own peculiar task. It will fulfil it by recognizing and obeying the Achaemenid kingship which has been ordained by God for Israel's best interest in the same way in which God ordained the Davidic kingship. The task itself is indicated by Scripture. Contemporary Judaism had to maintain its position and to be forerunner of a fulfilled Israel, as long as the other parts of such an integral Israel were still scattered, lost and had disappeared. The future reconstituted Israel—not only Judah, not only the kingdom of Judah!—would correspond to that Israel that, according to the citizenship-lists, had been in the beginning, that *confusione hominum* had largely perished, but that now *providentia Dei* had partially re-established in the form of the province Yehud, and that therefore one day *would again come to be.* Even under different conditions, the Chronicler's Judaism understands itself as part of

51. For a detailed interpretation see Willi, *Chronik*, pp. 53-55.

52. Cf. the recent investigation of R.G. Kratz, *Translatio imperii: Untersuchungen zu den aramäischen Danielerzählungen und ihrem theologiegeschichtlichen Umfeld* (WMANT, 63; Neukirchen–Vluyn: Neukirchener Verlag, 1991). On pp. 169-79 he compares the chronistic conception of the 'himmlische מלכו/מלכות' and its dispensation with the view of Dan. 1–6.

Israel. It is precisely its consciousness as Israel which goes to make up its Judaism. By readopting and retelling, by re-explaining and reinterpreting the old word, but equally by its attitude and self-consciousness this Judah passed on Israel's witness and heritage. It stands for an Israel which as in Gal. 6.16 we may call the Ἰσραὴλ τοῦ θεοῦ.

PROPHET AND SOCIETY IN THE PERSIAN PERIOD ACCORDING TO CHRONICLES

Harry V. Van Rooy

Introduction

This paper investigates the function of prophets and prophecy in a changing society, as reflected in 1 and 2 Chronicles. This is a complex issue, presenting many problems to the investigator.[1] One has to presuppose that the changing position and influence of the prophetic movement after the exile are reflected in these books. This presupposition is very problematic, as these books purport to tell the history of Israel, focusing on David, Solomon and the Kingdom of Judah. What we have is a text—and a vital question would be what can be deduced from a text like this one—about the time it deals with on the one hand and about the time it was written for on the other hand. What do we know about the writer's historiographic principles, the value of his sources and the way he used his sources?[2] There are many studies today using sociological approaches to answer questions like these,[3] but do we have enough data to develop a theory about the post-exilic society and the function of prophecy in that society? Is it possible to apply the results of anthropological and sociological field studies to the text of the Bible, a text that is highly edited and does not contain 'raw data'?[4] Do we only have a text, or can we read something from the text about the world in which it was written?

The problem can be illustrated by looking at modern history and texts about it, taking modern South African history as an example. In

1. Cf. R.P. Carroll, 'Prophecy and Society', in R.E. Clements (ed.), *The World of Ancient Israel: Sociological, Anthropological and Political Perspectives* (Cambridge: Cambridge University Press, 1989), pp. 203-25.

2. Carroll, 'Prophecy', pp. 204-206.

3. Cf. Carroll, 'Prophecy', p. 203.

4. A.G. Auld, 'Prophets and Prophecy in Jeremiah and Kings', *ZAW* 96 (1984), p. 66.

the course of history things happened, but the description and interpretation of those things are always done from a certain angle, causing diverse descriptions of the same 'history'. As the philosopher Karl Popper remarks, historians use sources, but every source has its own selection of material, using mainly that which fits into a preconceived theory.[5] Historiography, moreover, is always interpretation, and each interpretation presents a point of view.[6] There is no history as it happened, therefore, but only historical interpretations that can never be final. Every generation has the right to formulate its own interpretation of its history,[7] and these interpretations must formulate an answer to the question of how the current problems relate to the past and how progress towards a solution can be made.[8] It is the historian who selects and orders the facts of history;[9] therefore it can be stated that history has no meaning and that history in the normal sense of the word does not exist:[10] history has no meaning on its own, but we can give it meaning.[11]

Persons always look at the past from the point of view of their own complicated situation. This causes ongoing reinterpretation of history.[12] This reinterpretation can lead to a historical ideology in which a nation or a group can give themselves a history from which they emerged, a history that can differ from the history from which they really emerged.[13] Reinterpretation can then even be a recreation of history to sustain the struggle in the present time.[14]

As an example, four trends in South African historiography can be referred to.[15] In each of these four approaches an attempt is made to search for a scapegoat for the problems of the country.

5. K.R. Popper, *The Open Society and its Enemies*. II. *The High Tide of Prophecy: Hegel, Marx and the Aftermath* (London: Routledge & Kegan Paul, 1962), p. 265.

6. Popper, *Open Society*, p. 266.

7. Popper, *Open Society*, p. 268.

8. Popper, *Open Society*, p. 268.

9. Popper, *Open Society*, p. 269.

10. Popper, *Open Society*, p. 269.

11. Popper, *Open Society*, p. 278.

12. Cf. F.A. van Jaarsveld, *Omstrede Suid-Afrikaanse verlede: Geskiedenis ideologie en die historiese skuldvraagstuk* (Johannesburg: Lex Patria, 1984), p. 1.

13. Van Jaarsveld, *Omstrede Suid-Afrikaanse*, p. 5.

14. Van Jaarsveld, *Omstrede Suid-Afrikaanse*, p. 5.

15. Van Jaarsveld, *Omstrede Suid-Afrikaanse*, pp. 6-7.

1. In the traditional conservative historiography the white colonists and republicans are at the centre of the debate, with as scapegoat a progressive-imperialist approach focusing on Great Britain. The culprits were the British missionaries, imperialism and capitalism.
2. After World War I English-speaking historians adopted a more liberal historiography, with as point of reference the problem of colour in the British empire. In this approach the Afrikaners were the scapegoats.
3. After World War II, with the rise of decolonization and a proletarian world view, a more radical approach came to the fore. Ethnicity and colour as determining factors in the liberal approach were rejected in favour of class, with a Marxist frame of reference. The scapegoats were British imperialism and capitalism.
4. After 1948, with the disappearance of the colonial empires, a black radical approach to history surfaced in South Africa. For the first time the part played by black people in Southern Africa received attention, something that was absent especially from the first two approaches. From the expectation of a black dominated South Africa, the country received a new, exclusively black history, with history rewritten in terms of conquest, subjection, resistance and liberation.

The Afrikaners looked at their history as a struggle between Boer and British, with the nineteenth century being a century of wrong. Black radical historians interpret their history as a struggle between black and white, referring to three centuries of wrong.[16] The way history is perceived at a certain point in time is also a result of the circumstances of that time.[17] There can only be interpretations of history that can never be final interpretations.

For the purpose of this paper a few remarks on the history of Israel will suffice. In the history of Israel many things happened. In the Deuteronomistic History and in Chronicles attempts are made to describe this history—but these descriptions remain interpretations within a certain frame of reference. Each description and interpretation was directed at a certain community with a certain message. The

16. Van Jaarsveld, *Omstrede Suid-Afrikaanse*, p. 7.
17. Van Jaarsveld, *Omstrede Suid-Afrikaanse*, p. 175.

point of view from which this description was made is related to this message and reflects something of the circumstances in which the text was created. We have in front of us a text and the world created by the text. The text also speaks about the world of history and reflects something of the world for which it had a message. We have only the text in front of us, but it is not just a piece of fiction in the normal sense of the word. This text pictures the history of a nation, or better, recreates the history of a nation to bring a message in a new time. We have two texts about the history of this nation. By comparing them, the message of each in its own point in time becomes clearer. The text of Chronicles may have been a weapon in an ideological conflict at that time[18]—and we do not know enough about that period in the history of Israel to come to final conclusions. The reinterpretation in Chronicles remains linked to the context of that time, even though we are looking through the eyes of tradents and their developed tradition.[19]

A question remains of what kind of reliable historical information can be deduced from the books of Samuel, Kings and Chronicles. J.M. Miller is of the opinion that the historian can use these stories as they reflect the general religious, social and political circumstances of periods from which they originate, allowing for the changes affected during the editorial process.[20] It remains a problem, however, because it is often uncertain what must be ascribed to the editorial process.

In this paper the incidents, words and actions of prophets in Chronicles will be analysed, also in comparison with the Deuteronomistic History, looking at the world of the text and the world in which the text functioned when it was written. There are a number of studies dealing extensively with the prophets in these two books.[21] This paper will focus on what can be deduced from the text about the view on the role of prophets during the time when the books were written. This reflects a time when classical prophecy changed into a related but

18. R.P. Carroll, 'Prophecy and Society', p. 214.

19. B.O. Long, 'Prophetic Authority as Social Reality', in G.W. Coats and B.O. Long (eds.), *Canon and Authority: Essays in Old Testament Religion and Theology* (Philadelphia: Fortress Press, 1977), p. 5.

20. J.M. Miller, 'Israelite History', in D.A. Knight and G.M. Tucker (eds.), *The Bible and its Modern Interpreters* (Philadelphia: Fortress Press, 1985), p. 16.

21. Cf. R. Micheel, *Die Seher- und Prophetenüberlieferungen in der Chronik* (Beiträge zur biblischen Exegese und Theologie, 18; Frankfurt am Main: Peter Lang, 1983), and D.L. Petersen, *Late Israelite Prophecy: Studies in Deuteroprophetic Literature and in Chronicles* (SBLMS, 23; Missoula, MT: Scholars Press, 1977).

different phenomenon.[22] Chronicles reflects one of at least two positions, namely, the theocratic stream, while the visionary or eschatological stream is reflected in deutero-prophetic literature.[23] The way in which prophets appear in these books will be illustrated by discussing only a few representative examples, since space does not permit a complete treatment of all the examples.

Prophets in Regnal Resumés

At the beginning and end of the description of the time of a king the so-called regnal resumés frequently appear in Chronicles.[24] In the final resumés reference is often made to further sources. Of the fifteen final instances in Chronicles, eight have references to works (words) of prophets (1 Chron. 29.29; 2 Chron. 9.29; 12.15; 13.22; 20.34; 26.22; 32.32 and 33.18-19). In the other instances reference is made to the book of the Kings of Israel (and Judah).

Two examples will suffice for these references to prophets. The description of the reign of King David is concluded in 1 Chron. 29.29-30:

> Now the acts of King David, first and last, indeed, they *are* written in the book of Samuel the seer, in the book of Nathan the prophet, and in the book of Gad the seer, with all his reign and his might, and the events that happened to him, to Israel, and to all the kingdoms of the land (NKJV).

The conclusion to the reign of Jehoshaphat is as follows (2 Chron. 20.34):

> Now the rest of the acts of Jehoshaphat, first and last, indeed they *are* written in the book of Jehu the son of Hanani, which *is* mentioned in the books of the kings of Israel (NKJV).

The following prophets are mentioned in this way in Chronicles: Samuel, Nathan, Gad, Ahija, Iddo, Shemaiah, Jehu, Isaiah and Hozai.

It remains a question whether the works referred to must be regarded as separate works. This theory is explicitly rejected by Rosemarie Micheel.[25] It is also possible that these references point to

22. Cf. Petersen, *Late Israelite Prophecy*, p. 6.

23. Cf. Petersen, *Late Israelite Prophecy*, p. 13.

24. Cf. S.J. de Vries, *1 and 2 Chronicles* (FOTL; Grand Rapids, MI: Eerdmans, 1989), p. 434.

25. Micheel, *Prophetenüberlieferungen*, p. 79.

the Deuteronomistic History, even though all these prophets are not mentioned in that work.[26] A.G. Auld inclines to the view that these resumés in Kings and Chronicles can be regarded as cross-references between the two works at instances where they differ from a common source.[27] This needs further research. For the purpose of this paper, however, it is more important to ask what the purpose of these references to prophetic sources is. The text offers no reason, but it is quite clear that the text is placed squarely within the prophetic tradition.

Prophets in Chronicles with Parallels in the Deuteronomistic History

There are a number of instances where references to prophets in Chronicles have parallels in the Deuteronomistic History.[28] An example is in 1 Chronicles 17, which can be compared to 2 Samuel 7, regarding the prophet Nathan and David's desire to build a temple. There are only a few minor differences between the two texts (e.g. the omission of 2 Sam. 7.14, with its reference to the possible judgment of Solomon, one of the Chronicler's heroes[29]). In some instances the context of an episode in the two texts may differ, even though the data may correspond quite closely. This can be seen in 1 Chronicles 21. Its parallel in 2 Samuel 24 forms part of the appendix to 2 Samuel, while in Chronicles the story forms part of the main narrative.[30] It happens also in the case of Micaiah and the false prophets in 2 Chronicles 18. In Kings the episode forms part of the history of Ahab, while it forms part of the history of Jehoshaphat in Chronicles. The role of Ahab is minimized.[31] Chronicles ends with a prophetic word that a good king must trust YHWH, while Kings ends with the fulfilment of the prophetic word at the death of Ahab.

26. Cf. de Vries, *1 and 2 Chronicles*, pp. 109-10, and R.B. Dillard, *2 Chronicles* (WBC, 15; Waco, TX: Word, 1987), p. 74.

27. A.G. Auld, 'Prophets through the Looking Glass. Between Writings and Moses', *JSOT* 27 (1983), p. 17.

28. For a discussion of all the examples, cf. Micheel, *Prophetenüberlieferungen*, pp. 11-38.

29. Cf. de Vries, *1 and 2 Chronicles*, p. 153.

30. Cf. P.R. Ackroyd, *I & II Chronicles, Ezra, Nehemiah* (Torch Bible Paperbacks; London: SCM Press, 1973), p. 73.

31. Cf. Micheel, *Prophetenüberlieferungen*, p. 29.

R.B. Dillard says that we have two sermons with the same text.[32] Kings points to the fulfilment of the prophetic word as one of the causes of the exile, while Chronicles wanted to demonstrate the danger of alliances with other nations to the post-exilic community.[33]

A few examples occur in Chronicles where reference is made to events described in the Deuteronomistic History but not described in Chronicles. The reference to the prophecy of Ahijah in 2 Chron. 10.15 is one example. The prophecy itself is described in 1 Kgs 11.29-39, and Chronicles refers to the fulfilment of that prophecy without giving the prophecy. This supposes knowledge of the passage in Kings by the reader of Chronicles.[34] The reference to the word of God through Samuel in 1 Chron. 11.3 is another example, as Samuel's acts are not recorded in Chronicles.

Prophets in Chronicles without a Parallel in the Deuteronomistic History

In some instances Chronicles introduces new material.[35] In some of these instances there is some link with material in the Deuteronomistic History and in others no link at all. Examples of instances in Chronicles with no link at all include some general references to prophets, for example, in v. 22 of the psalm in 1 Chronicles 16 (with a parallel in Ps. 105.15), Jehoshaphat's exhortation to the people to believe in God and his prophets (1 Chron. 20.20), the reference in 2 Chron. 24.19 that God sent prophets to warn the people in the time of Joash, and the reference in 2 Chron. 36.16 that the people mocked the prophets.

In 1 Chron. 25.1-3 a unique use of the verb *nb'* occurs. It is used with reference to Levitical musicians, connecting prophetic action and liturgical music. This aspect of the cult was for the Chronicler part of the legacy of David, who decreed that these musicians should prophesy with musical instruments.[36] The temple musicians worked

32. Dillard, *2 Chronicles*, p. 139.

33. Dillard, *2 Chronicles*, p. 140.

34. Dillard, *2 Chronicles*, p. 87.

35. For a discussion of all the examples, cf. Micheel, *Prophetenüberlieferungen*, pp. 39-70.

36. J.H. Eaton, 'Music's Place in Worship: A Contribution from the Psalms', *Oudtestamentische Studiën*, XXIII (Pretoria, 1984), p. 97.

through prophetic inspiration and the composition and rendering of liturgical music were regarded as a form of prophecy.[37] The prophetic appellation of Levitical musicians is probably an innovation of the Chronicler and his contemporaries[38], giving them claim to a superior status.[39]

In Chronicles a number of prophets appear who are not mentioned in the Deuteronomistic History, like Jahasiel in 2 Chron. 20.14-17. He pronounced an oracle of salvation in the time of Jehoshaphat. The fulfilment of this oracle is described later on in the chapter. In v. 37 of the same chapter another prophet is mentioned, Eliezer the son of Dodavah, who prophesied against Jehoshaphat because of his alliance with Ahaziah the king of Israel. The fulfilment of this prophecy is described in the same verse. This rejection of alliances with foreign kings is one of the Chronicler's pet topics.[40] Other prophets mentioned in Chronicles without parallels in the Deuteronomistic History include the reference to a letter of Elijah in 2 Chron. 21.12-15, Zechariah the son of Jehoiada in 2 Chron. 24.20, another Zechariah in 2 Chron. 26.5, and Oded in 2 Chron. 28.9-11.

There are also some instances where the Chronicler refers to prophets known from the Deuteronomistic History, but introduces new material about them. The letter of Elijah could be an example of this type. In some of the instances reference is only made to a person known from the Deuteronomistic History. In 1 Chronicles reference is made to Heman, who is called the king's seer. His sons were among the musicians appointed by David. A person with the same name is mentioned in 1 Kgs 5.11 (MT) as a wise man. It is not clear whether the same person is meant, but what is important is the link between Levitical musicians and a seer. In 1 Chron. 26.28 reference is made to the seer Samuel who dedicated things that were given in the care of Levites. Again a link is made between a seer and Levites.

There are also instances where deeds of prophets known from the Deuteronomistic History are mentioned, where these deeds do not appear in that work. An example is the prophet Shemaiah in 2 Chron. 12.5, 7-8. He is mentioned in the previous chapter, with a parallel in

37. J. Blenkinsopp, *A History of Prophecy in Israel* (London: SPCK, 1984), p. 254.

38. Petersen, *Late Israelite Prophecy*, p. 62.

39. Petersen, *Late Israelite Prophecy*, p. 66.

40. Dillard, *2 Chronicles*, p. 160.

Kings. In this instance there is no parallel reference to the prophet. He pronounced judgment which resulted in conversion and the suspension of the judgment. 2 Chronicles 12 can be regarded as a chronistic interpretation of 1 Kgs 14.21-31, with the prophet being used to voice the interpretation.[41]

There are also instances where Chronicles expands material from Kings and introduces a prophet in the process. This is perhaps so in the case of 2 Chron. 15.1-8 and the prophet Azariah, the son of Oded.[42] The episode may be related to 1 Kgs 15.12, where reforms of Asa are mentioned. In Chronicles the prophet Azariah is introduced and his words were instrumental in causing the reform. Another example could be in 2 Chron. 16.7-10 with its reference to the seer Hanani. He may be the father of Jehu, mentioned in 1 Kgs 16.1. The cause of his words is Asa's treaty with Ben-Hadad. A parallel can be found in 1 Kgs 15.17-22. In the prophecy Hanani preaches against this treaty. In 1 Kgs 15.23 reference is made to Asa's illness. 2 Chron. 16.12 adds that he did not seek YHWH in his illness. The prophecy of Hanani may be an addition to give the cause of the illness. Dillard says that the Chronicler often uses speeches like this one to state his own theological convictions.[43] A similar example is in 2 Chron. 19.2-3, with its reference to Hanani's son Jehu. He admonishes Jehoshaphat for aiding Ahab, but praises him for his acts as regards the religion. Jehu is also mentioned in 1 Kings 16, but not in this connection. Dillard sees the key to the Chronicler's use of the story of Micaiah in 2 Chron. 19.1-3. He wants to illustrate the evil of foreign alliances and the failure to trust in YHWH.[44] For further examples, see 2 Chron. 25.7-9 and 35.25.

Micheel summarizes her findings on the prophetic material with no parallels in Kings in five points:[45]

1. They comment on and supply interpretations of events described in Kings, linking events to the king's relation to the Lord;
2. Their words are primarily directed at the king;

41. Cf. Micheel, *Prophetenüberlieferungen*, p. 41.
42. Cf. Micheel, *Prophetenüberlieferungen*, pp. 41-45.
43. Dillard, *2 Chronicles*, p. 126.
44. Dillard, *2 Chronicles*, pp. 143-44.
45. Micheel, *Prophetenüberlieferungen*, pp. 67-71.

3. Their message goes back to a theological view that trust in God results in blessing and mistrust brings judgment;
4. Two groups can be distinguished, namely, prophets also known from Kings and prophets introduced in Chronicles; and
5. Three of them had to suffer on account of their message.

Prophets in the Deuteronomistic History with no Parallel in Chronicles

There are a number of instances where prophets appear in the Deuteronomistic History without parallels in Chronicles. Some of them are in parts of the Deuteronomistic History that are omitted in Chronicles, like the time of Samuel and Saul, or pertaining to the kingdom of Israel. Examples of this are in Judg. 6.8-10, 1 Sam. 2.27-36 and 28.6. Reference was already made to the prophecy of Ahijah the fulfilment of which is mentioned in 2 Chron. 10.15, while the prophecy is found in 1 Kings 11. As regards prophets working in the Northern Kingdom, the following have no parallel in Chronicles: 1 Kings 13 (the man of God from Judah and the old prophet of Bethel), Elijah and Elisha, Jehu in 1 Kings 16, the reference in 1 Kgs 18.4 to the 100 prophets concealed by Obadiah, the prophets prophesying against Ahab in 1 Kgs 20, the sons of the prophets in 2 Kgs 2–5 and 9, Jonah in 2 Kgs 14.25 in the Deuteronomistic evaluation of the fall of Samaria in 2 Kings 17, with its reference to prophets in v. 13. Nathan is an example of a prophet appearing in the Deuteronomistic History in a number of instances, of which only one occurs in Chronicles. 2 Samuel 7 has a parallel in Chronicles, but there are no parallels to his deeds in 2 Samuel 12 and 1 Kings 1. This is an example of the omission of episodes that could reflect negatively on David.[46] On the other hand, 2 Chron. 9.29 has a book of Nathan among the sources of the time of Solomon, reflecting at least knowledge of 1 Kings 1.[47] In some instances the omission of these figures may simply be related to the fact that they were northern prophets, but on the other hand some northern prophets are used.[48] Some of the

46. Micheel, *Prophetenüberlieferungen*, p. 11.

47. Micheel, *Prophetenüberlieferungen*, p. 12.

48. Cf. C.T. Begg, 'The Chronicler's Non-Mention of Elisha', *BN* 45 (1988), p. 8.

instances may be related to the Chronicler's point of view. He omitted episodes that did not fit his picture of the people's history.[49] C.T. Begg thinks, for example, that Elisha's omission may be traceable to the episode described in 2 Kings 3,[50] where Elisha said that the alliance of Jehoshaphat, Jehoram and a king of Edom would receive victory from YHWH. This is in opposition to the Chronicler's stance against alliances with foreign nations. In the case of Ezekiel, the Chronicler's non-mention of him may also be ideologically based. Ezekiel subordinates the Levites to the Zadokite priests, while the Chronicler stresses the role of the Levites. In light of this, Ezekiel's description of Levitical apostasy versus Zadokite fidelity (Ezek. 44.10, 15) could be the cause of his non-mention by the Chronicler.[51]

As regards the classical prophets in Chronicles, another study by C.T. Begg deals extensively with the subject.[52] Isaiah's role is minimized in relation to that of Hezekiah. This is related to the special place of Hezekiah in these books. The initiative for his reform was his and he is pictured as a prophet. He can be regarded as the prophet of his time.[53] The treatment of Jeremiah corresponds with that of Isaiah, although he plays a more important part.[54]

Discussion and Conclusions

C.T. Begg distinguishes four general tendencies in the Chronicler's treatment of prophets:[55]

1. He goes much further than the Deuteronomistic History in emphasizing the prophetic dimension in Israel's history and introduces new material.

49. Begg, 'The Chronicler's Non-Mention of Elisha', p. 9.

50. Begg, 'The Chronicler's Non-Mention of Elisha', pp. 10-11.

51. Cf. C.T. Begg, 'The Non-Mention of Ezekiel in the Deuteronomistic History, the Book of Jeremiah and the Chronistic History', in J. Lust (ed.), *Ezekiel and his Book: Textual and Literary Criticism and their Interrelation* (BETL, 74; Leuven: Leuven University Press and Uitgeverij Peeters, 1985), pp. 342-43.

52. C.T. Begg, 'The Classical Prophets in the Chronistic History', *BZ* 32 (1988), pp. 100-107.

53. Begg, 'Classical Prophets', p. 102.

54. Begg, 'Classical Prophets', p. 103.

55. Begg, 'Classical Prophets', pp. 100-101.

2. Prophetic speeches are more closely related to the prophetic books.
3. The Chronicler's prophets have more resemblances to the classical prophets of the prophetic books than to the Deuteronomistic prophets.
4. He uses prophets to fill gaps in the Deuteronomistic succession of prophets in the South.

These four tendencies are fairly general, whereas this paper is intended to investigate the change in the interpretation of the function of prophets and what that reflects of the Chronicler. R.R. Wilson judges that prophets played an important role in the Chronicler's view of society.[56] Their appearance coincided with the founding of the monarchy.[57] A.G. Auld convincingly demonstrates the change in the way prophets were regarded.[58]

The many references to prophetic works in the regnal resumés are the writer's attempt to connect the work with the prophetic tradition. J. Blenkinsopp is of the opinion that the many seers and prophets mentioned as sources in Chronicles demonstrate the idea that prophets were regarded at that point as writers of historical books, whence the name *former prophets.*[59] Prophets are transformed into historians in Chronicles.[60] The writer of Chronicles must have had some link to the cult. The cult is often attacked in the words of the classical prophets in their books. But this aspect of the prophets' word does not function in Chronicles. This is due to the writer's attempt to demonstrate continuity between the prophets of history and those of his own tradition.

As regards the acts of prophets, the Chronicler often closely follows the Deuteronomistic History. For almost every Judaean king he presents a prophetic counterpart that admonished or encouraged him. When his source had a prophet suitable to his purpose, he followed it closely or adapted it to suit his purpose. Nathan in 1 Chronicles 17 is an example of the first possibility, while Gad in 1 Chronicles 21 is an example of the second. The story of Gad resulted in the choice of the

56. R.R. Wilson, *Prophecy and Society in Ancient Israel* (Philadelphia: Fortress Press, 1980), p. 292.

57. Wilson, *Prophecy and Society*, p. 293.

58. Auld, 'Prophets through the Looking Glass'.

59. Blenkinsopp, *A History of Prophecy in Israel*, p. 22.

60. Blenkinsopp, *A History of Prophecy in Israel*, p. 255.

site for the temple, which was very important for the Chronicler. He therefore made this story part of the main narrative. The story of Micaiah in 2 Chronicles 18 is another example of adaptation, as discussed above. As regards titles like prophet and seer, the Chronicler calls only one person a prophet in every king's reign. Other prophetic figures receive titles such as seer.[61]

Auld has a somewhat different view on the relation between Kings and Chronicles regarding the prophetic materials. He thinks that each of these books was developed from a common original. That original had a description of the Micaiah episode, but used the title prophet seldom.[62] According to him the Chronicler used a pre-final form of Kings as his source.[63]

Prophets in Chronicles are often linked to the progress of the theocracy. They played an important role in the founding of the monarchy.[64] They admonished kings and pronounced blessing or judgment, depending on the king's reaction. They were the guardians of the theocracy—and the rejection of their words resulted in judgment, as can be deduced from the reference in 2 Chron. 36.16 that the people mocked the prophets. The actions of the prophets were often linked to the Chronicler's doctrine of retribution. Disobedience resulted in judgment and obedience in blessing. In this regard the rejection of treaties with foreign nations played an important role. Examples of the prophets as guardians of the theocracy occur very frequently (cf. 2 Chron. 11.2-4; 24.19; 20.37; 21.12-15; 24.20; 28.9-11; 12.5, 7-8; 15.1-8; 16.7-10; 19.2-3; 25.7-9). This is the import of the letter of Elijah in 2 Chron. 21.12-15, with the Chronicler's idea of direct retribution placed in the mouth of one of the greatest prophetic figures. The Chronicler often periodizes the history of a king. In the beginning of his reign he was obedient and received blessing. After a time he sinned and received punishment. Between sin and judgment a prophet often appears, foretelling judgment.[65]

2 Chronicles 25 illustrates two aspects of the way prophets are introduced in these books. This chapter describes the history of

61. Cf. Micheel, *Prophetenüberlieferungen*, p. 19.

62. Auld, 'Prophets through the Looking Glass', pp. 7-8.

63. Auld, 'Prophets through the Looking Glass', pp. 8 and 15.

64. Petersen, *Late Israelite Prophecy*, p. 55.

65. S.L. McKenzie, *The Chronicler's Use of the Deuteronomistic History* (HSM, 33; Atlanta: Scholars Press, 1985), p. 114.

Amaziah, with the parallel passage in 2 Kings 14. In the description of Kings no prophets are mentioned. In Chronicles two prophets are introduced. In this way Amaziah gets his prophetic counterparts. In the first instance, in vv. 7-9, a man of God instructed the king not to use Israelite mercenaries against Edom. He obeyed the unknown man of God, with positive results. In vv. 15-16 the actions of another unknown prophet are described. After his return from his victory over Edom, Amaziah bowed down before the gods of the people of Seir. This prophet came to rebuke the king. The king refused to listen. The result was that judgment was pronounced on him. In the following passage the defeat of Amaziah in a battle against Israel is ascribed to his sin and disobedience. Positive and negative retribution is explained through the introduction of two unknown prophets in this chapter. In the theocracy the prophets had the task of proclaiming God's words to the kings of Judah, and they received blessing or judgment in accordance with their reaction to these words.[66] The fate of people and king often depended on their response to the prophetic word.[67]

In Chronicles an attempt is also made to connect Levites and prophets.[68] Sometimes it is done by way of a small remark in the course of the narrative. An example of this is the remark about the Passover, in the time of Josiah, that there had been no Passover like that one since the days of Samuel the prophet (2 Chron. 35.18). Kings refers to the time of the judges.

1 Chron. 25.1-3, discussed above, is an example of a more explicit link between Levites and prophets, between cultic activity and prophecy. The temple musicians worked through prophetic inspiration. Some of the prophets are also Levites in Chronicles: Samuel, Jahaziel in 2 Chron. 20.14-17 and Heman in 1 Chron. 25.4-6. Samuel is linked to the service of the Levites in 1 Chron. 26.28 where reference is made to objects consecrated by him that were later on preserved by Levites. In the cultic service prophetic and poetic inspiration coincided.[69] The Levites became more important in the hierarchy of the Second Temple, and the link between prophets and

66. Dillard, *2 Chronicles*, p. 301.

67. T.C. Eskenazi, 'The Chronicler and the Composition of 1 Esdras', *CBQ* (1986), p. 52.

68. Cf. Wilson, *Prophecy and Society in Ancient Israel*, p. 293.

69. Blenkinsopp, *A History of Prophecy in Israel*, p. 254.

Levites legitimated their place in the new society. Levites also performed the oracular function of prophets, for example, in 2 Chron. 20.13-23 on the battlefield. The fact that this oracle was given by a Levite may be an indication that the traditional prophets had disappeared in the Chronicler's time and that their functions had been taken over by temple personnel.[70] This is an example of the view of the hierocratic party on prophecy in their time.[71] In 2 Chron. 34.30 Levites are mentioned among the people who heard Josiah read from the book of the covenant. 2 Kgs 23.3 refers to prophets instead of Levites. In this way the Chronicler identifies the Levites of his day with the prophets of the nation's history.[72] The Levitical office received prophetic sanction.[73] This can be seen in Hezekiah's reorganization of the Levites. In 2 Chron. 29.25 the following is said:

> Then he stationed the Levites in the house of the Lord with cymbals, with stringed instruments, and with harps, according to the commandment of David, of Gad the king's seer, and of Nathan the prophet; for thus was the commandment of the Lord by his prophets.

In this instance king, prophets and Levites are linked. In v. 30 Hezekiah commanded the Levites to sing praise to the Lord with the words of David and of Asaph the seer. It can again be seen as a reflection of the decline of the prophetic order in the time of the Chronicler and of the rise of the Levites and the Levitical musicians.[74] The Levitical musicians receive Davidic authority for their prophetic activity.[75] A similar instance occurs in the time of Josiah, in 2 Chron. 35.15.[76] In this way practices from the Chronicler's time are retrojected into the past.[77]

In Chronicles the prophets also emphasized the true cult, almost on a par with the actions of kings.[78] Part of the prophetic message is that

70. Dillard, *2 Chronicles*, p. 157; cf. also Petersen, *Late Israelite Prophecy*, pp. 76-77.

71. Petersen, *Late Israelite Prophecy*, p. 77.

72. Petersen, *Late Israelite Prophecy*, p. 85.

73. Cf. Wilson, *Prophecy and Society in Ancient Israel*, p. 293.

74. Cf. Dillard, *2 Chronicles*, p. 236.

75. Petersen, *Late Israelite Prophecy*, p. 84.

76. Cf. Dillard, *2 Chronicles*, p. 291.

77. Eskenazi, 'The Chronicler and the Composition of 1 Esdras', p. 54.

78. J.D. Newsome, 'Towards a New Understanding of the Chronicler and his Purpose', *JBL* 94 (1975), p. 213.

Judah's prosperity is related to its fidelity to the cult. This can be contrasted to the many negative remarks of the classical prophets about the cult. The prophets are responsible for the reconstruction of the temple.[79] Kings also perform prophetic tasks in Chronicles. Hezekiah is a good example:[80] in his actions regarding the cult he is linked with great prophets from the past. J.D. Newsome has demonstrated the prophetic side of some of the kings, such as David, Hezekiah and Solomon.[81] The whole problem of the failure of prophecy is neatly sidestepped in Chronicles by letting prophets make only short-term predictions, with the description of fulfilment usually following soon after.

It remains a valid question whether the changes regarding the prophets in Chronicles against the Deuteronomistic history did not lessen the prophet's role. When a prophet's role is changed, something of his message is lost, or, as W. McKane put it, 'To revere a dead prophet and to confer orthodoxy on what he said in the past is essentially different from discerning the nature of truth attaching to prophetic utterances in the circumstances in which they were spoken'.[82] Prophets are often used in Chronicles to legitimate institutions of the writer's time. It is possible that this treatment of prophets, with only short-term predictions, must be seen as a reaction against the rise of the apocalyptic with its focus on the future and its use of unclear figures of speech. The development of prophecy into apocalyptic was not a unilinear development.[83] Chronicles refers to the prophets of the old days—and, as Auld put it bluntly, a good prophet is always a dead one.[84]

In the Persian period the role of the prophets became smaller and prophecy was transformed into apocalyptic.[85] If it is accepted that the apocalypticists and the Levites were opposing parties, the way prophets are pictured in Chronicles can be regarded as part of an ideological struggle. In history as recreated in Chronicles kings,

79. Petersen, *Late Israelite Prophecy*, p. 56.

80. Begg, 'Classical Prophets', pp. 102-103.

81. Newsome, 'Towards a New Understanding', p. 204.

82. W. McKane, 'Prophet and Institution', *ZAW* 94 (1982), p. 262.

83. Petersen, *Late Israelite Prophecy*, p. 55.

84. Auld, 'Prophets and Prophecy in Jeremiah and Kings', p. 67.

85. R.P. Carroll, *When Prophecy Failed: Reactions and Responses to Failure in Old Testament Prophetic Traditions* (London: SCM Press, 1979), pp. 204-205.

prophets and Levites played the major parts—and only the Levites remained in the new society and a changing world. They are the legitimate successors to the leaders of the pre-exilic community. The temple was to serve as the focal point of a new community[86] and prophets are used in Chronicles to emphasize this role accorded the temple.

It is therefore clear that prophets had a gradually diminishing role in the Persian period. The words of the prophets of former times became important because of a reinterpretation of their role in history too. Prophets became authoritative figures from the past who still had a message in a new time. The coupling of Levites with the prophets and the kings of the people's history also served to emphasize the more important role played by the Levitical hierarchy. Only they remained of the leading pre-exilic institutions. On account of their historical ties with prophets and kings, the Levites were fit to lead the people into a new future.

86. Petersen, *Late Israelite Prophecy*, p. 56.

HEBREW LITERATURE IN THE PERSIAN PERIOD

Giovanni Garbini

I feel I must begin by clarifying my view on the chronology of Hebrew literature, that is the writings which constitute the Bible. Today, it is still very widely held that the hypotheses put forward over a century ago by Julius Wellhausen on the *Torah* and those formulated half a century ago by Martin Noth on the historiographical texts have essentially retained their scientific validity, and for this reason it is not unusual to come across serious discussions of the Hebrew literature of the ninth and tenth centuries BCE. I must confess, however, to belonging to the small group of specialists who do not believe in the existence of the Yahwist, who consider the discovery of *Deuteronomy* in the Jerusalem temple not as a *pious fraud* by Josiah's priests but as a much later and entirely fictitious narrative; of those who see in the 'Succession Narrative' nothing but a very pleasant piece of romantic fiction; those, finally, who believe that the 'memoirs' of 'Nehemiah' were written only after Jerusalem had made acquaintance with a Greek literary genre of biographies and autobiographies. In summary, for me, Hebrew literature begins with the 'Song of Deborah' in the ninth century.

From this viewpoint, which sees pre-exilic texts as not very numerous and, moreover, as having been continually modified in the course of several centuries, it is easy to see the primary importance of the Persian period—two centuries that saw the writing and, most importantly, the reworking of a large part of Hebrew literature, both that which was retained in and that which was excluded from the religious canons established later.

During the pre-exilic period and actually in the course of the exile of Judah, the literary output of the Israelite states had inevitably reflected the ideological tensions that had existed at the heart of the dominant class, the only class capable of literary production. On the one hand there was the monarchy, with its structures, its political choices in relations with other states and its social attitudes at the heart of the state. On the other hand, there were groups opposed to the monarchy for various reasons (various options in foreign policy, the economic interests of an expanding merchant class, religious requirements which gave more weight to ethical values) and which in fact found themselves united in the struggle against the monarchic institution itself, as had been the case in Greece and as was soon to happen in Rome.

The particular nature of the transmission of Hebrew literature, which has come down to us in the form of a reduced *corpus* of religious writings of a normative character, gives us a very limited and very subjective vision of what is supposed to be the literary output of the kingdoms of Samaria and Jerusalem, to the virtual exclusion of the former and with the particular viewpoint of the latter. The writings redacted at the heart of the court—'annalistic', celebratory and liturgical works, having the king as the centre of public and therefore also religious life—have practically all disappeared, as have the works of the pro-monarchy prophets who were active there. There remain some all-but-faithful echoes of these in the distinctly anti-monarchic historiographic works which were written later, from the exile onwards.

Quite numerous, by contrast, and much more intense, are the voices of the opposition, those of the prophets in which are reflected the political passions of the Hebrew *intelligentsia* (oracles against the nations) and especially the anti-monarchic attitude of those who made themselves the apostles of a Yahwism different from this traditional and thus 'Canaanite' type, which was followed by the court: Yahweh Sebaoth versus Yahweh. It is perhaps in this milieu that the 'Book of the Wars of Yahweh' came into being, a work that was intended to present Hebrew national history in an exclusively religious way and thus reduce the figure of the king.

One can therefore affirm that the monarchy constituted the pivot around which all literary production gravitated; this is valid, in general terms, for all literatures of the ancient Near East where the same priestly milieux were in very close contact with the court, but this is particularly valid for the Hebrew literature of the monarchic period, if one thinks that the relative modesty of the two Israelite kingdoms did not permit the existence of a very large category of intellectuals/

functionaries which could have given rise to a literature not directly linked to the court.

This is the framework within which Hebrew literature developed when the two states of Israel and Judah existed. If the fall of Samaria put an end to the literature of the Northern Kingdom (a part of which was saved and collated by the natural heir, the south), the fall of Jerusalem had a very different effect. The political independence of the kingdom of Judah was over, but this was not true of the monarchy nor of the Jewish leading class, both transferred more or less comfortably to Babylon (if King Jeconiah was able there to beget the seven sons (1 Chron. 3.17-18) he had been unable to bring into the world during his three months' reign in Jerusalem (2 Kgs 24.8), this shows that life by the rivers of Babylon was not so bad after all). This indicates that Jerusalem's ideological tensions continued in the land of exile, though with one difference: the issues of foreign policy and social situation no longer existed, and conflict between the monarchy and its opponents became purely ideological and religious. By contrast, the events that had contributed to the end of political independence offered a further argument to the enemies of the monarchy, who found themselves for the first time in a clearly advantageous situation, faced as they were with a discredited king with no real way to defend himself. The conclusion of these troubles was that despite the support of a part of the prophetic milieu (Haggai and Proto-Zechariah), the last king of Judah, Zerubbabel, was removed from the throne by the priestly class led by Joshua, and with him was removed, for several centuries, the monarchy. On the literary level, these events found an eloquent echo in the writings of Deutero-Isaiah, of Ezekiel and of a historian who retraced in his own way all the stages of the monarchy—the exile marked the pinnacle of anti-monarchic literature. When, however, right at the beginning of the Persian period, the monarchy disappeared, Israel found itself lacking both a king and the motifs that had given birth to and sustained its literature over several centuries.

The first consequence of this new situation was the end of the monarchic period's two most important literary genres, that is, historiography and prophetic literature. Deprived of its king, Israel no longer felt the need to commit its own troubles to historical remembrance; only when there was a new monarchy with the Maccabeo-Hasmoneans did they start writing historiographical works again, such as the first book of the Maccabees. With the exception of the literary dissimulation of the memoirs of Nehemiah, entire centuries of Hebrew history were deliberately abandoned to oblivion and the good will of modern archaeologists. It is true that they continued to write history (as is testified to by the *Chronicles* in a period later than that which interests us here), but then it was only a question of rewriting, according to the new perspectives, an old history which was ever more distant in time and served increasingly as a pretext for the propaganda of the new ideologies.

As soon as the king had disappeared, even his opponents no longer had a *raison d'être*. Without an enemy to attack and criticise, with no direct responsibility in the conduct of political and economic life, the writing prophets no longer had a function to fill. Even in this case, however, there were attempts to take up the ancient texts again, to imitate them and, especially, to adapt them to the requirements of the new currents of thought. To conclude, at the beginning of the Persian period, Hebrew literature was at its lowest ebb.

It is well known that the Persian period is one of the least well-known periods in Hebrew history and, as far as Palestine is concerned, the poorest in archaeological material. The lack of direct sources on the most important centres of Hebraism should not surprise us unduly in the light of the apparent anomalies revealed by the Elephantine papyri. I say 'apparent', since it is clear that the reality was different from what was imagined later in Jerusalem. In this situation, it is impossible to determine precisely what were the Hebrew milieux in which the new literature developed.

The only historically identifiable point of reference is the priestly milieu of Jerusalem, which in fact exercised political dominion (under Persian tutelage) over a small part of the territory of Palestine. It is not difficult to imagine what might have been the literary output of the milieu in question: primarily a new redaction of liturgical texts and temple legislation corresponding to the requirements of the new situation, that is, that of a divine service in which the protagonist was no longer the King but a High Priest. It seems fair enough to assume that the latter took over many of the prerogatives of his predecessor; several Psalms and a large part of the non-narrative texts in the Torah would have had their first redaction at the start of the new age in the temple in Jerusalem. This type of literature, however, which one may consider routine and in its final form rather banal, only constituted a part of the conceptual re-elaboration practised by the post-exilic priesthood. Its new function as political guide, albeit in restricted terms, to a nation represented by the small group of people that had returned from the exile, went hand in hand in the new leading class with the need for deep reflection on the causes of the Hebrew people's tragedy (a tragedy moreover identical to that of many other peoples that had been victim to Assyrian and Babylonian imperialism) and especially on its own role and its own identity.

This is certainly not the place to trace, even in the broadest strokes, the development of Hebrew thought as it was shaped in Persian Jerusalem. Beyond the limits of this paper, we need to consider the extreme difficulty of identifying today how much in post-exilic Hebrew literature dates back to the Persian period and how much to the Hellenistic period. We may fairly assume however that many pre-exilic prophetic texts were taken up again, reworked and adapted to the experience of exile and return, while a current of thought that came in the wake of the ideas developed during the exile made the monarchy and the old leading class responsible for the political disaster. According to the teaching of Deutero-Isaiah, the people of Israel was from this point on the second contractual member of the pact with God, but it is important to enquire what this people's reality consisted in. What we know about the internal struggles that tore the priestly class apart in the Hellenistic period and about the political position which was then assumed by the Pharisees—whose support came from the popular classes—makes it easy to imagine that Jerusalem's new leaders must have identified Israel first and foremost with themselves, practically leaving aside the vast majority of the people of Judah and Samaria.

I believe I have thus identified a primary nucleus of Hebrew literary creation during the Persian period, in the need for self-definition within the group in power, which had taken the place of the monarchy. What had been the literature of the court is now replaced by the literature of the temple, perhaps less entertaining but certainly more self-conscious, in the name of national continuity, the most clear expressions of which can be seen in the use of the older Hebrew language, which was no longer spoken (with all respect to today's nationalists), and its ideological foundation in the cult of the old dynastic god Yahweh.

Even if the historical framework presented by the biblical writings, canonical or not—with the triumphant return of the survivors from Babylon and the total silence of the sources on the groups of Israelites who remained in Babylon or had moved away to Egypt despite Jeremiah's curses—aims to give the *impression* that the only Israel was that of Jerusalem and its environs, an objective analysis of the Hebrew writings reveals a quite different reality. In texts that can be reasonably dated to the Persian period, we find new concerns, unknown to both pre-exilic and post-exilic Palestinian Hebraism, which reveal a not insignificant level of contact with Babylonian culture. On the other hand, there exists a narrative literature, brilliant and suggestive, which springs from an originally Egyptian context. As was often the case in the history of Hebrew culture and thought, these developed in an original and creative way when they came into contact with particularly vivid forms of thought: just as it is impossible to envisage Philo without Greek philosophy, Ibn Gabirol without Arabic neo-platonism or Spinoza without Descartes, it is difficult to envisage the ethico-religious reflection of the first chapters of Genesis and that of the *Book of Watchers* without the Babylonian religious and literary tradition.

The existential problem of human beings, completely unknown to Egyptian literature, had been central in the Mesopotamian literature of the second millennium, both in the Sumerian and Akkadian languages; the human condition was defined at the very moment of the creation of humankind. With the arrival in Babylon of Iranian religious thought, focused on the problem of evil to the point of giving it its own metaphysical autonomy in the figure of Angra Mainyu (later Ahriman), anthropological reflection became closely interlinked with reflection on the origin of evil. It is from this perspective that the Hebrew story of the creation of human beings is written, such as it is presented to us in the second and third chapters of Genesis, where there is not infrequent explicit reference to Babylonian texts. The presence of evil in the world is subsequently developed differently in works such as the *Book of Watchers*, the subject-matter of which was clumsily taken up at the start of the sixth chapter of Genesis.

I do not want to turn my attention away from the importance of this viewpoint in the Hebrew thought that developed parallel to that which was retained in the canonical texts and which proved so important in the definition of this type of Judaism which developed into Christianity. What I want to underline is the fact that during the

Persian period an essential part of Hebrew literature, probably much more rich than one can imagine today, was created in Babylon by a Judaism that must certainly have had close links with Jerusalem but which nevertheless had its own individuality and, especially, a cultural make-up fed by daily contact with the most creative currents in oriental thought. If I may make a comparison, I would place the Babylonian Hebraism of the Achaemenid age next to the Spanish Hebraism of the Arabic period, and it is this Hebraism that seems to me to reveal the most original and, so to speak, the most modern traits—it is not by chance that the Babylonian Jews wrote in Aramaic.

I have just alluded to an Egyptian-inspired Hebrew narrative prose. It would be sufficient to cite the story of Joseph, but one must not neglect the hardly edifying Egyptian adventure of Abraham, the youth of Moses and the whole range of historical traditions relating to Egyptian Hebraism, of which there are some echoes in the Judeo-Hellenistic writers but otherwise virtual silence in what has come down to us. There certainly existed a significant and vibrant Egyptian Hebraism, since it is unthinkable that so many Jews might have arrived in Egypt only after the foundation of Alexandria. It is not easy to imagine, based on the few elements to which we have access, what might have been the characteristics of the literature expressed by the groups of Jews living in Egypt; we will, however, not be succumbing to speculation if we consider its attachment to the national tradition an essential aspect: as in Jerusalem, but unlike in Babylon, in Egypt they wrote in Hebrew, and, better still, they wrote about their own roots, all the more important since these reached back into just that Egyptian territory where this literature flourished. It seems that the ethical problems that fed the Babylonian Hebrew literature were not debated in Egypt; nor did they dig about in ancient history to justify the present, as was done in Jerusalem. The Jews who lived in Egypt had a sense of being, all things considered, in a place that was not entirely foreign to them and where it was in fact quite agreeable to live; further, since a pleasing narrative literature had flourished in Egypt, they also wanted to tell their stories, in an attractive way and without too many ideological complications.

Jerusalem, Babylon and an unknown vague locality in Egypt were therefore the places where Hebrew literature between the end of the sixth and the end of the fourth centuries most probably developed. If the reconstruction proposed here is correct, each of the three centres had its own cultural make-up and a particular type of intellectual requirement. It is however immediately apparent that the framework is far from complete: in the Hebrew Bible, we find a literature, a fascinating literature, which in all probability dates from that period and which has not been situated in the above scheme. This concerns large amounts of narrative prose that has subsequently come together in the books of Samuel and Kings, perhaps also in Judges. In certain cases, it is difficult to choose between the Persian and Hellenistic Periods (who could resolve with any certainty cases such as Ruth or the stories of Samson?), but in others the problem does not seem to present itself, at least within the limits of what we think we know: it is difficult to attribute to the Hellenistic period the 'Succession Narrative' or the stories about Elijah or Elisha. These narratives, which represent the highpoints of Hebrew narrative prose—where were they written, and by whom?

It seems very difficult to suppose that these narratives, written in Hebrew and situated in Palestine, could have been written anywhere other than in Jerusalem. It is equally difficult, however, to attribute them to the same priestly milieu that was in the process of revising the prophetic writings. We can gain an idea of the spiritual atmosphere in which at least some of these literary compositions matured (I am thinking particularly of that 'History of the Kings' of which the 'Succession narrative' is, at least in my opinion, only a part) by looking at the works themselves.

The original parts of these stories of kings and prophets (who appear in the current texts mixed with contaminations and later additions) are in the first place pleasant narratives, the work of writers who wanted above all to write attractive stories. The characters were drawn from the ancient national memory but the events must have been nearly all invented. One does not write what we call a historical novel without a certain political and moral vision, but this is subordinate to the story told, not a thesis to be defended. They spoke of kings because during the Persian period these were the only personages worthy of having stories told about them, as Herodotus shows us with figures such as Croesus and Gyges; that their troubles be dramatic is a basic requirement of the story itself: with good actions one earns paradise but bores the reader. Presenting the kings of Shechem, Jerusalem and Samaria in an unfavourable light was a part of the general atmosphere of post-exilic Jerusalem (it is hard to imagine that anyone might have been able to seriously sustain that the moral weaknesses of David and the political misdeeds of Solomon might have justified the accession to the throne of the latter); these kings acted like kings, without considering morality, which was a category foreign to their nature. If one wants to find details that might be able to illumine us on the political position of the author, one might mention sympathy for the tragic figure of Saul and interest for the sovereigns of the northern kingdom—the 'house of David' had not yet become a myth, and Samaria was not yet the arch-enemy.

On the hills of Jerusalem, a certain distance from the temple, some learned man, or perhaps priest who felt he was artistically gifted, gave new life to the distant and dramatic figures of the past, by breathing into them a humanity lacking in the annalistic tradition. He put next to them unforgettable female figures by also inventing love stories (Michal is perhaps the only woman in love in any ancient Near Eastern literature).

To conclude this analysis of Hebrew literature during the Persian period, if it is neither completely absurd nor lacking in evidence, I believe I can say that under the domination of the Achaemenids, Hebraism knew its magical moment and Hebrew literature its golden age. During the all too short interval between the ideological tensions that opposed prophecy to the monarchy and the yet greater tensions provoked in Hebraism as throughout the Near East by the arrival of Alexander the Macedonian with all that followed, Hebrew culture had the leisure to manifest itself according to the most authentic tendencies, without the exaggerations provoked by political and ideological struggles. Sense of tradition, piety, moral demands examined at the metaphysical level, richness of humanity and of understanding, these are the clearest traits that characterize the ground where the Hebrew literature of the fifth to fourth centuries was born, at the heart of this *Pax iranica* which was only marginally scratched away by the unfortunate Greek adventure. As ever in history, this was the calm before the storm, but it was at least calm. We should not regret that the Hebraism of the Persian period did not have a history; on the contrary, we should, for just that reason, consider that it has been fortunate and be grateful to it for having given us the most beautiful pages of Hebrew literature.

Composition and Chronology in the Book of Ezra–Nehemiah

Sara Japhet

Among the problems that concern scholars of the Book of Ezra–Nehemiah (= EN)—which is the main source for the period of the Restoration and the history of Judah under Persian rule[1]—are two that appear to be independent of each other: the literary or literary-historical question regarding the structure and composition of the book, and the historical or historiographical problem regarding the chronology upon which it is based and which emerges from it. Before explaining why I have chosen to present these two issues as dependent upon one another, I shall first present the central problems in each of the two areas.

I

The point of departure for any discussion of the question of composition is EN as a whole, before it was divided in two by later traditions.[2] From this compulsory point of departure, which is sometimes

1. This estimation is still valid, despite a certain increase in extra-biblical epigraphical and archaeological sources. On the history of criticism regarding the value of EN as a historical source, see S. Japhet, 'The Historical Reliability of Chronicles—The History of the Problem and its Place in Biblical Research', *JSOT* 33 (1985), pp. 83-107, esp. pp. 88-94; D.J.A. Clines, 'The Nehemiah Memoir: The Perils of Autobiography', in *What Does Eve Do to Help?* (JSOTSup, 94; Sheffield: JSOT Press, 1990), pp. 124-64; L.L. Grabbe, 'Reconstructing History from the Book of Ezra', in P.R. Davies (ed.), *Second Temple Studies*. I. *Pursian Period* (JSOTSup, 117; Sheffield: JSOT Press, 1991), pp. 98-106. Regarding the definition and subdivision of the period, see S. Japhet, 'The Temple in the Restoration Period: Reality and Ideology', *USQR* 43 (1991), pp. 196-97, 243.

2. See H.G.M. Williamson, *Ezra*, *Nehemiah* (WBC, 16; Waco, TX: Word, 1985), pp. xxi-xxii. Henceforth: Williamson.

termed 'canonical',[3] arise the questions regarding the book's structure, composition and author. Suggestions that the book should be viewed as a compilation of shorter, independent works, or, alternatively, as part of a larger work, as well as suggestions for identifying the author or authors and for reconstructing the process of its formation, have all been proposed as solutions to the problems that the book as it stands presents to the reader. In treating this question many scholars seem to hasten to advance immediately to the second stage;[4] we shall first dwell upon the book that we have before us.

On the basis of internal criteria such as contents, style, narrative technique and the like, and on the basis of formal criteria such as opening formulae, EN comprises three well-defined units:

1. Ezra 1–6, describing the history of the Temple from the first year of Cyrus (Ezra 1.1) until the sixth year of the reign of Darius (Ezra 6.15).
2. Ezra 7–10, the story of Ezra, which begins with a new opening phrase: 'After these events' (Ezra 7.1), presents new protagonists and is written in a different style.
3. Nehemiah 1–13, the story of Nehemiah, which also begins with a new opening phrase, 'The words of Nehemiah son of Hacaliah' (Neh. 1.1), and which ends with the last words of Nehemiah: 'O my God, remember it to my credit!' (13.31).

This simple structure presents events in chronological sequence: beginning with the building of the Temple, then Ezra the Scribe and his activities, and finally, the acts and achievements of Nehemiah. The non-critical reader will interpret this structure as an authentic reflection of historical events: the first told first, and the last, last. In a critical, literary-historical reading, however, this structure may be interpreted as an expression of the literary process, meaning that EN has been composed of the combination of three compositions, each

3. It seems that this term was coined following the general approach of Childs to the study of the Bible. See B.S. Childs, *Introduction to the Old Testament as Scripture* (Philadelphia: Fortress Press, 1979); J. Blenkinsopp, *Ezra–Nehemiah: A Commentary* (OTL; Philadelphia: Westminster Press, 1988), p. 41 (Henceforth: Blenkinsopp). The use of this term does not, of course, indicate acceptance of Childs's method.

4. On this matter see the criticism of T.C. Eskenazi, 'The Structure of Ezra–Nehemiah and the Integrity of the Book', *JBL* 107 (1988), p. 642.

of which existed independently before being joined together into the present work. This combination may be viewed as a single act or as a multi-staged process: first the two elements of the Book of Ezra were combined, and later the Book of Nehemiah was joined to it or placed adjacent to it. Indeed, those scholars who maintain that Ezra and Nehemiah are essentially two separate and independent works subscribe to this opinion or to one similar to it, arguing that their combination is merely a technical and late development.[5] The view of the book as a combination, in one or several stages, makes the question of authorship insignificant, leaving no good reason for seeking traces of the author in the creation of the book. The main focus of attention then shifts to each of the components of the book, with its structure, composition and authorship.

Indeed, each of the three components of EN is complex, and the topic of composition presents more than a few problems in each of them.[6] I shall present a number of these, following the order of the units:

5. Such as M.Z. Segal, 'The Books of Ezra and Nehemiah', *Tarbiz* 14 (1943), pp. 93-96, 103 (in Hebrew). In Segal's opinion the book of Nehemiah was written before the book of Ezra. S. Talmon, 'Ezra and Nehemiah (Books and Men)', *IDBSup*, p. 318 (but on p. 322 and following a different view is reflected); M. Kochman, 'Introduction to the Books of Ezra and Nehemiah', in N. Heltzer and M. Kochman, 'The Books of Ezra and Nehemiah', *The World of the Bible Encyclopedia* (Jerusalem: Revivim, 1985), p. 4 (in Hebrew). Kochman's remarks are not unequivocal. On p. 4 he says, 'It seems that the two books were not even edited by the same person', while on p. 5 he speaks of 'the editor of Ezra–Nehemiah'.

6. For detailed discussions of this subject one may consult the commentaries on EN, both the introductions and also the relevant passages of the commentary. In addition to commentaries that have already been mentioned (see nn. 2, 3 above), I might mention, among others, L.W. Batten, *A Critical and Exegetical Commentary on the Books of Ezra and Nehemiah* (ICC; Tübingen: Mohr, 1913), pp. 14-24; W. Rudolph, *Esra und Nehemia* (HAT; Edinburgh: T. & T. Clark, 1949), pp. xxii-xxiv (Henceforth: Rudolph); D.J.A. Clines, *Ezra, Nehemiah, Esther* (NCB; Grand Rapids: Eerdmans, 1984), pp. 9-12; A.H.J. Gunneweg, *Esra* (KAT; Gütersloh: Mohn, 1985), pp. 28-31. See also U. Kellermann, *Nehemia—Quellen, Überlieferung und Geschichte* (BZAW, 102; Berlin: Töpelmann, 1967), pp. 8-56; T.W. In Der Smitten, *Esra: Quellen, Überlieferung und Geschichte* (SSN, 15; Assen: Van Gorcum, 1973), pp. 3-26.

A. *For Ezra 1–6 three central problems may be presented:*
1. The change of language in the course of the unit: the story begins in Hebrew (1.1–4.7), passes over to Aramaic (4.8–6.18), and concludes in Hebrew (6.19-22). Hence the Hebrew part is a kind of framework within which the Aramaic portion is embedded.

2. The section comprises material of two major literary genres: narrative and document, and the transitions between them or their integration do not depend upon the change in language. The documents in the Hebrew part are Cyrus' proclamation (1.2-4), the list of the Temple vessels (1.9-11a), and the list of the returnees (2.2-67). In the Aramaic part they are: the correspondence of Rehum, the commissioner and Shimshai the scribe with Artaxerxes (4.[8]9-22), and the correspondence between Tattenai, governor of the province of Beyond the River and Darius (5.4[?], 7-17; 6.3-12). The rest of the text, both in Hebrew and in Aramaic, is narrative.[7]

3. Chapter 4 presents a particular difficulty, because of the evident lack of continuity in subject matter and chronology. The chapter passes from the construction of the Temple to the building of the city, and from the period of Cyrus to that of Ahasuerus and Artaxerxes and then to Darius (4.3, 5, 6, 7, 23, 24). In this chapter the problems of composition and chronology are closely connected, and we shall return to them below.[8]

B. *Ezra 7–10 also presents three central compositional problems*, and the first two are shared with the first section of the book. The transition from language to language is expressed in the literal citation of one document: the letter given by King Artaxerxes to Ezra the Scribe, which is written in Aramaic (Ezra 7.12-16). This document also expresses the combination of narrative and document. Additional documents include Ezra's genealogy (7.1-5), the list of returnees (8.1-14, and its appendices, 8.19-20), the list of donations (8.26-27), and the list of those who had married foreign women (10.18-43). However, a

7. The transitions from narrative to document and back are not always smooth. See for example Ezra 4.8, 9-11; 5.4; 6.6. In general it may be said that the documents are placed within the stories as in a frame, and on this matter see also: S. Japhet, 'Biblical Historiography in the Persian Period', in H. Tadmor and I. Eph'al (eds.), *WHJP*, VI (1983), pp. 181-82 (in Hebrew); H.G.M. Williamson, 'The Composition of Ezra I–VI', *JTS* 34 (1983), pp. 1-26.

8. See below, p. 206, and see S. Japhet, 'The Temple in the Restoration Period', pp. 203-206.

more complex problem in this section of the book is the shift in literary style from a first-person narrative of autobiographical character (7.27–9.15) to a third-person narrative, where Ezra is the main protagonist of the story but not its author (7.1-26; 10.1-44).[9] Thus the autobiographical unit is embedded within an overall literary framework. At the same time it must be noted that the shift in style from third-person to first-person and back does not influence either the continuity of the story or the plot, the unity of which is preserved, nor does it affect the combination of documents and narrative, which is found throughout the book.

C. *The most difficult problems relating to composition are found in the third section*, in Nehemiah 1–13, making its very definition as a single unit problematical. However, its opening with 'the words of Nehemiah' and its conclusion with Nehemiah's prayer delimit it clearly, demanding that it be seen from that viewpoint.

1. The major problem derives from the changes in style and literary genre. 'The words of Nehemiah' begins in Neh. 1.1 as an autobiographical composition with its own linguistic and stylistic stamp.[10] This style is preserved even, among other things, in the frequent transitions from singular to plural, which express the close identification of the speaker, Nehemiah, with the community for whom he speaks (Neh. 2.19, 20; 4.9-17 and elsewhere). The uniform autobiographical style dominates in Neh. 1.1–7.5 and 13.4-31 and determines the framework of this unit, whereas all the intervening material in Neh. 7.6–13.3 is characterized by variety and lack of uniformity. Here we find a mixture of genres and styles, and, as for the speaker, Nehemiah is still present from time to time, but in certain sections he is mentioned in the third person and in others he is not mentioned at all.[11]

9. See, among others, S. Mowinckel, '"Ich" und "Er" in der Esrageschichte', in A. Kuschke (ed.), *Verbannung und Heimkehr: Beiträge zur Geschichte und Theologie Israels im 6 und 5 Jahrhundert v. Chr.* (FS W. Rudolph; Tübingen: Mohr, 1961), pp. 211-33.

10. The definition of the work as 'the words of Nehemiah the son of Hacaliah' is found in the book itself, Neh. 1.1. The question of whether this is an authentic autobiographical work, written by Nehemiah, or a work written in autobiographical style, is of no concern in the present context. On questions of this type, see, for example, Clines, 'The Nehemiah Memoir'.

11. Nehemiah is mentioned in the third person in Neh. 8.9, 10.2, 12.26, 47—

2. The first question arising from this literary reality is that of the precise extent of 'the words of Nehemiah'. We may ask whether all of Nehemiah 1–7 should be included in it, or should the list of the builders of the wall of Jerusalem (Neh. 3.1-32), for example, be regarded as secondary to it?[12] From a different perspective, we may ask whether 'the words of Nehemiah' should be limited to Nehemiah 1–7 and 13.4-31, or should 'traces' of it be looked for in 7.6–13.3 as well? The considerations pertaining to this matter touch upon questions both of style and literary genre and also of the literary and topical continuity, and the decision is not always easy.[13] It is frequently determined by the scholar's preconceptions regarding the degree of stylistic uniformity and narrative continuity that may be expected in any work, and thus in 'the words of Nehemiah' as well.

In the light of the literary and topical continuity one may also join the list in Neh. 7.6-72 to 'the words of Nehemiah'. Nehemiah is certainly not the author of this list, as he himself says (Neh. 7.5), but some commentators would include the list in his work. The autobiographical style also shows in the description of the dedication of the wall (Neh. 12.31, 38, 40) and in the wording of the covenant (10.1-40). Thus it is possible that these passages, in their present form or in a different one, derived from Nehemiah's own words. However, even if we enlarge as much as possible the extent of the 'words of Nehemiah' and include controversial passages in it, we can only attribute to it Neh. 7.6-72, 10.1–11.2 and 12.27-43. This still does not cover all the material, and the resulting composition remains incomplete. Within it

that is, in each of the central components of this section (the reading of the Torah in chs. 8–9, the making of the covenant in ch. 10, and the lists in chs. 11–12). However these units themselves are complex, as we shall see below.

12. This question received a negative answer in the work of Torrey, who denies the list any historical value. See C.C. Torrey, *The Composition and Historical Value of Ezra–Nehemiah* (BZAW, 2; Berlin: J. Ricker, 1896), pp. 37-38. Mowinckel believes that it was inserted by a later editor; see S. Mowinckel, *Studien zu dem Buche Esra–Nehemia*, I (Oslo: Universitetsforlaget, 1964), pp. 109-16; Blenkinsopp also prefers the possibility that this material comes from another source (p. 47). But Rudolph, for example, maintains that this list, as well as Neh. 7.6-72, were already included in 'the words of Nehemiah' (Rudolph, p. 113), and see Williamson, pp. 201-202.

13. In all these matters there is no agreement among scholars, and we cannot expand upon this here. My remarks below are not intended to be conclusive but rather to suggest possibilities.

are passages that do not fit into any full continuity.[14]

3. What is the composition and source of the rest of the material in the Book of Nehemiah? It seems that at least three components are to be found in it, regarding whose existence and literary definition there is general agreement among commentators, although controversy persists regarding the original extent of each of them, its origin, and its relation to the final work. In general outline, and without taking a position with regard to controversial matters, these components are as follows:

a. A narrative describing the events of the seventh month in the time of Ezra. This certainly includes Neh. 8.1–9.3, but the question arises regarding the following two chapters, Neh. 9.4–10.40, which are combined with it into a single unit within the present narrative continuum. It seems probable that the great prayer in Neh. 9.5b-37 predated Ezra the Scribe;[15] but was it already included in the present narrative? As for Nehemiah 10, is its source in 'the words of Nehemiah' (see above), or did it have an independent literary existence? Despite these questions, in the existing literary reality, this component may be defined as 'the story of Ezra'. Ezra is the main protagonist of the narrative, and the story has a uniform character.[16]

b. Lists (Neh. 11.3–12.26). As we have thus far seen, various types of lists are included within the narrative continuum in each of the sections of the book; in Neh. 11.1–12.26, however, they constitute a

14. The connection of Neh. 11.1-2 to Neh. 7.5 or 72a creates continuity in content but not a textual one, and some link appears to be missing in the story. This combination also leaves Neh. 10 out of the sequence and emphasizes the question of where it originally belonged: should it be placed before Neh. 11.1-2 and joined in some way to Neh. 7.72a? Should it be regarded as the conclusion of Neh. 8–9, so that it is viewed as part of the 'story of Ezra'? Or should it be viewed as an independent unit? Also in the following two junction points—the story of the dedication of the wall in 12.27-43 and the account of Nehemiah's sccond term of office (13.4ff.)—the narrative sequence is not fully clear.

15. Concerning this prayer, see H.G.M. Williamson, 'Structure and Historiography in Nehemiah 9', *Proceedings of the Ninth World Congress of Jewish Studies, 1985 Panel Sessions* (Jerusalem, 1988), pp. 117-31; G. Rendsburg, 'The Northern Origin of Nehemiah 9', *Bib* 72 (1991), pp. 348-66.

16. See also Blenkinsopp's remarks on this subject. In his opinion, Nehemiah rather than Ezra is the hero of the story. He also separates Neh. 9–10 from the story of Ezra and sees Neh. 10 as the latest element in the book. But he argues that, nevertheless, this section (Neh. 7.5–10.40) 'has its own logic and preserves a kind of unity independent of its context' (p. 46).

different sort of literary phenomenon. This is a compilation of lists that are not integrated into the narrative but stand by themselves. They cannot be included in any of the earlier compositions, either in 'the words of Nehemiah' or in 'the story of Ezra'. Moreover, they themselves do not compose a complete unit.[17] This is essentially a compilation. Each of the lists undoubtedly has its own independent history, but it is difficult to assume that the compilation itself had any independent existence.

c. Some of the literary units do not belong to any of the components described above. First of all this refers to Neh. 12.44–13.3, but other passages may also be included in this category, depending on the definition of each commentator.

Thus we find that each of the component sections of EN is a composite, though there is a difference in degree, which becomes a difference in kind, between the units of the Book of Ezra and those of the Book of Nehemiah. Both in Ezra 1–6 and Ezra 7–10 one may find unity of style and literary method as well as overall continuity in narrative and subject matter which define these units as literary entities. This is not true of Nehemiah 1–13, where one does not find the same degree of literary uniformity overcoming the variety of its parts. Moreover, as shown above, one of the components of Nehemiah 8–13, which at least includes Nehemiah 8, is a literary entity similar in all its aspects to the 'Story of Ezra' in Ezra 7–10, and it may even be designated by that title. The natural conclusion here is that Nehemiah 8 initially belonged to the story of Ezra, and this position is adopted by practically all scholars.[18] The problem still remains of the place of

17. Neh. 11 is organized into a literary sequence. The list is preceded by a heading: 'These are the heads of the province who lived in Jerusalem—in the countryside of Judah, the people lived in their towns, each on his own property' (11.3). Then it proceeds to describe the inhabitants of Jerusalem (vv. 4-24) and those who lived in villages, in Judah (vv. 25b-30) and in Benjamin (vv. 31-36). Neh. 12.1-26 contains four lists, all of which present various information about the priests and Levites: the lists of the priests and Levites 'in the time of Jeshua'; the priests (12.1-7) and the Levites (12.8-9); the list of the High Priests (12.10-11), 'the list of the priests' in the time of Joiakim (12.12-21) and 'the Levites' in 'the time of Johanan son of Eliashib' (12.23-25), as well as two headings (vv. 22, 26), which perhaps serve as introductory and concluding phrases.

18. This includes scholars who believe that the Book of Ezra and the Book of Nehemiah are essentially two separate works. See for example Segal, 'The Books of Ezra and Nehemiah', p. 103; Kochman, 'The Books of Ezra and Nehemiah', p. 5.

Nehemiah 8 (or 8–10) in the context of the story of Ezra: is it a continuation of Ezra 10 or does it belong elsewhere?[19] But this problem is not sufficient to cast doubt upon the original connection of Nehemiah 8 to the story of Ezra. This association proves that in an earlier stage, prior to the literary reality of EN, Nehemiah 8 belonged to Ezra 7–10. The conclusion necessarily follows that the connection between the Book of Ezra and the Book of Nehemiah cannot be viewed as an entirely external combination. The connection between them belongs to the level of the sources from which the present book was constructed—a conclusion that brings us back to the question of the composition of EN as a whole, and to the role of its author. The tension between the final structure of the work and the continuity, uniformity and unity of its component parts necessitates the assumption of the existence and action of an author/editor. What were the function and aims of that author in composing the work?

II

A number of possible solutions are available to the scholar who seeks to answer the questions of composition and editing of EN. However, the most prevalent is the diachronic approach, according to which the composition of the book was a multi-staged process in which the literary units were compiled and joined to each other. Since the book is seen as being composed of various literary sources—whole works or isolated documents—deriving from various times and written by various authors, this approach does not distinguish sharply and unequivocally between the various stages of the literary process, some of which are 'creative writing', while others are 'editing'. The creation of the book is seen as one extended line upon which lie a large number of points, and it continues past what has been determined as the 'final' composition, in the figure of 'additions', inserted into the book in the course of transmission. Thus the 'Book', the final outcome of this process is not the planned result of a premeditated action. It is not a coherent composition whose plan was determined in advance so that a structural logic is reflected in it, but rather the result of a literary process, parts of which were quite coincidental. In

19. The most common suggestion is to view the reading of the Torah as Ezra's first action after his arrival in Jerusalem, that is, to place Neh. 8 after Ezra 8. See for example Rudolph, p. xxii, Blenkinsopp, p. 45, Williamson, p. xxxi, etc.

reconstructing this process, a scholar may define its 'final' point anywhere along the extended line, and, according to his or her inclinations, ignore everything that came afterward.

The great advantage of this conception is in its diachronical-historical aspect. It mitigates the difficulty presented by the contradictions and inconsistencies and permits maximum consideration of all the varieties that are evident in the work. Moreover, it liberates the authors and editors from the burden of the contradictions and inconsistencies and turns them into 'systematic' and 'rational' authors. Such a view gives the scholar a great deal of freedom in understanding the composition of the book, and thus in reconstructing its meaning. Let us illustrate this with two examples, from among many, those of Rudolph and Williamson. These two approaches differ from each other, but they have in common both the fact that they are examples of a 'middle line', not the extremes,[20] and also the clarity with which they are presented.

Rudolph assigns great importance to the author of Ezra–Nehemiah. He identifies him with the Chronicler and attributes great weight to him in molding the literary and theological character of the book. In his opinion, this author's method combined creative writing with use of sources, which are presented in their own language or reworked, and his hand as a writer and adapter is evident in all parts of the book.[21] In the light of this conception, which may explain the variety found in the book as a result of the author's use of sources, and which attributes great importance to the author, it might be expected that the 'book' to which Rudolph relates, that is, the product that left the hands of the writer/editor, would be EN as we have it—but that is not the case. Rudolph does not even try to clarify the structure and meaning

20. As a special group one should mention those scholars who believe that the original form of the book is that which is reflected in the apocryphal book of Esdras. After 2 Chron. 35–36, the book includes Ezra 1–10 and Neh. 8.1-12. See especially K.F. Pohlmann, *Studien zum dritten Esra* (FRLANT, 104; Göttingen: Vandenhoeck & Ruprecht, 1970), and in the same spirit, Dequeker (n. 29 below). Since I regard the secondary character of this work as firmly established, I shall not address this position and its conclusions in detail.

21. See Rudolph, pp. xxii-xxiii. The method itself is influenced strongly by the general approach of Noth. See M. Noth, *Überlieferungsgeschichtliche Studien* (Tübingen: Max Niemeyer Verlag, 2nd edn, 1957 [1943]), pp. 155-61 (= *The Chronicler's History* [trans. H.G.M. Williamson with an introduction; JSOTSup, 50; Sheffield: JSOT Press, 1987], pp. 75-81).

of EN as it is. He assumes that when the work left the author's hands it was different in two important points from the version in the biblical canon:

1. The order of the chapters, and thus the progress of the story were considerably different. The original order was: Ezra 1–8; Neh. 7.72b–8.18; Ezra 9.1–10.44; Neh. 9.1–10.40; Neh. 1.1–7.72a; 11.1–13.31. The subsequent change in the order and the creation of the present structure resulted from an error, the misunderstanding of a later editor.[22]
2. The book was much shorter than the present version, because certain passages were added after its completion. Among the additions are Neh. 10.2-28, 37b, 38b-40; 12.1-26, 46-47; 11.21-24, 25b-36, as well as verses and parts of verses throughout the book.

It is important to emphasize yet again that Rudolph does not attribute these changes in order and extent to the stratum of the sources but rather to the final redaction of the book. Therefore, although he emphasizes the importance of the author, this is not, in fact, the author of EN as we have it, but the hypothetical author of a reconstructed book. Consequently, a scholar such as Blenkinsopp, who accepts many of Rudolph's considerations and views, was able to present a different Book of Ezra–Nehemiah. He maintains, on the one hand, that the transfer of Nehemiah 8 from its original place after Ezra 8 to its present position was not the result of an error but rather the intentional doing of the author himself. However, on the other hand, he sees the end of the book not in Nehemiah 13 but in the story of the dedication of the wall (Neh. 12.27-43). Everything that comes afterward—the material written in the 'third-person' (Neh. 12.44–13.3) as well as authentic portions of Nehemiah's memoirs (Neh. 13.4-31)—was inserted into the book at a later date, after it was completed.[23]

22. It is interesting that in Rudolph's opinion, 'error' recurs on various levels of the composition of the book. According to him the author of the book, 'the Chronicler', as he defines him, also erred in understanding his sources and thus in composing the book. Rudolph maintains that in historical fact Nehemiah preceded Ezra and not vice versa. But because of an error in reading the date, the order of the sources was changed (p. xxiv). Thus the author first erred and reversed the order of Ezra and Nehemiah, and then a later editor erred and moved various chapters from their original (erroneous) place to their present positions.

23. Blenkinsopp, p. 47.

Williamson's position is considerably different, first of all because he is entirely free of the view that EN is a continuation of Chronicles. On the other hand, he does not attribute the same degree of importance to the author of the book as does Rudolph. In Williamson's opinion, after the stage of the primary sources, all of which are more or less contemporary with the events they describe,[24] there are two principal stages in the composition of the book. First the hypothetical work, Ezra 7–Nehemiah 11 and 12.27–13.31, was created by joining together the stories of Ezra and Nehemiah and the other materials that comprise this unit. This work was composed in approximately 400 BCE. The second stage took place about one hundred years later, when another author wrote Ezra 1–6 and joined it to the existing work, as an introduction. In addition to these two central stages, the book underwent a process of expansion, by the addition of the lists and short comments, which were added after Neh. 11.20 in 11.21–12.26 in a process of filling in,[25] which was concluded at the beginning of the Hellenistic period.[26]

It must be emphasized that there is no reason to reject in principle the formation of any biblical book as a multi-staged process, nor should one reject the possibility that a biblical book might have been expanded after the completion of its final form. The question is whether a scholar may completely ignore the canonical reality of EN and forego in advance any effort to find a structure or plan in it, and to determine *ex silentio* that the final state of the book has no significance. We are all well aware of the fear that may lurk in the heart of the critical scholar of adopting an excessively naive attitude to a book as it is. Such an approach courts the dangers of ignoring any signs of complexity, of pursuing harmonization, and of uncritical return to the orthodox position which denies the validity of literary-historical criticism in principle. However, in full awareness of the dangers of this approach, with full recognition of the complexity of the material in the book, and despite the unpopularity of this approach, I wish to suggest that it is possible—and hence obligatory—to explain the composition of EN precisely in that manner: as a book that was produced 'all at once', by an author, according to a clear

24. Williamson, p. xxxv.

25. Williamson, p. 349.

26. See Williamson, pp. xxxiii-xxxvi, 361, and also 'The Composition of Ezra I–VI'.

plan. Before doing so, however, I shall take up the second aspect of this article, the question of chronology.

III

One of the most difficult problems facing the student of EN and the history of Judah in the Persian period is the historical-chronological background of the events described in EN. This problem has two aspects: the 'objective', historical aspect—that is, the need to determine the correct order of historical events; and the historical-historiographical aspect—that is, the effort to understand the author of EN's conception of history as it is expressed in the chronology.

I have argued elsewhere, and others have argued before me, that EN differs from other historical books of the Bible in that it lacks a chronological skeleton, or a systematical chronological framework 'from which individual dates receive their meaning'.[27] We may contrast this situation to the Book of Kings, for example, where the chronological skeleton is composed of links—the kings of Judah and Israel in their synchronic positions, and the length of their reigns. This chronological structure is also the literary skeleton upon which the entire book is built. Things look different in EN. The book describes events one after the other, and occasionally provides the readers with various chronological facts,[28] but those facts do not appear to be combined within an overall chronological system.

Scholars wishing to determine the historical background and order of the events must do it on the basis of the unsystematic comments scattered through the book, comparing them with extra-biblical information derived from various sources, primarily the kings of Persia. Because of the importance of the Persian kings to the historical and theological outlook of EN, we find many references to these kings, and the question arises as to whether the analysis of these references may reveal the historical and chronological basis underlying the book.

The Persian emperors are mentioned in EN in the following order: Cyrus (Ezra 1.1, 2, 7, 8; 3.7; 4.3); Cyrus and Darius (Ezra 4.5), Ahasuerus (4.6), Artaxerxes (4.7, 8, 11, 23), Darius (4.24; 5.5, 6, 7; 6.1, 12, 13, 15), [Cyrus retrospectively (5.13, 14, 17; 6.3)], Cyrus,

27. 'Biblical Historiography in the Persian Period', p. 178.

28. As in Ezra 1.1; 3.8; 4.24; 5.13 and elsewhere. See Japhet, 'Biblical Historiography in the Persian Period', p. 177 and n. 9.

Darius, and Artaxerxes (6.14), Artaxerxes (7.1, 7, 11, 12; 8.1; Neh. 2.1; 5.14; 13.6), Darius the Persian (Neh. 12.22).

If we compare this list as it stands, and the sequence of the kings as they appear, to the list of the Persian kings as reconstructed from Persian, Babylonian and Greek sources, we find that—although the biblical list lacks a few names—except for one place,[29] the sequence of the kings is completely consistent with the correct order,[30] which is given below:

Order of the Kings of Persia[31]	*EN*
Cyrus (538–530)	Cyrus (Ezra 1.1ff.)
Cambyses (530–522)	–
Bardiya (522)	–
Darius I (522–486)	Darius (Ezra 4.5)
Xerxes/Ahasuerus (485–465)	Ahasuerus (Ezra 4.6)
Artaxerxes I (464–424)	Artaxerxes (Ezra 4.7ff.)
Xerxes II (423)	–
Darius II (423–404)	Darius (Ezra 4.24ff.)
Artaxerxes II (404–359)	Artaxerxes (Ezra 7.1ff.)
Artaxerxes III (358–338)	–
Arses (338–336)	–
Darius III (335–331)	Darius (Neh.12.22)

May we conclude from this apparent correspondence that the sequence of the Persian kings provided the historical basis for EN as we have it? If we fill in the historical events on the basis of this assumption, the following historical picture emerges:

29. Ezra 6.14. This verse mentions 'Cyrus and Darius and King Artaxerxes of Persia' in that order, which is the historical sequence of Darius I, Artaxerxes I, skipping Ahasuerus (Xerxes). But according to the structure proposed immediately below, it is necessary to replace this with the sequence between Artaxerxes II and Darius II, where the order is reversed. See on this matter L. Dequeker, 'Darius the Persian, and the Reconstruction of the Jewish Temple in Jerusalem (Ezra 4.24)', *Orientalia Lovaniensia Analecta* 55 (1993), pp. 75-76. I wish to thank Professor Dequeker for letting me read this article prior to publication.

30. Liver already took note of this: see J. Liver, 'Regarding the Problem of the Order of the Kings of Persia in the Books of Ezra and Nehemiah', in *Studies in Bible and Judean Desert Scrolls* (Jerusalem, 1974), pp. 264-65, 270-71 (in Hebrew).

31. Regarding the Persian chronology, see R.A. Parker and W.H. Dubberstein, *Babylonian Chronology 626 BC–AD 75* (Providence, RI, 1957, repr. 1971), pp. 10ff. See also E.J. Bickerman, 'En marge de l'écriture', *RB* 88 (1981), pp. 19-28. There are small differences among scholars regarding the calculation of the years, but none of these is significant in the present context.

1. In the history of the building of the Temple (Ezra 1–6), where the order of kings is: Cyrus, Darius, Ahasuerus, Artaxerxes, Darius, the necessary conclusion would be that the Temple was built at the time of Darius II, and the order of events would be as follows: the declaration by Cyrus (Ezra 1.2-4), which grants permission to build the Temple (538 BCE); the Return from Babylon; and the first steps in building the Temple (Ezra 1.5–3.13)—all took place at the time of Cyrus. Interruptions in the building of the Temple (Ezra 4.1-24) took place at the time of Cyrus, Darius, Ahasuerus and Artaxerxes, until the second year of the reign of Darius II (422 BCE). Renewal of work on the Temple, Darius' decree, the completion of the Temple and its dedication (Ezra 5.1–6.19) occurred from the second to the sixth year of the reign of Darius II (422–418 BCE).[32]
2. The King Artaxerxes, during whose reign, according to EN, both Ezra and Nehemiah were active, was Artaxerxes II (404–359). Ezra came to Judah in the seventh year of his reign (Ezra 7.7-8), that is, in 398 BCE, and Nehemiah did so in the twentieth year of his reign (Neh. 2.1-9), that is in 384 BCE.
3. The king called 'Darius the Persian' in Neh. 12.22 would most probably be Darius III, so that EN would reach the end of the Persian period.

As noted, this historical picture is the necessary conclusion from the assumption that the sequence of the kings of Persia is the historical and chronological basis of the events in EN. However, the difficulties it involves become evident the moment it is presented. We shall note the central problems:

1. With respect to objective evidence, the greatest difficulty is in placing Nehemiah during the reign of Artaxerxes II. Although some scholars have argued for such a dating,[33] the preponderance of extra-biblical evidence, mainly in the

32. This indeed is the picture suggested by Dequeker, 'Darius the Persian'.

33. See Kellermann, *Nehemia*, pp. 49-50; *idem*, 'Erwägungen zum Problem des Esra-datierung', *ZAW* 80 (1968), pp. 44-87; R.J. Saley, 'The Date of Nehemiah Reconsidered', in G.A. Tuttle (ed.), *Biblical and Near Eastern Studies: Essays in Honor of William Sanford LaSor* (Grand Rapids: Eerdmans, 1978), pp. 159-60.

Elephantine papyri, necessitate the placing of Nehemiah during the reign of Artaxerxes I, as is indeed the prevailing view.[34]

2. The question of the time of Ezra, which is an independent problem, is connected here to the transposing of Nehemiah to the reign of Artaxerxes I. Within the chronological sequence presented above, Ezra precedes Nehemiah (according to EN), but the period of his activity would fall in the reign of Artaxerxes II. Placing Nehemiah earlier, during the reign of Artaxerxes I, would immediately raise a methodological question: which details of EN must a scholar retain? Is one to accept the order of the Persian kings as a decisive datum, even after noting that the dating of Nehemiah deviates from that order, so that Ezra is left during the reign of Artaxerxes II? If so, the order of the Persian kings would be retained in the Book of Ezra but not in the Book of Nehemiah, which would completely detach Nehemiah 8 from the story of Ezra. Or, perhaps one should accept the order of events as described as obligatory and place Ezra during the reign of the same king as Nehemiah—that is, Artaxerxes I. By so doing, however, the order of the Persian kings would be disrupted. One way or another, the correspondence between the sequence of events as described in EN and the order of the kings of Persia is impaired, both in fact and in principle.
3. The third difficulty resides in placing the reconstruction of the Temple during the reign of Darius II. Historically this would mean that the Temple lay in ruins from its destruction in 586 BCE until 418 BCE, a period of 168 years. The interruption in the building lasted for more than 110 years, and the actions of Haggai and Zechariah the prophets, Zerubbabel the son of Shealtiel, and Jeshua the son of Jozadak the leaders of the people, all took place during the reign of Darius II. This view implies that other biblical evidence, such as the evidence in Ezra 3–4 or the genealogical lists in 1 Chron. 3.17-24 or 5.40-41, which seek to date Haggai, Zechariah, Zerubbabel, and Jeshua the son of Jozadak closer to Cyrus'

34. See the summary of the question, A.R.W. Green, 'The Date of Nehemiah: A Re-Examination', *AUSS* 28 (1990), pp. 195-209.

declaration or during the reign of Darius I, are all baseless, having either been falsified initially or misinterpreted later.[35]

Moreover, if we combine this difficulty with those we raised earlier and argue—following the common opinion—that Nehemiah is to be dated to the reign of Artaxerxes I, we would have to conclude that Nehemiah's actions in restoring the walls of Jerusalem preceded the reconstruction of the Temple, and that the figures mentioned above—Haggai and Zechariah, Zerubbabel and Jeshua—all acted at the time of Nehemiah or afterward. If we persist in claiming that Ezra, too, belongs to the reign of Artaxerxes I, these men would also be subsequent to Ezra. However, the difficulty of such a view is evident. It entirely contradicts not only the story of Ezra, but also that of Nehemiah, according to which it is abundantly clear that at his time the Temple already existed (see mainly Neh. 6.10-11). It also presents problems regarding other matters, such as the order of the High Priests, and the like.[36]

It seems, therefore, that there is tension which cannot be removed between the two structures within EN: on the one hand there is the list of the Persian kings in the order in which they appear, which seemed to correspond in every detail with the historical order, and, on the other hand, there are the historical development and the order of the various figures as they may be inferred from the details of the events and their specific contexts. What seemed at first glance to be full chronological correspondence cannot withstand historical criticism, and the conclusion demanded by these data is that the order of the kings of Persia cannot be viewed as the chronological foundation of EN.

Rejecting this chronological basis, however, raises another question. If one dates Nehemiah during the reign of Artaxerxes I and accepts the accumulating historical evidence that the construction of the

35. Generally speaking, this is the position of Dequeker: Nehemiah during the reign of Artaxerxes I, the building of the Temple during the reign of Darius II, the activities of Ezra during the reign of Artaxerxes II ('Darius the Persian', pp. 1ff.). He argues that the return of Zerubbabel must be dated to the time of Nehemiah, that is, in the second half of the fifth century BCE (p. 4), and that there is no decisive opposition to viewing Zerubbabel and Jeshua as contemporaries of Nehemiah (p. 12). See also p. 14 *et passim*.

36. Dequeker tries to respond to some but not all of these difficulties. Moreover, many of his proposed solutions are based on the repeated claim that various biblical authors distorted the facts or misunderstood them, and these do not seem convincing.

Temple did precede Nehemiah and is to be dated during the reign of Darius I—as is accepted by most scholars—one must face the question of the order of kings in Ezra 4. If we assume that the Darius who is mentioned in 4.24–6.15 is Darius I, we find that Ahasuerus and Artaxerxes, who ruled after him, are mentioned before him here (Ezra 4.6-23). However, this difficulty cannot outweigh all the problems that accrue according to the other approach. Several solutions have been proposed to this problem, and it seems that the literary arguments do provide a reasonable explanation.[37]

Another chronological question, which is not necessarily dependent upon the complex of problems raised above, is the dating of Ezra the Scribe. EN places him before Nehemiah, that is, during the reign of Artaxerxes I, but many considerations make it more plausible to date him to the period of Artaxerxes II.[38]

Does EN have another chronological skeleton? Theoretically its author could have used two other systematic structures for that purpose, and hints at their existence are indeed found in the book: the governors of Judah under the Persian regime and their terms of office,[39] and the High Priests and their terms of office.[40] By the nature

37. See, for example, Japhet, 'The Temple in the Restoration Period', p. 241 n. 99, and also Blenkinsopp, pp. 43 and 114.

38. Much has been written on this subject, and there is no need for us to go into detail. See, for example, the summary of the relevant considerations in Clines, *Ezra, Nehemiah, Esther*, pp. 16-24, or Williamson, pp. xxxix-xliv.

39. Here another historical question enters, which is considered by all those who deal with EN or the period of the Restoration: when did Judah/Jehud become an independent province under the Persian regime? Did this occur at the beginning of the Persian rule (as implied by the biblical evidence, such as EN, the headings of Haggai's prophecies, and the like)? Or was it only during the time of Nehemiah, when it was removed from the jurisdiction of the governor of Samaria? Debate on this matter persists, but it does not touch directly upon the subject under discussion here. We expressed our position in S. Japhet, 'Sheshbazzar and Zerubbabel against the Background of the Historical and Religious Tendencies of Ezra–Nehemiah', *ZAW* 94 (1982), pp. 80-82, 96-98. See also H.G.M. Williamson, 'The Governors of Judah under the Persians', *TynBul* 39 (1988), pp. 59-82. However, for the opposite opinion, see Dequeker, 'Darius the Persian', pp. 71-72.

40. This question is also a subject of prolonged controversy, especially since Cross proposed expanding the list of priests in Neh. 12.10-11 on the basis of the principle of 'paponymy'. See F.M. Cross, 'A Reconstruction of the Judean Restoration', *JBL* 94 (1975), pp. 9-18 and in other articles. Arguing against this position is J.C. Vanderkam, 'Jewish High Priests of the Persian Period: Is the List

of these positions, it is to be assumed that continuity both in office and registry were maintained. Evidence of the former is found in the 'words of Nehemiah', linking his rule to that of Artaxerxes ('in the twentieth year', Neh. 1.1; 2.1), and dating it ('From the twentieth year of King Artaxerxes until his thirty-second year, twelve years in all', Neh. 5.14, and also 13.6). However, this is the only evidence in this area, and it too is incomplete, since it does not indicate the end of Nehemiah's term of office.[41]

We learn of the succession of High Priests and their systematic listing from the presence of the list of priests (Neh. 12.10-11). From the headings of other lists, it can be also inferred that the terms of the High Priest provided the basis for administrative registries: 'In the time of Joiakim, the heads of the priestly clans were': (Neh. 12.12); 'But the Levite heads of clans are listed in the book of the chronicles to the time of Johanan son of Eliashib' (Neh. 12.23); and elsewhere. Nonetheless, despite the great importance of this material, it lacks chronological data and cannot be linked to the details of the historical picture in EN. It certainly does not provide the chronological or structural basis of the book.

Our discussion up to this point has led to similar conclusions in the two areas upon which we touched: the complex structure of the book presents the critical reader with such grave problems that one may doubt whether a coherent and planned structure exists, and in the matter of chronology it is clear that the book is not built on any chronological structure that can be verified in historical-political terms. Does this mean that the author of EN is a historian devoid of any sense of structure or any consciousness of time, that is, not a historian at all?

Such a conclusion would, in my opinion, be misguided. It would appear to derive from the separation of the two subjects that have so far been discussed and from the attempt to examine each of them in

Complete?', in G.A. Anderson and S.M. Olyen (eds.), *Priesthood and Cult in Ancient Israel* (JSOTSup, 125; Sheffield: JSOT Press, 1991), pp. 67-91.

41. This fact fits into the broader approach of EN. Surprisingly, the book presents not even a single detail about the end of its protagonists. Sheshbazzar, Zerubbabel, Jeshua, Ezra and Nehemiah all disappear from the stage of history without their deaths being recounted, in utter contrast to the other historical books of the Bible, which make a point of indicating the protagonists' deaths. See also S. Japhet, 'The Relationship between Chronicles and Ezra–Nehemiah' (VTSup, 43; Leiden: Brill, 1991), p. 308.

itself in terms as 'objective' as possible. It seems to me that the correct approach would be to examine these two subjects in terms of their relations with each other, that is, to examine the author's historical-chronological view not on the objective but rather on the historio-graphical-literary level. Then it would be clear that the author has a very clear conception of time, which provides the basis of the literary structure of EN. Hence we must turn back and discuss conjointly the two subjects to which we have so far devoted separate discussions, because they are bound up together and shed light upon each other.

IV

Analysis of the historical picture according to the chronological statements of EN shows that, with respect to historical periodization, the book is built in two parts: the first unit (Ezra 1–6) begins with Cyrus's decree in the first year of his reign (Ezra 1.1) and ends with the dedication of the Temple in the sixth year of the reign of Darius (Ezra 6.15). This is a period of twenty-two years: from 538 BCE to 517 BCE.

The second unit (Ezra 7–Nehemiah 13) begins with Ezra's arrival from Babylonia in the seventh year of the reign of Artaxerxes (Ezra 7.7), continues with Nehemiah, who went up to Jerusalem in the twentieth year of the reign of Artaxerxes (Neh. 1.1; 2.1), and finishes with Nehemiah's second term of office in the thirty-third year of the reign of Artaxerxes (Neh. 13.6-7). This is a period of twenty-six years, from 458 BCE until 432 BCE.

There are both similarities and differences in the formulation of these two periods. The most important similarity is the principle upon which the historical periodization is based: each of the periods lasts one generation, between twenty and thirty years. However, the two numbers are not equal, nor are they standard or typological. Rather they represent real numbers: twenty-two years and twenty-six years. The general chronological framework of the historical periodization is the reign of the Persian kings, and in both cases the length of the period is measured according to the years of the emperor. But this framework provides only the chronological *data* and not the *principle* upon which the historical periods are determined. The first period includes the full reign of two kings, one of whom is not even mentioned (Cyrus, who reigned in Babylonia from 538 BCE to 530

BCE, and Cambyses, 530–522 BCE), and part of the reign of a third king (Darius, 522–517 BCE); whereas the second period comprises part of the reign of one king (Artaxerxes), it does not begin with his ascent to the throne, nor does it end with the termination of his reign. Thus one must distinguish between the chronological reckoning, which is based on the reigns of the Persian kings, and the historical periodization, which defines the periods according to events in Judah.

Another feature common to these two periods is that in each of them the people were led by two leaders: Zerubbabel and Jeshua in the first period, Ezra and Nehemiah in the second. However, in this regard the portrayal of the periods is accomplished in different ways. During the first period the leaders were the heads of the establishment: Zerubbabel headed the secular establishment, and Jeshua the religious one—although there is no definition of their status throughout the unit. Jeshua is not called 'the High Priest', nor even simply 'the priest'; one learns of his status only from an indirect expression, 'Jeshua the son of Jozadak and his brothers the priests' (Ezra 3.2, and similarly also in 10.18). From other passages in the book of Nehemiah it may be inferred indirectly that Joshua was the High Priest (see Neh. 12.7, 10, 26), but in Haggai and Zechariah he is explicitly called 'the High Priest' (Hag. 1.1, 12, 14; 2.2, 4; Zech. 3.1, 8; 6.11). This is also true of Zerubbabel: in EN he holds no administrative title, and his leadership is indicated only by an indirect expression: 'They approached Zerubbabel and the chiefs of the clans' (Ezra 4.2), and by his comparison to Nehemiah in another passage (Neh. 12.47). However his status as a governor is indicated explicitly in Haggai[42] (Hag. 1.1, 14; 2.2, 21).

Furthermore, the definition of a 'generation' is not determined by its leaders. They are first mentioned in Ezra 2 (2.1), and the construction of the Temple finishes without them.[43] The definition of the

42. Therefore one cannot learn from Ezra 1–6 that Zerubbabel did not have the status of a governor, as argued by Alt and his followers: A. Alt, 'Die Rolle Samarias bei der Entstehung des Judentums', *KS* II, pp. 333ff. See also above, n. 39. The absence of titles is due to the author's particular outlook and he treats Zerubbabel similarly to Jeshua. See also Japhet, 'Sheshbazzar and Zerubbabel', pp. 80-86.

43. They are mentioned for the last time in Ezra 5.2. The rest of the story refers to 'the elders of the Jews' (Ezra 5.5; 6.8, 14), and conjointly to 'the governor of the Jews and the elders of the Jews' (Ezra 6.7), but Zerubbabel and Jeshua are not mentioned any more.

period is determined by its central project: the building of the Temple! The period begins with Cyrus's declaration permitting its construction and ends with the conclusion of construction and the dedication of the Temple. In contrast, the second period is defined clearly by its leaders, and not by its projects. The period begins with the commencement of Ezra's activity and concludes at the second part of Nehemiah's term of office. In the beginning Ezra works by himself (Ezra 7–10), in the end, Nehemiah works by himself (Neh. 13.4-31), and in between, Ezra and Nehemiah work in parallel or together.

The definition of the roles of these two men is also somewhat different from those of their predecessors. Without doubt, Nehemiah is the head of the secular establishment: he is the governor of Judah appointed by the Persian king (Neh. 5.14, 18; 12.26). Ezra is a priest, and he is represented as the spiritual leader of the people, but he is certainly not a High Priest, and he does not head the religious establishment. As indicated by his title, he is 'the priest-scribe' (Ezra 7.11, 12; Neh. 8.9, 12.26). Hence, during the time of their parallel activity, subjects such as construction of the walls, social reform, and the populating of Jerusalem belong to the field of Nehemiah's activity, and Ezra takes no part in them. By contrast, in the reading of the Torah and everything connected with that, as well as the dedication of the wall, they are presented at each other's side (Neh. 8.1, 2 etc.; 8.9; 12.36, and also Neh. 12.26).

The inner structure of these historical periods is also of importance. In the first period there is a concentration of events at two points in time, in the beginning of the period and at the end. The first chapters describe the events as a tight historical and chronological sequence, all of which takes place at the time of Cyrus. Immediately after Cyrus' proclamation the return to Jerusalem takes place. This migration is not dated explicitly, but as portrayed historically, it should be placed immediately after the proclamation: 'So the chiefs of the clans...got ready to go up and to build the House of the Lord...and King Cyrus of Persia released the vessels of the Lord's house', and so on (Ezra 1.5-7). Immediately after their arrival, 'When the seventh month arrived', preparations for construction of the Temple began, bringing in its wake active opposition by 'the people of the land' (4.1-5) and the cessation of construction (4.24).[44] Since the return from Babylonia is not dated, and the following events are described in relation to it ('in

44. On the literary and chronological problem of Ezra 4.6-24, see above, p. 206.

the second month', 'in the second year of their arrival', etc.), we cannot determine precisely to which year or years the author was attributing the events, but there is no doubt that it is soon after the proclamation by Cyrus, during the first years of his reign.

The two last chapters describe the events at the end of the period, from the second (4.24) to the sixth (6.15) year of Darius' reign. Between those two extremes is an interim period which, chronologically speaking, is the lion's share of the period, though there is nothing to tell about it. This is the time when construction of the Temple was stopped, 'all the years of King Cyrus of Persia and until the reign of King Darius of Persia' (4.5), and the author passes over it in a single sentence (4.24).

The second section is constructed according to the same historiographical principle: all the events are clustered at three very short points in time: two starting points and one conclusion. The first focus is Ezra's coming to Jerusalem, around which are concentrated all the events described in Ezra 7–10. The date at the beginning of the unit determines its setting in time: 'in the seventh year of King Artaxerxes' (7.7). The historical and chronological context of chs. 7–8 is established explicitly: 'On the first day of the first month the journey up from Babylon was started, and on the first day of the fifth month he arrived in Jerusalem' (7.9), and the affair of the foreign wives is linked to it in the narrative sequence: 'When this was over, the officers approached me, saying...' (9.1). Later two more dates are supplied ('the ninth month, the twentieth of the month' [10.9], 'the first day of the tenth month' [9.16]), and the affair is finished 'by the first day of the first month' (10.17). That is, the whole story of Ezra, in Ezra 7–10, takes place within a single year: from the first day of the first month in the seventh year of Artaxerxes until the first day of the first month one year afterward!

The second point in time is Nehemiah's arrival, which is set in the twentieth year of Artaxerxes' reign, that is—twelve years later. Here too, there can be no doubt concerning the close sequence of events. Nehemiah arrives in Jerusalem 'in the month of Nissan, in the twentieth year of the king' (Neh. 2.1). Three days after his arrival (2.11), he evaluates the situation, makes a plan, and begins constructing the wall, the completion of which is dated 'on the twenty-fifth of Elul, after fifty-two days' (6.15).[45] According to the given narrative

45. From this point it is possible to reconstruct the course of events in the prior

sequence the social reform is included in the same time period (Neh. 5), while Nehemiah begins preparations for populating Jerusalem immediately after the completion of construction (7.4-5). In parallel, the people gather in Jerusalem 'in the seventh month' (7.72), and in this context the reading of the Torah, the celebration of Sukkoth, the covenant, and populating Jerusalem are all bound together (chs. 7–11). Following all this comes the dedication of the wall (12.27-43). Although no dates are given, the spirit of the story and even the logic of the events require us to place it soon afterward. This means that all of Nehemiah's activities, from ch. 1 to ch. 12, are presented as the events of a single year!

The third point in time, which is about twelve years later, is the final one: the description in a single sequence of all the activities of Nehemiah in his second term of office: 'only after a while did I ask leave of the king [to return]. When I arrived in Jerusalem...' (Neh. 13.6-7).

The intermediate periods between these points in time are treated similarly; both the transition from the first to the second period and also the time intervening within each period itself. These are times when nothing is accomplished—according to the data of the book—and the role of the historian is just to bridge over them. This he does with a short sentence describing the situation, with a literary transitional phrase, or with utter silence.[46]

The historical concept of time is also the principle according to which one must understand the composition of EN. 'The first period' is presented by Ezra 1–6. The author apparently did not possess a complete and continuous literary source describing that period, but only miscellaneous documents that related to it. Therefore he wrote

months. According to this calculation, the construction of the wall began during the first days of the month of Av, leaving four months from Nissan until the end of Tammuz, for Nehemiah's journey to Jerusalem. These dates fit the data given in the book of Ezra, which are presented very precisely (Ezra 7.9).

46. An account of the situation is found in Ezra 4.24: 'At that time, work on the House of God in Jerusalem stopped and remained in abeyance until the second year of the reign of King Darius of Persia'. The transition between the completion of the Temple and Ezra's return is effected by the formula: 'After these events' (Ezra 7.1). The transition between Ezra and Nehemiah receives no attention, and that between Nehemiah's first and second terms of office is drawn indistinctly by the phrase: 'Earlier...' (Neh. 13.4), and then: 'During all this time I was not in Jerusalem' (13.6).

this unit using his own historiographical method, combining existing documents, as is, with a narrative framework.[47] For the description of the 'second period', however, two literary sources were available to the author: 'the words of Nehemiah' and the 'story of Ezra', which were apparently uniform and complete literary works, with a decided literary stamp, as well as lists of various sorts. According to the evidence of those sources, Ezra's activity began in the 'reign of King Artaxerxes' (Ezra 8.1; and also 7.11), but, lacking other identifying signs, this could have been any of the Persian kings of that name. This is also true of the king in whose time Nehemiah was active, for he too is called simply 'Artaxerxes' (Neh. 2.1; 5.14 *et passim*). Either following an accepted tradition or expressing his own opinion, the author placed both of these men at the time of the same king,[48] thus laying the chronological foundation upon which he built the 'second period'. In order to portray it as a single generation, and to express the synchronicity between Ezra and Nehemiah, he forwent the literary integrity of each of the two works that were in his possession. He broke them into smaller sections and combined them with each other. His cutting and editing is evident especially in 'the words of Nehemiah', from which he drew the longer sections. He placed the 'story of Ezra' at the beginning of the description, but after a series of events that included Ezra's coming to Jerusalem (Ezra 7–8) and the affair of the foreign women (Ezra 9–10), he interrupted the story and passed over to 'the words of Nehemiah'. Here, too, he did not present his source in a single sequence. First he severed the last part of 'the words of Nehemiah' (describing his second term of office) from the narrative continuum and placed it (or part of it) at the end of the work (Neh. 13.4-31).[49] By this means he expressed the historical view

47. For a more detailed account of this method of writing, see Japhet, 'Biblical Historiography in the Persian Period', in J.A. Emerton (ed.), *Congress Volume, Leuven 1989* (VTSup, 43; Leiden: Brill, 1991), pp. 181-82, Williamson, 'The Composition of Ezra I–VI', pp. 1-26.

48. On this matter see above, p. 206. It is likely that this refers to Artaxerxes I. Those who indeed maintain that Ezra was active at that time will assume that the author had a reliable tradition that reflected the historical facts (see for example Williamson, p. xliv), whereas those who place Ezra during the reign of Artaxerxes II will assume that the author was expressing his own opinion (see, for example, Blenkinsopp, *Ezra–Nehemiah*, p. 44).

49. The opening of this passage is doubtless truncated (see 13.4), and regarding the end it is hard to say whether the formula concluding the chapter, 'O my God,

that everything recounted from Nehemiah 1 to 13 refers to the period of Nehemiah. In a single sequence at the beginning of the description he presents the building of the wall, which also includes the story of the social reform (1.1–7.4 or 72),[50] but after beginning to tell about the populating of Jerusalem he interrupted the continuity of 'the words of Nehemiah' and assembled the continuation of the story from four components: an additional passage from 'the story of Ezra' about the reading of the Torah and everything pertaining to that (Neh. 8 or 8–9, or 8–10), a cluster of lists containing various information about the inhabitants of Jerusalem and of Judah (Neh. 11.1–12.26), passages from 'the words of Nehemiah' that are included within that sequence (Neh. 10 [?], 11.1-2; 12.27-43), and words of his own. By structuring the historical work in this way he created full synchronicity between Ezra and Nehemiah, presenting the events of 'the seventh month' of the story of Ezra as being anchored in the time of Nehemiah immediately after completion of the wall, and placing Ezra among those who celebrated at the dedication of the walls (Neh. 12.36). He also presented a comprehensive picture of settlement and administration during the time of Nehemiah, whether or not this was the original position of the material he used.

Evidently this compositional activity impaired the unity and integrity of the material that was taken from the sources, and it is

remember it to my credit' (13.31), which is repeated elsewhere in Nehemiah's memoir (4.19; 13.22) is indeed the concluding phrase.

50. We cannot deal here with the question of the source and function of the list of returnees in this context (Neh. 7.5-72) and its repetition in Ezra 2.1-70. Interestingly, in their understanding of the formation of EN, various scholars have attributed a decisive role to this list, or to the fact of its repetition, though they have come to entirely different conclusions. Kochman, for example, believes that the repeated appearance of the list is sufficient to prove that the books of Ezra and Nehemiah were originally separate works (p. 4, following Segal, pp. 93-96). Williamson (p. xxxiv) sees the relation between the lists as 'the most important single clue' for understanding the stages of the book's composition as we have presented them above, whereas Eskenazi, on the contrary, sees the repetition of the list as the key to understanding the book as a unified work (cf. her 'The Structure of Ezra–Nehemiah', and *In an Age of Prose—A Literary Approach to Ezra–Nehemiah* [SBLMS, 36; Atlanta: Scholars Press, 1988], pp. 37-88). I find no difficulty in assuming that the two appearances of the list might come from the author of EN himself, as is the opinion of Eskenazi, but, unlike her, I do not see the motivation for it in literary-rhetorical considerations but rather in historical and theological ones. However, I cannot expand on this here.

doubtful whether they can be fully reconstructed. For in his historical writing the author sought to give literary expression to chronological and historical principles that were alien to both of the sources he used. 'The words of Nehemiah' did not mention Ezra and covered a period of approximately thirteen years, and the 'story of Ezra' did not include Nehemiah, and its original historical framework is not clear from the material remaining from it. The lists in chs. 11–12 mentioned neither Ezra nor Nehemiah, and their historical background is described in other ways or not presented at all.[51] Hence, although, on the one hand, the author of the book chose to use existing literary sources and did not include much of his own writing, nevertheless, on the other hand, he sought to express his own views by placing this borrowed material within a chronological and historical framework that he himself created. Between these two traits there is tension, which persists no matter what, even if we assume that the author's historical view is consistent with the historical data of his sources. Without doubt the tension between the final framework and the sources augments as the deviation from the original material increases.

The historiographical method of EN in general and in detail forcibly raises the question of the relation between historical writing and historical reality.[52] The reader might ask, for example, why the structure of the book and its periodization is a 'historiographical principle' and not a faithful reflection of events 'as they happened'. This question would not relate, however, to the problem of reliability but to the very essence of historiography, and we can only touch upon it briefly. For even if we assume that all of the data is entirely dependable, down to the last detail, the historical periodization and the definition of these periods are historical concepts and not 'reality'. If the author wished to describe the restoration of life in Judah after the

51. The historical context of some of the lists is determined by their headings, such as: 'These are the priests and the Levites who came up with Zerubbabel son of Shealtiel and Jeshua' (Neh. 12.1, and elsewhere). See also above, pp. 195-96. However, the originality of the headings and their relations to the lists are not clear in every instance. The headings of the lists in ch. 11 lack all historical context.

52. I have dealt with various aspects of this question in several articles, such as those mentioned in nn. 1 and 39 above. See also S. Japhet, '"History" and "Literature" in the Persian Period: The Restoration of the Temple' in *Ah, Assyria...*: M. Cogan and J. Eph'al (eds.), *Studies in Assyrian History and Ancient Near Eastern History Presented to Hayim Tadmor* (ScHier, 33; Jerusalem: Magnes, 1991), pp. 174-88.

destruction of the Temple, why did he choose 'the construction of the Temple' as his topic and not some other subject? And why did he choose to begin his composition with the proclamation of Cyrus and not, for example, with the downfall of Jerusalem and the destruction of the Temple? Or with the history of Judah during the transitional period from 586 to 538 BCE? Or, on the contrary, with the very act of laying the foundations, which is now described in Ezra 3? The place where the author did decide to begin his account is a historical statement: the restoration of Judah and the reconstruction of Jerusalem begin with the proclamation of Cyrus and continue with the arrival of the returnees from the Babylonian Exile. Similarly, the other starting points are determined by the same criterion: the return of Ezra and his caravan with the permission from Artaxerxes and the coming of Nehemiah with the authorization and protection of the same king. By means of this time-structuring, the author expresses his historical view—which he also expresses in other ways—that change and renewal in the life of Judah were the result of initiative on the part of the Persian kings and the Jews of Babylonia, rather than any action in Judah itself, whether political or spiritual. God extended grace to Israel—that is to those who returned from exile—by means of the kings of Persia.

We may sum up briefly with the points at which we began: the literary composition of EN expresses the chronological-historical outlook of the author and was determined by it. Chronology and composition must be viewed as differing but complementary aspects of the historical writing, which can be understood only in their mutual relation and in their essence as one of the historian's means of expression.

THE STRANGE WOMAN (אשה זרה/נכריה) OF PROVERBS 1–9 AND POST-EXILIC JUDAEAN SOCIETY

Harold C. Washington

Introduction

Two female figures stand out in the Instruction of Proverbs 1–9: (1) Woman Wisdom, a divine personification whose moral, intellectual, and erotic appeal allures the (ostensibly male) student into pursuit of her (1.20-33; 3.13-18; 4.5-13, 8.1-31; 9.1-6), and (2) the 'Strange Woman' (אשה זרה) or 'Foreign Woman' (נכריה), the negative antitype of Wisdom, against whom the young man is warned in lurid terms (2.16-19; 5.1-23; 6.24-35; 7.5-27; cf. also 9.13-18). The following passage, with its double entendre in reference to the woman's 'feet', illustrates the sages' attitude toward the Strange Woman:

> For the lips of a Strange Woman drip honey,
> and her speech is smoother than oil;
> but in the end she is bitter as wormwood,
> sharp as a two-edged sword.
> Her 'feet' go down to death;
> her steps follow the path to Sheol (Prov. 5.3-5).[1]

1. Cf. L. G. Perdue's translation of v. 5:

> Her sexual organs descend upon Mot,
> Her aroused vagina embraces Sheol

(*Wisdom and Cult: A Critical Analysis of the Views of Cult in the Wisdom Literature of Israel and the Ancient Near East* [SBLDS, 30; Missoula, MT: Scholars Press, 1977], p. 148). The use in biblical Hebrew of רגלים, 'feet', as a veiled reference to the genitals is well known (Exod. 4.25; Deut. 11.10; 25.9; 28.57; Judg. 3.24; Ruth 3.4, 7, 8, 14; 2 Kgs 18.27 *Qere*; Isa. 6.2; 7.20; Jer. 2.25; Ezek. 16.25; for most of these, see *HALAT* [3rd edn], IV, p. 1106). Perdue's translation of צעדיה in v. 5b, based on the parallel with רגליה in v. 5a and an apparent meaning of Ugaritic *ṣǵd*, 'to make an erection' (J. Aistleitner, *Wörterbuch der ugaritische Sprache* [Berlin: Akademie-Verlag, 1963] #2339; cf. Perdue, *Wisdom and Cult*, p. 233) is less

Several recent studies have illumined the symbolic and ideological significance of the אשה זרה/נכריה in Proverbs. G. Yee, for example, demonstrates that the Strange Woman passages are arranged as a negative foil to Woman Wisdom, highlighting the virtues of the latter by displaying the vices of the Strange Woman in a parallel literary structure.[2] C. Newsom shows that the exploitation of sexual difference in Proverbs 1–9 solidifies the androcentric terms of sapiential discourse: 'Invoking the strange woman as a threat provides a basis for solidarity between father and son'.[3] For C. Camp, who emphasizes the multivalence of the figure as a symbol of chaos threatening the established social, economic, religious and moral orders, the Strange Woman 'is an archetype of disorder at all levels of existence'.[4]

Each of these studies advances our understanding of the Strange Woman as a function of the patriarchal need to control female sexuality. For the sage of Proverbs 1–9, any woman who wields her sexual powers outside the male-governed arrangements of marriage and family is construed as fundamentally Strange. Proverbs 1–9, moreover, magnifies the זרה from a mundane temptress with deadly erotic force into a symbol of primordial Evil. This articulation of death and evil in feminine language has grave consequences for the biblical tradition. As C. Camp puts it in a more recent study of the זרה figure, Proverbs portrays 'a force defined here as female that will ultimately split the religious cosmos of Judaism and Christianity into a dualistic moral system in which women can come out on only one side'.[5] We

convincing, but the sexually suggestive quality of the language of Prov. 5.3-5 is nonetheless quite clear. A similar use of רגלים appears in Prov. 7.11: 'Her "feet" do not stay at home'; and 6.28-29: 'Can one walk on hot coals without scorching the "feet"? So is he who sleeps with his neighbor's wife.' Note also in the latter context a play on the words אש, 'fire' (v. 27), and אשה, 'woman' (vv. 26, 29).

2. G.A. Yee, '"I Have Perfumed my Bed with Myrrh": The Foreign Woman (*'iššâ zārâ*) in Proverbs 1–9', *JSOT* 43 (1989), pp. 53-68.

3. C.A. Newsom, 'Woman and the Discourse of Patriarchal Wisdom: A Study of Proverbs 1–9', in P.L. Day (ed.), *Gender and Difference in Ancient Israel* (Minneapolis, MN: Augsburg Fortress, 1989), p. 149.

4. C. Camp, *Wisdom and the Feminine in the Book of Proverbs* (Bible and Literature, 11; Sheffield: Almond Press, 1985), p. 199, cf. pp. 112-20, 265-71.

5. 'What's So Strange about the Strange Woman?', in D. Jobling, P.L. Day and G.T. Sheppard (eds.), *The Bible and the Politics of Exegesis: Essays in Honor of Norman K. Gottwald on his Sixty-Fifth Birthday* (Cleveland: Pilgrim Press, 1991), p. 31.

might ask whether the presentation of Woman Wisdom in Proverbs 1–9 is in fact as affirmative as it is usually considered to be. Or are the Strange Woman and Woman Wisdom simply two sides of an ancient *meretrix/madonna* (prostitute/virgin) complex: two female figures of male fantasy, each highly charged erotically, but standing in tension with one another, one accessible but dangerous, the other remote and ethereal, both functioning ideologically to alienate the (presumed male) reader from the humanity of real women?[6]

With these broader interpretative issues in view, my aim in the present study is to narrow the focus to the most concrete facet of the gender politics of the Strange Woman: the economic. I propose to describe the particular social and economic interests that originally motivated the polemic against the Strange Woman in Proverbs 1–9. My contention is that during the early post-exilic period, when chs. 1–9 were fashioned as an introduction to the book of Proverbs,[7] the

6. The female reader of Prov. 1–9 confronts a more profound alienation—she is effectively banned from the pursuit of Wisdom by the categories of sapiential rhetoric. See Yee's concluding comments, 'The Foreign Woman in Proverbs 1–9', p. 67; and Newsom, 'Woman and the Discourse of Patriarchal Wisdom.'

7. Elsewhere I have examined the linguistic, structural and thematic evidence for dating the book of Proverbs and have concluded that the book must have been complete before the end of the Persian period, probably early in that era (*Wealth and Poverty in the Instruction of Amenemope and the Hebrew Proverbs: A Comparative Case-Study in the Social Location and Function of Ancient Near Eastern Wisdom Literature* [SBLDS; Atlanta: Scholars Press, forthcoming]; see ch. 6, 'Dating the Composition and Redaction of the Book of Proverbs'). It is not possible to review that entire discussion here, but some comments are necessary. Recent studies have reached a consensus that the final formation of Proverbs took place during the Persian period (cf. Camp, *Wisdom and the Feminine in the Book of Proverbs*, pp. 233-39). A. Wolters, however, argued convincingly that the G participle צופיה in Prov. 31.27 is an allusion to the Greek term σοφία ('*Ṣôpiyyâ* [Prov. 31.27] as Hymnic Participle and Play on Sophia', *JBL* 104 [1985], pp. 577-87; cf. G. Rendsburg, 'Bilingual Wordplay in the Bible,' *VT* 38 [1988], p. 354), leading some scholars to move their judgment of the date of composition to a later period, since Greek influence would seem to indicate that the book of Proverbs was still in formation after the conquest of Alexander the Great (e.g. R.C. Van Leeuwen, *Context and Meaning in Prov. 25–27* [SBLDS, 96; Atlanta: Scholars Press, 1988], p. 143; and Camp, 'What's So Strange about the Strange Woman?', p. 303). This conclusion does not necessarily follow, however. Wolters himself allows that an earlier date, before Alexander, is possible ('*Ṣôpiyyâ* [Prov. 31.27] as Hymnic Participle and Play on Sophia', p. 586 n. 44).

During the two centuries before Alexander's invasion in 332 BCE, there was a

אשה זרה/נכריה represented women who did not belong to the גולה community. Liaisons between Judaean men and these 'foreign' women posed economic problems: since genealogical lineage, land tenure and cultic membership were linked in the post-exilic period, the prospect

heavy influx of Greek cultural influence, brought by trade, Greek settlements on the coast, and the presence of Greek soldiers in the Persian imperial army (M. Smith, *Palestinian Parties and Politics that Shaped the Old Testament* [London: SCM Press, 2nd edn, 1987], pp. 42-54; D. Auscher, 'Les relations entre la Grèce et la Palestine avant la conquête d'Alexandre,' *VT* 17 [1967], pp. 8-30. For the extent of imported Greek pottery during the period, see E. Stern, *Material Culture of the Land of the Bible in the Persian Period, 538–332 BCE* [Warminster: Aris & Phillips, 1982], pp. 137-42, 283-86; and R. Wenning, 'Attische Keramik in Palästina. Ein Zwischenbericht,' *Transeuphratène* 2 [1990], p. 157-168. Also of value is J. Elayi, *Pénétration grecque en Phénicie sous l'Empire perse* [Nancy: Presses Universitaires de Nancy, 1988]). Greek coins appear in the vicinity of Jerusalem well before the beginning of the Hellenistic period proper. The earliest was minted in Athens by Pisistratus, c. 550 BCE (Y. Meshorer, 'An Attic Coin from Jerusalem,' *'Atiqot* 3 [1961], p. 185). The spread of Greek names among the Semitic populations of pre-Hellenistic Palestine reflects the advance of the Greek language before 332 BCE (M. Hengel, *Judaism and Hellenism: Studies in their Encounter in Palestine during the Early Hellenistic Period* [Philadelphia: Fortress Press, 1974], I, p. 61; II, p. 44). Likewise the Samaritan papyri discovered at Wadi Daliyeh attest to the penetration of Hellenistic culture deep into northern Palestine before Alexander's arrival (the papyri are not published, but see the introductory description of F.M. Cross, Jr, 'The Discovery of the Samaria Papyri', *BA* 26 [1963], pp. 110-21). Since Proverbs contains only this single Hebrew–Greek wordplay, but shows no thematic interaction with Greek ideas, we should conceive of an author with some knowledge of the Greek language, but only the remotest sense of Greek culture. This fits best with the Achaemenid era.

C. Camp mentions three other grounds for dating Prov. 1–9 to the Hellenistic era ('What's So Strange about the Strange Woman?', pp. 23, 303 n. 22). These are: (1) the biblical author's familiarity with the deuteronomic and priestly legislation of the Pentateuch; (2) the presupposition in the poems of a walled Jerusalem, along with the urban setting of the prostitute; and (3) the possibility that the author models the literary structure of Prov. 1–9 after the dimensions of the Temple in 1 Kgs 6 (cf. P. Skehan, 'Wisdom's House', *Studies in Israelite Poetry and Wisdom* [CBQMS, 1; Washington, DC: Catholic Biblical Association, 1971], pp. 27-45). None of this is inconsistent with a Persian period date for the composition of Prov. 1–9. I would argue that the third item, the possibility that the author has created in the Proverbs scroll a literary replacement for the Temple, suggests a date *before* the reconstruction of the Second Temple. (Cf. the flying scroll of Zech. 5.1-2, too large for an actual scroll, but conforming to the dimensions given in 1 Kgs 6 for the front porch of the temple, as well as the area of the inner sanctum occupied by the cherubim; C.L. and E.M. Meyers, *Haggai, Zechariah 1–8* [AB, 25B; New York: Doubleday, 1987],

of exogamous marriages brought the danger of outside encroachment upon the land holdings of the Judaean congregation. Thus the Strange Woman was off-limits to Judaean men of the Persian period not only for moral and religious reasons: the אשה זרה represented a threat to the social and economic integrity of the post-exilic Judaean collective.[8] The material applied to the Strange Woman in Proverbs 1–9 is not unitary in origin. Rather, traditional warnings against diverse types of illicit women have been gathered in service of the polemic against the זרה. The effect of this redactional combination is to obscure the identity of the זרה, apart from the essential feature of her alien status. The economic anxiety provoked by this alien figure thus motivates an assortment of slurs, sexual and religious, against her.

The Origins of the Strange Woman Motif

First it must be recognized that warnings against strange women are not new to Hebrew wisdom literature. The Instruction texts of ancient Egypt and Mesopotamia are intrinsically androcentric, set in the form of a father's teaching to his son, so warnings against women, especially unfamiliar women, are as old as the genre. Typically in these earlier traditions the strange woman appears as a prostitute. Since women were chiefly excluded from the public sphere in ancient Near Eastern societies, one of the few socially sanctioned female roles outside the patriarchal household was that of the prostitute. If a woman in public view was not patently accountable to a man, she was liable to be presumed a prostitute.[9] Thus the New Kingdom Egyptian Instruction

pp. 279-83; D.L. Petersen, *Haggai and Zechariah: A Commentary* [OTL; Philadelphia: Westminster Press, 1984], p. 247).

8. This paper was written before I had access to J. Blenkinsopp, 'The Social Context of the "Outsider Woman" in Proverbs 1–9', *Bib* 72 (1991), pp. 457-73, but it is worth noting that Blenkinsopp's thesis has much in common with the view presented here.

9. P. Bird describes the prostitute's marginal status as the consequence of men's conflicting claims both to exclusive control of their wives' sexuality and sexual access to other women: 'Her social status is that of an outcast, though not an outlaw, a tolerated, but dishonored member of society... The harlot is that "other" woman, tolerated but stigmatized, desired but ostracized' ('The Harlot as Heroine: Narrative Art and Social Presupposition in Three Old Testament Texts', *Semeia* 46 [1989], pp. 120-21; cf. S. Niditch, 'The Wronged Woman Righted: An Analysis of Gen. 38', *HTR* 72 [1979], p. 147).

of Any warns against unfamiliar women as follows:

Beware of a woman who is a stranger,
One not known in her town;
Don't stare at her when she goes by,
Do not know her carnally.[10]

The ancient Egyptian scribal miscellanies frequently chide young male students for spending their energies on (as the Egyptians would put it), 'beer, women and dance'.[11] Similar passages can be found in the Mesopotamian Instruction literature (e.g. in the Babylonian 'Counsels of Wisdom', ll. 72-79).[12] In all of this material the woman is viewed as enticing but disreputable. For teacher and pupil alike, she is a distraction from study and should be avoided.

Among the various sub-collections of Proverbs 10–31, only three sayings invoke the warning against women that becomes a leitmotif in Proverbs 1–9. Prov. 29.3 establishes an opposition between wisdom (חכמה), and illicit women (זונות, prostitutes):

The lover of wisdom gladdens his father,
but the associator with prostitutes wastes his wealth.

Here, however, there is no identification of the woman as strange (זרה) or foreign (נכריה). Two sentences present the figure of the strange woman as a treacherous watery pit (also known already from the Egyptian Instruction of Any):[13]

The speech of strange women (זרות) is a deep pit;
The curse of Yhwh is on him who falls into it (22.14).

10. M. Lichtheim, *Ancient Egyptian Literature*. II. *The New Kingdom* (Berkeley: University of California Press, 1976), p. 137. For additional examples, see H. Brunner, *Altägyptische Weisheit: Lehren für das Leben* (Bibliothek der alten Welt, Reihe der alte Orient; Zurich: Artemis, 1988), p. 463.

11. E.g. Pap. Anastasi IV.11,9–12,1, 'Rebuke Addressed to a Dissipated Scribe' (= Pap. Sallier I.9,9ff; cf. Pap. Anastasi V,1b,1-2); in R. A. Caminos, *Late-Egyptian Miscellanies* (Brown Egyptological Studies, 1; London: Oxford University Press, 1954), p. 182.

12. W. Lambert, *Babylonian Wisdom Literature* (Oxford: Clarendon, 1960), pp. 102-103.

13. Any describes the woman as 'a deep water whose course is unknown' (Lichtheim, *Ancient Egyptian Literature*, II, p. 137).

> For a strange woman[14] is a deep pit;
> and a foreign woman (נכריה) a narrow well (23.27).

These sentences are likely to be of pre-exilic origin, and thus it would seem that the warning against unfamiliar women was already a traditional theme for the post-exilic sages. This does not, however, account for the singular intensity of the concern in Proverbs 1–9. Only in Proverbs 1–9 does זרה/נכריה become the technical terminology for a type of woman who endangers the very community. How are we to identify this female figure who inspires such alarm?

The Problem of the Identity of the זרה *in Proverbs 1–9*

No consensus has been established concerning the identity of the אשה זרה/נכריה in Proverbs 1–9. Earlier debate revolved around the question whether the זרה is an allegorical or actual figure. The Strange Woman was interpreted either as a personification, opposed to Wisdom but with no mundane referent, or as the literal representation of a real type of woman. Literalists favored the view that the זרה represents Greek ἑταίραι, common prostitutes brought into the region by the armies of Alexander and his successors.[15] Neither of these alternatives proved adequate. Commentators dropped the allegorical line of inquiry as anachronistic and focused on efforts to identify the historical and cultural setting of the figure. Much credence has been given to G. Boström's proposal that the זרה is a not an ordinary prostitute, but a foreign devotee of the goddess Ishtar who engages in cultic prostitution as a fertility rite.[16] Boström's theory rests solely, however, on details from Prov. 7.5-27, where references to sacrifices, paying of vows (7.14), lunar phases (7.9, 20), and the distinctive behavior of the woman might seem to imply a cultic background. The hypothesis cannot be applied to Prov. 2.16-19, 5.1-23, 6.24-35 and

14. Reading זרה (cf. LXX ἀλλότριος οἶκος), but MT here reads זונה. One could argue in favor of MT as the *lectio difficilior*, since the LXX is likely to have conformed to the tendency of the adjectives זרה and נכריה to occur as a pair in Prov. 1–9 (2.16; 5.20; 7.5; cf. L.A. Snijders, 'The Meaning of זר in the Old Testament', *OTS* 10 [1954], p. 67).

15. For a review of earlier research, c. 1894–1929, see G. Boström, *Proverbiastudien: Die Weisheit und das fremde Weib* (Lund: Gleerup, 1935), pp. 15-41.

16. Boström, *Proverbiastudien*, pp. 103-34.

9.13-18, which lack the features that led Boström to associate the זרה with a foreign cult.[17]

Recent studies, moreover, have raised doubts about the existence of cultic prostitution in ancient Israel and its environs. R. Oden, for example, argues that the Deuteronomistic charge of 'sacred prostitution' is an example of what some anthropologists have defined as 'ethnic boundary marking'.[18] This is a process by which an ethnic group develops sensational accounts, often erroneous, of the customs of other groups as a way of delineating its own self-understanding. Sexual and dietary practices are the most common subjects for ethnic boundary marking. Oden maintains that if we prescind from the biblical suggestions of cultic prostitution, no clear evidence remains for the practice in the ancient Near East. Most of the evidence for cultic prostitution from ancient Mesopotamia, for example, is irredeemably vague. The variety of Akkadian terms which have been interpreted as designations for cultic prostitutes (e.g. *ēntu, nadītu, qadištu*) simply denote female cultic functionaries—there is little basis in the texts for assuming that these individuals are prostitutes. It appears that celibacy rather than compulsory sexual intercourse was a condition of the status of *ēntu* and *nadītu*.[19] Virtually all the post-biblical evidence for cultic prostitution, Oden argues, is dependent upon Herodotus' account of rites at the Babylonian temple of Ishtar (*Histories* 1.199), which is not reliable as historical evidence.[20] Herodotus' colorful stories, I

17. W. McKane, *Proverbs: A New Approach* (OTL; Philadelphia: Westminster Press, 1970), pp. 284-85. McKane also gives an incisive critique of Boström's treatment of Prov. 7.5-27; see pp. 334-39.

18. R.A. Oden, 'Religious Identity and the Sacred Prostitution Accusation', in *The Bible without Theology: The Theological Tradition and Alternatives to it* (San Francisco: Harper & Row, 1987), pp. 131-53. Oden draws on the discussion of anthropologist F. Barth (ed.), *Ethnic Groups and Boundaries: The Social Organization of Culture Difference* (Boston: Little, Brown, 1969); see especially Barth's 'Introduction', pp. 9-38.

19. Oden, 'Religious Identity and the Sacred Prostitution Accusation', pp. 148-52.

20. Oden, 'Religious Identity and the Sacred Prostitution Accusation', 146-47. For recent surveys of opinion on the historical reliability of Herodotus, see S. Flory, *The Archaic Smile of Herodotus* (Detroit: Wayne State University, 1987), p. 170; and H.R. Immerwahr, 'Herodotus', in P.E. Easterling and B.M.W. Knox (eds.), *The Cambridge History of Classical Literature*, I, Part 3, *Philosophy, History, Oratory* (Cambridge: Cambridge University Press, 1989), pp. 26-29 (each with additional bibliography).

would suggest, are themselves probably examples of ethnic boundary marking, delineating the virtues of the Greek world by describing the exotic practices (from the Greek perspective) of the distant East.

The biblical texts which have generally been regarded as witnesses to the practice of cultic prostitution (Hos. 1–3, 4.13-14; Amos 2.7; Deut. 23.18-19; 1 Kgs 14.24; 2 Kgs 23.7 etc.) are equally uncompelling. P. Bird has recently shown, for example, that the root זנה in Hosea has no intrinsic cultic connotations; the religious indictment of זנונים in Hosea 1–4 is a metaphorical and polemical innovation of the prophet.[21] K. van der Toorn concludes in a recent study that '"sacred prostitution" as a magical rite in the context of fertility cults...is a myth of historiography in the case of ancient Israel'.[22] If we accept this conclusion, Boström's interpretation of the אשה זרה/נכריה must be rejected.

Van der Toorn offers an alternate scenario for Prov. 7.5-27: far from being a professional prostitute, the woman is engaged in an extraordinary act of prostitution for the sake of paying a vow. For ancient Israelite women living in the margin of the official cultus, van der Toorn argues, the vow was a popular form of devotion. Women were typically dependent upon men, however, to supply the means of payment.[23] If a husband or father refused, one of the few means of access to resources outside the household economy was incidental prostitution. Thus the woman of Prov. 7.5-27 says that she is obliged

21. P. Bird, '"To Play the Harlot": An Inquiry into an Old Testament Metaphor', in P.L. Day (ed.), *Gender and Difference in Ancient Israel* (Minneapolis: Augsburg Fortress, 1989), pp. 75-94.

22. K. van der Toorn, 'Female Prostitution in Payment of Vows in Ancient Israel', *JBL* 108 (1989), p. 205. Because of their association in some biblical contexts with the root זנה, the substantives קדשה and קדש have been misconstrued as designations for cultic prostitutes. It can be asserted with confidence, however, only that the terms denote consecrated individuals. See van der Toorn, 'Female Prostitution in Payment of Vows', p. 203; Bird, '"To Play the Harlot"', pp. 86-88; and M.I. Gruber, 'The *qādēš* in the Book of Kings and in Other Sources', *Tarbiz* 52 (1983), pp. 167-76 (Hebrew).

23. This would naturally have been a source of tension between husband and wife. Van der Toorn ('Female Prostitution in Payment of Vows', p. 196) adduces cross-cultural evidence from contemporary Islamic societies: A.H. Betteridge, 'The Controversial Vows of Urban Muslim Women,' in N.A. Falk and R.M. Cross (eds.), *Unspoken Worlds: Women's Religious Lives in Non-Western Cultures* (San Francisco: Harper & Row, 1980), pp. 141-55.

to pay a vow (7.14, the D perfect שלמתי has a modal sense: 'today *I must fulfil* my vows'), and in the absence of her husband, who has taken the money bag with him (7.19-20), she invites a young man to exchange money for sex.[24] Van der Toorn's reading of the passage is instructive, but there is reason to question whether women were so relegated to the fringe of the Israelite cultus.[25] The combination of piety and unabashed adultery envisioned in this scenario also strains credibility.[26] Whatever its merits, Van der Toorn's reading of Prov. 7.5-27, like Boström's cultic prostitution theory, cannot be applied to the larger complex of Strange Woman passages in Proverbs 1–9. None of the distinctive particulars of the scene in 7.5-27 appear outside this passage.

Above all it must be recognized that prostitution, whether cultic or mundane, is neither the sole nor central concern of the Strange Woman passages as a group. Although Prov. 7.5-27 compares the forbidden woman to a prostitute—she is 'dressed like' one (שית זונה, 7.10)—never in Proverbs 1-9 is the אשה זרה/נכריה explicitly identified as a prostitute. Prov. 6.26 *contrasts* the forbidden woman (נכריה, 6.24) to a זונה:

> For a prostitute (אשה זונה) may be had for a loaf of bread,
> But the wife of a man (אשת איש) stalks a man's life.

The immediate concern in this context is adultery not prostitution, as 6.32 makes clear:

> But he who commits adultery has no sense;
> he who does it destroys himself.

It is likewise impossible, however, to interpret all the Strange Woman passages in Proverbs 1–9 as prohibitions of adultery. P. Humbert suggests that the expressions אשה זרה and נכריה denote a woman who is 'strange' because she belongs to another man (i.e. she is 'alien' in a forensic sense). He translates the terms זרה and נכריה as 'femme d'autrui' or 'femme autre (que la sienne)', and refers them to

24. Van der Toorn, 'Female Prostitution in Payment of Vows', pp. 193-201.

25. See P. Bird, 'The Place of Women in the Israelite Cultus', in P.D. Miller, Jr, P.D. Hanson and S.D. McBride (eds.), *Ancient Israelite Religion: Essays in Honor of Frank Moore Cross* (Philadelphia: Fortress Press, 1987), pp. 397-419.

26. Cf. C. Camp: 'The scenario of a proper Israelite matron picking up some pocket change with a little harlotry on the side seems improbable' ('What's So Strange about the Strange Woman?', p. 21).

adultery.[27] Not all of the material in Proverbs 1–9 allows this explanation, however. Two of the Strange Woman passages indicate that the זרה is married (6.29; 7.19), but the others do not.[28] Neither the expression אשה זרה nor נכריה occurs outside Proverbs with the meaning that Humbert would assign to them here: 'belonging (i.e. married) to another'. The terminology of biblical Hebrew for a woman with whom a man commits adultery is unambiguous: אשת רעהו, 'the wife of one's neighbor' (Lev. 20.10; Deut. 22.24; Jer. 5.8; Ezek. 18.6, 11, 15; 22.11; 33.26; cf. אשת רעך, 'the wife of your neighbor', Exod. 20.17; Deut. 5.21; אשת עמיתך, 'the wife of your kinsman', Lev. 18.20); אשת איש, 'the wife of a man' (Lev. 20.10); נאפת, 'adulterer' (G participle feminine, Lev. 20.10; Ezek. 16.38; 23.45); מנאפת, 'adulterer' (D participle feminine, Ezek. 16.32; Hos. 3.1; Prov. 30.20). In Proverbs 1–9 such designations for a woman involved in adultery appear only in Prov. 6.24-35 (אשת איש, 6.26; אשת רעהו, 6.29; the man is designated נאף אשה, 'one who commits adultery with a woman', 6.32). There is no basis for assuming that the terms זרה/נכריה denote an adulterous woman in the other Strange Woman texts. Nowhere in these passages are the penalties for adultery alluded to (Lev. 20.10; Deut. 22.22); rather the sanctions that are invoked (Prov. 5.14) deal with other offenses, as we shall see below.

The richness of detail concerning the Strange Woman in Proverbs 1–9 only vexes attempts to identify her. The descriptions of 2.16-19, 5.1-23, 6.24-35, 7.5-27 and 9.13-18 differ so greatly among themselves that despite the efforts of some commentators, it is impossible to reconcile them.[29] No actual woman would possess all the traits

27. P. Humbert, 'La "femme étrangère" du livre des Proverbes', *Revue des études sémitiques* 2 (1937), pp. 49-64; 'Les adjectifs "*zâr*" et "*nokrî*" et la "femme étrangère" des Proverbes biblique', *Mélanges syriens offerts à M. René Dussaud*, I (Bibliothèque Archéologique et Historique, 30; Paris: Librarie Orientalisk Paul Geuthner, 1939), pp. 259-66.

28. The term אלף in 2.17 might be taken in the sense of 'friend, companion', and thus 'husband', but an equally convincing argument can be made for referring the term to Yhwh. Other evidence suggests a meaning of 'teacher' or 'instruction' for the word here (McKane, *Proverbs: A New Approach*, pp. 286-87). For the semantic development of the verbal root אלף in the sense associated with instruction, see M.D. Coogan '**'lp*, "To be an Abecedarian"', *JAOS* 110 (1990), p. 322.

29. The description of the אשת כסילות in 9.13-18 might be excluded from the group, since the terms זרה and נכריה are absent from this passage. G. Yee's study, however, has shown that a strategic arrangement groups the five passages, including

assigned to the זרה. She is instead a subtly crafted composite literary figure, 'a rather motley character', as L. Perdue characterizes her, whose 'fusing of different types seems most comparable to a similar blending together of the same types in the prophetic literature where they are again lumped together in an indistinguishable maze'.[30] These tensions in the portrayal of the אשה זרה/נכריה most likely reflect the independent origins of some of the passages now referred to her. Drawing upon the traditional motif of the warning against unfamiliar women, the sages have constructed their polemic against the Strange Woman by combining originally independent units in a redactional process parallel to that through which a composite portrait of divine Wisdom was assembled in Proverbs 1–9, relying in part upon older units of tradition.[31]

Three of the Strange Woman passages are introduced by strikingly similar formulaic bi-colons:

> להצילך מאשה זרה מנכריה אמריה החליקה
> To save you from the strange woman
> from the foreign woman with her smooth words (2.16).
>
> לשמרך מאשת רע מחלקת לשון נכריה
> To preserve you from the evil woman,
> from the smooth tongue of the foreign woman (6.24).
>
> לשמרך מאשה זרה מנכריה אמריה החליקה
> To preserve you from the strange woman,
> from the foreign woman with her smooth words (7.5).

The references to the woman's seductive words mark these introductory lines as part of the editorial framework of Proverbs 1–9, which structurally opposes the treacherous speech of the Strange Woman to

9.13-18, chiastically in opposition to the figure of Wisdom ('The Foreign Woman in Proverbs 1–9,' pp. 55, 67). Thus, by editorial design if not in original composition, the אשת כסילות belongs to the same complex as the other accounts of the אשה זרה and נכריה.

30. Perdue, *Wisdom and Cult*, p. 154; cf. O. Plöger, *Sprüche Salomos* (BKAT, 17; Neukirchen–Vluyn: Neukirchener Verlag, 1984) pp. 79, 82; and Camp, *Wisdom and the Feminine in the Book of Proverbs*, pp. 115-17.

31. Prov. 8.1-36, for example, has ancient roots and some portions of the text may have been composed as early as the period of the united monarchy (see C. Kayatz, *Studien zu Proverbien 1–9: Eine form- und motivgeschichtliche Untersuchung unter Einbeziehung Ägyptischen Vergleichsmaterials* [WMANT, 22; Neukirchen–Vluyn: Neukirchener Verlag, 1966], pp. 76-118; cf. p. 13).

the salutary words of Woman Wisdom.[32] Apart from these formulaic introductory lines, the extended accounts of Prov. 6.24-35 and 7.5-27 make no mention of the woman as זרה or נכריה, and, as we have seen, their pictures of the figure are quite divergent. This is easily explained if the editors of Proverbs 1–9 have appropriated independent traditions for the purposes of their campaign against the זרה. Before their incorporation into Proverbs 1–9 these compositions warned against involvement with particular types of women: Prov. 6.25-35 focused on adultery, while 7.6-27 addressed a special circumstance tantamount to prostitution. In their present context, the traditions are adapted for the purpose of denouncing the זרה.[33]

Proverbs 1–9 thus gathers under the umbrella of the זרה an assortment of warnings against unfamiliar women. Because of the composite nature of her portrait, the proscribed figure has no consistent identity, and sexual slur is only the most prominent of a variety of tactics used to disparage her. The woman is depicted as 'alien, harlotrous, evil, adulterous, and foolish'.[34] She is also noisy, deceitful, disrespectful, ignorant and perilous unto death. Why does this figure arouse such attention? The essential attribute unifying the accounts of the forbidden woman in Proverbs 1–9 is her designation as זרה/נכריה; thus to ascertain the sages' motivation for denouncing her we must examine the semantic value of these terms with special reference to the post-exilic period.

In biblical Hebrew the adjective זר denotes 'otherness', referring to what is outside a field of recognition or of legitimacy.[35] In cultic contexts, for example, we find references to 'illicit incense' (קטרת זרה, Exod. 30.9) or 'unlawful fire' (אש זרה, Lev. 10.1). As a social designation, זר refers chiefly to those outside the pertinent kinship group, whether family, tribe or nation. Thus the law of levirate marriage stipulates that 'the wife of the deceased shall not be married outside

32. J.N. Aletti, 'Séduction et parole en Proverbes I-IX,' *VT* 27 (1977), pp. 129-44; G. Yee, 'The Foreign Woman in Proverbs 1-9.'

33. Other commentators have suggested composite origins for chs. 6 and 7. Cf. for example G. Boström, *Proverbiastudien*, pp. 143-44; R.N. Whybray, *Wisdom in Proverbs: The Concept of Wisdom in Proverbs 1–9* (SBT; Naperville, IL: Allenson, 1965), pp. 48-50.

34. Yee, 'The Foreign Woman in Proverbs 1–9,' p. 54.

35. Snijders reviews all occurences of the term in 'The Meaning of זר in the Old Testament', pp. 1-154; cf. Snijders, 'זור/זר', *TDOT*, IV, pp. 52-58; for נכרי, cf. 'The Meaning of זר in the Old Testament', pp. 60-68.

(the family) to a stranger' (לאיש זר, Deut. 25.5). Priestly rules designate men of non-Aaronic descent (e.g. Num. 3.10), or those outside the tribe of Levi (Num. 1.51; 18.4) as זר. Frequently in the prophetic literature the term זר denotes non-Israelites (as such, usually Israel's enemies), for example, Ezek. 31.12: 'foreigners from the most terrible of nations', זרים עריצי גוים.

The adjective נכרי has a similar range of meanings to those of זר. The term can indicate 'strangeness' simply with regard to the household (Ps. 69.9), but as a social designation נכרי typically denotes foreignness by reason of nationality or ethnicity (e.g. Exod. 21.8; Deut. 17.15; 29.21; Judg. 19.12; 1 Kgs 8.41 = 2 Chron. 6.33). In exilic and post-exilic contexts the word-pair זר/נכר becomes prominent, especially in the prophetic literature where it designates the foreign opponents of Judah (Obad. 11; Isa. 61.5; Jer. 5.19; cf. Lam. 5.2). The frequent collocation in Proverbs 1–9 of זרה with נכריה suggests that here too the terminology denotes a 'foreign' adversary of the Judean community. Most significant for comparison with Proverbs 1–9 are Ezra 10.2, 10-11, 14, 17-18, 44; and Neh. 13.26-27 where the phrase נשים נכריות, 'foreign women' (cf. also 1 Kgs 11.1, 8), refers to women outside the גולה group whom men within the community had married. The original context of Proverbs' disparagement of the זרה/נכריה, I will now argue, was this circumstance of Ezra's and later Nehemiah's drive to free the post-exilic community 'of everything foreign' (מכל נכר, Neh. 13.30). The polemic against the אשה זרה/נכריה in Proverbs 1–9 corresponds in terminology and in substance to the post-exilic campaign against exogamous marriages described in Ezra chs. 9–10, Neh. 10.30; 13.23-27; and Mal. 2.10-16.[36]

36. A connection between the polemic against the Strange Woman in Prov. 1–9 and the marriage reforms of Ezra–Nehemiah was first suggested, to my knowledge, by H. Oort, who argued that Prov. 1–9 reflects conditions later in the post-exilic era, when the measures instituted by Ezra and Nehemiah had lost force ('Spreuken 1–9', *TT* 19 [1885], pp. 412-17). C. Camp suggests that while deviant sexuality was preeminent in the earlier tradition of warnings against strange women, the secondary interpretation of the זרה as ethnically foreign came to the fore in support of the post-exilic marriage reforms (*Wisdom and the Feminine in the Book of Proverbs*, pp. 269-70; cf. Camp, 'What's So Strange about the Strange Woman?', p. 18).

The Social-Historical Context of the Post-Exilic Campaign against Foreign Women

Conventionally the prohibition of exogamous marriage in post-exilic Judah has been understood as religiously motivated: the aim was to preserve authentic Yahwist observance against the syncretist influences of the 'peoples of the land'. The post-exilic community, however, was not only a religious association. J. Weinberg has advanced the thesis that the Restoration community was organized as a *Bürger-Tempel-Gemeinde* (civic–temple community), a religio-political unit fictively constituted as an agnatic lineage of property-holding men and their families.[37] Membership in the temple community was determined by ostensible descent within a paternal estate (בית אבות; Ezra 1.5; 2.59 = Neh. 7.61; 2.68; 4.2-3; 8.1; 10.16; Neh. 7.70-71; 11.13; 12.12, 22, 23).[38] Real property (נחלה/אחזה, Neh. 11.3, 20) was distributed according to the divisions of this lineage.[39] Thus in the *Bürger-Tempel-Gemeinde* participation in the temple cult, land tenure and citizenship were linked under the leadership of the heads of the paternal estates (ראשי האבות), who presumably were among the larger property holders of the community.[40]

37. J.P. Weinberg, 'Demographische Notizen zur Geschichte der nachexilischen Gemeinde in Juda', *Klio* 54 (1972), pp. 45-58; 'Das *bēit 'abōt* im 6.–4. Jh. v.u.Z.', *VT* 23 (1973), pp. 400-14; 'Der *'am hā'āreṣ* des 6.–4. Jh. v.u.Z.', *Klio* 56 (1974), pp. 325-35; 'Die Agrarverhältnisse in der Bürger-Tempel-Gemeinde der Achämenidenzeit', in J. Harmatta and G. Komoróczy (eds.), *Wirtschaft und Gesellschaft im Alten Vorderasien* (Budapest: Akademiai Kiadö, 1976), pp. 473-86; 'Zentral- und Partikulargewalt im achämenidischen Reich', *Klio* 59 (1976), pp. 24-43; 'Die Mentalität der jerusalemischen Bürger-Tempel-Gemeinde des 6.–4. Jh. v.u.Z.', *Transeuphratène* 5 (1992), pp. 133-41. Weinberg's theory is summarized by D.L. Petersen, *Haggai and Zechariah 1–8: A Commentary* (Philadelphia: Westminster Press, 1984), pp. 30-31; and D.L. Smith, *The Religion of the Landless: The Social Context of the Babylonian Exile* (Bloomington, IN: Meyer–Stone, 1989), pp. 106-108. Important criticisms of the *Bürger-Tempel-Gemeinde* model are given by J. Blenkinsopp, 'Temple and Society in Achaemenid Judah', in P.R. Davies (ed.), *Second Temple Studies*. I. *Persian Period* (JSOTSup, 117; Sheffield: JSOT Press, 1991), pp. 22-53.

38. J. Weinberg, 'Das *bēit 'abōt* im 6.–4. Jh. v.u.Z.'

39. Weinberg, 'Die Agrarverhältnisse in der Bürger-Tempel-Gemeinde der Achämenidenzeit', pp. 481-84.

40. Note the prominence of the ראשי האבות in contributing to the rebuilding of the

Land tenure was a critical issue for the early post-exilic community. The deportees to Babylon had comprised only a small proportion of the total Judaean population, perhaps 10 per cent.[41] After the deportations, the remaining Judaean majority appears to have made claims to the land holdings left behind by the exiles (cf. 2 Kgs 25.12; Jer. 39.10; 40.4-12).[42] During the exile Ezekiel quotes the assertion of those remaining in Judah that 'the land has been given to us as a possession' (11.15), to which Ezekiel counters vigorously that the land of Israel will be given back to the exiles (11.17; cf. 33.23-29). Thus as members of the גולה community began to return and re-establish themselves, conflict over the land was inevitable.[43]

The returning exiles responded to local opposition by conceiving themselves typologically as the generation of a new conquest (Ezra 9.1-2, 10-15). The true Israel, now identified with the גולה (Ezra 1.11; 2.1; 9.4; 10.6; Neh. 7.6), had entered the land from the outside, and those presently occupying the land, like the Canaanites during the first conquest, were excluded from the covenant community.[44] The 'children of the גולה' (בני הגולה, Ezra 4.1; 6.19-20; 8.35; 10.7, 16; בני גלותא, Ezra 6.16) were opposed to the 'peoples of the land' (עמי הארץ, Ezra 10.2, 11; Neh. 9.24; 10.31-32) or 'peoples of the lands' (עמי הארצות, Ezra 3.3; 9.1-2, 11; Neh. 9.30). By referring to the local non-גולה Judaeans as 'peoples of the land(s)', the returning exiles effectively classified their Judaean rivals, together with the neighboring non-Judaean peoples (Ammonites, Moabites, Edomites, residents of

temple and the maintenance of its treasury (Neh. 7.70-71; Ezra 2.68).

41. This is J. Weinberg's estimate ('Demographische Notizen zur Geschichte der nachexilischen Gemeinde in Juda', p. 47); for other reviews of the evidence, see W. Schottroff, 'Zur Sozialgeschichte Israels in der Perserzeit', *VF* 27 (1982), p. 49; and P. Ackroyd, *Exile and Restoration: A Study of Hebrew Thought of the Sixth Century BC* (Philadelphia: Westminster Press, 1968), pp. 22-23 n. 24.

42. See especially E. Janssen, *Juda in der Exilszeit: Ein Beitrag zur Frage der Entstehung des Judentums* (FRLANT, 69; Göttingen: Vandenhoeck & Ruprecht, 1956), pp. 49-54.

43. Weinberg, 'Die Agrarverhältnisse in der Bürger-Tempel-Gemeinde der Achämenidenzeit', pp. 479-81.

44. H.G.M. Williamson, 'The Concept of Israel in Transition', in R.E. Clements (ed.), *The World of Ancient Israel: Sociological, Anthropological and Political Perspectives* (Cambridge: Cambridge University, 1989), p. 155. Perhaps this 'new conquest' ideology reflects the influence of Deutero-Isaiah's conception of the return as a new Exodus.

Samaria, etc.), as alien to Israel.[45] S. Japhet summarizes the situation:

> According to Ezr.–Neh. only one Israelite community exists in the land of Israel: that of returned exiles!... Who, then, are the other inhabitants of the land, according to Ezr.–Neh.? They are all foreigners (נכרים), peoples of the lands (עמי הארצות)... Anyone who does not fall under the definition of Israel according to Ezra's view, that is, anyone who is not a member of the 'community of exile', belongs to the 'peoples of the lands, with their abominations which have filled it from end to end' (Ezr. 9.11). The dichotomy is sharp: the 'exiles' are Israel, and all others 'the peoples of the lands'.[46]

The efforts of the returned exiles to regain control of the land were buttressed by Persian endorsement of their control over the Jerusalem temple (Ezra 1.1-4; 6.1-12; 7.12-26). Ezek. 11.15-17 already portrays both the non-deported Judaeans and the exiles acknowledging that legal right to the land accrues to those with access to the cult (cf. Lev. 25.23).[47] Now as the post-exilic Judaean *Bürger-Tempel-Gemeinde* began to take shape under Persian sponsorship, those who established membership in the temple community likewise secured their land rights.[48] Cultic membership and the attendant land rights were established genealogically, thus a technical terminology for genealogical registry (ספר היחש, התיחש, Neh. 7.5) first appears in the sources of the early post-exilic period.[49] According to the accounts of Ezra 2 and Nehemiah 7, some families were excluded because 'they could not prove their paternal estates (בית אבות) nor their descent, whether they belonged to Israel' (Ezra 2.59-60 = Neh. 7.61-62).

45. Cf. J. Blenkinsopp, *Ezra–Nehemiah: A Commentary* (OTL; Philadelphia: Westminster Press, 1988), p. 108.

46. 'People and Land in the Restoration Period,' in G. Strecker (ed.), *Das Land Israel in biblischer Zeit* (Göttinger Theologische Arbeiten, 25; Göttingen: Vandenhoeck & Ruprecht, 1983), pp. 112-15.

47. M. Smith, *Palestinian Parties and Politics That Shaped the Old Testament* (London: SCM Press, 2nd edn, 1987), pp. 75, 81-82; cf. J. Blenkinsopp, *Ezra–Nehemiah*, p. 60.

48. Besides the studies of J. Weinberg cited above, see J. Blenkinsopp, *Ezra–Nehemiah*, pp. 69, 83. For comparative evidence from Persian period Babylonia, where hereditary citizenship, cultic participation and land tenure were linked, see M. Dandamayev, 'Babylonia in the Persian Age', in W.D. Davies and L. Finkelstein (eds.), *The Cambridge History of Judaism*. I. *Introduction: The Persian Period* (Cambridge: Cambridge University Press, 1984), pp. 330-31.

49. Weinberg, 'Das *bēit 'abōt* im 6.–4. Jh. v.u.Z.', p. 406.

Although the genealogical idiom dominates the accounts of Ezra–Nehemiah, many of the genealogical relations that defined the temple community were fictive expressions of political or social solidarity rather than blood lineage.[50] This is evident in the גולה lists of Ezra 2.1-70//Neh. 7.6-63, where groups identified by patrilineage are combined with those identified by geographical location (e.g. Ezra 2.21-35). The fluidity of the גולה concept is evident in the exclusion of some families who were unmistakably part of the exilic group (note the Babylonian place names of Ezra 2.59), while other local groups who dissociated themselves from the 'peoples of the lands' were eventually admitted to the cultic assembly (Neh. 10.29; Ezra 6.21). The volatility of the definition of the authentic גולה group is also reflected in the case of the family of Hakkoz, which according to Ezra 2.61 was banned, but in Ezra 8.33 seems to have been readmitted (cf. Neh. 3.4, 21; 1 Chron. 24.10). Gradually the word גולה was converted from a term proper to those who underwent exile or their immediate descendants (e.g. Ezra 1.11; 2.1), to a designation for all recognized members of the community (Ezra 6.19-21).[51]

Genealogical reckoning thus provided an 'ideology of descent' for the post-exilic civic–temple community similar to that found in pre-exilic Israel and in other tribal cultures.[52] The גולה community's ideology of descent, however, differed from that provided by the oral genealogies of tribal cultures because it was subject to the control of writing. Through their administration of the genealogical registry, the leaders of the post-exilic community had the decisive word in the debate over the identity of the true Israel, who would belong to its

50. See especially Smith, *The Religion of the Landless*, pp. 99-105.

51. R.J. Coggins, 'The Origins of the Jewish Diaspora,' in R. Clements (ed.), *The World of Ancient Israel: Sociological, Anthropological and Political Perspectives* (Cambridge: Cambridge University Press, 1989), pp. 166-67. J. Weinberg attempts to trace in some detail the progressive incorporation of local Judaean populations into the civic–temple community. See especially 'Demographische Notizen zur Geschichte der nachexilischen Gemeinde in Juda', pp. 53-58.

52. The phrase 'ideology of descent' is from cultural anthropologist M. Sahlins, *Tribesmen* (Englewood Cliffs, NJ: Prentice–Hall, 1968), p. 55. Compare the assessment by anthropologist M. Fortes of the segmented oral genealogies of tribal groups: the lineage genealogy is not 'historically accurate', but takes its shape as a 'conceptualization of the existing lineage structure... projected backwards as pseudo-history' ('The Structure of Unilineal Descent Groups', *American Anthropologist* 55 [1953], p. 27).

temple, and who would possess its land. This control which the heads of the paternal estates exercised over community membership and over land allotments among the divisions of the lineage was frustrated, however, by exogamous marriages by some members of the community. Marriage alliances had always had implications for property holdings among the families involved, but the economic stability of the *Bürger-Tempel-Gemeinde* was especially vulnerable to disruption by marriages outside the community.[53] In the voluble social circumstances of the early post-exilic period, any unauthorized disturbance of the genealogical integrity of a בית אבות would have been an economic threat. Exogamous marriages could result in alien claims to land belonging to the Judaean collective.[54]

The post-exilic rules prohibit marriage to either men or women outside the community: 'We will not give our daughters to the peoples of the land or take their daughters for our sons' (Neh. 10.30 [Heb. 10.31]; cf. 13.25; Ezra 9.12); yet the record of offenses in Ezra–Nehemiah focuses, like Proverbs 1–9, on women outside the community as the principal danger (Ezra 9.2; 10.2-3, 10-11, 14, 17-18, 44; Neh. 13.23, 26-27). This emphasis in Proverbs 1–9 and Ezra–Nehemiah on avoiding women outside the community addresses a concrete threat to the real property holdings of the Judaean collective, because within the patrilineal land tenure system women were capable of inheriting and disposing of property. For example, Priestly law confirms female inheritance in the case of the daughters of Zelophehad (Num. 27.1-11; 36.1-9). In the absence of a male heir, the provision for these women aims to secure the inheritance within the bounds of its rightful patrilineal tribe, thus female heirs are required to marry within the lineage of their late father (see especially Num. 27.7-8; 36.6-9). These laws, presumably post-exilic in their present form, make clear that it was possible for women to inherit real property,

53. While not adopting Weinberg's *Bürger-Tempel-Gemeinde* model for the post-exilic period, K.G. Hoglund recognizes marriage 'as a means of transferring property and social status from one group to another', and relates the marriage reforms of Ezra–Nehemiah to concern over property rights ('Achaemenid Imperial Administration in Syria-Palestine and the Missions of Ezra and Nehemiah' [PhD dissertation, Duke University, 1989], pp. 436, 451-52); cf. Hoglund, 'The Achaemenid Context', in P.R. Davies (ed.), *Second Temple Studies*. I. *Persian Period* (JSOTSup, 117; Sheffield: JSOT Press, 1991), p. 67; and Camp, *Wisdom and the Feminine in the Book of Proverbs*, p. 242.

54. Cf. Blenkinsopp, *Ezra–Nehemiah*, p. 176.

and moreover that this possibility introduced conflicts over land tenure even among Israelite tribes. In the post-exilic setting, if families outside the recognized paternal estates became related to community members through marriage, there could be no assurance that such laws would preserve the economic base of the Judaean collective.

T.C. Eskenazi has recently drawn attention to additional evidence from Elephantine that Jewish women of the Persian period could own land. The archives of Mibtahiah daughter of Mahseiah, for example, attest to a woman who in her lifetime acquired three houses. Through the course of several marriages she was able to buy, sell and inherit property. Another amply documented case is that of a fifth-century Egyptian slave woman named Tamut, who was married to the Jewish temple official Ananiah son of Azariah. Tamut had extensive real property rights, including the ability to bequeath to her daughter Jehoishma even when a male heir existed.[55] The marriage contracts from Elephantine leave no doubt that women married to Jewish men of the Persian period could dispose of real property, and might at least partially disinherit the families of their husbands as a result of divorce.[56]

There are further indications of the considerable degree of economic power that women in the Judaean community could possess. At least one בית אבות listed in Ezra 2.1-70//Neh. 7.6-63 descends from a woman (Ezra 2.61; Neh. 7.63; 1 Esdr. 5.38).[57] This group was excluded from the community (Ezra 2.62), but not apparently because it derived from a woman. The group was marginal because of its descent from a Transjordanian family. This capacity within a

55. T.C. Eskenazi, 'Out from the Shadows: Biblical Women in the Postexilic Era', *JSOT* 54 (1992), pp. 25-43. For additional details of the archives of Mibtahiah and Tamut, see B. Porten, 'The Jews in Egypt', in W. Davies and L. Finkelstein (eds.), *The Cambridge History of Judaism*, I, pp. 399-400; and *Archives from Elephantine: The Life of an Ancient Jewish Military Colony* (Berkeley: University of California Press, 1968), pp. 190-263.

56. See also the study of Elephantine marriage contracts in E. Lipiński, 'Marriage and Divorce in the Judaism of the Persian Period', *Transeuphratène* 4 (1991), pp. 63-71.

57. On the 'descendants of Barzillai, who had married one of the daughters of Barzillai the Gileadite, and was called by their name,' see Eskenazi, 'Out from the Shadows', pp. 37-38; Camp, *Wisdom and the Feminine in the Book of Proverbs*, p. 260; H.G.M. Williamson, *Ezra, Nehemiah* (WBC, 16; Waco, TX: Word, 1985), p. 37.

patrilineal system to recognize segments derived from females is another feature shared by the post-exilic Judaean social organization and the segmentary lineages of genuine tribal cultures.[58] In both contexts the lack of a legitimated patriarch for a lineage segment does not necessarily prejudice against the property rights of the segment within the larger social group.

Several commentators have noted the presence in Ezra–Nehemiah of women at the assembly (קהל) that convenes at crucial moments in the life of the people and appears to constitute the broadest authority of the community.[59] Women belong to the קהל before which Ezra reads the Law (Neh. 8.2-3), and which later takes an oath of allegiance to the Law (Neh. 10.29). Women also attend the assembly that makes a covenant to expel illicit wives and their children from the community (Ezra 10.1). Also significant is Neh. 5.1-13, where women are explicitly mentioned along with the men (v. 1) as crying out for their threatened possessions, 'our fields, our vineyards and our houses' (v. 3). It appears therefore that despite the ostensibly patriarchal social organization of the post-exilic period, women in the community were significantly enfranchised. In order to preserve the collective economic base of land holdings, however, women outside the community were prevented from gaining access by marrying into the group.

It would overdraw the case to maintain that internal management of land tenure was the sole motive for Ezra and Nehemiah's marriage reforms. Religious self-definition must have been an urgent concern for the exiles, and this would have remained an issue in its own right for the post-exilic temple community. Moreover, K. Hoglund has adduced evidence in his study of Achaemenid imperial administration that the Persians, to facilitate ease of identification of the ruling group and regularity of administration and taxation, enforced a guarded ethnic identity among those, such as the גולה community, to whom they

58. For the inclusion of segments descended from women within patrilineal tribal groups, see Sahlins, *Tribesmen*, p. 55. An example from the Tiv of central Nigeria is illustrated in the genealogical diagram provided by L. Bohanan, 'A Genealogical Charter,' *Africa* 22 (1952), p. 302 fig. 1.

59. E.g. Eskenazi, 'Out from the Shadows', pp. 41-42; Camp, *Wisdom and the Feminine in the Book of Proverbs*, p. 259. For Deuteronomic antecedents (Deut. 29.10, 17; cf. 31.12; 12.12, 18; 16.11, 14), see M. Weinfeld, *Deuteronomy and the Deuteronomic School* (Oxford: Oxford University Press, 1972), p. 291.

entrusted regions of the imperial domain.[60] Hoglund sees in the community's lament of their status as 'people in bondage' (Ezra 9.9) and as 'slaves in the land' (Neh. 9.36) the self-awareness of a dependent population who occupy Judaean territory at the pleasure of the Persians. If Hoglund is correct, the גולה Judaeans risked losing their land entirely if they did not maintain themselves as a distinct community.

Since, for all these reasons, exogamous marriage was perceived as a threat to the survival of the civic–temple community, unprecedented sanctions were imposed against the practice. The received legal tradition, however, did not contain a universal ban of exogamy, nor was there any existing provision for the expulsion of foreign wives. Ezra's citation of the law in 9.1-2 is an exegetical combination of Exod. 34.11-16 and Deut. 7.1-4, each of which contains a stock catalogue of traditional enemies of Israel, including 'the Canaanites, Hittites, Perizzites and Jebusites' (Ezra 9.1), in addition to Deut. 23.2-9, which excludes Ammonites and Moabites from the assembly of Yhwh (but which admits Egyptians, in conflict with Ezra 9.1).[61] Although Ammonites and Moabites were obviously covered by Ezra and Nehemiah's intermarriage ban, the names of the proscribed peoples were not the essential feature of this adaptation of the law. There had been been no Canaanites, Hittites, Perizzites or Jebusites in Judah for centuries, so the question of intermarriage with them was moot. The critical aspect of this development was the assertion of ethnic difference from all local non-גולה populations ('peoples of the lands', vv. 1, 2 and 11), whereby Judaeans outside the temple community were classed together with the traditional enemies of Israel.

60. 'Achaemenid Imperial Administration in Syria-Palestine', pp. 437-42; 'The Achaemenid Context', pp. 65-66.

61. For the universal prohibition of exogamy as a post-exilic innovation, see S.J.D. Cohen, 'From the Bible to the Talmud: The Prohibition of Intermarriage', *HAR* 7 (1983), pp. 23-39. On the development of the legal exegetical tradition in Ezra 9 and Neh. 10, cf. M. Fishbane, *Biblical Interpretation in Ancient Israel* (Oxford: Oxford University Press, 1985), pp. 114-29; and D.J.A. Clines, 'Nehemiah 10 as an Example of Early Jewish Biblical Exegesis', *JSOT* 21 (1981), pp. 111-17.

The Strange Woman of Proverbs 1–9 as a Threat to the Judaean Temple Economy

Against the social-historical background I have just described, it becomes clear that the terminology of the polemic against the Strange Woman in Proverbs 1–9 coincides with the ideological strategy of Ezra–Nehemiah. The terms זרה and נכריה can denote both 'strangeness' to the immediate kinship group and 'foreignness' to the nation—the rhetoric of Ezra–Nehemiah exploits these two senses as one. Although the גולה community is only fictively constituted as a kinship group, anyone outside the community is classified in the language of ethnicity as a foreigner and thus excluded. A Judaean of illicit background is as alien to the community of Ezra–Nehemiah as a Moabite or Egyptian. Proverbs 1–9, proscribing relations with any woman deemed זרה, admonishes Judaean men to preserve this narrow definition of the community.

We saw above that Prov. 6.24-35 and 7.5-27 are traditional units related to the אשה זרה/נכריה only by means of their introductory formulae (6.24; 7.5). These two passages could easily have originated as pre-exilic compositions. Prov. 2.16-19 and 5.1-23, however, show a closer correspondence to the circumstances of Ezra–Nehemiah. Here not only is the prescription of Ezra–Nehemiah against outside women echoed, but also the consequences of failing to heed the prohibition are indicated. In Proverbs 2 the signal warning against the זרה/נכריה אשה, whose 'house sinks down to death' (2.18), is linked with possession of the land.[62] Prov. 2.21 identifies the 'upright' who will 'inhabit the land' (ישכנו הארץ) as those who avoid the Strange Woman; 'but the wicked', the text continues, 'will be cut off from the land'. This is traditional language, the stock phraseology of Deuteronomic theology (e.g. Deut. 4.1; 5.16; 6.18; 11.9; 16.20).[63] The juxtaposition, however, of this stereotypical language of inhabiting the land with the warning against foreign women in Proverbs reflects precisely the anxiety over land tenure which was a motivating factor in Ezra–Nehemiah's campaign against exogamy.

62. Cf. Camp, *Wisdom and the Feminine in the Book of Proverbs*, p. 251.

63. Cf. Plöger, *Sprüche Salomos*, p. 28; Weinfeld, *Deuteronomy and the Deuteronomic School*, pp. 313-16.

In Prov. 5.8-10 involvement with the Strange Woman is associated with the alienation of Judaean wealth:

> Keep your way far from her (i.e. the זרה)
> and do not go near the door of her house;
> lest you give your honor to others (אחרים)
> and your years to the merciless (אכזרי);
> lest strangers (זרים) take their fill of your wealth,
> and your labors go to the house of an alien (נכרי).

The series of masculine references in vv. 9-10 (אחרים, אכזרי, זרים, נכרי) has puzzled commentators.[64] One would expect feminine forms if the text grew out of concern that Judaean men might spend their resources on foreign prostitutes or illicit lovers. The passage makes sense, however, if we connect it with the fear that Judaean property will fall under the control of alien families (i.e. the control of alien men), via liaisons and eventual marriages to women outside the community. The prominence of the בית אבות in post-exilic social organization, and the tumultuous social process through which various paternal estates rivalled one another for position in the temple community may account for the frequency with which the Strange Woman is denounced by reference to her 'house' (בית, 2.18; 5.8; 7.8, 27; cf. 5.10, 'the house of an alien', בית נכרי).

Ezra reports that the 'heads of the paternal estates' (Ezra 10.16) convened in order formally to identify and prosecute all members of the collective who had married outside the group. The penalties for failure to submit to these proceedings included expulsion from the temple assembly (קהל) and the confiscation of property (רכוש, Ezra 10.8). The latter term often refers to movable goods and it is usually interpreted so here.[65] The Chronicler, however, uses the word to include real estate (e.g. 1 Chron. 27.31, the summary holdings of the king including vineyards and orchards) and the term most likely refers to real property in Ezra 10.8. Since membership in the קהל entailed title to land, the dedication (חרם) of property which here accompanies expulsion from the assembly would involve the forfeiture of immovable property to the temple collective. This is a severe penalty indeed, and its currency in the post-exilic period illumines the sage's warning in Prov. 5.14. Stay away from the Strange

64. E.g. McKane, *Proverbs: A New Approach*, p. 316; Plöger, *Sprüche Salomos*, p. 56.

65. E.g. Hoglund, 'Achaemenid Imperial Administration', p. 431.

Woman, he says, lest at the end of your life in weakness and poverty you look back and say: 'I was at the point of utter ruin in the assembled congregation' (קהל, 5.14). This plight of impoverishment combined with disgrace before the assembly is clearly reminiscent of the punishment stipulated in Ezra 10.8.[66]

Mal. 2.10-16 condemns the practice of Judaean men divorcing their legitimate wives in order to marry women outside the community.[67] Prov. 5.15-20 uses remarkably similar vocabulary to urge marital fidelity as opposed to involvement with strange (זרה) and foreign (נכריה) women.[68] The 'wife of your youth' (אשת נורך) to whom Prov. 5.18 urges fidelity is mentioned twice in this section of Malachi (2.14, 15). Malachi's reference to 'the wife of your youth, to whom you have been faithless, though she is your companion and wife by covenant' (2.14) can also be compared to Proverbs' charge that the Strange Woman 'forsakes the companion of her youth and forgets the covenant of her God'.[69] Malachi's rhetorical question in 2.10 reflects the post-exilic setting common to Ezra–Nehemiah and Proverbs where there is an overarching need to preserve the genealogical integrity of the Judaean lineage. Malachi asks, 'Have we not all one father?' (i.e. are we not all of the same lineage?; v. 10a). He continues, 'Why then are we faithless to one another?' (i.e. by engaging in exogamous marriages; v. 10b).

Conclusion

The attack on the Strange Woman of Proverbs 1–9 thus belongs originally to a social milieu in which an ideology of descent preserved the socio-economic integrity of the community by branding outside

66. Cf. Camp: 'Whatever the range of possible meanings of Prov. 5.10-14, it is hard to disassociate it completely from Ezra 10.2-11 (cf. esp. Ezra 10.8 and Prov. 5.14)' (*Wisdom and the Feminine in the Book of Proverbs*, p. 269).

67. The identity of the בת אל נכר (Mal. 2.11) is disputed, but the best solution remains that she is a woman outside the recognized גולה community (see B. Glazier-McDonald, 'Intermarriage, Divorce, and the בת אל נכר', *JBL* 106 [1987], pp. 603-11; and *Malachi: The Divine Messenger* [SBLDS, 98; Atlanta: Scholars Press, 1987], pp. 81-120). As in Ezra–Nehemiah, those outside the temple community are charged with the religious abominations of the 'peoples of the lands'.

68. A. Robert, 'Les attaches littéraires Bibliques de Prov. I–IX', *RB* 44 (1935), p. 508.

69. Camp, *Wisdom and the Feminine in the Book of Proverbs*, p. 236.

women as זרה/נכריה. The negative language directed against the זרה in Proverbs 1–9 persisted in Hebrew wisdom literature even after it had outlived its former purpose. Ben Sira, for example, preserves the זרה as a negative stereotype (9.3), but no trace of her earlier socio-economic significance remains. Here the זרה is included indiscriminately in a catalog of types of women who according to Ben Sira should be avoided, including women singers, virgins, prostitutes, beautiful women, other men's wives, and women *per se* (Sir. 9.2-9). Thus this זרה figure is merely a misogynistic rhetorical device. From Qumran has survived a sapiential work (4Q184, *DJD* 5: 82-85) that draws upon the images associated with the זרה in Proverbs 1–9, but the terminology of strangeness has disappeared. Despite her depiction with features borrowed from the זרה of Proverbs 1–9, here the figure is named only הזונה. Perhaps, like the prostitute of the Apocalypse, she symbolizes Rome.[70]

In post-exilic Judah, however, the Strange Woman represented a more immediate and specific threat. The condemnation of the נכריה/אשה זרה in Proverbs 1–9 was motivated by concern for economic and corporate survival. This accounts for the vehemence of the attack which has impressed so many commentators, and reminds us of some of the social costs by which biblical Israel was reconstituted in the wake of the Babylonian destruction.[71]

70. J.M. Allegro, '"The Wiles of the Wicked Woman": A Sapiential Work from Qumran's Fourth Cave', *PEQ* 96 (1964), pp. 53-55.

71. Earlier versions of this paper were presented at meetings of the Society of Biblical Literature in 1990 and 1991. For kindly giving me copies of their articles before publication, I would like to thank Tamara C. Eskenazi, 'Out from the Shadows: Biblical Women in the Postexilic Era'; Kenneth G. Hoglund, 'Sociology of the Second Temple Period: The Achaemenid Context'; and E. Lipiński, 'Marriage and Divorce in the Judaism of the Persian Period'; and also Ben C. Ollenburger, whose work on Trito-Isaiah in the post-exilic context afforded me with many of the insights pursued here.

The Mixed Marriage Crisis in Ezra 9–10 and Nehemiah 13: A Study of the Sociology of the Post-Exilic Judaean Community*

Daniel L. Smith-Christopher

Introduction

Mixed marriage, and societies' reaction to it, can often reveal significant lines of stress within a social group, and between social groups—particularly when power is unequally shared between those groups. Because of this, sociological observations of the mixed-marriage crisis in the book of Ezra–Nehemiah may contribute to our understanding of post-exilic Judaean society. Furthermore, however, sociological analysis can often reveal many modern assumptions of the biblical scholars who are themselves engaged in studying the historical events in question.

If proof is needed that the interests of the scholarly reader can influence his or her reading of the biblical text, surely we need look no further than the mixed marriage crisis in Ezra 9–10, for example, in order to find emotionally charged comments such as Williamson's view that 'The treatment described in these two chapters of how Ezra tackled the problem of mixed marriages is among the least attractive parts of Ezra–Nehemiah, if not the whole Old Testament'.[1]

Similarly, D. Clines is 'appalled by the personal misery brought into so many families by the compulsory divorce of foreign wives [and] outraged at Ezra's insistence on racial purity, so uncongenial to modern liberal thoughts'.[2] Clearly, there are a number of social assumptions operant in these views, such as western, liberal-minded

* This article, on the subject of marriage, is dedicated to my wife Zsa Zsa, to celebrate the occasion of our marriage this past June, 1992.

1. H.G.M. Williamson, *Ezra, Nehemiah* (Waco, TX: Word, 1985), p. 159.

2. D.J.A. Clines, *Ezra, Nehemiah and Esther* (NCB; Grand Rapids: Eerdmans, 1984), p. 116.

toleration of 'mixed' marriages in the name of democratic, and perhaps romantic, idealism. But sociological analysis can also guide historical analysis—and force us to ask questions about the meaning and significance of mixed marriages in the Persian period, the biblical attitude toward mixed marriages, and the meaning and significance of mixed marriages for *modern* readers of these texts—particularly in racially segregated modern societies.

The Texts

Although there is some debate about whether Neh. 13.3 really deals within the mixed marriage issue, it is dealt with at great length in Ezra 9–10, and again in Neh. 13.23-31. This issue has usually been approached by commentators as two examples of the same problem with the post-exilic community. As I will argue below, however, there is good reason for reading the accounts in Ezra quite differently from the account in Nehemiah.

Many of these discussions of the dissolution of mixed marriages have tended to focus on two main points. First, the Deuteronomic legal basis for the action taken by Ezra in Ezra 9–10 and Nehemiah in Nehemiah 13, and the fact that the Deuteronomic laws are being stretched to justify this action.[3] Second, the social meaning of this action in the context of the post-exilic community and its attempt to preserve its 'purity' and/or maintain its economic holdings without threat of foreigners 'inheriting' land.[4] T.C. Eskenazi, for example,

3. See W. Horbury, 'Extirpation and Excommunication', *VT* 35 (1985), pp. 13-38, who argues that an interpretation that combines laws regarding admission to the temple congregation *and* penalties for breach of covenant (Deut. 17, 18, 19 and 20 as well as Deut. 7) could result in such a justification; and G. Blidstein, 'Atimia: A Greek Parallel to Ezra X 8 and to Post-Biblical Exclusion from the Community', *VT* 24 (1974), pp. 357-60, who argues that Ezra may well have been given just such an authority to exile offenders in Artaxerxes' letter in Ezra 8. At least since Batten's commentary, scholars have noted that the Torah does not really authorize Ezra's action. See L. Batten, *Ezra and Nehemiah* (ICC; Edinburgh: T. & T. Clark, 1980 [1913]), p. 331; W. Rudolph, *Esra und Nehemia* (HAT; Tübingen: P. Siebeck, 1949), pp. 87-97; J. Blenkinsopp, *Ezra–Nehemiah* (London: SCM Press, 1988), p. 176; Williamson, *Ezra, Nehemiah*, pp. 130-32.

4. Note Fensham, and others, who state that 'The reason for this attitude had nothing to do with racism, but with a concern for the purity of the religion of the Lord... [I]n the end it was a question of the preservation of their identity', *The*

recently argued in support of the view that inheritance may have been a major concern in the post-exilic community since Jewish women could inherit land, as shown in the Elephantine Papyri.[5] Similarly, K. Hoglund's important work on the imperial nature of the military mission of Nehemiah in the context of Persian policy after the Egyptian Revolt has lent new and important information about the nature of the community within which Nehemiah had royal authority. Hoglund states that:

> systems of allocating territories to dependent populations will work as long as the imperial system is capable of maintaining some clarity as to who is allowed access to a particular region and who is not. Intermarriage among various groups would tend to smudge the demarcation between the groups...the community possesses land tenure only at the will of the empire.[6]

That land tenure was a significant factor in *all* marriages in ancient Israel can hardly be doubted, although, as C. Meyers points out in her analysis of exogamy and endogamy in ancient Israel, the *cultural influences* of 'foreign' women must also be considered.[7]. If we follow the land tenure issue—or more broadly the economic issue—then modern analyses of mixed marriages raise some very interesting questions that apply to a historical analysis of Ezra and Nehemiah's cases. Thus, between the two points noted—legal and social—this essay attempts to contribute to the dialogue on the second point.

Books of Ezra and Nehemiah (Grand Rapids: Eerdmans, 1982), p. 124; Cf. Batten, *Ezra and Nehemiah*, p. 331; Blenkinsopp, *Ezra, Nehemiah*, p. 176. The economic issues have also been noted by Blenkinsopp, and by J. Weinberg, 'Die Agrarverhältnisse in der Bürger-Tempel-Gemeinde der Achämenidenzeit', *Acta Antiqua* 22 (1974), pp. 473-85.

5. See T.C. Eskenazi, 'Out from the Shadows: Biblical Women in the Post-Exilic Era', *JSOT* 54 (1992), pp. 25-43. See also J. Blenkinsopp, 'The Social Context of the "Outsider Woman" in Proverbs 1–9', *Bib* 74 (1991), pp. 457-73.

6. K. Hoglund, 'Achaemenid Imperial Administration in Syria-Palestine and the Missions of Ezra and Nehemiah' (PhD dissertation, Duke University, 1989), p. 416. I wish to thank Dr Hoglund for allowing me to consult this manuscript ahead of its much anticipated publication during 1992.

7. See C. Meyers, *Discovering Eve* (Oxford: Oxford University Press, 1988), pp. 180-88.

Methodology

The method applied in this study is comparative and sociological. I have discussed this method at some length elsewhere,[8] so it is important only to summarize the main methodological argument here. In brief, the comparative sociological approach does not seek to make direct comparisons across cultural or chronological distances, as if such comparisons would constitute a 'proof'. Rather, this method seeks to deal with the fact that *all* modern biblical scholarship is dependent on the biases of the reader of the text, and the success of biblical analysis can as often depend on the breadth as well as the depth of the knowledge and experience that a reader brings to a text. Comparative analysis seeks to raise new questions for exegesis by suggesting new directions for research, or previously unknown approaches, by crossing disciplines for new perspectives.

The present study will illustrate this approach by surveying a sample of the relevant sociological and anthropological literature on mixed marriage and then taking cues from this survey to ask questions about the biblical case of the mixed marriage 'crisis' in Ezra 9–10 and Nehemiah 13.

The Sociology of Mixed Marriage

It seems self-evident that mixed marriages will be much more common in mixed societies where the availability of endogamous (same group) marriage partners is low. Indeed, biblical commentators have often suggested this as a possible explanation for the mixed marriages in the first case. L. Batten, in his earlier commentary, attributed the motive to an actual scarcity of Jewish women who were returning exiles within the acceptable boundaries of the community. 'There is no hint that Jewish women had married foreign men. The condition is attributable to the scarcity of women in the new community.'[9]

W. Rudolph also thought that the ratio was to the disadvantage of young men seeking marriage. It seemed to Rudolph that Jewish

8. D.L. Smith, *Religion of the Landless* (Bloomington, IN: Meyer–Stone, 1989), pp. 5-16.

9. Batten, *Esra and Nehemiah*, p. 331.

women were available in the exile in sufficient numbers, whereas in Palestine it was clearly not always easy to find a full-blood Jewish woman '...weil unter den Heimkehrern wohl die Männer überwogen hatten und die im Lande zurückgebliebene Bevölkerung rassisch gemischt war'.[10] But it is clear from recent sociological analysis that the matter is certainly much more complex than simply the relative numbers of available spouses. The sociologist R.K. Merton describes mixed marriages as 'marriage of persons deriving from those different in-groups and out-groups other than the family which are culturally conceived as relevant to the choice of a spouse'.[11]

This definition immediately raises further questions about the biblical case by pointing to those 'relevant' considerations that defined the marriage 'crisis'. Ezra, for one, defines the terms both ethnically (by citing the national/ethnic categories of Canaanite, Hivite, Perizzite, etc.) *and* religiously (by citing such terms as 'the Holy Seed'). In this case, 'endogamy' would refer to marrying within a religious and ethnically defined group. *It is clear that Ezra conceived of this group as consisting only of former exiles* (Ezra 9.4). But even if this was a rigid definition for the writers of Ezra,[12] the possibility remains that these 'mixed-marriages' were considered 'mixed' *only* by Ezra and his supporters, and not in the first case by the married persons themselves. The issue is made more precise by Merton's considerations of 'endogamy':

> Endogamy is a device which serves to maintain social prerogatives and immunities within a social group. It helps prevent the diffusion of power, authority and preferred status to persons who are not affiliated with a dominant group. It serves further to accentuate and symbolize the 'reality' of the group by setting it off against other discriminable social units. Endogamy serves as an isolation and exclusion device, with the function of increasing group solidarity and supporting the social structure by helping to fix social distances which obtain between groups. All this is not

10. Rudolph, *Esra und Nehemiah*, p. 87.

11. R.K. Merton, 'Intermarriage and the Social Structure: Fact and Theory', *Psychiatry* 9 (1941), pp. 361-74 (362).

12. Although I accept the notion that the books of Ezra and Nehemiah are now actually one work, I think that differences in the history of the Nehemiah materials which were later edited by the addition, among other things, of the Ezra material, allows us to still speak of 'Ezra' as opposed to 'Nehemiah'.

meant to imply that endogamy was deliberately instituted for these purposes; this is a description in functional, not necessarily purposive, terms.[13]

Furthermore, in a comment that virtually defines Ezra's attitude as it appears in the biblical texts, Merton suggests that public outcries against mixed marriage are 'outbursts of moral indignation [that] are defensive devices which stabilize the existing organization of interpersonal relations and groups...'[14]

There has been a considerable discussion of mixed marriage in sociological and anthropological literature, often in dialogue with Merton's programmatic article, in which he outlined his functionalist perspective to guide further study.[15]

In his discussion two significant parts of his theoretical formulation are 'exchange theory' and the related 'hypergamy' theory drawing on the 'commodity exchange' approach to marriage formulated in the structuralist anthropological analysis of Levi-Strauss. Other social scientists emphasize group identity as the main factor in protecting 'boundaries'. On a secondary level, it is also important to mention romantic/democratic 'violations' of ethnic boundaries, and the argument that violations of group identity in mixed marriages result from deviance or alienation from the strictures of a specific ethnic or

13. Merton, 'Intermarriage', p. 368.

14. Merton, 'Intermarriage', p. 369.

15. Among the more helpful articles consulted for this essay, see C. Bagley, 'Patterns of Inter-Ethnic Marriage in England', *Phylon* 29 (1968), pp. 347-50; S. Benson, 'Interracial Families in London', in *Ambiguous Ethnicity* (Cambridge: Cambridge University Press, 1981), pp. 146-49; N. Gist, 'Cultural versus Social Marginality: The Anglo-Indian Case', *Phylon* 28 (1967), pp. 361-75; J. Golden, 'Patterns of Negro–White Intermarriage', *American Sociological Review* 19 (1954), pp. 144-47; G.A. Kourvetaris, 'Patterns of Generational Subculture and Intermarriage of Greeks in the United States', *International Journal of Sociology of the Family* 1 (1971), pp. 34-48; B. Lobodzinska, 'A Cross-Cultural Study of Mixed Marriages in Poland and the United States', *International Journal of Sociology of the Family* 15/1-2 (1985), pp. 94-117; S. Marcson, 'Theory of Intermarriage and Assimilation', *Social Forces* 29 (1950), pp. 75-78; J. Mayer, 'Jewish–Gentile Intermarriage Patterns: A Hypothesis', *Sociology and Social Research* 45/2 (1961), pp. 188-95; T.P. Monahan, 'Interracial Marriage in the United States: Some Data on Upstate New York', *International Journal of Sociology of the Family* 1 (1971), pp. 94-105; E. Porterfield, 'Perspectives on Black–White Intermixture', *Black and White Mixed Marriages* (Chicago: Nelson–Hall, 1978), pp. 1-184; G.D. Sandefur, 'American Indian Intermarriage', *Social Science Research* 15/4 (1986), pp. 347-71.

cultural group.[16] Finally, many studies have proven the more self-evident notion that intermarriage increases as the numbers of single population in a mixed society decrease.[17] I will comment on many of these and their relevance to the Ezra–Nehemiah texts in turn.

Hypergamy Theory

In his analysis of black–white intermarriages, E. Porterfield works with Levi-Strauss's idea that marriages are an effective control of human commodities and that they are 'exchanged' in order to gain certain advantages. This 'exchange' basis for the analysis of mixed marriages has led to the so-called 'hypergamy' theory. When applied to black–white marriages in the USA, for example, it is suggested that typically the black male 'exchanges' educational/financial success for the white female's racial status.[18] The advocates of the 'hypergamy' theory argue that success- or status-minded males from low status groups will attempt to 'marry up' among females of the majority or higher status groups.[19]

16. Social deviance is cited as a major factor in mixed marriages in many studies. This approach seems less promising as a guide to biblical research, but is important to mention. In discussing Arab–Jewish marriages in Israel, Erik Cohen states that in nearly every case he found, 'the Jewish women had in some respect been marginal in Jewish society' (E. Cohen, 'Mixed Marriage in an Israeli Town', *Jewish Journal of Sociology* 11 [1969] pp. 41-50 [49]) Similarly, Kuo and Wong point to couples who share a certain disregard of social norms in Singapore, and mixed couples of Malay and Chinese and occasionally Indians, occur (E.C.Y. Kuo, 'Population Ratio, Intermarriage and Mother Tongue Retention', *Anthropological Linguistics* 20/2 [1978], pp. 85-93; E.C.Y. Kuo and A.K. Wong, 'Ethnic Intermarriage in a Multiethnic Society', in *The Contemporary Family in Singapore* [Singapore: Singapore University Press, 1979], pp. 168-88). There is very little in the Hebrew Bible, however, that would support the supposition that those who engaged in mixed marriages were social outcasts or marginal to the society in question. In the one possible example, Ruth, her poverty and compassion make her exceptionally positive rather than negative; that is, her alienation from Moabite society is not a negative factor. She certainly is a case of alienation from her native traditions, however, and is honoured in the Hebrew Bible. Indeed, the shock of mixed marriage in Ezra 9–10 is precisely to be attributed to Ezra's horror that it is the leaders who are involved, most especially the priests.

17. Kuo and Wong, 'Ethnic Intermarriage', p. 86.

18. D.P. Aldridge, 'Interracial Marriages', *Journal of Black Studies* 8/1 (1977), pp. 361-68.

19. Males from the majority, higher status groups, it is argued, usually do not

This theory of intermarriage as the attempt to 'marry up' in status is supported by studies in India, where

> The predominant pattern of intercaste marriage involved a low caste husband and a high caste wife... between the professional male of low caste group and the non-professional female of high caste group.[20]

> Most intermarriages in India between caste and outcaste people mirrored the pairings for American blacks and Jews—that is, subordinate group males and dominant group females—although none of the observers of this phenomenon have come up with a convincing rationale for this situation.[21]

Within the USA, the same pattern has been noted for the Asian upperclasses, who marry advantaged members of the majority population.[22] Finally, J. Mayer's work on Jewish–Gentile marriages in times of antisemitism concluded that there was a rise in specifically Jewish male–Gentile female mixed marriages in the data from Europe between 1876 and 1933.[23]

Typically, the hypergamy theory predicts that it will be males of the disadvantaged population who marry females from the majority population. But this is not necessarily a gender issue. In the Asian population, it is the female who is much more likely to attempt to 'marry up'. This is argued by Siyon Rhee, for example, who notes the pattern of 'marrying up' for Asian females (in his case, Vietnamese and Korean):

> By marrying Americans, preferably Caucasians, some females may attain the more egalitarian marital relationships and status. They might be a good example of hypogamy... [which]... implies the pattern wherein the female

need to legitimate mixed liaisons with formal marriage, but have tended to keep concubines instead. But this point may be open to question. The data about Asian women shows that the issue is not simply gender, but which of the two genders in a particular context has a sense of freedom to pursue 'mixed' associations. In the Asian context it is the women who seek to 'marry up' in greater number.

20. D. Singh, 'An Exploratory Study of Touchable–Untouchable Intercaste Marriage in India', *Indian Journal of Sociology* 1/2 (1970), pp. 130-38.

21. P.R. Spickard, *Mixed Blood: Intermarriage and Ethnic Identity in Twentieth Century America* (Madison: University of Wisconsin Press, 1989), p. 350.

22. L. Hagime Shinagawa and G. Young Pang, 'Intraethnic, Interethnic, and Interracial Marriages among Asian Americans in California, 1980', *Berkeley Journal of Sociology* 33 (1988), pp. 95-114.

23. J. Mayer, 'Jewish–Gentile Intermarriage Patterns: A Hypothesis', *Sociology and Social Research* 45/2 (1961), pp. 188-95.

> marries into a higher social stratum. For some Korean and Vietnamese females, interracial marriage acts as a means of achieving better status in the family. On the contrary, the Asian American male is likely to give up his dominant status by outmarrying.[24]

Similarly, Kim's data from studies of the Korean minority in Japan note that Korean females are seeking higher status by marrying in greater numbers with Japanese males. Kim concluded his study by finding that Koreans in general accepted the notion of mixed marriage in much higher percentages than the Japanese majority.[25]

Finally, J.N. Tinker's data on Japanese and American mixed marriages tend to confirm the data for the Asian population:

> The most persuasive explanation may be... that they [Asian women] had, or thought they had, something to gain by intermarriage. Their traditional role in the Japanese-American family was less rewarding to them than the dominant American definition of the female role. Several students of Japanese-American subculture have remarked about an expectation that women be submissive and subordinate...
>
> Thus, looking at marriage as an exchange, it would not be surprising if some Japanese-American females should conclude that they could get a better bargain on the open market. Just as some Caucasian males might have seen that it was to their advantage to enlarge the field of those eligible for marriage to include the Japanese, so some Japanese-American women might have found it to their benefit to consider intermarriage.[26]

Thus, 'exchange theory' asks the reader of the biblical text to consider what 'upward' advantages were perceived by those men of the exilic community who 'married out'. As E.L. Cerroni-Long observes:

> the rationale of exogamy is the extension of a society's standing through creation of new links and alliances and renewal of old ones while that of endogamy is the maintenance of group boundaries by forbidding the introduction of outsiders in the kinship network and the reinforcement of intra-group ties and sense of identity.[27]

24. S. Yoo Rhee, 'Korean and Vietnamese Outmarriage: Characteristics and Implications' (PhD dissertation, UCLA, 1988), pp. 150-68.

25. Y. Shin Kim, 'Marriage Pattern of the Korean Population in Japan', *Journal of Biosocial Science* 17/4 (1985), pp. 445-50.

26. J.N. Tinker, 'Intermarriage and Ethnic Boundaries: The Japanese-American Case', *Journal of Social Issues* 29/2 (1973), pp. 49-81.

27. E.L. Cerroni-Long, 'Marrying Out: Socio-Cultural and Psychological Implications of Intermarriage', *Journal of Comparative Family Studies* 15/1 (1984), pp. 25-46.

The hypergamy theory, if applied to Ezra–Nehemiah, raises interesting questions about the relative advantages of the post-exilic community vis-à-vis the surrounding communities. We shall return to these questions, but the second main theoretical approach to mixed marriages is also helpful for our analysis.

Group Boundary Maintenance

Some sociologists prefer to see prohibitions against mixed marriage as a socio-psychological indicator of worries by a group about its own identity and cultural survival. Cerroni-Long, for example, observes that

> When a human group finds itself uprooted and isolated and faced by a strong pressure to conform to alien standards it instinctively falls back on the primary ties of the kinship network both to reaffirm its individuality in the face of threats of extinction and to maintain some form of normal existence amidst unforeseeable and stressful contingencies.[28]

I have already commented on relative numbers as an important aspect of intermarriage. But Spickard observes that, while intermarriage is low in circumstances of high ethnic concentration, large numbers can often be compensated for by highly active small group socialization.[29] R.J. Lazar developed the following schema:[30]

Selectivity Low	Socialization Low = High Intermarriage
Selectivity High	Socialization Low = Low Intermarriage
Selectivity Low	Socialization High = Low Intermarriage

This seems borne out by the fact that in cases where socialization skills have been radically disrupted, intermarriage can be high even in cases of high concentration, such as the high instances of Native-American intermarriages (even in geographical locations where numbers are high), and the dramatic increase of Japanese and Filipino women marrying into the 'victorious' white society of the occupation soldiers.[31]

C.E. Glick notes that early immigrant men often are more willing

28. Cerroni-Long, 'Marrying Out', p. 28.

29. Spickard, 'Mixed Blood', p. 347.

30. R.J. Lazar, 'Toward a Theory of Intermarriage', *International Journal of Sociology of the Family* 1 (1971), pp. 1-9.

31. See Bok-Lim C. Kim, 'Casework with Japanese and Korean Wives of Americans', *Social Casework* (May 1972), pp. 273-79.

to marry local women, until the immigrant group can establish itself as a viable community.[32] Once the pressure of being a disadvantaged group eases, endogamous marriage becomes more common. This is also supported by D.D. Smits's historical/sociological studies of Puritan horror of early colonial intermarriage with Indians. Smits concluded his survey of the available data by indicating that 'The most formidable barriers to Anglo–Indian marriage were intrinsic to seventeenth-century New England culture and demonstrate its ethnocentrism, exclusiveness, insecurity, and materialism'.[33] This approach to mixed marriage analysis also raises interesting questions for understanding the biblical community—such as the possible breakdown of communal boundaries and socialization (until Ezra and/or Nehemiah attempted to reinforce them) which would otherwise have discouraged these relationships more effectively. Again, the patterns suggest a traumatized community, whose 'socialization' is low.

The Mixed Marriage Crisis in the Post-Exilic Community

Requisite to understanding the mixed marriages issue in the Persian period is clarification of the differences between the accounts given in Ezra 9–10 and in Nehemiah 13. In general, we are dealing with a similar phenomenon, but the details suggest important differences of emphasis. To begin, however, we need to ask if there is a general biblical attitude toward 'mixed marriage'. Interestingly enough, there does appear to be a 'romantic streak' running through ancient Hebrew narrative on this issue, an attitude that certainly appears to change in the post-exilic context, at least for more conservative leaders like Ezra and Nehemiah.

On Romance in the Bible

As we have observed earlier, sociologists take certain values seriously as factors that may mitigate the separation of social groups, such as romantic values or democratic idealism. Indeed, Merton already pointed out that romantic or democratic notions may lead to violations

32. C.E. Glick, 'Intermarriage and Admixture in Hawaii', *Social Biology* 17/4 (1970), pp. 278-91.

33. D.D. Smits, '"We are not to Grow Wild": Seventeenth-Century New England's Repudiation of Anglo–Indian Intermarriage', *American Indian Culture and Research Journal* 11/4 (1987), pp. 1-31.

of group solidarity,[34] and Glick noted that 'romantic' attachments increased among minorities of generations following the immigrant generation.[35] Certain societies will also tolerate mixed marriages as a democratic value, or as an expression of equality. It is clear that normative social sanctions against mixed marriages sometimes conflict with equally strong values of romantic idealism ('true love conquers all'), and the latter can occasionally overcome the group boundaries for some, if not all, of the persons involved (obviously the couple itself, and perhaps the immediate family, etc.).

It is therefore important to point out that a romantic basis of marriage (or a romanticized setting for a relationship) is recognized in the Bible as a cause for mixed marriages. Notable examples are Moses and Zipporah (Exod. 2.21), Joseph and Asenath (Gen. 41.45) and Samson's marriage to a Philistine woman (Judg. 14). Proverbs' famous warnings against the 'foreign woman' (even though clearly an analogy) includes the assumption that the foreign woman will exert an exotic romantic attraction. Clearly not *all* of these 'mixed marriages' are condemned but 'love' is almost *always* mentioned or implied (again, by a romanticized setting, e.g., Moses and Zipporah at the well, etc.) in cases of mixed marriage.

The same list of nationalities represented among the foreign women in Ezra 9 and 10 is also found in 1 Kgs 11.1-2, where Solomon's wives are mentioned, among whom were Ammonite, Moabite, Edomite, Sidonian and Hittite.[36] Here, interestingly, we have one of the few references to romantic love in the entire Bible (note also Isaac's love for Rebekah, Gen. 24.67; Jacob's love for Rachel, Gen. 29.18, 20, 30; Amnon's love for Tamar in 1 Sam. 13.1, 4) outside of Song of Solomon. The vast majority of cases deal with pious or religious 'love' between God and the people. Furthermore, the only example of the phrase 'I love you' between a man and woman is Judg. 16.4, 15, which is *also* dealing with a 'mixed marriage' between Samson and Delilah.[37]

34. Merton, 'Intermarriage', pp. 366-67.

35. P.C. Glick, 'Intermarriage among Ethnic Groups in the United States', *Social Biology* 17 (1970), pp. 292-98.

36. There is a good discussion of this in Blenkinsopp, *Ezra–Nehemiah*, pp. 174-79.

37. Although Delilah is never explicitly identified as Philistine, when one notes the parental concern over Samson's love for a Philistine woman in ch. 14, this

Finally, the increasing interest in Proverbs 1–9 (but especially ch. 5) shows how love/romance can lead to assignations with the 'alien' woman, the results of which may be that 'your labors will go to the house of an alien'. It appears to be the case, then, that romantic love is dealt with in the Hebrew Bible with a certain circumspection, because it can lead to unwise marital ties with 'foreigners'. Blenkinsopp has suggested that the warnings about Solomon's wives now found in the Deuteronomistic Historian may come from the post-exilic era.[38]

The typical examples of romantic attachments in the Hebrew Bible are dealt with in individual stories, but we are dealing with a group in Ezra 9–10 (in Nehemiah 13 the situation is a bit more specific). Perhaps we can conclude from this *group* interest in Ezra that the editors are intentionally focusing attention away from the individual level of possible romantic relationships, but with an emphasis instead on the disobedience of 'the people'. This group focus in Ezra, especially when read in the context of the explicit mention of Solomon's wives in Nehemiah, suggests an unwillingness of post-exilic editors to accept 'romance' as an acceptable excuse for mixed marriages. The later texts, such as Proverbs, show an increasing suspicion toward mixed marriage in a romantic/erotic setting.

The Ezra Account

In Ezra, reflecting an interest in priestly terminology and concerns, the sins of the priests and Levites are prominent among the guilty (9.1, and note that the priests and Levites are listed first among the guilty). The foreign peoples are blamed for abominations, תּוֹעֵבוֹת, a term from תָּעַב. Note the frequent cultic context of this term. Ezekiel uses it to describe the sins of the people, particularly their ritual/religious sins in Ezek. 5.9, 11; 7.3, 8; 16.22; describing idols in 16.36 and 14.6. In Proverbs, the term is used in reference to things that God 'hates' (Prov. 3.32; 15.8, 9; 6.16) but this includes justice issues, such as a false balance or financial cheating (Prov. 11.1, 20 and 20.23). In ritual law, Lev. 18.24-30 associates foreign practices (of the 'nations I am casting out before you') with 'abominations'. The term seems predominantly *late*, with some 33% of all instances found in Ezekiel alone.

appears to be a logical conclusion. See E. Lipiński, 'Love in the Bible', *EncJud*, XI, cols. 523-27.

38. Blenkinsopp, *Ezra–Nehemiah*, p. 175.

Ezra's orientation reflects the Priestly writer's obsessions with 'separations' (note the use of the term *bdl* 'to separate'[39]) between the pure and impure. Such concern with separation and identity maintenance in much of the Priestly legislation is consistent with a group under stress. Yet, this sociological picture in the Ezra account of the breakup of mixed marriages is not at all compatible with a tendency among modern scholars to see the exiles as a privileged elite.[40] I would want to argue that Ezra's action was an attempt at inward consolidation of a threatened minority:

> Die realitäten in der nachexilischen Gemeinde bestätigen offenbar nicht den im heirokratischen Lager genährten 'offiziellen' Gemeindeglauben an das schon vorhandene Heil, dessen Schutzherren die Perserkönige sein sollen... Die disillusionaierten Heimkehrer suchten mit alle Mitteln, nicht zuletzt durch Einheirat in vermögende Familien, deren Adstammung und Zugehörigkeit zur Jahwegemeinde umstritten war, ihren Sozialstatus aufzubessern.[41]

> Den Landbesitz der Golah-Mitglieder hatten sich die Nichtexilierten und die Kanaanäer geteilt, die von Babylon mitgebrachten Geldmittel der Heimkehrer wurden von Tag zu Tag weinger; es gab kaum Handel, dafür aber schlechte Ernten, zerstörende Dürre und Trockenheit. Kein wunder, dass die Euphorie, welche die Heimkehrerbewegung eingeleitet hatte, zesehends einfror und jeder zunächst auf das eigene Sichdurchschlagen bedacht war. Die mit dem Tempelbau erwartete Parusie was ausgeblieben, Resignation und Apathie drohten die Junge Gemeinde in 'Fromme' und 'Abtrünnige' zu spalten.[42]

The Ezra texts reveal a profound consciousness of 'us' and 'them', and describe a group intent on its internal affairs and survival. Terms such as 'the holy seed' clearly indicate a *group* xenophobia. Why would there be such an emphasis in the Ezra material? One answer may well be, in agreement with In Der Smitten's work, that the Ezra material represents another perspective from the Nehemiah material, since Ezra is largely a fictional 'midrash' on the Letter of Artaxerxes, the goal of which was to 'override' the Nehemiah material from a

39. Smith, *Religion of the Landless*, pp. 145-49.

40. N. Gottwald, *The Hebrew Bible: A Socio-Literary Introduction* (Minneapolis: Fortress Press, 1985), p. 433.

41. T.W. In Der Smitten, *Esra: Quellen, Überlieferung und Geschichte* (Assen: Van Gorcum, 1973), p. 138.

42. In Der Smitten, *Esra*, pp. 143-44.

priestly perspective.[43] But if Ezra is from a 'priestly' perspective, this raises troubling questions after considering the modern sociological material. Why are the priests involved in this mixed marriage problem in the first place? We can establish quite clearly that it is the priestly writer of the exilic/post-exilic period that is *most* passionately concerned with the maintenance of boundaries of separation. Ezekiel's concerns with purity are an excellent example of this, as are the concerns of Haggai and Zechariah. Are we to believe, then, that the mixed marriage 'crisis' of Ezra, where the priests are so heavily implicated, represents a mass dereliction of duty on the part of exilic priests who abandon one of their central defining concepts? Or do the priests involved simply *disagree* with Ezra as to what constitutes a marriage that is actually 'mixed'? There are good grounds for seeing the presence of a disagreement *between Jews*, as noted by Blenkinsopp as well. Essentially, the *only* basis for Ezra's objection is that the foreigners were simply Jews who were not in exile. This is supported by two categories of evidence: first, the presence of texts that clearly argue for a more lenient attitude toward some of the people of foreign origin who affiliate with Israelites; (cf. Isa. 60.1-5; Jonah; Ruth, etc.) second, the fact that the groups with which these 'mixed' marriages are taking place are identified with old terms that almost surely have become stereotypically pejorative slurs referring to those ethnic groups who have long since either disappeared or assimilated, having been condemned historically as those unclean peoples 'justifiably' destroyed by Joshua in the legendary patriotic tales of the founding of the Davidic House.

Pejorative slurs and the presence of counterarguments thus suggest a debate within the community about the identity of the community itself in relation to others in the land. In short, I would argue that 'boundary maintenance' theories about mixed marriage lead us to question whether the Ezra documents are really talking about 'foreigners' at all. Could it be that the Ezra documents, rather, represent a later time in Jewish post-exilic life, when we are dealing with a rise of 'denominations', 'sects' within the life of the community who are vying for the title of 'true Jew'?[44]

Finally, we return to the issue of Ezra's authority to dissolve these

43. In Der Smitten, *Esra*, p. 88.

44. See T.C. Eskenazi and E.P. Judd, 'Marriage to a Stranger in Ezra 9–10', in this volume, pp. 266-85.

marriages. As many commentators have noted, Artaxerxes' letter did *not* give Ezra the explicit power to dissolve marriages. Blenkinsopp, for example, wondered if Ezra exceeded his authority:

> Since exogamous marriage involved community leaders lay and clerical, both they and the equally distinguished families of the women threatened with divorce must have been offended... the likelihood of stirring up a hornet's nest would not have been welcomed by the Persian authorities who sent Ezra out precisely as an instrument of the pax Persica at a difficult moment and to a sensitive part of the empire. This may explain why the story breaks off suddenly rather than, as we might have expected, on an upbeat note. We do not know the outcome, but it would be a reasonable guess that Ezra was recalled after a stay of no more than a year...[45]

My suggestions would lend further support to Blenkinsopp's supposition, if Ezra was a historical figure as Blenkinsopp believes. However, if the Ezra material is a midrash on the Artaxerxes' letter as In Der Smitten suggests, we are dealing with largely political and religious propaganda about an internal struggle.

The Nehemiah Texts

An internal struggle, however, is not the issue with the Nehemiah material, where 'the chief danger was perceived to come from outside Judah...'[46] Political considerations seem predominant in Nehemiah, giving the impression of treacherous power-grabbing in both temple and government through strategic marriages. With Nehemiah, we are dealing with specific cases again, which is, as we noted, the more typical biblical form for describing mixed marriage.

Tobiah ('the Ammonite') and Sanballat ('the Horonite'), for example, were leaders of the opposition to Nehemiah's work of rebuilding Jerusalem. It appears that they have local authority, although the precise nature of their authority is not clear. Williamson suggests that 'the context clearly presupposes that they were the leaders of those already in the land and not part of the group who returned with Ezra. Thus the suggestion that they were district governors...is attractive'.[47]

Only Nehemiah names the officials Tobiah and Sanballat. But are they foreigners? The actual descent of Tobiah and Sanballat is in

45. Blenkinsopp, *Ezra-Nehemiah*, p. 179.
46. Blenkinsopp, 'Social Context', p. 460.
47. Williamson, *Ezra, Nehemiah*, p. 130.

question. On onomastic grounds, it is typically supposed that at least Tobiah must be a Yahweh-worshipper.[48] But Williamson has objected, stating that 'Ammonite' should be taken as an ethnic categorization. He believes that Sanballat is governor of Samaria, and Tobiah is a lesser official under him, although he rejects the idea that he is governor of Ammon. Sanballat himself is probably of Moabite origin (linking him with the Horonaim).[49] It is interesting to note, in this context, the explicit association of Jewish 'nobles' (*hōrîm*) who 'spoke well of Tobiah' to Nehemiah *because of marital ties* (Neh. 6.17-19). When, in Nehemiah 13, we meet Tobiah again, it is in the context of Nehemiah ejecting him from temple accommodation (13.4-9), where we also find a breakup of foreign marriages (13.23-27) and another statement about intermarriage between the family of Sanballat and Eliashib the High Priest (v. 28). The example that Nehemiah chooses to illustrate the problems of foreign marriage is an example of political leadership: Solomon. From Nehemiah, much more clearly than from Ezra, we gain the strong impression that the problem of foreign marriages is centrally a political problem, involving the Jewish aristocracy and local governmental leadership. In his recent commentary, Blenkinsopp also considered the political and economic advantages of such marriages: 'As sparse as our information is, it reveals a network of relationships cemented by *marriages de convenance* between the Sanballats, Tobiads, and important elements of the lay and clerical aristocracy in Jerusalem'.[50]

What we are clearly dealing with in Nehemiah is the attempt to intermarry the leadership of the temple with the local political leadership, while in Ezra, we have no such suggestion. Indeed, the example of Solomon is only cited in Nehemiah, which suggests an even more explicitly political concern in the Nehemiah texts. The politics of associating with the descendants of Ammon and Moab is also much more a reference to local leadership than is the case with Ezra, where the ethnic categories are more pejorative than informative.

This has led some commentators to speculate on the socio-political goals that may have been sought through these 'alliances'. Rudolph, for example, suggested that community leaders, while aware of the

48. See P.R. Ackroyd's comments in 'Tobiah', *Harper's Bible Dictionary* (New York: Harper & Row, 1985), p. 1080.

49. Williamson, *Ezra, Nehemiah*, pp. 182-83.

50. Blenkinsopp, *Ezra–Nehemiah*.

negative implications of foreign wives, 'had no desire to sacrifice good relations with neighbors, or financial ties, for the sake of a principle'.[51]

As noted above, recent investigations have tended to move in the direction of inheritance laws, and the worry that the land belonging to the returned community should not pass into 'foreign' control by inheritance.

> We should...bear in mind the important social and economic factors involved. Since according to Priestly law (Num. 27.1-11) daughters could in certain circumstances inherit, exogamous marriage could lead to alienation of family property, a concern also reflected in the stories in Genesis 12–50 about the ancestors. The situation obtaining at the time of Nehemiah, when the priesthood was involved in intermarriage with non-Judean families (Neh. 13.4, 28) reminds us also that control of the temple, an obviously crucial issue, could have played a part in discouraging such marriages in the ranks of the clerical and lay aristocracy.[52]

The assumption here, however, is that the exile community is an 'advantaged' group, since they are supported by the Persians. On the other hand, Williamson presents the possibility of a reverse scenario, with economic/social advantages being on the side of the surrounding community who did not go into exile:

> [the danger of assimilation]...was heightened by the economic power wielded by some of those who are here labelled 'the peoples of the land'. During the exile foreign landlords had apparently assumed control of a good deal of the territory of Judea, and the difficult economic circumstances that the returned exiles faced could soon have placed them at the mercy of these powerful neighbours.[53]

In the Nehemiah case—which we have seen is arguably the case actually dealing with 'foreign marriage'—the exchange theory raises the issue of what advantages would have been gained by the post-exilic community 'marrying up' among those defined as 'outsiders'. The guilty are males who are presumably attempting to 'marry up' to exchange their low status of 'exiles' for participation in aristocratic society. This suggests that members of the exilic community perceived themselves in a disadvantaged position vis-à-vis the 'peoples of the land'.

51. Rudolph, *Esra und Nehemiah*, p. 160.
52. Blenkinsopp, *Ezra–Nehemiah*, pp. 176-77.
53. Williamson, *Ezra, Nehemiah*, p. 160.

Once again, sociological inferences lead one to conclude that the mixed marriages are built on the presupposition that the exile community was the relatively *disadvantaged* one of the two (or more) groups involved in the marriages. Their marriages were an attempt to marry 'up' in status, or perhaps regain lost status. Our model, constructed from contemporary sociological models of hypergamy/hypogamy, tends to support this assumption.

An examination of the Ezra and Nehemiah cases in relation to modern sociological studies of mixed marriage has strongly suggested that the post-exilic community shows signs of disintegration and trauma, which was responded to by the attempts to 'shore up' boundaries, and remove economic or political temptations by pointing to their dire consequences in Israel's past. The Nehemiah texts, however, raise a further possibility because of their specific attention to political, and foreign, leadership.

Were the Persian Officials Directly Involved in Mixed Marriages?

Does the fact that the leaders and priests are specifically singled out among the guilty indicate involvement by a 'higher authority'? Weinberg has argued convincingly that the priesthood emerged at this time as both the spiritual and political leadership of the 'Temple Community',[54] and the Achaemenid rulers themselves are known to have encouraged intermarriage *among the leadership* of the Persian empire—particularly seeking to relate the satrapial governors to the royal family. As G. Walser has argued, 'Für den Grosskönig war die Verschwägerung mit den Satrapen ein Element der politischen Sicherheit und entsprechend die Beleihung von nahen Verwendten aus der königlichen Familie mit grossen Satrapien das Mittel der Machterhaltung'.[55] Walser refers particularly to the experience of Pausanias, king of Lacedaemon, who attempted to marry into the Achaemenid aristocracy to seek a position under Persian rule.[56] But

54. See my English translation of Weinberg's work, *The Citizen-Temple Community* (JSOTSup, 151; Sheffield: JSOT Press, 1992). For the original German version, consult J. Weinberg, 'Zentral- und Partikular- gewalt im achaemenideischen Reich', *Klio* 59 (1977), pp. 25-43, and 'Die Agrarverhältnisse' (reference in n. 4).

55. G. Walser, 'Heiraten zwischen Griechen und Achämeniden-Prinzessinnen', in *Kunst, Kultur und Geschichte: Der Achämenidenzeit und Ihr Fortleben* (Berlin: Dietrich Reimer, 1983), pp. 87-90.

56. Herodotus, *The History* 5.32 (trans. D. Greene; Chicago: University of Chicago Press, 1987), p. 368.

perhaps the best example of this policy of intermarriage, and certainly the most dramatic recorded, comes from an episode in the career of Alexander soon after his conquest of Persia. In 324 BCE, immediately following the Northern India campaign, Alexander stopped at Susa, where he arranged for a massive wedding ceremony uniting himself, and many of his Macedonian officers, to Persian wives. This event is mentioned in most of the classical sources on Alexander, excerpts of which serve to clarify the nature of the event.

Diodorus of Sicily, for example, writes that, after Alexander gave Caranus a magnificent funeral, he 'then proceeded to Susa, where he married Stateira, the elder daughter of Darius, and gave her younger sister Drypetis as wife to Hephaestion. He prevailed upon the most prominent of his friends to take wives, also, and gave them in marriage the noblest Persian ladies...'[57]

Athenaeus recounts the detailed description of the ceremony itself by Chares, including the number of bridal chambers, the furniture, and money involved in the five day ceremony/festivity.[58] The descriptions of Arrian are perhaps the most helpful, when he points out that

> These weddings were solemnized in the Persian fashion; chairs were placed for the bridegrooms in order; then after the health-drinkings the brides came in, and each sat down by the side of her bridegroom; they took them by the hand and kissed them, the King setting the example; for all the weddings took place together. In this, if ever, Alexander was thought to have shown a spirit of condescension and comradeship...[59]

The suggested significance of this event for our study is the fact that the classical sources emphasize that Alexander's action *was part of his growing fascination with, and adoption of, Persian imperial policies and formalities*. Arrian, for example, continued his narrative by describing the growing alarm among Alexander's Macedonian soldiers as Alexander continued to indulge his growing fondness for Persian custom:

57. *Diodorus of Sicily* 17.107.5-6 (trans. C.B. Welles; LCL; London: Heinemann, 1963).

58. Athenaeus, *The Deipnosophists* 12.538 (trans. C.B. Gulick; London: Heinemann, 1933). Note that the Persian rulers' festivities went on for days, as in Est. 1.4.

59. Arrian, *Anabasis of Alexander* 7.4.2-7 (trans. E.I. Robson; London: Heinemann, 1912–13).

> In fact they had long been pained to see Alexander wearing the Median robes, and his Persian marriage ceremonies had not given satisfaction to most of them; indeed, not even to some of the bridegrooms... [A]ll this caused indignation to the Macedonians, as giving an idea that Alexander's heart was growing entirely Orientalized, and that he paid little consideration to Macedonian customs and Macedonians themselves.[60]

Alexander's intermarriage of officials was seen as part of his mimicry of Persian policies. This is clear from the fact that, prior to this, intermarriage of Macedonians with foreign women was considered unacceptable. In his study of Alexander, for example, A.B. Bosworth noted that

> apart from Seleucus' wife, Apame, none of the Persian ladies is recorded playing any role in the age of the Successors. Taking wives from the vanquished, even the nobility of the vanquished, was a degradation, and there was hostility to Alexander's Asian consorts.[61]

Walser, too, noted the late, urban, and literary aversion to foreign women in Greek thought: 'Für die Polisgriechen und ihre Theoretiker Platon und Aristoteles sind nichtgriechische Frauen ein Greuel und die Verbindung mit ihnen ein nationales Sakrileg'.[62] Clearly, we are not dealing with a Greek innovation, and all the Greek officers except Seleucus divorced their wives at the death of Alexander.[63]

In addition to Walser's references in classical sources, there is also biblical reference to Persian intermarriage particularly in Esther. Although Esther's ethnic identity is at first hidden, the search for new wives for the king was conducted 'throughout the provinces', suggesting openness to intermarriage (Est. 2.1-3). Est. 1.20 also indicates that

60. Arrian, 7.2.8-12.

61. A.B. Bosworth, *Conquest and Empire: The Reign of Alexander the Great* (Cambridge: Cambridge University Press, 1988), pp. 157-58.

62. Walser, 'Heiraten', p. 88.

63. R.D. Milns, *Alexander the Great* (London: Robert Hale, 1968), p. 240; V. Tcherikover, *Hellenistic Civilization and the Jews* (New York: Atheneum, 1959), p. 8. W.W. Tarn would argue, however, that the mixed marriages at Susa were indicative of Alexander's own vision of world unity. Although his arguments are compelling, he did not consider the possibility of Persian influence in the context of the Susa marriages. See his chapter 'Brotherhood and Unity', in *Alexander the Great.* II. *Sources and Studies* (Cambridge: Cambridge University Press, 1979 [1948]), pp. 399-449. This notion has been disputed for some time. Wilcken denies that Alexander had any such cosmopolitan visions (See U.P. Wilcken, *Alexander the Great* [trans. G.C. Richards, London: Chatto & Windus, 1932], p. 208).

the marriage ceremony between Esther and the Persian ruler was a 'communal event' which reminds one of the opulent descriptions of Alexander's Susa weddings. But whereas the wedding in Esther is not a wedding of multiple couples (at least it is not mentioned), one does have the sense that this description contains the notion of following the king's example in the festivities. Thus Esther's wedding, however fictional the story itself may be, is a description that sounds authentically Persian when compared with classical sources.

Did the Jewish leaders mentioned in Nehemiah intermarry with the encouragement of the Persian imperial leadership? We are probably not to assume that the intermarriage was general, that is, among a large number of the population, but precisely among the leaders. We have seen that the book of Nehemiah stresses precisely this. Batten, for example, considered the number involved to be 'insignificant'[64] compared to the population as a whole—perhaps no more than 103 persons. Furthermore, it is significant that the opposition to Nehemiah's construction program came from the local officials, among whom were undoubtedly officials now 'related' to members of the post-exilic community.

One does not have to imagine some officially sanctioned mass wedding of local Jewish officials in order to suppose that the Persian authorities would have approved of the intermarriage of local leadership. If there was such encouragement, then the breakup of foreign marriages must be understood not only as an indication of the social status of the community, but also as an act of political defiance. Such a political implication should be added to the framework of the discussion. The suggestions made herein about the possible encouragement of the Persian political leadership are not meant to finally solve the controversy about the meaning of the foreign marriages, but simply to introduce a possible further complication in the circumstances.

Conclusions

In my own attempt to better understand the post-exilic Judaean society, this study has raised even more questions about the nature of the Ezra material. Sociological comparisons make me highly suspicious of the actual lines of the debate in Ezra. If, as has been suggested at least since Torrey, Ezra is a fictionalized response to the Nehemiah texts,

64. Batten, *Ezra, Nehemiah*, p. 351.

then this would explain some of the difficulties with understanding Ezra's accounts, and especially the polemics against the priests. If the Ezra material is an intra-communal partisan document drafted with Nehemiah as the foil, then historical interests should focus on the Nehemiah texts. But *sociological* analysis of both Nehemiah and Ezra continues to raise questions about the supposed high status of the post-exilic community vis-à-vis the surrounding communities and its self-consciousness as a group with social boundaries throughout the Persian period. Neither the Ezra nor the Nehemiah texts make sociological sense if the community was a greatly privileged one, especially when the mixed marriage crisis is viewed with an eye toward contemporary cross-cultural mixed marriage behaviour.

MARRIAGE TO A STRANGER IN EZRA 9–10*

Tamara C. Eskenazi and Eleanore P. Judd

> When they [women] marry they do not become members of their husband's lineage—only their children do. Thus women could be termed a 'foreign element' in their husbands' families—an element recruited in order to perpetuate the lineage, but simultaneously potentially dangerous to it in the event of the husband's death.[1]

As Katarzyna Grosz observes, there is an important sense in which all marriages are marriages with foreigners. This essay, however, focuses on marriage with so-called foreign women in Ezra 9–10. As a collaboration between a sociologist (Judd) and a biblical scholar (Eskenazi), the paper uses sociological perspectives as tools for identifying Ezra–Nehemiah's own definition of the term stranger or foreigner. In particular, the paper seeks to explore more fully the nature of the conflict in Judah between those who returned from exile (the *gōlâ*) and the people(s) of the land(s).

The Problem

The basic story of Ezra 9–10 is all too familiar. Taken at face value, it relates a simple yet disheartening story:[2] Ezra, who arrives in Judah

* A version of this paper was originally presented at the Annual Meeting of the Society of Biblical Literature, Kansas City, 1991. The authors thank Bridget Wynne and Rachel Benjamin (HUC) for their comments on a draft of this paper.

1. K. Grosz, 'Some Aspects of the Position of Women in Nuzi', in B. Lesko (ed.), *Women's Earliest Records from Ancient Egypt and Western Asia: Proceedings of the Conference on Women in the Ancient Near East, Brown University, Providence, Rhode Island November 5–7, 1987* (BJS, 166; Atlanta: Scholars Press, 1989), pp. 167-80 (178).

2. Readers, modern or ancient, may not necessarily concur as to what is disheartening here: the marriages or the objections to them? For a discussion of diverse responses, see D. Smith-Christopher, 'The Mixed Marriage Crisis in Ezra 9–10 and

in 458 BCE, learns that leaders of the community had married women from 'the peoples of the lands' (Ezra 9.1). He and his informants interpret these marriages as religiously pernicious and influence the community to expel the women.

Behind this simple and familiar tale of woe lie several uncertainties. Despite the confidence of many interpreters, we finally do not really know some of the basic facts about the charge against mixed marriages. We do not know how many members of the community actually married so-called foreign women; we do not know what proportion of the population they constituted; we do not know why men married such women; and we do not know whether women also married so-called foreign men.[3] Our most decisive ignorance grows from ambiguities in the first and last verses of this episode. As a result, we do not know the ethnic or religious background of the women and we do not know what happened to the marriages. Consequently, it is not self-evident who counts as a foreigner and therefore, conversely, also who counts as a member of Israel.

The two key phrases at the beginning and the end of this episode (Ezra 9–10) are strikingly ambiguous—a phenomenon that is itself suggestive of a larger story, possibly deliberately obfuscated. Introducing the problem is the crucial (yet ambiguous) phrase in Ezra 9.1 in which certain officials report the following to Ezra:

Nehemiah 13: A Study of the Post-Exilic Judaean Community', in this volume.

3. Did women also marry foreigners? Theoretically there are at least three possible answers:

A. Such marriages were only prohibited for men; hence, although some women also married spouses perceived as foreigners, they did not violate community law.

B. Only men actually married outsiders, in which case we must wonder why. Were women less able or less motivated to enter such marriages?

C. Although both men and women intermarried and thereby violated a law, the magnitude of the threat to the community was deemed less severe in the case of women.

Given the paucity of information, no certainty can be achieved. Nevertheless it seems most probable that the prohibition applied equally to men and women. Sex-ratio imbalance and greater control over women's marriage choices may explain the absence of reports about such violations by Judahite women (but see Neh. 6.18, which refers to the marriage of Tobiah's son to a Judahite woman of a prominent lineage).

לא נבדלו העם ישראל והכהנים והלוים מעמי הארצות כתועבתיהם לכנעני החתי
הפרזי היבוסי העמני המאבי המצרי והאמרי

Many translations render this verse essentially like the NRSV, saying 'The people of Israel, the priests, and the Levites have not separated themselves from the peoples of the lands with their abominations, from the Canaanites, the Hittites, the Perizzites, the Jebusites, the Ammonites, the Moabites, the Egyptians, and the Amorites'. The Hebrew in Ezra 9.1, however, is more complicated. The JPS Tanakh renders it more accurately: 'The people of Israel and the priests and the Levites have not separated themselves from the peoples of the land whose abhorrent practices are like those of the Canaanites, the Hittites, the Perizzites, the Jebusites, the Ammonites, the Moabites, the Egyptians, and the Amorites'. The interpretative difference comes from recognizing that the כ in כתועבתיהם לכנעני indicates a simile which leaves the actual ethnic background of the women unspecified; they are not necessarily Canaanites, Hittites and the rest, but rather like them.[4]

Since Ezra 9.1, surprisingly, does not divulge the precise ethnic identity of the women, and hence the kind of 'stranger' that they were, one can postulate several possible referents for these 'peoples of the lands'.[5] Given what we *do* know about the demographic composition of Judah in the Persian period, the women could have come from any of the following groups:[6]

4. See also H.G.M. Williamson, '[they] have not kept themselves separate from the peoples of the lands, but have acted according to the abominations of the Canaanites, the Hittites' (*Ezra, Nehemiah* [WBC, 16; Waco, TX: Word, 1985], p. 125). It is true that women from some of these nations appear in Neh. 13.23-24 as wives of Judahites. But it is methodologically unsound to suppose (automatically) that Ezra and Nehemiah face an identical situation, especially given the fact that they take differing measures to combat the 'problem'. Each case needs to be examined in its own context prior to comparing their function in the final form of the book. The literary and historical issues need to be kept distinct. Our concern here is with plausible historical reality.

5. On the terminology for groups in Israel in the post-exilic era, see H.C.M. Vogt, *Studie zur nachexilischen Gemeinde in Esra–Nehemia* (Werl: Dietrich & Coelde, 1966) and J.P. Weinberg, 'The Am Ha-Aretz of the 6–4 Century BCE', in *The Citizen–Temple Community* (JSOTSup, 151; Sheffield: JSOT Press, 1992), pp. 62-74. The original German version appears in *Klio* 57 [1974]). See also E. Wurthwein, *Der 'Am ha'arez im Alten Testament* (BWANT 4/17; Stuttgart: Kohlhammer, 1936).

6. We can say with certainty that all three groups were present in the province of Judah during the time of Ezra. We have no information, however, as to the numbers

1. The women could have been Judahites or Israelites who had not been in exile or who differed along particular ethnic and socio-economic lines from the returnees (e.g. Jer. 52.16). The controversy would concern Jewishness defined as a peoplehood based on ancestry or on the experience of exile (masking, perhaps, a conflict over land rights), rather than on specific religious beliefs and practices. This distinction is suggested by Ezra 4.1-4, where the so-called 'adversaries of Judah and Benjamin' (Ezra 4.1), who offer to participate in building the house of God, describe themselves as worshippers of Israel's God ever since they had been brought to the land by King Esarhaddon. Although Ezra 4.3 does not specify why the offer was rejected, the ethnic origin of this group seems to be an issue. The rejection leads to hostility. As Ezra 4.4 reports, 'Thereupon the people of the land undermined the resolve of the people of Judah and made them afraid to build'.[7]
2. The women could have been members of foreign nations. They could have been Ammonites, Moabites and the like (as in Neh. 13), that is, from nations that had been long time neighbors,[8] or they could also have come from more distant

and proportion of these populations or their patterns of settlements. What is crucial for this examination is that we do not have a clear notion of the terminology used by each group for itself or by others for each group. The very ambiguity about terminology that frustrates scholars may mirror an historical uncertainty about identity and boundaries in the transitions during the post-exilic era. See, e.g., D.L. Smith, *The Religion of the Landless: The Social Context of the Babylonian Exile* (Bloomington, IN: Meyer–Stone, 1989).

7. Note the singular form of 'people of the land'. Does it intend the same 'peoples of the lands' in Ezra 9–10? Several commentators assume that it does (see, e.g., Williamson, *Ezra, Nehemiah*, p. 130, and J. Blenkinsopp, *Ezra–Nehemiah: A Commentary* [OTL; Philadelphia: Westminster Press, 1988], pp. 174-75). Others (e.g. Weinberg) argue for different groups. The safest conclusion seems to be that the double plural of 'peoples of the lands' in Ezra 9.1 includes but may not be limited to these 'people of the land'.

8. One of the best analyses of this situation is Williamson's *Ezra, Nehemiah*. Williamson notes that members of the religious community, presumably those who had previously returned from exile, had both married and adopted some of the religious practices of the rest of the Palestinian population (p. 130). Commenting on Ezra 3.3 (but cross-referencing the passage to Ezra 9.1), Williamson states that this population comprised (generally speaking) 'those who were not part of the returned

lands (Phoenicia, Persia, Greece and/or Egypt), some perhaps brought along from Babylonia by exiles.[9] The presence of such diverse groups in the region is evident in biblical texts and all other sources.[10]

3. The women could have come from Judahite and Israelite families in the land who developed (or persisted in) religious practices and beliefs different from those of the *gōlâ* community. The conflict would thus revolve around Judaism as religion rather than peoplehood. The origin of the women would be less significant than their actual religious practices.

It should be noted that these three patterns of tension find their parallels in modern Israel and contribute to social and political friction there—a topic to which we shall return.

Not only is the first verse vague about the origin of the women, but the concluding verse is unclear about their fate. The MT simply states,

כל אלה נשאו נשים נכריות ויש מהם נשים וישימו בנים

community, both within the province of Judah and their near neighbors (cf. Vogt, *Studie*, pp. 152-54). The possibility of true Jews being among them is simply not envisaged in these books' (*Ezra, Nehemiah*, p. 46). He also notes that Ezra himself, who carefully avoids identifying the people of the land as Canaanites (p. 130), interprets the violation as religious, not racial. In the end, Ezra 'urges them [the community] to confess and to conform to God's will by redrawing the community's lines of demarcation' (p. 155).

9. But note R. Carroll, who suggests that 'the anti-Canaanite ideology which informs the attack on the foreign wives confines the polemic to people from neighboring territories around Jerusalem and does not apply to foreign wives from further afield. At least, the books of Ezra and Nehemiah are silent about such wives... [H]aving a Babylonian or Persian wife was no obstacle to success in the Second Temple Period!' ('Textual Strategies and Ideology', in P.R. Davies [ed.], *Second Temple Studies*. I. *Persian Period* [JSOTSup, 117; JSOT Press, 1991], p. 124).

10. See Neh. 13.16 for the presence of Tyrian traders in Jerusalem and Herodotus for the international blend of populations in the region during the fifth century BCE. Archaeological excavations such as those at Dor and Ashkelon attest to the presence of highly cosmopolitan cities along the coast of the Mediterranean, a short distance from Jerusalem and surely within the range of Judah's provincial towns. For a recent summary of some such finds, see E. Stern, 'The Dor Province in the Persian Period in Light of the Recent Excavations in Tel Dor', *Transeuphratène* 2 (1990), pp. 147-55.

The JPS translates the concluding verse as follows: 'All these had married foreign wives, among whom were some women who had borne children' (Ezra 10.44), noting in a footnote that the Hebrew of the last four words is 'uncertain' (p. 1507). Many modern translations (e.g. NRSV) and commentators (e.g. Blenkinsopp) follow the reading in LXX and 1 Esdras, which eliminate the ambiguity by stating, 'All these had married foreign women, and they put them away with their children' (1 Esdr. 9.36). The MT, however, remains silent about the outcome of the inquiry. Blenkinsopp suggests that the silence hides a specific problem:

> The narrator wishes to leave us with the impression that the matter was settled amicably, almost unanimously, but the real situation was probably rather different. Since exogamous marriage involved community leaders lay and clerical, both they and the equally distinguished families of the women threatened with divorce must have been offended. Moreover such action, which was not required by any law known to us, exceeded Ezra's mandate. The likelihood of stirring up a hornet's nest would not have been welcomed by the Persian authorities who sent Ezra out precisely as an instrument of the pax Persica at a difficult moment and to a sensitive part of the empire. This may explain why the story breaks off suddenly rather than, as we might have expected, on an upbeat note. We do not know the outcome, but it would be a reasonable guess that Ezra was recalled after a stay of no more than a year.[11]

Williamson responds differently to this abrupt conclusion. He comments on Ezra 10.44 as follows:

> The text of this verse is so uncertain... that it would be unwise to build much on it... [T]here is no need to emend this verse into a statement that the wives were dismissed (as 1 Esdr. 9.36 does), and the MT may stand as an indication that the narrator was not insensitive to the personal tragedies he was recording.[12]

Although Ezra 9–10 interprets the danger of these marriages in religious terms (and also in what some have called racial terms), modern scholars have noted socio-economic factors at play, especially a concern over land belonging to the Jewish province. Weinberg's analysis of the Bürger-Tempel-Gemeinde in particular, and studies by J. Blenkinsopp, K. Hoglund and D. Smith-Christopher, develop some of the implications of these considerations. The present essay is clearly

11. *Ezra–Nehemiah*, p. 179.
12. *Ezra, Nehemiah*, p. 159.

indebted to them.[13] Nevertheless, as observers of twentieth-century Middle Eastern politics know, religious sentiments and language can play a visible and often volatile role. Therefore it is important to be cautious about dismissing religious fervor or subsuming it prematurely under more pragmatic, material considerations.

Insights from Sociology

Social scientists who have long studied ethnic groups and ethnicity shed important light on the complex situation of mixed marriages in post-exilic Judah. Critically used, their findings can help analyze the post-exilic era because sociology provides a perspective that is fundamental for understanding any human society. As C. Goldscheider points out, sociology 'can be applied to all societies at all points in time'.[14]

Sociological studies identify certain patterns in the survival mechanisms of groups and in intergroup harmony and conflict. Two prominent theories in ethnic research are system theory and power-conflict theory. System theory views society as a system of tension-management between dominants and subordinates in which the dominants have responsibility as well as privilege; the dominants are responsible for managing society so that the subordinates will not rebel or revolt. Power-conflict theory also views society in terms of dominants and subordinates but assumes groups whose interests clash over scarce resources such as economic goods, prestige and power; this theory stresses inequality in most interactions. Whether approached

13 See esp. J.P. Weinberg, 'Problems der sozialökonomischen Struktur Judäas vom 6. Jahrhudert v.u.Z. bis zum 1 Jahrhundert u.Z.', *Jahrbuch für Wirtschaftsgeschichte* (1973), pp. 237-51 and 'Die Agrarverhältnisse in der Bürger-Temel-Gemeinde der Achämenidenzeit', in J. Harmatta and G. Komoróczy (eds.), *Wirtschaft und Gesellschaft im alten Vorderasien*, (1976), pp. 473-86 (for English translation, see Weinberg's *Citizen-Temple Community*, pp. 92-104); Blenkinsopp, *Ezra–Nehemiah* (see also his 'The Social Context of the "Outsider Woman" in Proverbs 1–9', *Bib* 72 [1991], pp. 457-73, for a summary pertinent to this issue); K.G. Hoglund, *Achaemenid Imperial Administration in Syria-Palestine and the Missions of Ezra and Nehemiah* (SBLDS, 125; Atlanta: Scholars Press, 1992); and Smith, *The Religion of the Landless*.

14. C. Goldscheider, 'Theoretical Issues in the Sociology of Contemporary Jewries: Comments on "What is Conceptually Special about a Sociology of Jewry"', *Contemporary Jewry* 9/1 (Fall/Winter 1987/1988), pp. 91-100 (92).

from the perspective of systems theory and maintenance of equilibrium or that of conflict and struggle for dominance, analyses of intermarriage are integral to discussions of ethnic groups.[15]

Milton Gordon defines an ethnic group as a collectivity within a larger society 'with a shared sense of peoplehood' based on presumed shared socio-cultural experiences and/or geographical roots.[16] F. Barth adds that dichotomization of others as strangers implies a recognition of limitations on shared understandings.[17] R. LeVine and D.T. Campbell observe that there are always areas of ethnic complexity without clear group boundaries. The lack of defined boundaries emerges as a result of nomadism, migrations and conquests. The well-bounded ethnic entity is associated with advanced stages of political development and with the existence of a state.[18]

Ethnic interpenetration occurs when groups move to seek specialized economic opportunities, flee from war, or respond to other environmental pressures that disperse peoples without homogenizing them. In the absence of physical barriers it is nearly impossible to delimit ethnic groups. Intermarriage is a classic example of crossed ethnic boundaries. In some cases such crossing is appreciated for its value in cementing alliances; in others it is viewed as a violation of group integrity.

In analyzing patterns of intermarriage, sociologists suggest that we identify three processes: (1) the structure and function of the current norms, namely who benefits and how; (2) the sources of deviations from those norms, namely the practices; and (3) the pattern of deviation, especially in terms of religion, race and class (the latter denoting cases of hypergamy or hypogamy).[19]

Robert Merton offers us a conceptual framework within which we can examine ancient or modern intermarriage. As he observes, the incest taboo, which appears to be universal, restricts marriage to

15. E.P. Judd, 'Raising Jewish Children: Maintaining Ethnic Identity' (PhD dissertation, University of Denver, 1986).

16. M. Gordon, *Assimilation in American Life* (New York: Oxford University Press, 1964), p. 24.

17. F. Barth, *Ethnic Groups and Boundaries* (Boston: Little, Brown, 1969), p. 18.

18. R. LeVine and D.T. Campbell, *Ethnocentrism: Theories of Conflict, Ethnic Attitudes and Group Behavior* (New York: Wiley, 1972), p. 88.

19. R.K. Merton, 'Intermarriage and the Social Structure', *Psychiatry* 4 (1941), pp. 361-74 (366).

members of different family groups.[20] Merton cautions that a literal interpretation would consider every marriage an 'intermarriage' because the contractants come from different social groups of one sort or another.[21] The norms of each society determine which differences between marriage partners are relevant-to-mate-selection. Therefore, one must discriminate between the specific norms and practices of a society to know which marriages are acceptable to the community and which ones are not. Neither endogamy nor exogamy is uniformly interpreted. The value placed on them (positive or negative) and on any of the other factors within a given society is not stable but rather varies, depending on conditions of survival, economy and politics. Hence the very definition of intermarriage and attitudes toward it are culturally determined, as is the definition of 'stranger'.

Marriage practices might deviate from norms because of immigration laws which influence the size of the nationality groups and therefore regulate the opportunities for socially prescribed marriages. A disproportionate sex-ratio also exerts pressure for out-marriage.[22] Such pressures may be mitigated by in-groups' pressures to conform, but, Merton cautions, analytically it is necessary to recognize their significance.[23] When the pool of acceptable marriage partners is small, those who want to marry must find partners outside the group or

20. Merton, 'Intermarriage and the Social Structure', p. 362. See also K. Grosz's comment on the first page of this article.

21. Merton, 'Intermarriage and the Social Structure', p. 361.

22. Merton, 'Intermarriage and the Social Structure'. See also P. Russell Spickard ('Mixed Marriage: Two American Minority Groups and the Limits of Ethnic Identity, 1900–1970' [PhD dissertation, University of California, Berkeley, 1983]), who examines specifically Jewish groups, and confirms that the size of the community does seem to be important, for where the community is large intermarriage seems to be lower; even where Jews were a small percentage of the population they were able to form tightly knit communities. S. Della Pergola (*Jewish and Mixed Marriages in Milan 1901–68* [Jerusalem: The Institute for Contemporary Jewry, 1972], p. 86) says the smaller the size of the community, the greater the age disparities, and this contributes to intermarriage; among Blalock's propositions the 20th proposition states that, in the case of minorities that are not highly visible, the greater the size and heterogeneity of the community, the less the status loss resulting from equal-status contacts with the minority. Note: this proposition is less likely to hold true for highly visible minorities or for members of elite sub-groups within the dominant group (H. Blalock, *Toward a Theory of Minority-Group Relations* [New York: John Wiley, 1967], p. 69.

23. Merton, 'Intermarriage and the Social Structure', p. 363.

remain single. J. Macer says that the exogamy rates increase as the size of the ethnic group decreases.[24] We know from research in contemporary societies that in communities with few available partners within the group but also many shared symbols and values with outgroups, intermarriage will occur apace. M. Rokeach found the frequency of inter-ethnic marriage is directly related to such similarity.[25]

These sociological observations illumine Ezra–Nehemiah by placing it in the larger context of immigrant communities seeking to establish boundaries when previous signposts have been lost. Norms must be determined in light of new circumstances. Religion, race and class are all grist for the mill of controversy in Ezra 9–10, exemplified here by references to religion, holy seed, and intermarriage among the leaders.[26] Several crises about boundaries occur even before Ezra 9–10 (see Ezra 2.59-63 and 4.1-5), yet from Ezra 6.21 we learn that some sanctioned crossings of these boundaries did exist.[27]

With the help of sociological categories we are able to place the conflict over intermarriage in Ezra 9–10 within the complex network of intricate variables that shape communities in periods of transition. The chapters reflect certain typical patterns and concerns that link the situation in Judah with other communities in similar transition. At the same time, sociological insights alert us to the kind of data we must have—but do not—for a secure analysis of the specific situation in post-exilic Judah. Constructing credible models for analysis is therefore both hazardous and necessary.

We do not know, for example, the sex-ratio in post-exilic Judah. Possibly the discrepancy of approximately 10,000 persons between the number given in individual units in Ezra 2//Nehemiah 7 and the sum total of returnees specified in the text (Ezra 2.64 and Neh. 7.60) represents accompanying families, mostly women and children, coming with about 30,000 heads of household.[28] Such a ratio would

24. J. Macer, *Jewish–Gentile Courtships* (Glencoe: Free Press, 1961), p. 91.

25. M. Rokeach, *The Open and Closed Mind: Investigations into the Nature of Belief Systems and Personality Systems* (New York: Basic Books, 1960), p. 325.

26. According to Della Pergola intermarriages in modern Jewish communities in Milan tend to be upper-class phenomena (*Jewish and Mixed Marriages*, p. 91).

27. It is possible that this very crossing of boundaries precipitated Ezra's mission but the text does not place the issue of mixed marriages on the agenda of Ezra's initial mission (Ezra 7).

28. The number of returnees based on adding up the distinct groups totals 29,818 according to Ezra 2 and 31,089 according to Neh. 7. The sum total of the returnees

closely parallel the sex-ratio among Jewish immigrants to Israel in the twentieth century, prior to the establishment of the state, where only one third of immigrants arrived with families.[29] This kind of a ratio helps explain the need to go outside the *gōlâ* community of returnees to find wives.[30]

Perspectives on Ezra–Nehemiah from Modern Israel

Who are those outsiders, women acceptable to some but unacceptable to others as marriage partners? How did it happen that many respectable citizens violated communal boundaries at that particular time? To examine the subject further we turn to contemporary analogues for the situation in Judah during the fifth century BCE. We draw upon S.N. Eisenstadt, who emphasizes the recurrence of cultural patterns indigenous to a particular society, persisting through time and distinguishing it from others.[31] According to Eisenstadt, social

reported in both Ezra 2.64 and Neh. 7.66 is 42,360.

29. It need not be surprising if the number of women and children is relatively small. The immigrants to Israel prior to the establishment of the state, like the immigrants from Babylonia, were pioneers. Only one third of the arrivals came accompanied; approximately 60% of these came with only one person (indicating a very limited number of wives and children). This stands to reason, since such immigration would be primarily undertaken by young men. See J. Matras, 'Demographic Perspectives on Integration in Israel', in *The Integration of Immigrants from Different Countries of Origin in Israel: A Symposium Held at the Hebrew University on October 25–26, 1966* (no editor listed; Jerusalem: Magnes, Hebrew University, 1969), pp. 131-42, esp. p. 133.

30. The lists of Ezra 2 and Neh. 7 pose another set of problems: We do not know whether the lists encompass males only or complete families. We also cannot establish the date for the groups themselves. Do these lists record the first return or several different waves? Or do they reflect the total population at a particular juncture, compiled for tax purposes or for other political reasons? Theories abound and no consensus has been reached. Weinberg, for example, has drawn important demographic conclusions on the basis of these numbers (see esp. his 'Demographische Notizen zur Geschichte der nachexilischen Gemeinde in Juda', *Klio* 54 [1972], pp. 45-59 and 'Das Bet Abot im 6.–4. Jh. v.u.Z.', *VT* 23 [1973], pp. 400-414; English translation in Weinberg's *Citizen–Temple Community*, pp. 34-48, 49-61); uncertainty about the basis for these data leaves doubt as to the results of Weinberg's analyses. For a different approach to demographic data, see C.E. Carter's essay, 'A Social and Demographic Study of Post-Exilic Judah', in this volume. Carter's conclusions revise the ways the lists of Ezra 2 // Neh. 7 are to be interpreted.

31. See, e.g., S.N. Eisenstadt, 'Comments on the Problems of Continuity of

patterns and meanings in a particular culture will often persist under differing guises and continue to demarcate that society from other (seemingly similar) groups.

With this in mind, we examine developments in another Jewish society which, like the post-exilic community, had undertaken a return to the land. We suggest that developments in twentieth-century Israel provide a singularly vital data base as well as useful sociological models for the analysis and understanding of Ezra–Nehemiah. We do not claim that such a source should be used exclusively; we simply seek to take advantage of it in light of striking historical and demographic parallels which, we believe, are illuminating.[32]

Eisenstadt claims that patterns characteristic of Jewish society took shape during the Second Temple Period.[33] Given such a hypothesis, an analysis of modern Israel, where data are available, is therefore pertinent. Examining modern Israel is uniquely useful for understanding post-exilic phenomena for yet another reason: twentieth-century Israel re-lives some of the conditions, developments and events that had led to the formation of post-exilic Judah and defined it.

Both communities are products of resurgence of immigration in response to new possibilities for self-determination. In the earlier part of this century the seemingly benevolent British Empire replaced the Ottomans as rulers of the Middle East, mirroring the takeover of the area by the Persians in the sixth century BCE. As Judah was a strategic doorway for Persia in its dealings with Egypt and Greece, so this land became an important gateway for the British.[34] The Balfour Declaration (1917), in which the British government promised the Jews a Jewish homeland, compares with Cyrus' Edict, authorizing the Jews to return to Judah (Ezra 1). In both instances, immigration to

Jewish Historical Patterns in Israeli Society', in R. Kahane and S. Kopstein (eds.), *Problems of Collective Identity and Legitimation in the Israeli Society: A Reader*, (Jerusalem: Academon, 1980), pp. 381-96 (Hebrew).

32. For a similar principle at work but different criteria and issues, see C.E. Carter, 'A Social and Demographic Study of Post-Exilic Judah' (PhD dissertation, Duke University, 1991), especially ch. 4, dealing with 'Palestine in the Ottoman and Mandatorial Periods' (pp. 167-215). See also Carter's article in the present volume.

33. Carter, 'A Social and Demographic Study', p. 389. Eisenstadt himself focuses on the later part of the Second Temple Period; nevertheless his observations apply to the earlier part as well.

34. Especially to the 'Crown Jewel', i.e., India.

Israel followed. New opportunities (and changing conditions in Europe) stimulated Jews from Christian Europe to go to Israel in growing numbers. They represented a particular form of Judaism (in contradistinction to those from Muslim countries). As a result of new arrivals, tension developed in the land between Jews and non-Jews as well as among different types of Jews. Politics and religion proved to be hopelessly entwined.

In this new mixture of population, three different intermarriage patterns bear analysis. Each provides a possible analogue to the controversy over 'foreign wives' in Ezra 9–10; each corresponds to a different demographic division in the land and hence exemplifies a different kind of tension:

1. Tension between Jews from different ethnic backgrounds, now enacted between Ashkenazi and Sephardi Jews.[35] These dynamics suggest parallels to ethnic/cultural tension in the Persian period between Jews who had been exiled and those who stayed in the land, irrespective of specific religious practices.[36]

35. Ashkenazi Jews (name based on *Ashkenaz*, 'Germany') have lived for generations in European countries under the influence of Christianity; Sephardic Jews (name based on *sepharad*, 'Spain'), mostly from the Mediterranean region and the Middle East, trace their roots to Spanish Jewry expelled in 1492, and have lived primarily under Muslim influence. These two groups of Jews developed different ethnic cultures, practices and identity as a result of living in dramatically different worlds. For centuries since the middle ages, the Sephardi Jews constituted the dominant group in the land of Israel. In the first decades of the twentieth century they have been overrun by European, Ashkenazi immigrants who brought different customs which then became the norm. Marriages between members of the two groups are officially sanctioned. In practice, however, they meet with opposition by traditional members from each group. Socio-economic factors, language and cultural traditions separate the two groups and create levels of conflict which affect the range of acceptable marriage partners (see Y. Peres below).

36. Statistics about the marriage rates among Jews from different countries of origin and about the attitudes towards marriages between people from different countries of origin indicate the persistent tension in Israel concerning such marriages, although marriages between members of these groups are officially sanctioned, even encouraged. Tension is especially high when it comes to marriages between Sephardi and Ashkenazi Jews. See Y. Peres, 'Communal Identity and Inter-Communal Relations in Israel', *The Integration of Immigrants from Different Countries of Origin in Israel*, pp. 74-87 (Hebrew).

2. Tension between Jews and non-Jews, the latter being mostly Muslims and Christians or people from Muslim or Christian background. Some opponents of Jewish immigrants have been longtime settlers in the land and consider themselves native. Others are newcomers. These groups have their counterpart in Persian-period Judah. All of them have been involved in intermarriages that have incurred formal and informal opposition.
3. Tension between orthodox and non-orthodox Jews on account of different religious perspectives. The basic conflict among these groups pertains to issues of authority and interpretation of Torah (theoretically separate from matters of ethnic background), paralleling different religious practices and interpretations in the Persian period.

Although all three sets of tension need to be investigated in order to discern the fuller complexity of the post-exilic situation, this essay focuses only on the third: it examines modern inner Jewish *religious* tension, and, in particular, the modern phenomenon of the Haredim as an interesting analogue to Ezra 9–10.

The term *haredim* literally means 'those who tremble', presumably in awe of God. This word occurs in Ezra 10.3, where it refers to the pious supporters of Ezra (see also Ezra 9.4).[37] In modern Israel the term designates ultra-orthodox Jewish movements, noted, among other things, for their separatist lifestyle coupled with an aggressive program to impose their interpretation of Judaism upon other segments of the society, a situation that has led to intense inner Jewish conflict in Israel.

According to Charles Liebman, the tension among Israelis between religious and non-religious Jews is perceived as second only to Arab–Jewish relations as a cause for civil conflict. As Liebman observes, 'In fact, in March, 1988, 58 percent of a random sample of Jews in Jerusalem identified religious–secular relations as the most serious problem in the city, whereas only 23 percent stated that Jewish–Arab relations were the most critical problem'.[38]

37. 'And around me gathered all who tremble (כל חרד) at the word of the God of Israel' (Ezra 9.4). Blenkinsopp suggests that these were an organized group in the post-exilic era (*Ezra–Nehemiah*, pp. 177-79).

38. C.S. Liebman, 'Introduction', in C.S. Liebman (ed.), *Religious and Secular: Conflict and Accommodation between Jews in Israel* (Jerusalem: Keter,

The rise of the Haredim in Israel presents suggestive parallels to Ezra–Nehemiah. The emergence of this movement in modern Israel goes back to the time when Israel, as Palestine, first became part of the British Empire. Although the British Mandate, from a Jewish perspective, cannot be equated with the purportedly benign Persian rule (but see A. Kuhrt's legitimate reservations about the benevolence of Cyrus),[39] several interesting parallels exist. Norman Gottwald suggests the parallel when he refers to Israel in the Persian era as 'Colonial Israel'.[40] Like post-exilic Judah, the modern land of Israel that the British acquired contained diverse ethnic, religious and political groups. As noted above, for both Empires, this strip of land served as a gateway to an important part of the Empire (to India for the British, to Egypt and Greece for Persia). In both instances, tension between earlier settlers established on the land and Jewish newcomers flared up and required imperial intervention.

Of the many different aspects that bear a comparative analysis, we limit ourselves to tracing the relation between what sociological studies call 'secularist' and 'orthodox' Jews.[41] Orthodoxy in Israel first

1990), p. xi. See also S.M. Cohen, *Unity and Polarization in Judaism Today: The Attitudes of American and Israeli Jews* (New York: American Jewish Committee, 1988) and C.S. Liebman and E. Don-Yehiya, *Religion and Politics in Israel* (Bloomington: Indiana University Press, 1984).

39. A. Kuhrt, 'The Cyrus Cylinder and Achaemenid Imperial Policy', *JSOT* 25 (1983), pp. 83-97.

40. N.K. Gottwald, *The Hebrew Bible: A Socio-Literary Introduction* (Philadelphia: Fortress Press, 1985), pp. 409-590. For a sociological analysis of patterns in ancient and modern empires on a comparative basis, see S.N. Eisenstadt (ed.), *A Sociological Approach to Comparative Civilizations: The Development and Directions of a Research Program* (Jerusalem: Hebrew University Press, 1986). Also see his 'Observations and Queries about Sociological Aspects of Imperialism in the Ancient World', in M.T. Larsen (ed.), *Power and Propaganda: A Symposium on Ancient Empires* (Mesopotamia Copenhagen Studies in Assyriology, 7; Copenhagen: Akademisk Forlag, 1979), pp. 21-33, and *The Political Systems of Empires* (New York: The Free Press of Glencoe, 1963).

41. The modern divisions only roughly parallel M. Smith's distinction between the so-called 'syncretists' or 'assimilationists' and the Yahweh Alone Party (see his *Palestinian Parties and Politics That Shaped the Old Testament* [New York: Columbia University Press, 1971). It seems to us that Smith's categories can be helpfully revised in light of modern developments in Israel, particularly in terms of labels for the 'liberal' position. In addition, as we will suggest below, the modern situation does not follow his bipolar opposition for the ancient conflict. Reducing the tension

gained official power when British pressure led to the formation of the Chief Rabbinate as the highest religious authority for the Jewish sector. The British government saw the Jewish settlement, above all, as a religious community.[42] With British patronage, the Chief Rabbinate fought against other Jewish groups for complete control over marriage and divorce laws. In the early period, however, these laws and their applications were somewhat flexible in practice (even when not so in theory).

In the mid 1930s, immigration from Poland and Lithuania brought to Israel great orthodox rabbis whose religious authority (often dynastically shaped) was not official or governmental but rather based upon spontaneous recognition by certain religious communities.[43] The greatest among them refused official position within the Chief Rabbinate. Yet, within a short time they, not the official structures, came to exert great religious power and authority in Israel: practices within many religious communities depended on the decisions of the Eastern European orthodox rabbis rather than those of the official Chief Rabbinate. Over a period of time, the name Haredim ('those who tremble'—see Ezra 9.4 and 10.3) came to designate these groups.

In the meantime, the sphere of control by the Chief Rabbinate grew beyond its initial limits. By 1948, every Jewish citizen of the newly founded state of Israel (not only those who voluntarily affiliated themselves with the Jewish Community) had to marry in accordance with the laws as determined by the Chief Rabbinate.[44] This represented a shift from an earlier vagueness in the legal structure under which one could bypass rabbinic authority. Prior to the establishment of the state, the definition of who was under the jurisdiction of the Chief Rabbinate was still flexible. As M. Friedman says, practically speaking, 'a Jew living in the land of Israel could have circumvented the Chief Rabbinate and not require its services even on a subject as sensitive as marriage'.[45]

to two groups as Smith does may therefore reflect a misleading oversimplification.

42. M. Friedman, 'The Chief Rabbinate—Dilemma without Solution', *Problems of Collective Identity and Legitimation*, pp. 253-67 (Hebrew).

43. These men were anti-Zionist, seeing Zionism as the secularization of the land (see also the chapter on 'Religious Orthodoxy's Attitudes toward Zionism', in Liebman and Don-Yehiya, *Religion and Politics in Israel*, pp. 57-78.

44. Friedman, 'The Chief Rabbinate', p. 263.

45. 'The Chief Rabbinate', p. 256; our translation.

For the purpose of regulating family laws and for the sake of the 'Law of Return', it eventually was deemed necessary to determine more definitely who is a Jew. A struggle led to a specific legal definition in 1970, and, ironically, to intensification of the problems. As D. Segre observes, 'In practice there were two problems confronting the government: one was the definition of the Jew with reference to the Law of the Return, which grants immediate citizenship to any Jew returning to his ancestral land; the other was the definition of the Jew with reference to the competence of the religious courts in matters of marriage and divorce'.[46]

On March 10, 1970, the state of Israel ruled that it will recognize as a Jew 'only a person who has been born to a Jewish mother or who has been converted to Judaism and is not a member of another religion'.[47] Prior to 1970, self-definition allowed persons to declare themselves Jews and be registered as such. Nevertheless, the Chief Rabbinate could reject the legitimacy of such identity when it came to questions of marriage. Since only a Jew could marry a Jew, and only the Chief Rabbinate could authorize such marriages, most adults depended on the Chief Rabbinate for their legally recognized Jewish identity.

It did not take long for the fuller repercussions of a clash between the earlier flexibility and the newer definition to surface. After 1970, many persons who had always considered themselves Jews and had been legally considered Jews by the state—including the granddaughter of Israel's Prime Minister David Ben Gurion—found themselves legally outside the pale in Israel, unable to marry other Jews.[48] The chief Rabbinate could (and did) accept or reject candidates for marriage on the basis of *its* interpretation of the law as to who is a Jew. Since the authority of the Chief Rabbinate on questions of marriage is higher than that of the Supreme Court, it has voided

46. D.V. Segre, *A Crisis of Identity: Israel and Zionism* (Oxford: Oxford University Press, 1980), p. 124.

47. The Law of Return (Revision §2) March 10, 1970, Definition 4B (cited by M. Amon, 'Israel and Jewish Identity Crisis' [PhD dissertation, Claremont Graduate School, 1972], p. 16).

48. For a litany of cases in which families were no longer considered legal, and for a report about the sorrowful consequences, see Amon, 'Israel and Jewish Identity Crisis', esp. pp. 16-121. See also the chapter on 'Religious Leaders in the Political Arena', in Liebman and Don-Yehiya, *Religion and Politics in Israel*, pp. 79-99, and S. Aloni, ההסדר: ממדינת חוק למדינת הלכה (Tel Aviv: Otpaz, 1970), which focuses primarily on these cases.

marriages even after the Supreme Court had sanctioned them.

Nevertheless, the Chief Rabbinate, which is orthodox, on occasion appeared too moderate for the Haredim. Its authority declined and its rulings were superseded for the Haredim by the teachings of the European rabbis and their disciples. Examples from the *haredi* press reveal the degree of alienation between them and the general population outside their camp.[49] The Haredim have called non-orthodox Jews 'gentiles' and denied their Jewish identity. From a *haredi* perspective, a marriage between a *haredi* and a non-*haredi* constitutes a mixed marriage.[50]

Although for the purpose of comparison we have greatly simplified the complexities of the modern situation, three aspects of that situation are significant for our present purpose: first, the evolving definition of who is a Jew, moving from a broad category to a narrow one; second, the inter-religious gap that leads one group of Jews to characterize the other formally and publicly as gentiles and strangers; third, the dynamics and particular pace of such developments.

In the 1990s, almost 45 years after the establishment of the state of Israel, 55 years since the arrival of ultra-orthodox Eastern European rabbis, and 74 years after the Balfour Declaration (compare with Ezra's arrival 80 years after Cyrus's declaration), the Jewish community in Israel is divided into at least four important groups: Haredim, orthodox, religious liberals, and non-religious.[51] It is important to

49. See A. Levi, 'The *Haredi* Press and Secular Society', in Liebman (ed.), *Conflict and Accommodation between Jews in Israel*, pp. 21-44. In *Yated Neeman*, a major Haredi newspaper (lit. 'a faithful tentpeg'; note the unmistakable allusion to Isa. 22.23 and possibly also Ezra 9.8) we read the following about Jewish Israeli youth: 'we have noted that norms have changed here, that Jewish antisemitism is almost official policy today... and these Israelis who are indifferent to Jews, allow themselves to express emotions only when matters affect Arabs' (cited by Levi, *Conflict and Accommodation between Jews in Israel*, p. 27).

50. Similarly, in Israel marriage between orthodox and non-orthodox is perceived as mixed marriage (even when legally accepted). See L. Weller and S. Topper Weller, 'Strange Bedfellows: A Study of Mixed Religious Marriages', in Liebman (ed.), *Conflict and Accommodation between Jews in Israel*, pp. 173-92.

51. Although the most severe battles are still *defined* in terms of two categories, secular and religious, the categories themselves are subject to a variety of definitions. The four major groups are (I) the Haredim who heed the teachings of their own, usually European, rabbis; (II) the orthodox (III) religious liberals and (IV) the 'non-religious'.

note that from *haredi* or orthodox perspectives, everyone who does not follow the Halakah (Jewish rabbinic law) as interpreted by them is 'non-religious'.

As a result of the evolving definition of who is a Jew, many modern marriages in Israel have been declared illegal because people who had considered themselves Jews have been otherwise defined by the new laws. In some cases the results have been tragic.[52] In others, mechanisms such as conversion have enabled partners to remarry (although some children of the earlier union are forbidden to marry most other Jews).[53]

Conclusions

The phenomenon of the modern Haredim illustrates striking parallels to Ezra–Nehemiah, all the more noteworthy when we recall that the noun *hared* or (plural) *haredim* ('those who tremble' in relation to God's teachings) occurs only in Ezra 9–10 and Isaiah 66.[54] As the British established the Chief Rabbinate for Jewish affairs, so, we can suppose, the Persians created a structure for Jewish affairs (or elevated an already existing one), that is, the priesthood.

Like the illustrious *haredi* European rabbis in the 1930s, Ezra arrived from diaspora late, after certain patterns had been established. He offered a more stringent definition of who is a Jew, which gained

52. Note the case of Enoch Langer, for example. Langer, who serves in the Army, has been termed a *mamzer*, i.e., a descendant of a prohibited relationship. Although the Chief Rabbi found evidence to dispute the *mamzer* appellation, all rabbis asked to sit on the court and review the evidence refused to do so (Amon, 'Israel and Jewish Identity Crisis', p. 38). Karaites (Jews from Egypt) and Bnei Israel (Indian Jews from a very old settlement) are not fully recognized by the orthodox Rabbinate (*ibid*., p. 60). For further details see Amon as well as Amnon Levi, החרדים (Jerusalem: Keter, 1989) and Aloni, ההסדר: ממדינת חוק למדינת הלכה .

53. There is an official list of children considered *mamzerim* (plural of *mamzer*) because of the circumstances of the parents' divorce and subsequent remarriage; they are forbidden to marry other Jews (Amon, 'Israel and Jewish Identity Crisis', p. 37). However, they are allowed to marry other *mamzerim* or converts to Judaism (*ibid*., p. 36).

54. Ezra 9.4 and 10.3 and Isa. 66.2 and 66.5. It is possible that the modern Haredim modeled themselves consciously after their particular interpretation of Ezra. Such modeling would underscore rather than vitiate parallels with Ezra 9–10: it would provide an example of twentieth-century 'returned exiles' interpreting their religious community in terms of a fifth-century BCE model.

popular support among some segments of the population, leading to further legal reformulation of the issues and to communal tension. In this process, previously sanctioned relations had to be re-evaluated.

Given this interpretation, the women of Ezra 9–10 could have been Judahites or Israelites who had not been in exile and who, in the eyes of the early returnees, were appropriate marriage partners. Ezra 9.1-2 does not refer to these women as Canaanites or Ammonites because they are not. Nevertheless, on the basis of a redefinition, they come to be regarded as those outsiders and shunned accordingly. We are not alone in pointing to the likelihood that the women were not members of foreign groups.[55] What we add to earlier interpretations is an illustration of how it can happen that well-intentioned, loyal Jews marry persons who, in the course of time, lose their legitimacy in the Jewish community. Using the example of the Haredim we also delineate a process—gradual and often tragic—by which some women, caught in the drama of shifting concepts of identity, can be transformed from spouses to strangers.

55 For a summary of these views, see H.C. Washington, 'The Strange Woman of Proverbs 1–9 and Post-Exilic Judaean Society', in this volume. See also C. Camp, 'What's So Strange about the Strange Woman?', in D. Jobling, P.L. Day and G.T. Sheppard (eds.), *The Bible and the Politics of Exegesis: Essays in Honor of Norman K. Gottwald on his Sixty-Fifth Birthday* (Cleveland: Pilgrim Press, 1991), pp. 17-31.

WHAT WAS EZRA'S MISSION?

Lester L. Grabbe

In the consensus that has prevailed in English language scholarship,[1] Ezra's mission has usually been accepted as historical with at most a few brief comments about the character of the mission. It is seldom presented as a major problem. Yet the plethora of suggestions about what Ezra was commissioned to do should have aroused suspicion. When we compare him with Nehemiah, whose overall purpose in going to Jerusalem has not occasioned much doubt or controversy, it is quite surprising that Ezra's aim has mustered such a legion of explanations. The more theory, the less clarity.

The problem is not just a hypothetical one. Although the prevailing consensus has accepted the historicity of the commission, another scholarly tradition, represented mainly in German language scholarship, has been more skeptical.[2] Thus, a judgment about what Ezra was up to seems central to the question of historicity.

1. On the consensus, see L.L. Grabbe, 'Reconstructing History from the Book of Ezra', in P.R. Davies (ed.), *Studies in the Second Temple* (JSOTSup, 117; Sheffield: JSOT Press, 1991), pp. 98-106. Works that can be said to represent, more or less, this consensus include L.W. Batten, *A Critical and Exegetical Commentary on Ezra and Nehemiah* (ICC; Edinburgh: T. & T. Clark, 1913); W. Rudolph, *Esra und Nehemia* (HAT, 20; Tübingen: Mohr [Siebeck], 1949); D.J.A. Clines, *Ezra, Nehemiah, Esther* (CBC; London: Marshall, Morgan & Scott; Grand Rapids: Eerdmans, 1984); H.G.M. Williamson, *Ezra, Nehemiah* (WBC, 16; Waco, TX: Word, 1985); J. Blenkinsopp, *Ezra–Nehemiah* (OTL; London: SCM Press, 1989)

2. See the review in L.C.H. Lebram, 'Die Traditionsgeschichte der Esragestalt und die Frage nach dem historischen Esra', in H. Sancisi-Weerdenburg (ed.), *Achaemenid History*. I. *Sources, Structures and Synthesis* (Proceeding of the Gröningen 1983 Achaemenid History Workshop; Leiden: Nederlands Instituut voor het Nabije Oosten, 1987), pp. 103-138, especially pp. 104-117.

The Text

Although traditio-historical questions must be given due weight, there is considerable value at this point in taking a synchronic look at the Ezra material (= EM). What is the picture presented by the text as it now stands?[3] Is it a consistent one? For convenience, the following table attempts to integrate the data by roughly paralleling the decree of Artaxerxes with the EM proper (naturally, such a schematic summary cannot give the whole story):

Decree	*Activities of Ezra*
Ezra = 'scribe of the law of the God of heaven' (Ezra 7.12)	Law read and Sukkot kept (Neh. 8)
'People of Israel', priests, Levites allowed to go to Jerusalem (7.13)	Ezra collects 'the people', priests, Levites for the journey (Ezra 8.15-20)
Ezra to 'inquire' (*lebaqqārâ*) concerning Judah and Jerusalem according to the law of God in his hands (7.14)	Mixed marriages dissolved (Ezra 9–10)
Gifts of silver, gold, vessels from king, counsellors, people for temple (7.15-19)	Twenty-five and a half tons of gold and silver plus vessels transported, delivered (Ezra 8.24-34)
Other necessities for temple to come from state treasury (7.20-23)	Ezra gives thanks for putting it in the king's heart to beautify (*lepā'ēr*) the temple (Ezra 7.27)
No tribute on temple or personnel (7.24)	—

3. There is general agreement that the EM is found essentially in Ezra 7–10 and Neh. 8, though disagreement exists on the original order of the material. Since C.C. Torrey's discussion in *The Composition and Historical Value of Ezra–Nehemiah* (BZAW, 2; Giessen: Ricker, 1896), pp. 28-34, the original order has been widely held to be Ezra 7–8, Neh. 8, Ezra 9–10. However, many still accept the present order: M. Noth, *The Chronicler's History* (*Überlieferungsgeschichte*, chs. 14–25, trans. and ed. H.G.M. Williamson; Sheffield: JSOT Press, 1987), pp. 62-66, and S. Mowinckel, *Studien zu dem Buche Ezra–Nehemiah III* (Skrifter utgitt av Det Norske Videnskaps–Akademi i Oslo II. Hist.-Filos. Klasse. Ny Serie., 7; Oslo: Universitetsforlaget, 1965), pp. 7-11; K. Koch, 'Ezra and the Origins of Judaism', *JSS* 19 (1974), pp. 173-97, specifically p. 192. For our purposes, however, the exact original order is irrelevant.

Ezra to appoint judges over whole of Ebir-Nari to judge by laws of his God (7.25-26)	Initiative to dissolve mixed marriages comes from leaders and people (Ezra 9–10)

First, the decree of Artaxerxes (Ezra 7.12-26): after the address to Ezra, the first statement allows all those so desiring to return to Jerusalem with Ezra (v. 13). Only then is it stated that Ezra himself is sent by 'the king and his seven counsellors'. This is done for two reasons: first, to 'investigate Judah and Jerusalem by the law of God which is in your hand' (v. 14) and, second, to bring the gifts of silver and gold from the king and his counsellors, any silver and gold found in Babylon, the gifts of the people and the priests to the temple of God (vv. 15-16), as well as vessels for the service of God's house (v. 19). The bullion is to be used to acquire animals for offering on the altar (v. 17). Anything left over can be used as desired (v. 18), though other needs are also to be catered for, up to 100 talents of silver from the royal treasury (v. 20). A message to the governor(s) of the territory further states that no tax is to be imposed on temple personnel (v. 24). Ezra himself is empowered to appoint judges and magistrates to judge those who know God's laws and to teach those who do not, with severe penalties for non-observance (vv. 25-26), this being done for the whole of the satrapy (despite v. 14, which limits his activities to Judah and Jerusalem). As an appendix to the decree, Ezra blesses God who put it in the king's mind to glorify the temple in Jerusalem (vv. 27-28).

In Ezra 8 the journey to Jerusalem is described. Ezra finds there are no Levites in the company of the priests and Israelites, and must find some. He then entrusts the bullion—over 22 metric tons of silver plus another $3\frac{1}{2}$ tons of gold—to a group of priests; the journey is made, the gifts turned over, offerings offered, and his orders delivered to the satraps (*sic*) and governors. In Ezra 9–10 the problem of mixed marriages is handled. 'The officials' (*haśśārîm*) tell Ezra that some of the *gōlâ* have contracted marriages with the 'peoples of the land'. His reaction is to go into public mourning and prayer, followed by fasting in the chamber of Johanan. The *gōlâ* is commanded (by the officials and elders) to assemble in Jerusalem, an investigation is ordered, and the guilty individuals (only 111 are named) renounce their wives. Nehemiah 8 describes the reading of 'the book of the law of Moses', after which Sukkot is kept, not having been so celebrated since the days of Joshua (v. 17).

Analysis

Preliminary Considerations

Before looking at specific proposals, it is important to consider some general points.

1. *Religious bias of Ezra–Nehemiah.* The books of Ezra-Nehemiah have apologetic aims, including the desire to present the Persian kings and government as acting under the divine guidance of Yahweh to support the Jewish community and temple.[4] The writers and compilers would naturally use any authentic documentation to demonstrate this, but it is not inconceivable that they might also use forged or doctored documents or reinterpret matters to the advantage of their own viewpoint. Thus, the information of the books must be sifted critically and not simply taken at face value. Alleged favor from Persian officials in particular must be scrutinized with care. This is an elementary point but one seemingly forgotten in some discussions of the subject. As M. Dandamaev and A. Lukonin have noted, there are 'no grounds for speaking of a special benevolence towards Judaism on the part of the Persian kings'.[5] It was noted some time ago that what Artaxerxes is alleged to have done is modelled on what Hezekiah and Josiah did.[6]

2. *Development of the Ezra tradition.* The EM must not be interpreted in light of the later Jewish tradition, as is shown by even a quick glance at how the traditions about Ezra and Nehemiah developed. Already 1 Esdras had begun to elaborate by emphasizing Ezra and ignoring Nehemiah. The book of Ezra itself refers to the 'law which is in Ezra's hand', without further specification. According to a later development of the tradition, though, Ezra's esteem had grown to the point of single-handedly restoring the law after it had been burned (*4 Ezra* 14.21-48). However, another tradition cut Ezra out

4. See especially S. Japhet, 'Sheshbazzar and Zerubbabel—Against the Background of the Historical and Religious Tendencies of Ezra–Nehemiah', *ZAW* 94 (1982), pp. 66-98; 95 (1983), pp. 218-30.

5. M.A. Dandamaev and V.G. Lukonin, *The Culture and Social Institutions of Ancient Iran* (Cambridge: Cambridge University Press, 1989), p. 249.

6. J.M. Myers, *The World of the Restoration* (Englewood Cliffs, NJ: Prentice–Hall, 1968), p. 136.

altogether. Ben Sira made no mention of him, though he cited Nehemiah (49.13), which makes it difficult to believe that the present Ezra tradition was the only one available to him. He may well have known some sort of Nehemiah tradition such as surfaces in 2 Macc. 1.18-36 in which Nehemiah had not only displaced Ezra but had even become the founder of the Second Temple. Even this brief information shows that there were also negative views of Ezra in circulation—or at least ones that gave him little or no place in the restoration. The role of Ezra as lawgiver and founding teacher was not a universal one in early Judaism.

3. *Persian support of religion and local cults.* It is often stated that 'it was Persian policy to support religion'.[7] One can respond with both a 'yes' and a 'no'. On the affirmative side, the Persians continued what was already general policy in the Near Eastern empires: to tolerate local cults as long as they did not threaten insubordination. They also granted special favors (not necessarily permanent) to certain specific cults for political reasons.[8] On the negative side, the alleged support of cults is often exaggerated in modern literature because of the propaganda of the Persian kings themselves.[9] Overall Persian policy was rather to reduce the income of temples.[10] Little evidence exists that cults generally received state support (as sometimes alleged), which is hardly surprising since temples usually had their own

7. R. de Vaux, 'The Decrees of Cyrus and Darius on the Rebuilding of the Temple', *The Bible and the Ancient Near East* (London: Darton, Longman & Todd, 1971), pp. 63-96 (= translation from *RB* 46 [1937], pp. 29-57), quote from pp. 77-78). Cf. J. Blenkinsopp, 'The Mission of Udjahorresnet and Those of Ezra and Nehemiah', *JBL* 106 (1987), pp. 409-421, esp. p. 413.

8. For example, the cults of certain temples in Egypt, according to the Demotic Chronicle: W. Spiegelberg, *Die sogenannte demotische Chronik des Pap. 215 der Bibliotheque Nationale zu Paris; nebst den auf der Ruckseite des Papyrus stehenden Texten* (Demotische Studien, 7; Leipzig: Hinrichs, 1914), pp. 32-33. For examples from Mesopotamia, see C. Tuplin, 'The Administration of the Achaemenid Empire', in I. Carradice (ed.), *Coinage and Administration in the Athenian and Persian Empires: The Ninth Oxford Symposium on Coinage and Monetary History* (BAR International Series, 343; Oxford: BAR, 1987), pp. 109-166, esp. p. 150.

9. A. Kuhrt, 'The Cyrus Cylinder and Achaemenid Imperial Policy', *JSOT* 25 (1983), pp. 83-97.

10. Dandamaev and Lukonin, *Culture and Social Institutions*, pp. 362-66; Tuplin, 'Administration of the Achaemenid Empire', pp. 149-53.

incomes.[11] On the contrary, temples were regulated and taxed, both in goods and services.[12]

4. *The Artaxerxes decree (Ezra 7.12-26).* Recent English language publications have generally taken the Artaxerxes decree regarding Ezra as an authentic document; in actuality it has often been questioned or rejected.[13] This is not the place for a thorough discussion of the question, but there are definite Jewish elements that cannot be eliminated as simply 'due to Ezra',[14] as has been recognized most recently by Blenkinsopp who otherwise accepts the decree as authentic.[15] This strongly suggests that—even if the decree is based on a genuine one—it has been retouched to give a different message in its

11. Some documents of the Persepolis Treasury and Fortification Texts mention the issuance of rations for cultic purposes, though the exact significance of this is unclear. See R.T. Hallock, *Persepolis Fortification Tablets* (Chicago: University of Chicago, 1969), especially texts 336–77, 741–74. It may be that these are only for certain official state cults; cf. G.G. Cameron, *Persepolis Treasury Tablets* (Chicago: University of Chicago Press, 1948), pp. 5-9 and texts 10–11.

12. Tuplin, 'Administration of the Achaemenid Empire', pp. 149-53; Dandamaev and Lukonin, *Culture and Social Institutions*, pp. 362-66; S. Hornblower, *Mausolus* (Oxford: Clarendon, 1982), pp. 161-63; G. Posener, *La première domination perse en Egypte* (Bibliotheque d'Etude de l'Institute Français d'Archeologie Orientale, 11; Cairo: Institut Français d'Archeologie Orientale, 1936), pp. 164-76.

13. Eduard Meyer was the main one who has influenced a positive evaluation of the decree (*Die Entstehung des Judenthums* [Halle: Niemeyer, 1896; repr. Hildesheim: Olms, 1965], pp. 60-71). Recent commentators who have accepted this evaluation include Rudolph, *Esra und Nehemiah*, pp. 73-77; Clines, *Ezra, Nehemiah, Esther*, pp. 101-106; Williamson, *Ezra, Nehemiah*, pp. 98-105. Those who have rejected it include A.H.J. Gunneweg, *Esra* (KAT, 19.1; Gütersloh: Mohn, 1985), pp. 129-40; Lebram, 'Die Traditionsgeschichte der Esragestalt', esp. pp. 117-20.

14. This was originally argued by Meyer, *Entstehung*, p. 65, but others have often repeated the proposal. One of the most glaring incongruities is the amount of state aid allowed for the Jerusalem cult: up to 100 talents of silver ($3\frac{1}{2}$ metric tons), a fantastic sum considering that the tribute for the whole of Ebir-nari was only about 350 talents (Herodotus 3.91). The figure in Ezra is most easily explained as an element of Jewish propaganda.

15. J. Blenkinsopp, 'The Sage, the Scribe, and Scribalism in the Chronicler's Work', in J.G. Gammie and L.G. Perdue (eds.), *The Sage in Israel and the Ancient Near East* (Winona Lake, IN: Eisenbrauns, 1990), pp. 307-15, esp. pp. 312-13; *Ezra–Nehemiah*, pp. 148-52.

present form. However much the decree may fit generally the Persian period documents, it cannot be taken at face value.[16]

Various Proposals

A variety of proposals have been made as to Ezra's mission. These suggestions have been passed down in the literature, but not always with critical examination. If the historicity of Ezra and his mission is not taken for granted, however, the need for careful scrutiny of such proposals is obvious. In evaluating these proposals, two sorts of questions must be considered. First, what does the text say? Second, what can be argued on the basis of analogy and inference? As will become clear, a number of proposals are nothing more than hypothetical constructs with little or no basis in the text itself.

High priest. The text nowhere states that Ezra was high priest. Because no high priest is named in the EM, however, one might assume that Ezra held this office. Indeed, he takes on many of the functions that one would expect the high priest to carry out: settling the issue of mixed marriages, reading the law, declaring a religious festival. Nor is the presence of anyone else as high priest indicated. Yet no list of high priests contains Ezra in it (e.g. Neh 12.10-11, 22, 26), nor is he said to be high priest in any of the later Ezra legends. It seems unlikely that his status would have been suppressed in the tradition in the same way that reference to him as governor might have been (see next section).[17]

16. It is often commented that the decree 'fits' the Persian decrees. Yet it must be acknowledged that we have only *one* royal letter generally admitted as genuine, and this is only in Greek translation (Thucydides 1.128-29). Herodotus is doubted by many (e.g. M. van den Hout, 'Studies in Early Greek Letter-Writing', *Mnemosyne* 2 [4th series] [1949], pp. 19-41, pp. 138-53), while the Gadatas inscription continues to be controversial (cf. O. Hansen, 'The Purported Letter of Darius to Gadatas', *Rheinisches Museon* 129 [1986], pp. 95-96 [against its authenticity] and J. Wiesehöfer, 'Zur Frage der Echtheit des Dareios-Briefes an Gadatas', *Rheinisches Museon* 130 [1987], pp. 396-98 [in favor of it]).

17. Koch, 'Ezra and the Origins of Judaism', pp. 190-92, sees Ezra as a high priest from indications in the text (e.g. the genealogy) but recognizes that no explicit reference to this occurs.

Governor. It is almost universally agreed that Nehemiah held the post of governor.[18] Not surprisingly, some have proposed—or simply assumed—that Ezra was also governor.[19] Although no reference to such an office for Ezra is made in the text, it might have been suppressed in the narrative, just as it seems to have been for Sheshbazzar and Zerubbabel.[20] The decisions Ezra allegedly made fit well the role of governor, in particular intervening to force those with mixed marriages to divorce and having the right to set up judges. Also, no governor seems to be around during his activity. On the other hand, the commission in the alleged document from Artaxerxes makes no mention whatsoever of the office of governor, which would seem to clinch the matter.

Also, from what we know of Persian administration the royal judges were under the authority of the satrap who is completely ignored in the text.[21] This leads to another interesting point, for if Ezra should be thought of as governor, from the plain sense of the text one could go even further and suggest that Ezra held the office of satrap. The idea that Ezra was satrap might be thought absurd by most, but the narrative implies that he had similar authority because he was able to give orders to the 'king's satraps and to the governors' (Ezra 8.36) and to set up judges in the whole of the satrapy. (Naturally, this was done in the name of the king, but did any satrap govern with any other authority, at least in theory?) Therefore, just as good a case could be made for Ezra as satrap as for Ezra as governor.

Commissioner for Jewish Affairs. H.H. Schaeder proposed that Ezra was a Persian official with responsibility for Jewish affairs, a thesis that is still often cited with favor.[22] This conclusion is based on two

18. An exception is R. North, 'Civil Authority in Ezra', in *Studi in onore di Edoardo Volterra* (Publicazioni della Facoltà di Giurisprudenza dell'Università di Roma; Milan: Giuffrè, 1971), VI, pp. 377-404.

19. Most recently O. Margalith ('The Political Role of Ezra as Persian Governor', *ZAW* 98 [1986], pp. 110-12), though he asserts this without arguing the question. Cf. also M. Smith, *Palestinian Parties and Politics That Shaped the Old Testament* (New York: Columbia, 1971), p. 152.

20. On this question, see S. Japhet, 'Sheshbazzar and Zerubbabel', *ZAW* 94 (1982), pp. 66-98.

21. Hornblower, *Mausolus*, p. 150.

22. H.H. Schaeder, *Esra der Schreiber* (BHT, 5; Tübingen: Mohr [Siebeck], 1930), pp. 39-59.

main arguments: first, the meaning of 'scribe of the law of the God of heaven' and, second, the analogy of the much later *reš galuta* in the Sassanian empire. In fact, both arguments and Schaeder's basic conclusions have been criticized over the years.[23] Although the term 'scribe' alone can be applied to an official high in the administration, there is no such analogy for Ezra's title which is 'scribe of the law of the God of heaven'. In fact, Schaeder has to suppose that the identity of Ezra's office in the decree is different from that in the rest of the EM (cf. 7.6, 10-11), where the emphasis is on Ezra's knowledge of the Torah. A further question: Why should we believe that there was a special commissioner for Jewish affairs? The Jews were only one of hundreds of small ethnic groups throughout the Persian empire. Did each have its own commissioner? Why should the Jews be special? In any case, I am unaware of any evidence of such a concept as a commissioner for Jewish affairs from anything we know about Persian administration. The analogy from the later Sassanian empire seems rather far-fetched.[24] In short, this much-quoted theory actually has little to support it.

The Analogy of Udjahorresnet. Although this suggestion has been around for a long time, it has been discussed most recently by J. Blenkinsopp.[25] Udjahorresnet was an admiral in the Egyptian navy who went over to the Persian side with the invasion of Cambyses. As a reward he was honored by Cambyses who made him his adviser and royal physician. Later on under Darius he was sent back to Egypt with authority to found the 'House of Life'. Like Ezra he was a scribe and also probably a priest.

This interesting proposal is not without difficulties, however. From the textual side, one can make a major objection: Artaxerxes' decree does not suggest the same sort of commission for Ezra as for Udjahorresnet; for example, Ezra is not said to restore anything,

23. See especially Mowinckel, *Studien*, III, pp. 121-24; K. Galling, *Studien zur Geschichte Israels im persischen Zeitalter* (Tübingen: Mohr [Siebeck], 1964), pp. 166-67; Blenkinsopp, *Ezra–Nehemiah*, pp. 136-38; 'The Sage, the Scribe, and Scribalism', pp. 312-14.

24. A problem already noted by Mowinckel, *Studien*, III, p. 122; Koch, 'Ezra and the Origins of Judaism', p. 183.

25. J. Blenkinsopp, 'Mission of Udjahorresnet'; however, the most striking parallels which he notes are those with Nehemiah rather than Ezra.

whether temple or other institution, nor (as already noted) is there any indication that he set up the system of judges supposedly commissioned in the decree. In any case, he would have had no way of enforcing any of his actions, since he came without military aid of any sort.[26]

One must also ask how far such analogies can be pressed. Although it does seem helpful in understanding Nehemiah and his commission, because of a common literary form, a number of considerations detract from its usefulness for Ezra:

1. Egypt was newly conquered and needed to be granted certain concessions to soften the new state of subjection, whereas Judah had long been under Persian rule.
2. Udjahorresnet had been a useful quisling and could expect certain offices as a reward for services rendered; such is not suggested in the EM for Ezra, for whom any grant was likely to be the result of a petition to the king.
3. Egypt was a large and important satrapy, whereas Judah was a small province (if indeed it was a province at this time[27]).
4. Udjahorresnet made a request to Cambyses at a time when the Egyptian temples were having their revenues reduced, whereas the temple and cult of Jerusalem had long been in operation and did not need setting up again after a recent war or conquest. If Ezra was alleged to have come at the time of Darius, the parallel might be more interesting, but the restoration of temple, cult and priesthood was at least half a century—perhaps even more than a century—earlier.

26. This is a point well made by Smith, *Palestinian Parties and Politics*, p. 194 n. 116.

27. A. Alt, 'Die Rolle Samarias bei der Entstehung des Judentums', *Kleine Schriften zur Geschichte des Volkes Israel* (Munich: Beck, 1953), II, pp. 316-37 (reprinted from *Festschrift Otto Procksch zum 60. Geburtstag* [Leipzig: Deichert & Hinrichs, 1934], pp. 5-28) argued that Judah was a part of the province of Samaria until the time of Nehemiah, a thesis still maintained (e.g. by S.E. McEvenue, 'The Political Structure in Judah from Cyrus to Nehemiah', *CBQ* 43 [1981], pp. 353-64). However, others have strongly defended the view that Judah was a separate province from the beginning of Persian rule. See Smith, *Palestinian Parties and Politics*, pp. 147-53; H.G.M. Williamson, 'The Governors of Judah under the Persians', *TynBul* 39 (1988), pp. 59-82.

Defense of the Frontier. It is often stated that Ezra's mission was believable because the Persians wanted to make the frontier province of Judah secure. No doubt the security of Judah was an important matter to the state, but it is difficult to see how Ezra's mission could have been of much use to it. Gifts to the temple would presumably generate a certain amount of goodwill toward the Persian administration but not much else. Ezra brought no soldiers, refusing even to ask for a military escort. He was supposed to 'investigate' according to the law in his hand; whatever that law was, this instruction seems unlikely to have produced a tranquil province. In fact, the measures instigated with regard to marriages divided the people, creating discontent and potential unrest.

Lawgiver. Although this may seem to receive some support from the text, this support is actually less than generally assumed. The most interesting thing about the decree is that it concentrates on the temple and cult, not on Ezra's duties with regard to the law. *Later* Jewish tradition makes Ezra the lawgiver *par excellence*, as noted above, but this does not emerge from the EM itself.[28] This is reinforced by a closer consideration of Ezra's law. Exactly what it constituted is much debated, but whatever it was,[29] it was not basically new. It is hard to believe, for example, that Sukkot was being celebrated for the first time in the mid-fifth or early fourth century BCE.

The analogy of Darius I's codification of Egyptian law has often been cited. Certainly, several sources mention this accomplishment.[30] Darius is also credited in general with being a 'lawgiver'.[31] Yet, as with Udjahorresnet, it is difficult to know how far this analogy can be

28. This point was made by Koch, 'Ezra and the Origins of Judaism', p. 185.

29. The identification has been much debated. In addition to the commentaries cited in n. 1 above, see R. Rendtorff, 'Esra und das "Gesetz"', *ZAW* 96 (1984), pp. 165-84; C. Houtman, 'Ezra and the Law: Observations on the Supposed Relation between Ezra and the Pentateuch', *OTS* 21 (1981), pp. 91-95.

30. W. Spiegelberg, *Die sogenannte demotische Chronik*, pp. 30-32; E. Meyer, 'Ägyptische Dokumente aus der Perserzeit', *SPAW* (1915), pp. 287-311, esp. pp. 304-11; N.J. Reich, 'The Codification of the Egyptian Laws by Darius and the Origin of the "Demotic Chronicle"', *Mizraim* 1 (1933), pp. 178-85.

31. See especially A.T. Olmstead, *History of the Persian Empire* (Chicago: University of Chicago Press, 1948), pp. 119-34, for references; however, Olmstead's own argument for a Darian law code based on Hammurabi is completely hypothetical and has found little support among scholars.

pressed. As already noted, Ezra was long after Darius, nor did the king actually create new laws. It is known that Persian law was being applied in Egypt years before his alleged codification, and in any case he had the traditional Egyptian law only codified, not created anew.[32]

Internal Rivalry in the Priesthood and Community. That Nehemiah had a continual battle with various of the priests and other officials in Jerusalem is clear, but such has also been suggested for Ezra.[33] This is very hypothetical because such a conflict does not immediately stand out in the EM. Yet, paradoxically, this thesis, which is perhaps the most hypothetical, seems also the most plausible because it takes account of the nature of the books before us: the apologetic aim which might well attempt to cover up strife, as well as not to give publicity to the side it opposed; a perhaps genuine document allowing Ezra to return to Jerusalem but tampered with to support the story of the EM; and the hints of strife in both Ezra (10.15) and Nehemiah (6.10-19; 13.4-9).

Conclusions

The closer one looks, the more enigmatic Ezra's mission becomes. As soon as one solution starts to look interesting, it is undermined by further considerations or by paradoxical data. Ezra is not sent as high priest, but he acts like a high priest. He is not a satrap, yet he is not required to pay any attention to the satrap. He is not the governor of Judah, but the powers conferred make him equal or superior to the governor. He has authority to appoint judges and magistrates over the whole satrapy, but when a problem is brought to his attention he can only sit in the street in mourning before retiring in pique to a friend's room. It is the elders and officials who make the decisions and take the actions. He gathers priests and coerces Levites to come to a community already well supplied, reads a 'new' law actually long known and commands supposedly unfamiliar celebrations of hoary antiquity. He

32. Dandamaev and Lukonin, *Culture and Social Institutions*, p. 125, point out that there is no sign of significant changes to Egyptian law during Achaemenid times. See also Tuplin, 'Administration of the Achaemenid Empire', pp. 112-13.

33. Especially by Smith, *Palestinian Parties and Politics*, pp. 92-95. This is a part of his thesis of a 'Yahweh-alone' party versus a 'syncretistic' party conflict going back well into pre-exilic times.

comes to 'restore' a cult that has been functioning for decades and brings along temple vessels even though the original ones had been returned at the end of the exile. This is not to mention the king's ransom in gold and silver that he carries with him.

This is all at the king's express command—or, rather, the decree is alleged to have been written by Ezra himself, with the king merely having to make his mark. Indeed, Ezra is pictured as only one individual in a veritable Jewish network enveloping the throne—along with the royal cupbearer Nehemiah, Mordecai who was second only to the king, the queen Esther and perhaps even an aged Daniel and friends still pottering about the court with the odd royal *pesher*. With such powerful support, one wonders how Ezra could have been content with extracting a mere 25½ tons of bullion from the court and treasury (though, granted, he did have another 100 talents of credit for miscellaneous expenses).[34]

We have to conclude that Ezra's mission is a puzzle, whether we look at the text itself or by analogy suggest some hypothetical construct. This result might seem banal; 'so what?' one might ask. But in the light of recent commentaries and histories of Israel, this is not an insignificant conclusion.[35] Most of the histories of Persian Judah have been paraphrases of Ezra–Nehemiah, more or less. Few have broken free from this configuration, but even the practitioners of the 'new history' must ask and answer the old-fashioned questions of sources and reliability. The books of Ezra and Nehemiah are not straightforward history. They represent a mixture of the historical, the literary and the theological—probably only the last two in parts. If the Ezra material is assumed to be more or less historical, it is easy to persist with a traditional quasi-Pharisaic view of the origins and growth of Judaism. On the other hand, if there is good reason to question the basis of the consensus, we are forced back to giving

34. It may be objected that this picture requires one to draw on other books of the canon, some of them long after the Persian period. This illustrates my point precisely, since the books of Ezra and Nehemiah themselves contain a diversity of traditions which arose at different times. They represent in miniature what the canon represents in macro-form.

35. See, for example, J. Bright, *A History of Israel* (London: SCM Press, 3rd edn, 1980), S. Herrmann, *A History of Israel in Old Testament Times* (London: SCM Press, 1975), A. Soggin, *A History of Israel: From the Beginnings to the Bar-Kokhba Revolt, AD 135* (London: SCM Press, 1984), and even J.M. Miller and J.H. Hayes, *A History of Ancient Israel and Judah* (London: SCM Press, 1986).

greater attention to the social and religious dynamics of the time. Therefore, deciding that the historical Ezra is not so accessible as current fashion has it is itself a conclusion worth taking the time to argue.

INDEXES

INDEX OF REFERENCES

INDEX OF AUTHORS

JOURNAL FOR THE STUDY OF THE OLD TESTAMENT

Supplement Series

55 THE ORIGIN TRADITION OF ANCIENT ISRAEL:
1. THE LITERARY FORMATION OF GENESIS AND EXODUS 1–23
T.L. Thompson

56 THE PURIFICATION OFFERING IN THE PRIESTLY LITERATURE:
ITS MEANING AND FUNCTION
N. Kiuchi

57 MOSES:
HEROIC MAN, MAN OF GOD
George W. Coats

58 THE LISTENING HEART:
ESSAYS IN WISDOM AND THE PSALMS
IN HONOR OF ROLAND E. MURPHY, O. CARM.
Edited by Kenneth G. Hoglund, Elizabeth F. Huwiler, Jonathan T. Glass and Roger W. Lee

59 CREATIVE BIBLICAL EXEGESIS:
CHRISTIAN AND JEWISH HERMENEUTICS THROUGH THE CENTURIES
Edited by Benjamin Uffenheimer & Henning Graf Reventlow

60 HER PRICE IS BEYOND RUBIES:
THE JEWISH WOMAN IN GRAECO-ROMAN PALESTINE
Léonie J. Archer

61 FROM CHAOS TO RESTORATION:
AN INTEGRATIVE READING OF ISAIAH 24–27
Dan G. Johnson

62 THE OLD TESTAMENT AND FOLKLORE STUDY
Patricia G. Kirkpatrick

63 SHILOH:
A BIBLICAL CITY IN TRADITION AND HISTORY
Donald G. Schley

64 TO SEE AND NOT PERCEIVE:
ISAIAH 6.9-10 IN EARLY JEWISH AND CHRISTIAN INTERPRETATION
Craig A. Evans

65 THERE IS HOPE FOR A TREE: THE TREE AS METAPHOR IN ISAIAH
Kirsten Nielsen

66 SECRETS OF THE TIMES:
MYTH AND HISTORY IN BIBLICAL CHRONOLOGY
Jeremy Hughes

67 ASCRIBE TO THE LORD:
BIBLICAL AND OTHER STUDIES IN MEMORY OF PETER C. CRAIGIE
Edited by Lyle Eslinger & Glen Taylor

68 THE TRIUMPH OF IRONY IN THE BOOK OF JUDGES
Lillian R. Klein

69 ZEPHANIAH, A PROPHETIC DRAMA
Paul R. House
70 NARRATIVE ART IN THE BIBLE
Shimon Bar-Efrat
71 QOHELET AND HIS CONTRADICTIONS
Michael V. Fox
72 CIRCLE OF SOVEREIGNTY:
A STORY OF STORIES IN DANIEL 1–6
Danna Nolan Fewell
73 DAVID'S SOCIAL DRAMA:
A HOLOGRAM OF THE EARLY IRON AGE
James W. Flanagan
74 THE STRUCTURAL ANALYSIS OF BIBLICAL AND CANAANITE POETRY
Edited by Willem van der Meer & Johannes C. de Moor
75 DAVID IN LOVE AND WAR:
THE PURSUIT OF POWER IN 2 SAMUEL 10–12
Randall C. Bailey
76 GOD IS KING:
UNDERSTANDING AN ISRAELITE METAPHOR
Marc Zvi Brettler
77 EDOM AND THE EDOMITES
John R. Bartlett
78 SWALLOWING THE SCROLL:
TEXTUALITY AND THE DYNAMICS OF DISCOURSE
IN EZEKIEL'S PROPHECY
Ellen F. Davies
79 GIBEAH:
THE SEARCH FOR A BIBLICAL CITY
Patrick M. Arnold, S.J.
80 THE NATHAN NARRATIVES
Gwilym H. Jones
81 ANTI-COVENANT:
COUNTER-READING WOMEN'S LIVES IN THE HEBREW BIBLE
Edited by Mieke Bal
82 RHETORIC AND BIBLICAL INTERPRETATION
Dale Patrick & Allen Scult
83 THE EARTH AND THE WATERS IN GENESIS 1 AND 2:
A LINGUISTIC INVESTIGATION
David Toshio Tsumura
84 INTO THE HANDS OF THE LIVING GOD
Lyle Eslinger
85 FROM CARMEL TO HOREB:
ELIJAH IN CRISIS
Alan J. Hauser & Russell Gregory

86 THE SYNTAX OF THE VERB IN CLASSICAL HEBREW PROSE
Alviero Niccacci
Translated by W.G.E. Watson

87 THE BIBLE IN THREE DIMENSIONS:
ESSAYS IN CELEBRATION OF FORTY YEARS OF BIBLICAL STUDIES IN THE UNIVERSITY OF SHEFFIELD
Edited by David J.A. Clines, Stephen E. Fowl & Stanley E. Porter

88 THE PERSUASIVE APPEAL OF THE CHRONICLER:
A RHETORICAL ANALYSIS
Rodney K. Duke

89 THE PROBLEM OF THE PROCESS OF TRANSMISSION IN THE PENTATEUCH
Rolf Rendtorff
Translated by John J. Scullion

90 BIBLICAL HEBREW IN TRANSITION:
THE LANGUAGE OF THE BOOK OF EZEKIEL
Mark F. Rooker

91 THE IDEOLOGY OF RITUAL:
SPACE, TIME AND STATUS IN THE PRIESTLY THEOLOGY
Frank H. Gorman, Jr

92 ON HUMOUR AND THE COMIC IN THE HEBREW BIBLE
Edited by Yehuda T. Radday & Athalya Brenner

93 JOSHUA 24 AS POETIC NARRATIVE
William T. Koopmans

94 WHAT DOES EVE DO TO HELP? AND OTHER READERLY QUESTIONS TO THE OLD TESTAMENT
David J.A. Clines

95 GOD SAVES:
LESSONS FROM THE ELISHA STORIES
Rick Dale Moore

96 ANNOUNCEMENTS OF PLOT IN GENESIS
Laurence A. Turner

97 THE UNITY OF THE TWELVE
Paul R. House

98 ANCIENT CONQUEST ACCOUNTS:
A STUDY IN ANCIENT NEAR EASTERN AND BIBLICAL HISTORY WRITING
K. Lawson Younger, Jr

99 WEALTH AND POVERTY IN THE BOOK OF PROVERBS
R.N. Whybray

100 A TRIBUTE TO GEZA VERMES:
ESSAYS ON JEWISH AND CHRISTIAN LITERATURE AND HISTORY
Edited by Philip R. Davies & Richard T. White

101 THE CHRONICLER IN HIS AGE
Peter R. Ackroyd

102 THE PRAYERS OF DAVID (PSALMS 51–72):
STUDIES IN THE PSALTER, II
Michael Goulder

103 THE SOCIOLOGY OF POTTERY IN ANCIENT PALESTINE:
THE CERAMIC INDUSTRY AND THE DIFFUSION OF CERAMIC STYLE IN THE BRONZE AND IRON AGES
Bryant G. Wood

104 PSALM STRUCTURES:
A STUDY OF PSALMS WITH REFRAINS
Paul R. Raabe

105 RE-ESTABLISHING JUSTICE
Pietro Bovati

106 GRADED HOLINESS:
A KEY TO THE PRIESTLY CONCEPTION OF THE WORLD
Philip Jenson

107 THE ALIEN IN ISRAELITE LAW
Christiana van Houten

108 THE FORGING OF ISRAEL:
IRON TECHNOLOGY, SYMBOLISM AND TRADITION IN ANCIENT SOCIETY
Paula M. McNutt

109 SCRIBES AND SCHOOLS IN MONARCHIC JUDAH:
A SOCIO-ARCHAEOLOGICAL APPROACH
David Jamieson-Drake

110 THE CANAANITES AND THEIR LAND:
THE TRADITION OF THE CANAANITES
Niels Peter Lemche

111 YAHWEH AND THE SUN:
THE BIBLICAL AND ARCHAEOLOGICAL EVIDENCE
J. Glen Taylor

112 WISDOM IN REVOLT:
METAPHORICAL THEOLOGY IN THE BOOK OF JOB
Leo G. Perdue

113 PROPERTY AND THE FAMILY IN BIBLICAL LAW
Raymond Westbrook

114 A TRADITIONAL QUEST:
ESSAYS IN HONOUR OF LOUIS JACOBS
Edited by Dan Cohn-Sherbok

115 I HAVE BUILT YOU AN EXALTED HOUSE:
TEMPLE BUILDING IN THE BIBLE IN LIGHT OF MESOPOTAMIAN AND NORTHWEST SEMITIC WRITINGS
Victor Hurowitz

116 NARRATIVE AND NOVELLA IN SAMUEL:
STUDIES BY HUGO GRESSMANN AND OTHER SCHOLARS 1906–1923
Translated by David E. Orton
Edited by David M. Gunn

117 SECOND TEMPLE STUDIES:
1. PERSIAN PERIOD
Edited by Philip R. Davies

118 SEEING AND HEARING GOD WITH THE PSALMS:
THE PROPHETIC LITURGY FROM THE SECOND TEMPLE IN JERUSALEM
Raymond Jacques Tournay
Translated by J. Edward Crowley

119 TELLING QUEEN MICHAL'S STORY:
AN EXPERIMENT IN COMPARATIVE INTERPRETATION
Edited by David J.A. Clines & Tamara C. Eskenazi

120 THE REFORMING KINGS:
CULT AND SOCIETY IN FIRST TEMPLE JUDAH
Richard H. Lowery

121 KING SAUL IN THE HISTORIOGRAPHY OF JUDAH
Diana Vikander Edelman

122 IMAGES OF EMPIRE
Edited by Loveday Alexander

123 JUDAHITE BURIAL PRACTICES AND BELIEFS ABOUT THE DEAD
Elizabeth Bloch-Smith

124 LAW AND IDEOLOGY IN MONARCHIC ISRAEL
Edited by Baruch Halpern and Deborah W. Hobson

125 PRIESTHOOD AND CULT IN ANCIENT ISRAEL
Edited by Gary A. Anderson and Saul M. Olyan

126 W.M.L.DE WETTE, FOUNDER OF MODERN BIBLICAL CRITICISM:
AN INTELLECTUAL BIOGRAPHY
John W. Rogerson

127 THE FABRIC OF HISTORY:
TEXT, ARTIFACT AND ISRAEL'S PAST
Edited by Diana Vikander Edelman

128 BIBLICAL SOUND AND SENSE:
POETIC SOUND PATTERNS IN PROVERBS 10–29
Thomas P. McCreesh

129 THE ARAMAIC OF DANIEL IN THE LIGHT OF OLD ARAMAIC
Zdravko Stefanovic

130 STRUCTURE AND THE BOOK OF ZECHARIAH
Michael Butterworth

131 FORMS OF DEFORMITY:
A MOTIF-INDEX OF ABNORMALITIES, DEFORMITIES AND DISABILITIES IN TRADITIONAL JEWISH LITERATURE
Lynn Holden

132 CONTEXTS FOR AMOS:
PROPHETIC POETICS IN LATIN AMERICAN PERSPECTIVE
Mark Daniel Carroll R.

133 THE FORSAKEN FIRSTBORN:
A STUDY OF A RECURRENT MOTIF IN THE PATRIARCHAL NARRATIVES
Roger Syrén

135 ISRAEL IN EGYPT:
A READING OF EXODUS 1–2
G.F. Davies

136 A WALK THROUGH THE GARDEN:
BIBLICAL, ICONOGRAPHICAL AND LITERARY IMAGES OF EDEN
Edited by P. Morris and D. Sawyer

137 JUSTICE AND RIGHTEOUSNESS:
BIBLICAL THEMES AND THEIR INFLUENCE
Edited by H. Graf Reventlow & Y. Hoffman

138 TEXT AS PRETEXT:
ESSAYS IN HONOUR OF ROBERT DAVIDSON
Edited by R.P. Carroll

139 PSALM AND STORY:
INSET HYMNS IN HEBREW NARRATIVE
J.W. Watts

140 PURITY AND MONOTHEISM:
CLEAN AND UNCLEAN ANIMALS IN BIBLICAL LAW
Walter Houston

141 DEBT SLAVERY IN ISRAEL AND THE ANCIENT NEAR EAST
Gregory C. Chirichigno

142 DIVINATION IN ANCIENT ISRAEL AND ITS NEAR EASTERN ENVIRONMENT:
A SOCIO-HISTORICAL INVESTIGATION
Frederick H. Cryer

143 THE NEW LITERARY CRITICISM AND THE HEBREW BIBLE
David J.A. Clines and J. Cheryl Exum

144 LANGUAGE, IMAGERY AND STRUCTURE IN THE PROPHETIC WRITINGS
Philip R. Davies and David J.A. Clines

145 THE SPEECHES OF MICAH:
A RHETORICAL-HISTORICAL ANALYSIS
Charles S. Shaw

146 THE HISTORY OF ANCIENT PALESTINE FROM THE PALAEOLITHIC PERIOD TO ALEXANDER'S CONQUEST
Gösta W. Ahlström

147 VOWS IN THE HEBREW BIBLE AND THE ANCIENT NEAR EAST
Tony W. Cartledge

148 IN SEARCH OF 'ANCIENT ISRAEL'
Philip R. Davies

149 PRIESTS, PROPHETS AND SCRIBES: ESSAYS ON THE FORMATION AND HERITAGE OF SECOND TEMPLE JUDAISM IN HONOUR OF JOSEPH BLENKINSOPP
Eugene Ulrich, John W. Wright, Robert P. Carroll and Philip R. Davies (eds)

150 TRADITION AND INNOVATION IN HAGGAI AND ZECHARIAH 1–8
Janet A. Tollington
151 THE CITIZEN-TEMPLE COMMUNITY
J.P. Weinberg
152 UNDERSTANDING POETS AND PROPHETS: ESSAYS IN HONOUR OF GEORGE WISHART ANDERSON
A.G. Auld
153 THE PSALMS AND THEIR READERS: INTERPRETIVE STRATEGIES FOR PSALM 18
D.K. Berry
154 MINHAH LE-NAHUM: BIBLICAL AND OTHER STUDIES PRESENTED TO NAHUM M SARNA IN HONOUR OF HIS 70TH BIRTHDAY
M. Brettler and M. Fishbane (eds)
155 LAND TENURE AND THE BIBLICAL JUBILEE: DISCOVERING A MORAL WORLD-VIEW THROUGH THE SOCIOLOGY OF KNOWLEDGE
Jeffrey A. Fager
156 THE LORD'S SONG: THE BASIS, FUNCTION AND SIGNIFICANCE OF CHORAL MUSIC IN CHRONICLES
J.E. Kleinig
157 THE WORD *HESED* IN THE HEBREW BIBLE
G.R. Clark
158 IN THE WILDERNESS
Mary Douglas
159 THE SHAPE AND SHAPING OF THE PSALTER
J.C. McCann
160 KING AND CULTUS IN CHRONICLES: WORSHIP AND THE REINTERPRETATION OF HISTORY
William Riley
161 THE MOSES TRADITION
George W. Coats
162 OF PROPHET'S VISIONS AND THE WISDOM OF SAGES: ESSAYS IN HONOUR OF R. NORMAN WHYBRAY ON HIS SEVENTIETH BIRTHDAY
Heather A. McKay and David J.A. Clines
163 FRAGMENTED WOMEN: FEMINIST (SUB)VERSIONS OF BIBLICAL NARRATIVES
J. Cheryl Exum
167 SECOND ZECHARIAH AND THE DEUTERONOMIC SCHOOL
R.F. Person
168 THE COMPOSITION OF THE BOOK OF PROVERBS
R.N. Whybray
174 A LITERARY APPROACH TO BIBLICAL LAW
J.M. Sprinkle
175 SECOND TEMPLE STUDIES: 2. TEMPLE AND COMMUNITY IN THE PERSIAN PERIOD
T. Ezkenazi and K.H. Richards